Praise for a previous ed
BRITAIN BY BRITR

"Both *[Europe by Eurail]* and *Britain by BritRail* are great all-in-one choices for those who use the popular rail passes to get around. The books combine detailed information on trains, accommodations, and stations with good general guidebook-type descriptions of destinations. . . . If you are riding the rails in Europe or Britain, don't leave home without these two guides."

—*Orange County* (Calif.) *Register*

HELP US KEEP THIS GUIDE UP TO DATE

We would love to hear from you concerning your experiences with this guide and how you feel it could be improved and kept up to date. Please send your comments and suggestions to:

editorial@GlobePequot.com

Thanks for your input, and happy travels!

BRITAIN BY BRITRAIL 2012/13

TOURING BRITAIN BY TRAIN

THIRTY-FIRST EDITION

Written by
LaVerne Ferguson-Kosinski

Edited by
C. Darren Price

Rail Schedules by
C. Darren Price

Guilford, Connecticut

To buy books in quantity for corporate use
or incentives, call **(800) 962-0973**
or e-mail **premiums@GlobePequot.com.**

The author and the publisher gratefully acknowledge the kind permission of Eurostar Passenger Services and its Web site, Deutsche Bahn and its Web site, Brittany Ferries, Irish Ferries U.K. Limited, P&O Stena Line, SeaFrance Limited, DFDS Seaways, and Stena Line to use their resources in the compilation of the timetables in this text.

The rail map on pp. vi–vii is reproduced courtesy of the Thomas Cook European Timetable; www.thomascookpublishing.com.

Text design: Nancy Freeborn

ISSN 1081-1117
ISBN 978-0-7627-7299-5

Printed in the United States of America

Train schedules, prices, and conditions of use appearing in this edition are updated at press time and are subject to change without notice by the railways. Prices are estimates and are based on exchange rate at time of printing. The information is to assist with trip planning only. We cannot be held responsible for its accuracy. Please check with the railways for the most recent information.

ABOUT THE AUTHOR

LaVerne Ferguson-Kosinski and her late husband, Lt. Col. George Ferguson, first coauthored this unique and comprehensive how-to guide in 1980.

After battling a long illness, George, who was globally and affectionately known as "Mr. Eurail," passed away in 1997 and was buried at Arlington National Cemetery.

LaVerne wanted to ensure that accurate British and European rail travel information would continue to be available. She is devoted to producing comprehensive, practical, yet friendly guidebooks for the independent rail traveler or armchair dreamer. Her technical writing and editorial background; academic education in English, world history, and communications; and experience in research and development for an international research institute have added considerable substance to her three decades of traveling the rails in Britain and Europe.

Her dream of exploring the world began in third-grade geography class when she first began collecting travel brochures. After attending Ohio State University, LaVerne lived in and traveled throughout Europe. She resides in Fort Myers Beach, Florida, with her husband, Joe "Cool" Kosinski, a structural engineer.

Heartfelt thanks and appreciation go to you, the readers, whose comments, suggestions, and corrections help keep both guidebooks accurate and up to date.

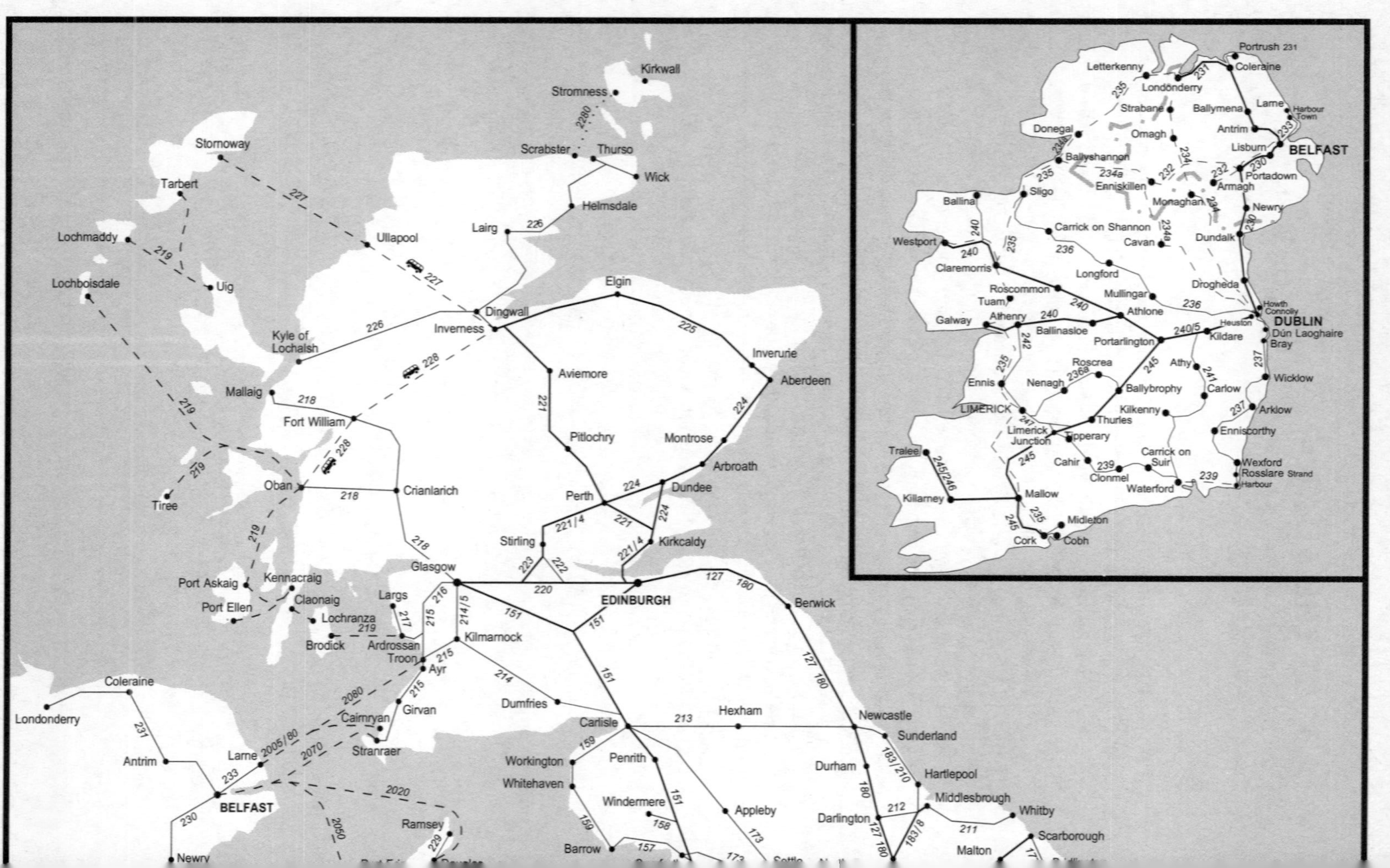

Kirkwall
Stromness
Stornoway
Scrabster
Thurso
Wick
Tarbert
Helmsdale
Lairg
Ullapool
Lochmaddy
Uig
Lochboisdale
Dingwall
Inverness
Elgin
Kyle of Lochalsh
Inverurie
Aberdeen
Aviemore
Mallaig
Fort William
Pitlochry
Montrose
Arbroath
Oban
Crianlarich
Dundee
Tiree
Perth
Stirling
Kirkcaldy
Glasgow
Port Askaig
Kennacraig
Port Ellen
Claonaig
Largs
Lochranza
EDINBURGH
Berwick
Brodick
Ardrossan
Troon
Kilmarnock
Ayr
Coleraine
Londonderry
Girvan
Dumfries
Cairnryan
Stranraer
Carlisle
Hexham
Newcastle
Sunderland
Antrim
Larne
Workington
Penrith
Durham
Hartlepool
Whitehaven
BELFAST
Windermere
Appleby
Middlesbrough
Darlington
Whitby
Ramsey
Barrow
Malton
Scarborough
Newry
Settle
Portrush
Letterkenny
Londonderry
Coleraine
Strabane
Ballymena
Larne
Harbour Town
Donegal
Omagh
Antrim
Lisburn
BELFAST
Ballyshannon
Enniskillen
Armagh
Portadown
Ballina
Sligo
Monaghan
Newry
Carrick on Shannon
Cavan
Dundalk
Westport
Claremorris
Longford
Drogheda
Roscommon
Mullingar
Tuam
Howth
Connolly
Galway
Athenry
Athlone
DUBLIN
Ballinasloe
Heuston
Portarlington
Kildare
Dún Laoghaire
Bray
Roscrea
Athy
Ennis
Nenagh
Ballybrophy
Carlow
Wicklow
LIMERICK
Kilkenny
Arklow
Thurles
Limerick Junction
Tipperary
Enniscorthy
Tralee
Carrick on Suir
Cahir
Clonmel
Wexford
Rosslare Strand
Harbour
Waterford
Mallow
Killarney
Midleton
Cork
Cobh

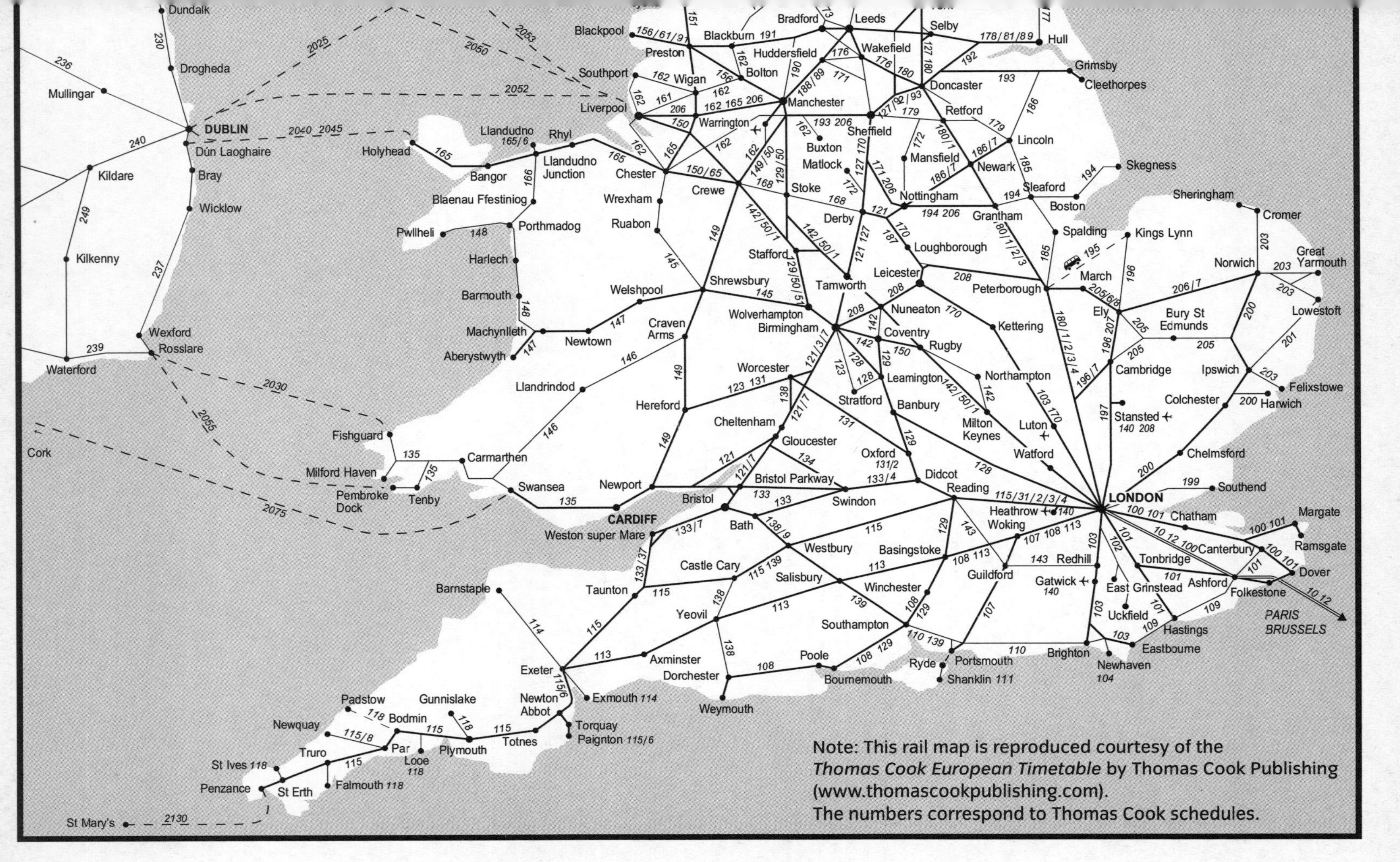
Dundalk
Drogheda
Mullingar
DUBLIN
Dún Laoghaire
Bray
Wicklow
Kildare
Kilkenny
Wexford
Rosslare
Waterford
Cork
Blackpool
Preston
Southport
Wigan
Liverpool
Blackburn
Bolton
Huddersfield
Bradford
Leeds
Wakefield
Selby
Hull
Doncaster
Grimsby
Cleethorpes
Manchester
Warrington
Sheffield
Retford
Lincoln
Skegness
Holyhead
Llandudno
Rhyl
Llandudno Junction
Bangor
Chester
Crewe
Wrexham
Ruabon
Blaenau Ffestiniog
Porthmadog
Pwllheli
Harlech
Barmouth
Machynlleth
Aberystwyth
Newtown
Welshpool
Shrewsbury
Buxton
Matlock
Mansfield
Newark
Stoke
Stafford
Derby
Nottingham
Grantham
Sleaford
Boston
Spalding
Kings Lynn
Sheringham
Cromer
Norwich
Great Yarmouth
Lowestoft
Loughborough
Leicester
Peterborough
March
Ely
Bury St Edmunds
Tamworth
Wolverhampton
Birmingham
Nuneaton
Coventry
Rugby
Kettering
Cambridge
Ipswich
Felixstowe
Harwich
Colchester
Stansted
Chelmsford
Southend
Craven Arms
Llandrindod
Hereford
Worcester
Leamington
Stratford
Banbury
Northampton
Milton Keynes
Luton
Watford
Fishguard
Milford Haven
Pembroke Dock
Tenby
Carmarthen
Swansea
Newport
CARDIFF
Cheltenham
Gloucester
Oxford
Didcot
Reading
Bristol Parkway
Bristol
Swindon
LONDON
Heathrow
Woking
Chatham
Margate
Ramsgate
Canterbury
Dover
Weston super Mare
Bath
Westbury
Basingstoke
Tonbridge
Redhill
Guildford
Gatwick
East Grinstead
Ashford
Folkestone
Castle Cary
Salisbury
Winchester
Uckfield
Hastings
PARIS BRUSSELS
Barnstaple
Taunton
Yeovil
Southampton
Axminster
Dorchester
Poole
Bournemouth
Ryde
Portsmouth
Shanklin
Brighton
Newhaven
Eastbourne
Exeter
Exmouth
Weymouth
Padstow
Gunnislake
Newton Abbot
Torquay
Paignton
Newquay
Bodmin
Plymouth
Totnes
Truro
Par
Looe
St Ives
Falmouth
Penzance
St Erth
St Mary's
Note: This rail map is reproduced courtesy of the *Thomas Cook European Timetable* by Thomas Cook Publishing (www.thomascookpublishing.com).
The numbers correspond to Thomas Cook schedules.

CONTENTS

IN THE BEGINNING

"My heart is warm with the friends I make,
And better friends I'll not be knowing;
Yet there isn't a train I wouldn't take
No matter where it's going."

—EDNA ST. VINCENT MILLAY

Like thousands of other discerning visitors, you are about to learn that the British rail system offers a delightful way of traveling throughout the length and breadth of Europe's only English-speaking nation—Britain. So welcome aboard *Britain by BritRail*! You are embarking on a unique and rewarding traveling experience.

Train travel is an anomaly for most Americans. Millions of Americans have either forgotten or have never had the opportunity to learn what travel by train can be like. The British and Europeans' outlook on train travel is different. They need trains for transport; thus, they have created trains with the simplest and yet most extravagant amenities of their culture. In so doing, they provide fast, economical, and often elegant modes of transportation.

Britain is a rather compact nation. It's about two-thirds the size of California or approximately one-third larger than the New England area of Maine, Vermont, New Hampshire, Massachusetts, Rhode Island, and Connecticut—the North American area to which Britain has contributed much of its heritage since colonial days.

This thirty-first edition of *Britain by BritRail* encompasses rail travel in England, Scotland, and Wales. Although the Republic of Ireland and Northern Ireland are, of course, a part of the British Isles, Ireland's railways do not accept the BritRail Pass. They do, however, accept the BritRail Pass + Ireland add-on, which provides for rail travel within England, Scotland, Wales, Northern Ireland, and the Republic of Ireland. The Republic of Ireland also accepts Eurail passes. For rail travel information about the Republic of Ireland, please consult *Europe by Eurail: Touring Europe by Train*.

In Britain you'll find more than 18,700 trains traveling to more than 2,500 destinations daily. The service is so frequent that if you miss a train, chances are you won't have to wait more than a half hour to an hour for another. The British frequently seize such an opportunity to nip into a nearby pub for a quick pint and a game of darts. So follow the adage "When in Rome, do as the Romans do." After all, Britain inherited some of Rome's customs too!

Aboard a British train the driver (that's what the British call their train engineers) takes care of all the driving while you sip a beverage, enjoy an uninterrupted view of the countryside, and stretch out in a comfortable seat. You may even respond to "nature's call" at your own option rather than waiting for the closest petrol (gas) station.

Few places in Britain cannot be reached by train. By employing the base cities of London, England; Edinburgh or Glasgow in Scotland; or Cardiff in Wales, the splendor of Windsor Castle, the legendary Loch Ness Monster, or the natural beauty of Swansea Bay is an easy, comfortable train ride away.

London is a tourist magnet, but despite what other writers say, London is not Britain. A visit to Britain that does not include at least a few days in the countryside is unthinkable. Britain has some of the most beautiful countryside in the world. The mountains may not be a match in size to the Alps and the seas not azure blue like the Mediterranean, but all of this is offset by a magical quality of green so peaceful and picturesque that, in a mere glance, the visitor becomes aware that he or she is seeing history.

How to Use *Britain by BritRail*

Britain by BritRail is the perfect traveling companion for visitors using the BritRail Pass. This guidebook is written to provide detailed train-related information to readers in a direct, pragmatic manner. *Britain by BritRail* is devoted to the visitor who goes to Britain expecting its train services to provide the necessary transportation for a holiday that is exciting and different. We have gone ahead of you, probed what can be done, and solved the problems of doing it long before you arrive. We personally experience every city and day excursion, and our researchers pledge to constantly recheck and revise subsequent editions. This is accomplished by personal visits and through a British and European network of correspondents.

Britain by BritRail presents a concept for comfortable, unhurried travel by train in Britain. By utilizing the economy of a BritRail Pass, along with the innovative, fully described Base City–Day Excursion method, you really see Britain at its best—by train.

This book helps to introduce and establish the reader in the base cities of London, Edinburgh, Glasgow, and Cardiff. Establish yourself in affordable, comfortable accommodations. Then, when you have finished your sightseeing and shopping in the base city, let *Britain by BritRail* guide you to recommended day excursions. For the most part these interesting places are based on train schedules and geographic locations that assure your return each night to the same hotel room. With a BritRail Pass and a current copy of this book, you become your own tour guide and avoid the constant packing and unpacking that accompanies most bus tours attempting to cover the same territory. *You* call the shots and set the pace.

Britons and their continental cousins have employed rail services for "holiday-making" for decades. Train travel is too fast for any possible chance of boredom setting in, yet it is leisurely enough to enjoy fully the constantly changing scene of hills and hamlets, farms and forests, countrysides and cities—everything that forms Britain's fascinating landscape.

Should you pause to ponder why, for example, the English leave their cars at home when they're "off on holiday," you will find the answer very quickly when your train parallels a major highway or flashes across a bridge through the center of a British city. The superhighways—right down to the ancient, narrow streets—are packed with vehicles, all proceeding at a much slower pace than you and your train.

In the chapters describing the base cities and day excursions, *Britain by BritRail* meets you upon arrival at the base-city airport or train station, then leads you step by step to those essential facilities such as tourist information sources, currency exchanges, and hotel accommodations.

Britain by BritRail does not include comprehensive hotel listings, but it does include quaint bed-and-breakfasts and personally selected hotels convenient to the rail services. The primary purpose, insofar as accommodations are concerned, is to point out the most convenient tourist information center or hotel booking (reservations) facility and how to get there.

Restaurants are treated in the same manner. We appreciate good food and good service. With few exceptions, however, the choice of what to eat and where to find it remains the option of the reader perusing the wealth of excellent publications catering to this most worthy pursuit. We do, however, include some of our own personal recommendations.

Each day-excursion section begins with the distance and average train time for the trip, along with the tourist information office location and hours of operation. You'll also find explicit walking or easy transport directions on how to get from the train station to the city tourist information office.

Readers requiring advance information regarding the base cities should contact the closest British Tourist Authority office listed in the Appendix of this edition, or visit the BTA Web site on the Internet at www.visitbritain.com. Country and individual city contacts and Web sites are included in each chapter and in the Appendix.

Train schedules in Britain and those appearing in this edition are shown in twenty-four-hour style. For example, a train departing at 1935 leaves at 7:35 p.m. Schedules between the base cities of London, Edinburgh, Glasgow, and Cardiff are included with each base-city description. This particular information should prove helpful when you are initially planning your BritRail trip.

Train schedules for the day-excursion trips out of the base cities are also provided in the text describing each day excursion. With a few exceptions for overnight excursions, we chose trains departing from the base cities on morning schedules and trains returning from the day excursions usually in the late afternoon or early evening.

Please remember the timetables and schedules appearing in this edition are provided for planning purposes only. Every care has been taken to make the timetables and schedules correct at printing, and the information is checked with authoritative sources up to press time. *Britain by BritRail* and/or its publisher cannot, however, be held responsible for the consequences of either changes or inadvertent inaccuracies.

Current rail schedules are posted in all British rail stations. Timetables from the base cities to each day-excursion point are available free for the asking in the base-city train stations. Please consult them. You may also visit the point-to-point rail schedule pages of www.networkrail.co.uk or www.nationalrail.co.uk.

PLANNING A BRITRAIL TRIP

A plan is often defined as "a program of action." Plans vary in detail and complexity, according to the nature of the user. We have observed two general types of rail travelers: one conservative, the other adventurous. One traveler may require a detailed, hour-by-hour schedule for each day's activities; another may merely plan to get up in the morning and see what the day brings.

One of the first questions to answer when planning a trip is "When can I go, and how much time can I spend?" In Britain April through October are the most popular months for tourists and for many events; plus during the Christmas and New Year's holidays, London literally sparkles.

When planning your trip, take British bank holidays into consideration because banks, postal services, and most shops and many attractions are closed, and some transportation services are reduced. Bank holidays include New Year's Day, Good Friday, Easter Sunday, Easter Monday, May Day, Spring Holiday, Queen's Official Birthday, Summer Holiday, Christmas Day, and Boxing Day. (See the "2012/13 Bank and Public Holidays" section in the Appendix.)

Whether you admit it or not, everyone has a problem budgeting vacation time. Human nature is to try to see as much as possible in as little time as possible. This "sightseers' syndrome" could be dangerous to your vacation. Avoid it by planning an itinerary that allows ample free time. Also, vary the day excursions by going on a short one following a particularly long outing away from the base city. Press too hard by trying to see and do too much, and you will return home looking as if you desperately need another vacation.

How long should your BritRail tour be? There are many factors bearing on such a determination. How much annual vacation time do you have? How do you use it—all at one time or in two or more segments? BritRail Passes can accommodate just about anyone's personal needs, with consecutive passes ranging from four days to one month of travel and flexible passes ranging from four to fifteen days of travel in two months. BritRail Passes permit travel on all scheduled British trains.

Even if you don't have two weeks or more for a grand tour of Britain, travel magazines and the travel sections of the Sunday newspapers are usually loaded with one-week bargain airfares to almost anywhere, Britain and mainland Europe included. By coupling our Base City–Day Excursion mode of easy travel with a four-day BritRail Flexipass, you can maximize the time you do have to spend in Britain.

Once you know how much time you have for your BritRail trip, the next step is to develop a clear idea of where you want to go in Britain, what you want to see, and what you want to do. Develop your objectives well before your departure date.

We disagree with those who believe that anticipation of travel is more rewarding than its realization. But we do agree that the planning phase can also be a fun part of your trip. Properly done, this "homework" will pay substantial dividends when your travel actually begins.

To get things started, write to, e-mail, or telephone the British Tourist Authority (BTA) at (800) GO 2 BRIT (800-462-2748) for information. (BTA office addresses in North America are listed in the Appendix.) Be specific. In your request indicate when you will be going, where you wish to go within Britain, and what in particular you would like to see. If you have any special interests or hobbies, be sure to mention them in your request. By spelling out your information needs, you will obtain better responses.

Don't overlook the Internet and your local library as valuable information sources. Travelers who have computers and access to the Internet can do an incredible amount of research and planning in the comfort of their own homes or offices. The great "information highway" is at your disposal.

You may want to start with some basic Web sites about Britain in general, then do subject-specific searches. For example, to obtain general information on Britain, start with the British Tourist Authority's Web site: www.visitbritain.com. Other sources of information may be found in the Appendix of this edition, including city tourist information sites.

Seek out friends and neighbors who have been to Britain. No doubt you'll find their experiences flavored by their own likes and dislikes. Nevertheless, any and all information gathered before your trip will eventually find its place in your memory bank. You'll find yourself recalling many of these fragments of information during your own journey.

Now comes the decisive phase of your trip planning—constructing an itinerary. The moment of truth is at hand! Your only limitation during this portion of the planning phase is the lack of more than twenty-four hours in a day.

Draw a blank calendar-style form covering a period from at least one week before your departure to a few days following your return. Make extra copies of the form—you'll need them. (Perfection is a long time coming in this project!) Begin to block your itinerary into calendar form, being mindful that the itinerary can be changed, but the number of days in a week remains fixed at all times. Possibly by the third time through the exercise, you'll begin to "see the light at the end of the tunnel." Remember, it is only human to try to cram too many activities into a day, but better to discover planning errors before starting your trip rather than during the middle of it.

With your itinerary in a calendar format, you can determine housing requirements, seat and sleeper reservations, and the other facets of your forthcoming trip. The days blocked out in advance of your departure show your "countdown" items, such as stopping the newspaper, having mail held at the post office, getting prescriptions filled, taking pets to the kennel, shopping, arranging legal documents and credit cards, and so on. Make several copies of your completed itinerary, and leave some behind for the folks with whom you want to stay in touch. Above all, take copies of your itinerary with you—you'll refer to them frequently.

If there have been any break-ins in your neighborhood, you should take steps to ensure it doesn't happen to you while you are gone. Alert the neighbors to keep a watchful eye for suspicious people and their activities. Many professional thieves have been known to park in a driveway in broad daylight with a moving van. The police should be advised regarding your absence. Check with the insurance agency that writes your homeowners policy. Ask the same question they ask in those television commercials: "Am I covered?" You may need additional coverage during your absence. Some travelers have a trusted friend or family member "housesit" while abroad. This option eliminates having to stop the paper and mail, and perhaps even sending Fluffy to the kennel. One final caution: Don't announce your forthcoming vacation, in the newspapers or online. If you use any social media websites, such as Facebook or Twitter, wait until you return from your trip to brag about it. You may trust all of your online friends, but do you trust all of their friends, who may also be able to see your information?

U.S. citizens are required to have a passport to be admitted into Britain; a visa is not necessary. If you do not have a passport or if yours has expired, write immediately to one of the U.S. passport offices listed in the Appendix. Allow at least six weeks to obtain your passport. There are ways to expedite the process by going online to **www.passportsandvisas.com,** at a substantially higher cost. Passport Services through the U.S. Department of State, Bureau of Consular Affairs offers the brochure *Passports: Applying for Them the Easy Way.* Call the National Passport Information Center (NPIC) at (877) 487-2778 to request the pamphlet, to receive applications, or to check on passport status or emergency passport procedures. See "Passport Information" in the Appendix.

Travel Economy

"Know before you go," the slogan of the U.S. Customs Service concerning what you may return with, also applies to the financial aspects of vacation planning. The fluctuation of the dollar's purchasing power abroad over the past few years has left a lot of us wondering whether we could afford a vacation on the other side of the Atlantic. It is sometimes difficult to determine what effect Britain's inflation will have on your dollars once you're there.

Advance planning pays off. Purchasing most of your vacation needs in advance (particularly transportation) in American dollars is probably the most effective way to combat inflation and price fluctuations. Buy as much of your vacation needs before you go, and plan to limit your out-of-pocket costs paid in foreign currency to a minimum. In this way you are protected against fluctuating currency values.

Train travel in Britain is one of the best means of effectively stabilizing your travel dollars. Prepayment plans, such as the BritRail Pass, are ideal. Not only do you purchase the pass with American dollars before departure, but the BritRail Pass also provides the most inexpensive way to travel in Britain—the quickest too!

Most travel agents still have a penchant for wanting to sell a "fly-drive" program to clients who want to vacation in Britain. But, in general, car rentals have one basic flaw—the price you see is not the price you pay; it always seems to be higher. As a general rule, add to the quoted price another 20 percent for personal accident insurance, collision insurance, and taxes. After that, consider fuel costs at about three times that of fuel in the United States. Don't forget about the 20 percent value-added tax (VAT). Remember, driving is on the left in Britain.

Accommodations usually account for the greatest share of a traveler's budget. Low-cost air fares and transportation bargains like the BritRail Pass can get the traveler to and around Britain, but the real bite out of the buck comes when the visitor pays for a night's lodging. Attractively priced accommodations packages are being offered by some tour operators, but too few suit the needs of individual itineraries, as is the case for travelers on a BritRail vacation. With advance planning and advance payment, however, you can realize significant savings if you are willing to put forth the extra time and effort to do your homework.

Well ahead of your intended departure date—preferably two months in advance, but no less than six weeks—write, call, or visit the Web sites of one of the British Tourist Authority (BTA) offices listed in the Appendix of this edition, or contact the tourist offices of your specific destination and request information regarding lodging (including the bed-and-breakfasts) in the areas you intend to visit during your BritRail journey. You may make reservations, or "bookings," as the British call them, in a variety of ways.

The best assurance you will have a room waiting upon arrival is to make an advance deposit directly to the hotel, then take care of the balance with the hotel's cashier when checking out. Always ask the hotel to confirm the room rate upon check-in, and be sure to ask what is included in the rate (for example, is breakfast included?). This will avoid delays and possible financial embarrassment when leaving.

One final bit of advice on reducing the cost of accommodations in Britain: Use your BritRail Pass. Too many of us overlook the fact that the BritRail Pass can actually provide exceptional savings in housing costs by permitting you to stay outside the base city's center, where hotel rooms, pensions, bed-and-breakfasts, and the like are far less expensive than their in-town counterparts.

London particularly lends itself to such a suburban arrangement because there are many areas outside the city's center that are readily accessible by rail. Anytime downtown accommodations become difficult to find, or too demanding on the budget, tell the housing people you have a BritRail Pass and can easily stay in the suburbs.

Staying in London's northern or western suburbs has other advantages too. From many of the suburban stations, you can board a fast InterCity train for a day excursion without ever going into a London terminus. You can return to the suburbs in the evening, too, without becoming involved in London's rush hours.

Watford Junction, 16 miles from London's Euston Station, is one of the stations in London's suburbs that offers excellent InterCity connections to such day-excursion points as Birmingham and Coventry, as well as the base city of Glasgow. Most InterCity departures from Euston Station on weekday mornings pick up at Watford Junction sixteen minutes later. On weekday evenings most InterCity trains set down at Watford Junction twenty minutes ahead of their arrival times in Euston Station.

Going to St. Albans, Perth, or the base cities of Edinburgh and Cardiff, we recommend transferring to King's Cross or Paddington from Euston to continue the trip.

Other rail points in London suburbs are Luton, for direct rail connections to Nottingham and Sheffield; Stevenage, along the main line to Edinburgh via York; and Slough or Reading, for connections to Bath as well as the Welsh cities of Cardiff and Swansea.

There are times when accommodations in the base cities are very limited. Edinburgh, during its annual Military Tattoo and Festival every August, is an excellent example. Lodgings in the suburbs, a la BritRail Pass, can be more economical and just as convenient as those in the base cities. If you have your heart set on lodgings in London, when inquiring as to availability you will be asked the inevitable question, "What do you want to be near?" Naturally, when you're traveling by rail, your response will be, "The rail station." You are in for a surprise: At last count, London had seventeen primary rail stations. Because these terminals rim the vast, sprawling city, a better site-selection statement would be to ask for a hotel near one of the major lines of the Underground (the "Tube").

How to Get There

Transatlantic air traffic is so frequent and varied today that no description of it—short of an entire book—could do it justice. Excursion fares are available in a multitudinous variety. Charter flights are available too, but some excursion rates are less expensive than charters. On a regularly scheduled airliner winging its way to Europe, it is not uncommon to find every passenger in your row of seats paid a different fare for the same flight with the same service.

We refer readers to their travel agents for airline tickets. Since many airlines no longer pay commissions to travel agents, you may have to pay a service fee. If you've dealt with a reputable travel agency over the years, contact it for air-excursion fare options. Or, if you have lots of time, you can call the various airlines' toll-free telephone numbers and ask them for fare information or visit their Web sites. We have listed contact information for a few airlines in the Appendix. Don't be disturbed if you receive a variety of responses. Sift them out until you find what you're looking for. Internet users can search online for those bargain fares with consolidators, travel portals, and the actual airlines as well. Remember that not all airlines allow their fares to be quoted on other sites. Additionally, we have seen prices obtained at the same time vary by up to 10 percent, depending on the website used to find them, with the airline site itself most often being the cheapest.

Regarding charter flights, inquire about them but investigate thoroughly before making any final decisions. Here again, get your travel agent involved, even if it's only to obtain the tickets. Even some of the most reputable air-charter carriers still operate on a "Go–No Go" basis. This means that if enough passengers sign up for the flight, it will go as scheduled; if there are not enough passengers booked, the flight will be scrubbed. Look up the airline in your phone book, or dial (800) 555-1212 and tell the operator the name of the airline information office with which you wish to speak, or use the search engines on the Internet to find specific Web addresses.

BritRail Passes

A BritRail Pass provides unlimited train travel for a specified number of days in England, Scotland, and Wales. You don't have to purchase a rail pass to travel by train in Britain; having one, however, is very convenient and economical. For example, with a BritRail Pass, you do not have to purchase a rail ticket every time you want to make a trip somewhere by train. Just board any train going your way and travel whenever, wherever, and as often as you like throughout the period your BritRail Pass is valid.

BritRail Passes are not available in Britain and must be purchased in North America before departure. You may order directly from one of the companies listed in the Appendix. You may also purchase some of the passes through some travel agents. A list of British and European rail passes and their corresponding prices at press time is available in the Appendix.

Visitors to Britain should consider purchasing a BritRail Pass if they plan to travel primarily by train. To help you decide whether to purchase a rail pass, we have included a selection of British one-way rail fares in the Appendix. Compare the individual fares for your itinerary with the cost of the type of BritRail Pass best for your trip.

Keep in mind when comparing the point-to-point rail fares to the cost of the rail pass that convenience has a value too. Standing in line ("queuing") to purchase train tickets is an inconvenience that can be avoided. With a BritRail Pass, you need do this only once—when you validate your pass at the station.

Even short-time visitors to the British Isles may find it advantageous to purchase a BritRail Pass in lieu of point-to-point tickets. For example, the cost of point-to-point tickets for a circuitous journey—like a quick dash out of London for a look around Edinburgh and Bath—exceeds the cost of an eight-day first-class or standard-class adult BritRail Consecutive Pass. The economy of the pass becomes immediately apparent when doing such comparisons. Also, consider the London–Edinburgh–Bath–London circuit could be made comfortably in as little as three days, leaving five more days of unlimited rail travel available to the pass holder. Even if you could not extend your stay, you would still save money, in this case, by purchasing a BritRail Pass.

BritRail Passes are available for first- or standard-class rail travel. First-class seats are wider; consequently, first-class coaches are more spacious since they accommodate fewer passengers. BritRail's standard class, however, is also very comfortable. Some trains in Britain have entirely standard-class carriages. One thing in common to both classes is the view. Whether in first or standard class, you can lounge ensconced in comfort while watching the countryside glide by. Expand your horizons—don't leave home without a rail pass!

When traveling in Britain on certain peak days, holidays, or summer Saturdays, seat reservations are recommended. You may make them at most rail stations or at the rail counters in Heathrow, Gatwick, Birmingham, and Manchester Airports by giving destination and departure times of the train (train numbers are not used in Britain). Although you can make seat reservations in the United States after purchasing a BritRail Pass (at least two weeks before departure is necessary), it is more economical to make them in Britain. Trips less than two and a half hours and overnight sleeper trains must be booked in Britain directly.

There are two basic types of passes to choose from: BritRail Consecutive Pass and BritRail Flexipass. Prices are listed in the Appendix.

BritRail Consecutive Pass. The Consecutive Pass offers unlimited consecutive-day rail travel in England, Scotland, and Wales. Choose to travel for three, four, eight, fifteen, or twenty-two days or one month. The BritRail Senior Consecutive Pass (available to adults age sixty and older) offers a 15 percent discount off the first-class BritRail Adult Consecutive Pass. The BritRail Youth Consecutive Pass offers a 25 percent discount in both first and standard class for those age sixteen through twenty-five.

BritRail Flexipass. This pass provides exactly what its name implies: flexibility. Travel on any three, four, eight, or fifteen days within the two-month validity period in either first or standard class. Unlike the Consecutive Pass, your travel days need not be consecutive, thus enabling you to stay in your favorite location for several days until you continue your journey.

A BritRail Senior Flexipass (age sixty and older) offers first-class rail travel at a discount off the adult BritRail Flexipass price. A Youth Flexipass (age sixteen through twenty-five) is available in either first or standard class for any three, four, eight, or fifteen days of travel within a two-month period.

BritRail Family Passes. With the purchase of each adult or senior pass, one accompanying child (age five through fifteen) gets a pass of the same type and duration free. Passes for additional children may be purchased at a 50 percent discount off the regular adult pass price. Children younger than age five travel free. The BritRail Family Pass program is available with BritRail Consecutive, BritRail Flexipass, BritRail Senior, BritRail Pass 'n Drive, BritRail Pass + Ireland, and BritRail Party Pass.

BritRail Party Pass. Offers a 50 percent discount for the third to ninth person's pass when parties of three to nine passengers are traveling together at all times. Applies to the BritRail Consecutive and Flexipass, first class only.

BritRail Pass 'n Drive. Although Britain's compactness makes it convenient to take the train and see the sights, there are a few nooks and crannies that cannot be reached by train. Those who want to combine the thrill of driving on the left-hand side of the road with rail travel can opt for the BritRail Pass 'n Drive. Use the fast, comfortable British trains for the longer journeys and the freedom of a rental car to explore the beautiful British countryside.

First, purchase your BritRail Pass 'n Drive voucher from one of the companies listed in the Appendix. The price includes a BritRail Flexipass for unlimited rail travel (choice of first or standard class) for any four or eight days within a two-month period and car rental vouchers for any two days within the same period. Then, at least seven days before departure, telephone Hertz toll-free at (800) 654-3001 to reserve your first car rental date. Be certain to state that you have already purchased a BritRail Pass 'n Drive and mention the program code IT-BRIT. Reservations should be made as soon as possible, particularly if you want a car with an automatic transmission. For the remainder of your car rental reservations, Hertz has rental offices at rail stations throughout England, Scotland, and Wales.

Since your car rental vouchers may be used only during the validity period of your BritRail Flexipass, the most economical way of utilizing them is to arrange for a car to meet your train at a day-excursion point, do your exploring, and return the car to the same station before returning to your base city by train. Prebooked requests for a car to meet your train will be honored seven days a week, but note that some Hertz offices are closed on Sunday.

Each car rental voucher includes a twenty-four-consecutive-hour rental with unlimited mileage, no drop-off charge, and government tax (VAT) of 20 percent. The renter is responsible for collision damage, personal accident insurance, gasoline, and road tax. Payment of these charges may be made by credit card or a deposit at the start of each rental period. Aside from gasoline, other additional charges are a minimum of approximately $15 (U.S.) per day. Two or more persons traveling together receive a substantial discount.

BritRail Pass + Ireland. For unlimited travel on the rail networks of England, Scotland, Wales, Northern Ireland, and the Republic of Ireland, this is the pass for you. Choose to travel for any five or ten days within a one-month validity period in either first or standard class.

BritRail England Consecutive Pass. Valid for unlimited consecutive-day travel on England's rail network for three, four, eight, fifteen, or twenty-two days or one month in either first or standard class. Includes transportation from Heathrow,

Gatwick, or Stansted Airports, but it counts as one day of travel on your pass. Special youth, senior, and family rates. Party passes allow 50 percent discount for the third to ninth person traveling together at all times.

BritRail England Flexipass. Valid for unlimited three, four, eight, or fifteen days of flexible (nonconsecutive) rail travel in a two-month period throughout England (Scotland and Wales not included) in either first or standard class. Includes transportation from Heathrow, Gatwick, or Stansted Airports, but it counts as one day of travel on your pass. Special youth, senior, and family rates. Youth age sixteen to twenty-five. Senior age sixty and older. Family passes allow one child to travel free with each adult. Party passes allow 50 percent discount for the third to ninth person traveling in a group.

BritRail London Plus Pass. Casual, short-term, or business visitors to Britain may benefit from this special flexible rail pass tucked in their pocket before leaving home. The London Plus Pass offers unlimited rail travel throughout a large portion of southern England for any two or four days out of an eight-day period or for any seven days within a fifteen-day period. Choose first- or standard-class rail travel; special youth, senior, and family rates are applicable. *The pass is **not** valid for travel on London Underground.* It is, however, valid on the Heathrow Express, Gatwick Express, and Stansted Express rail services (constitutes one day of travel on your pass). It does not extend to Bath and is not valid on First Great Western Trains services. Party passes provide 50 percent discount for the third to ninth person traveling as a group.

The **London Travelcard** provides access to the London Underground (subway, or "Tube," as the Britons say) and buses for one or seven days. **The Central Zone Travelcard** is valid for travel in London's two inner zones; the **All Zone Travelcard** covers all six zones, the Docklands Light Railway, and Heathrow Airport transfers (but not on Heathrow Express).

BritRail Freedom or Scotland Pass. The Freedom Pass offers unlimited standard-class rail travel in Scotland on ScotRail's network, including travel to and from Berwick and Carlisle for any four days within an eight-day period or any eight days within a fifteen-day validity period. The pass includes transportation on all Caledonian MacBrayne and Strathclyde ferries to the islands of Scotland, key bus links, Glasgow Underground, and a discount on some P&O ferry routes. Passholders are not allowed to travel before 0915 Monday through Friday. Family discount allows children age five through fifteen to receive a free pass with each accompanying adult; additional children are half fare; children younger than age five travel free.

Great Heritage Pass. This pass provides entry to more than 600 of Britain's public and privately owned historic sites, castles, homes, and gardens, available in consecutive increments of three, seven, or fifteen days or one month.

Travel Tips

Planning Pays Off. Careful planning is key to every successful thing we do, and planning a rail vacation in Britain is no exception.

For rail travelers we recommend the *Thomas Cook European Timetable* (www.thomascookpublishing.com), which contains timetables covering major rail routes in Britain honoring the BritRail Pass. In Britain the timetable may be purchased at most Thomas Cook Travel Agencies and Bureaux de Change (money exchange offices). Free rail schedules for Britain may be found online at www.networkrail.co.uk, or www.nationalrail.co.uk. Also, free schedules may be obtained at any British rail station. Plus, you may purchase the *Great Britain Railway Passenger Timetable* in rail-station book stalls (however, you'll also need to buy a magnifying glass!).

How Much to Take? Half the clothes and twice the money! Obviously, practical advice would be "as little as possible." We usually tend to pack everything we conceivably might use during a vacation, lug it everywhere, use it very little, and return home with longer arms. In these days of wash-and-wear fabrics (and deodorants), this is not necessary. A good rule is to take a shoulder bag and one medium-size suitcase with wheels or two small bags. Hold to this rule, and you will have a more comfortable trip.

Regardless of how comfortable you expect the weather at your destination to be, pack a sweater. Brief cold spells in Britain are not uncommon. Stow a small pocket flashlight in your shoulder bag together with a collapsible umbrella or rain hat in the "unlikely event" that you may need them. Remember where you're going, chap!

Bring a washcloth if you normally use one; washcloths are not frequently found in hotels abroad. Take an electrical converter and adapter plugs for your appliances such as razors and hair dryers. Travel-size dual-voltage hair dryers are convenient; you only need to switch the voltage to the European 220 and add the adapter plug for Britain.

If you must take expensive jewelry with you (which we do not recommend), take a copy of its insurance appraisal as proof of purchase to customs officials upon your return. Same for watches produced by foreign manufacturers. You may have bought that solid-gold Rolex in a St. Louis pawnshop for a song, but the customs inspector may have you singing a different tune if you can't come up with the paperwork!

If you wear prescription eyeglasses or contact lenses, take a copy of your prescription. The same applies to prescription medications. Even if you use only over-the-counter drug products, we suggest taking an adequate supply of the item in its original container. Many such products may not be available or are sold under a different label or packaging.

Cash, Cards, and Credentials. Don't carry more cash than you can afford to lose; use ATMs (automated teller machines), or carry traveler's checks. You will, of course, need both U.K. and U.S. cash to pay for tips, snacks, refreshments, and taxi fares at your arrival and departure gateways. Distribute your currency around in pockets, briefcase, money clip, and money belt. A money belt is an ideal way to carry the larger notes.

ATMs offer the best exchange rate on foreign currencies, but if you plan to use them, do your homework first. Ask your bank for a list of ATM locations in Britain and whether your magnetic imprint needs to be modified to work in foreign ATMs. Be certain to know your PIN number, and inquire if the bank will charge you per overseas cash withdrawal. Although U.S. banks levy surcharges for the luxury of using their machines, these charges do not extend to U.S.–issued cards at machines overseas. Remember, though, that a cash withdrawal on a credit card is like a "temporary miniloan," and there is an interest charge. Get more information online at www.visa.com or www.mastercard.com for Visa and MasterCard charge cards, or contact the issuing institution of your card directly for specific details. For ATM locations click on www.mastercard.com/atmlocator or www.visa.com/atm.

You can avoid interest charges by using a debit card (cash withdrawals and purchases are deducted from your checking account). You probably will still pay a fee per withdrawal.

If you do carry traveler's checks, cash them at the branch-bank facilities located in or near railway stations and airports. Banks and official currency-exchange services are government supervised and are required to pay the official exchange rates. Hotels and stores seldom give you the full exchange value and often add substantial service fees. Credit cards are handy for paying the larger expenses such as hotels and restaurants. The charge is converted into dollars at the applicable exchange rate on the date the charge is posted.

Make a list of credit card, traveler's check, rail pass, and airline ticket numbers that you plan to take. Leave a copy at home, and pack one in your suitcase or carry-on bag. When purchasing your BritRail Pass, inquire about Pass Protection, a type of optional travel insurance covering any unused portion of the pass in case of loss or theft while abroad. Make two copies of your passport. Leave one copy at home, and take the other one with you. Carry a certified copy of your birth certificate and a few extra passport photos. Taking the time to do this will save you days of delay on your trip if your passport is lost or stolen. If your passport is lost or stolen, report it to the local police and contact the nearest U.S. embassy or consulate.

Cameras and Film. If you plan to take an expensive foreign-made camera purchased in the United States, take the sales slip with you. Otherwise, go to a U.S. Customs Office before leaving the country and register your equipment. Carry a copy of the sales slip or the registration form with your passport, and keep a spare copy tucked away in the camera case or your shoulder bag.

Some quick thoughts for those of you considering bringing or buying a digital camera. Unless you are serious about cameras, don't get caught up in buying the newest, best camera, with the most megapixels. Find a reasonably sized camera that is easy to use and fits your budget. (Currently, $200–$300 will buy you an excellent portable model, without expensive extra features you are unlikely to use.) Spend time before your trip getting comfortable with at least the basic features of your camera. You don't want to be desperately fumbling with it while speeding by a shepherd with his flock in the highlands of Scotland! Your digital camera will probably take a memory card of some kind. Given that taking your laptop abroad is probably not a good idea, our suggestion is to buy 4 to 5 smaller cards instead of 1 or 2 larger cards. This reduces the number of pictures that you lose if your camera is lost or stolen, or if a card goes bad. Several companies make small padded wallets that carry your extra memory cards independent of your camera and camera bag, and can stay on your person to keep your pictures from being lost. If your camera uses rechargeable batteries, an extra set is recommended. Further, be sure to have the necessary adapters for charging the camera battery in your hotel room.

Phones & Communication. The days of spending an arm and a leg to call home from your hotel room in Europe are gone for good. Now, thanks to the wonders of modern technology, there are a variety of inexpensive options for communicating with friends and family back home. There is also no reason for you to give up your cell phone addiction, make local calls from your hotel, or look for one of the few remaining pay phones.

If you have an AT&T or T-Mobile mobile phone in the U.S., check with your carrier to see if your phone can be used internationally. Often, your carrier will provide you with an "unlock" code, (possibly for a fee) so that your phone can be used with a SIM (Subscriber Identification Module) Card from another carrier. This could allow you to buy a SIM, or a prepaid SIM, from the local carrier in the country or countries to which you travel. Verizon and Sprint phones, which use a separate technology, rarely work abroad (those that might are often labeled as "world phones"). Some prepay phones that you can buy will work across European borders, particularly if you remain within a few countries. We would recommend buying a prepaid cell phone or SIM card directly from the mobile company, or from a reputable shop. Most major train stations and airports now have one or more of this type of store. Check with the clerk in the store to see if the phone that you are thinking of buying will work throughout your itinerary.

Buying prepay phones in Europe is relatively inexpensive, with the phone being very affordable and additional minutes available for a small cost. You are probably best off not using this phone for international calls, unless you have read the fineprint regarding international rates associated with the phone and/or SIM card. There are other choices for a mobile phone, with several companies providing rental European phones, which can be shipped to you before you depart. Prices start around $50 for a week-long rental, not including airtime.

Depending on how long you will be gone, and how much you need to see loved ones back home, an Internet cafe and video conferencing may be the way to go. While there are several available services, Skype (www.skype.com) is the largest and most reliable one. If you use the service computer-to-computer only, it is necessary to set up an account (for free). Some Internet cafes will have Skype software and a webcam preinstalled on their computers, and your loved one(s) will need the same equipment on their computer back home. If you are planning on using Skype extensively, an inexpensive headset with a microphone may be an easily packable purchase to give you some privacy and protect you from distractions. Of course, this assumes that you need to talk to your loved ones while you are gone. If you just need to check in, a few E-mails from Internet cafes may be perfectly sufficient.

En Route Tips

With all the luxuries of flight that modern airplanes offer, there is still something about flying that makes it more demanding than a similar amount of time spent at home or in the office. A transatlantic trip with a minimum of incidents and inconveniences is what we're after. Here are some suggestions we've found helpful.

Arrival and Security. For international flights (which include domestic flights where you then connect to an international flight) arrive at the airport at least two hours before your flight time. If you are departing from a major airport, with corresponding congestion, an earlier arrival may be in order. Be sure to follow all of the most recent TSA guidelines for travelers, found at www.tsa.gov/travelers/index.shtm. Our goal is to get through the security checkpoint with minimal fuss. To this end, wear loose fitting clothes without a belt that needs to be taken off, and comfortable, easy to remove shoes. Minimize the items carried on your person to include jewelry, keys, and change. Be sure you do not have any prohibited items in your carry-on baggage, and remember that any liquids must be in 3 ounce or smaller containers. Any electronics should be accessible, as they may be x-rayed separately. Patience is key; take your time and remember that you are on your way to a great vacation.

In-Flight Comfort. If you plan to catch some shut-eye en route, ask for a seat alongside a bulkhead. Bulkheads don't mind being leaned on, but passengers do. If you need more legroom, sit in an emergency exit row, but be prepared to accept the responsibility for being physically capable of standing and opening the exit hatch if necessary. Also, be sure your seat reclines. On some planes the seats forward of the emergency exits do not recline. Opt for seats in the forward section of the airplane; passengers in the forward section generally experience less vibration and engine noise.

Wear loose clothing. Unfasten your shoes, but don't take them off. Your feet will swell following several hours of immobility. The best remedy is to walk the length of the aisle in the airplane every hour or so. Try deep knee bends. To reduce swelling, consider wearing elastic stockings.

Flying dehydrates your body. Drink lots of water, and watch what you mix with it—alcohol dehydrates too. Special meals for special diets are no problem with the airlines, but requests should be made at the same time as reservations.

Tax-Free Purchases. Tax-free shopping in Europe was abolished in 1999 between European Union (EU) countries. This change had little if any effect on U.S. and other non–EU travelers as long as travel is to or from a non–EU destination. The EU consists of Austria, Belgium, Bulgaria, Cyprus, Czech Republic, Denmark, Estonia, Finland, France, Germany, Greece, Hungary, Ireland, Italy, Latvia, Lithuania, Luxembourg, Malta, Poland, Portugal, Slovakia, Slovenia, Spain, Sweden, The Netherlands, and the United Kingdom. Every international airport, as well as many ferry ports and train stations, has a "tax-free" shopping service. The routine is generally the same. You select your purchases, pay for them and add them to your carry-on luggage, find safe storage for them during the flight, then haul them off the airplane. There are variations.

For example, at JFK in New York, you select the items from a sample or catalog. The items are then delivered "for your convenience" to your departure gate for pickup. The hazards of this system are many. If the delivery person gets things mixed up and fails to make the right gate at the right time, you'll be off into the wild blue yonder sans purchases. Or, if you are late passing the pickup point, sometimes an unknown "benefactor" tries to help by taking your purchases on board the plane ahead of you. Finding this so-called benefactor can prove to be difficult.

Solution? Buy your "booty" aboard the airplane while en route. Most international airlines carry aboard a good stock of tax-free items, which you may purchase from the cabin crew. It's always best to check at the airline counter, however, to be certain that this in-flight service will be available on your particular flight.

Many airports have created specialty shopping outlets to compensate for revenue losses. Look for the British Airport Authority to be a trendsetter in this area. "Tax free," by the way, is a misused term. Many items, with the exception of alcohol and tobacco, normally may be purchased cheaper in the arrival city. The U.K. can be a bit pricey, so you may wish to purchase before departure. If taking any Eurostar or channel-crossing trips while abroad, the taxes are lower in Belgium and France than in Britain.

Keep in mind everything you purchase, "tax free" or otherwise, is subject to customs duty when returning home. Items shipped are processed separately. Consequently, know your quotas and attempt to stay within them to avoid paying duty and the ensuing delays involved. Remember, honesty is always the best policy.

Before Landing. Fill out all the customs forms your flight attendant gives to you, and keep them with your passport and airline ticket. Keep this packet handy, but secure, until your credentials are required by the customs officials at the airport.

What to Do about Jet Lag

For North Americans it usually takes an entire day to reach Britain by air and an entire day to return. Although the flying time aboard most jet airplanes ranges from seven to eight hours, airport to airport, it will be day two before you arrive in Britain. Most eastbound transatlantic flights depart at night and arrive the following morning. There is, however, limited daytime service on some airlines. The idea is to find a flight that will get you to your European destination as close as possible to bedtime according to the clock in your arrival city. Westward bound, try to get a flight as late as possible so you can go straight to bed when you arrive home in North America.

During the flight, you will be exposed to a cocktail hour, a dinner hour, a break for an after-dinner drink, followed by a full-length feature movie. In the morning, as the sun rises in the east over Britain, you'll be awakened for breakfast an hour or so before landing.

Add up the time consumed by all the scheduled events while en route, and you'll quickly conclude that your night spent in the sky over the Atlantic Ocean consisted of many things—except sleep. Even if you did manage to sleep during the entire trip instead of eating, drinking, and watching movies, your body and all its functions will be arriving in Britain a few hours after midnight by North American time. You will crave adjustment to the phenomenon known as "jet lag," which will try its best to interrupt your plans for a carefree vacation.

The following explanation of what jet lag is and some means to combat it should prove helpful to any traveler undergoing four or more hours of time change.

The human body has numerous rhythms; sleep is one of them. Even in a cave without sunlight, your body will still maintain a twenty-four-hour wake/sleep cycle. The heart rate falls to a very low ebb in the early hours of the morning, when you are usually asleep. Body temperature, which affects the mental processes, also drops during this time. Consequently, if an air traveler is transported rapidly to a time zone five or six hours ahead of that of the departure point, even though it may be eight or nine o'clock in the morning at the arrival point in local time, the traveler's body functions are at a low ebb. The result is a subpar feeling that can persist for as long as two or three days unless something corrects it.

To cope effectively with jet lag, start varying your normal sleep–eat–work pattern a week or so before your departure. If you are normally up by 7:00 a.m. and in bed around 11:00 p.m. or so, get up earlier and go to bed later for a few days. Then reverse the procedure by sleeping in a bit in the morning and going to bed ahead of your normal time. Vary your mealtimes, possibly putting off breakfast until lunchtime. This will condition your body to begin accepting changes in routines. In turn, when the big transatlantic change comes, it won't be as much of a shock on your system.

To lessen the effects of jet lag en route, avoid excessive drinking and eating. Set your watch to local time at your destination as you depart on your flight. By doing this, you subconsciously accelerate your adjustment to the new time zone in advance. For example, how many times have you looked at your watch and then realized you were hungry? After your arrival, exercise the first day by taking a vigorous walk, followed by a long nap. Then take it easy for the rest of your arrival day, and begin doing everything you normally do back home according to the new local time.

Some seasoned transatlantic travelers take even stronger precautions to avoid jet lag. They follow the rule of "no coffee, tea, food, wine, beer, or liquor" on the day of the flight to Europe. They do, however, advocate lots of fruit juices, vegetable juices, and water (no carbonated drinks). This method follows the theory that your body clock will then go on hold, waiting for you to restart it with breakfast the day you arrive in Europe. We emphasize slow and easy the first day to avoid personal crash and burn.

Resist the temptations of the airlines up to the point of breakfast and try to get some sleep. Some current studies have shown the hormone melatonin to be useful in combating jet lag, but as with any other over-the-counter drug, you should first consult your physician. And then there's the "light theory"—using a blue light source behind your elevated knee caps. Regardless of which remedies you choose, respect jet lag by taking some precautions, and you'll enjoy your vacation.

Train Travel Tips

Arriving in Britain for the first time, you may experience a confusion of terminology and learn too late that what you sought was really available throughout your visit. The problem may have merely been not knowing where to look or what to call the desired object. The following information may further ease and enhance the pleasure of your BritRail adventures.

Travel for the Disabled. First know that the British rail system is a leader in providing facilities and accessibility for the disabled in its stations and aboard its trains. Rail travel therefore has become an increasingly chosen method of transportation and recreation for disabled persons. Many aids for accessibility have been incorporated into rail-station design. Trains are designed with wider doors for wheelchair access; some even have a removable seat to make room for a wheelchair. Spaces for wheelchairs are at no extra charge and should be prearranged with the railway. Ramp access to toilets, buffets, and other facilities is provided. Folding wheelchairs are also available at main stations so occupants may be transferred to a regular seat once aboard the train.

Stationlink provides ramp-equipped, low-floor buses between the rail terminals and Victoria Coach Station. *Tel:* (020) 7918 4300; www.tfl.gov.uk. Just follow the signs in the main concourse of the rail station to board. Stationlink circular service operates in both directions and honors the London Visitor Travelcard.

The railways of Britain are most eager to provide as comfortable a journey as possible for the disabled passenger. To do this, prior notice of intended travel plans helps both the traveler and the authorities.

Those readers who want to learn more about this innovative approach should write to the Royal Association for Disability and Rehabilitation (RADAR), 12 City Forum, 250 City Road, London, England EC1V 8AF for details, or call from the United States 011 44 20 7250 3222; *Fax:* 011 020 7250 0212; *E-mail:* radar@radar.org.uk; Web site: www.radar.org.uk.

In the United States contact Mobility International USA, 132 E. Broadway, Suite 343, Eugene, OR 97401; *Tel:* (541) 343-1284; Web site: www.miusa.org for information about services and referrals to international affiliates. The organization produces the book *A World of Options: A Guide to International Educational Exchange, Community Service and Travel for Persons with Disabilities.*

If you plan to travel in Britain with a disabled person, call the British National Rail Enquiries at (0845) 748 4950 (from the United States, dial 011 44 845 748 4950) for information on the train company you will be using (British Train-Operating Companies are listed in the Appendix), or contact one of the British Tourist Agency (BTA) offices as soon as you establish your itinerary and begin making arrangements. For example, call Virgin Trains Journey Care at (0845) 744 3366 if traveling on their lines. Many others will prearrange assistance as well for those with any special needs or requirements. Sleeper services offer compartments efficiently designed for the traveler in a pushchair (wheelchair) regardless if traveling with or without a companion.

The same applies to the airline you'll be using for your transatlantic flight. Provide all the details of your itinerary, the nature of the disability, and any other information that will help them help you, such as if a wheelchair is needed at departures and arrivals. Specifically, tell them about special diets, medications, and toilet and medical-attention requirements. With these details attended to, you can look forward to a pleasant journey.

Baggage Carts. Many otherwise able train visitors to Britain impose a severe disadvantage upon themselves by arriving with more luggage than three men and a small boy could possibly carry. Train porters are nearly an extinct species, and their demise was expedited by the luggage trolley—Britain's version of our baggage cart—an elusive device that, whatever your position on the train platform, haunts the extreme opposite end and requires insertion of £1 sterling (coin) to use.

Our number one trip tip to all train travelers is to "go lightly." At most, take one medium-size suitcase with wheels, or two small bags, augmented by a modest shoulder bag. There still will be times when you will wish you could discard your suitcase. Pack lightly and leave room for souvenirs, or you might just need to purchase another piece of luggage for gifts.

If you have purchased a suitcase with built-in wheels, it usually will follow at your heels like a well-trained dog as you apply minimum pulling power. Unlike a dog, the wheeled suitcase cannot climb stairs, so be prepared to lift it on and off the train, and up and down the steps of stations without lifts (elevators).

Rather than relying on the trolleys in the train stations, consider investing in your own baggage cart to take with you if your suitcase does not have built-in wheels. There are many types available.

When loading your luggage onto a baggage cart or station trolley, keep the load as narrow as possible. You may need to pass through rather narrow ticket barriers to and from the trains. A Samsonite suitcase loaded sideways on a baggage cart or one of the station's trolleys will just clear, but a wardrobe case is trouble each and every time.

The trolleys provided by the station should not be taken aboard the train, although we've seen it tried. Again, if you are taking your own cart with you, fold it before boarding. If you don't, you may spend an embarrassing ten minutes or so on the station platform extracting a hapless fellow traveler from it as your train eases out of the station without you.

Using the Lifts (Elevators). The greatest problem in using the train station's luggage trolleys (or your own baggage cart) is traversing the station hall to the platform area, because practically every station has stairs. You can overcome this problem by using the station's lift (elevator). This polite announcement is found posted in most British rail stations: LIFTS ARE AVAILABLE FOR PASSENGERS WHO HAVE DIFFICULTY IN USING THE STAIRS. PLEASE CONTACT STATION STAFF IF ASSISTANCE IS REQUIRED.

In searching for a lift, don't always look for a modern, automatic-door elevator brightly lit with soft music playing. Instead, sometimes you will find the old-fashioned, double-door, manually operated freight elevator, large enough to hold a Mack truck and usually illuminated with a single, bare lightbulb—but it works. As the sign says, STATION STAFF WILL ASSIST YOU.

If you use lifts frequently, however, you will develop the knack of handling them all by yourself. A note of caution: Lifts will not operate until both barriers (usually a door and a gate) have been closed securely. Furthermore, the lift will be left inoperative if you fail to close the doors after you have used it. Be considerate of other passengers and the station staff by making certain all doors are secure.

Porter Services. Porter service is on the wane but still available in some train stations, particularly in the larger ones. We found Virgin Train personnel provided the best service and assistance, particularly with luggage. The best way to locate a porter is to inquire at the Left Luggage (baggage storage) area or at the station's incoming taxi stand. Waterloo, Gatwick, and Liverpool Street Stations have left luggage areas; some stations may offer luggage lockers, but most have stopped this service and even removed trash containers for security reasons.

If your luggage has been checked in at the station, there will be a handling charge, but the tip remains a personal item between you and the porter. We suggest £1.50 minimum per bag as a reasonable gratuity. Most porters will take your bags to the train and place them aboard in the luggage racks over your seats. Porters are rather scarce on arrival platforms. If you must have assistance, approach the stationmaster's office or the train conductor before departure with the request that a porter be asked to meet your train upon arrival at your destination.

If you are transferring between base cities or changing hotels from one city to another, you can request the hall porter at the hotel you are leaving to arrange for the arriving hotel's hall porter to meet your train upon arrival. A small tip should arrange everything.

A Few More Train Tips. The following train travel tips should make your trip more enjoyable:

- "Mind the gap!" when boarding and disembarking.
- Show your BritRail Pass or rail ticket upon request, and in the case of the rail pass, have your passport handy should the conductor ask to see it.
- Don't place your feet on the seats of the train unless you have removed your shoes or have provided a protective covering for the seat.
- Place your luggage in the overhead racks or the racks at the ends of the carriages provided for that purpose—not on the seats so other passengers won't be able to crowd you.
- All British trains are now nonsmoking. Rather stiff fines are imposed for those who violate nonsmoking rules.
- Observe seat reservations. They are usually marked by a ticket inserted at the top of the seat. Even though it is apparent that a seat is unoccupied, if there are other passengers seated opposite, ask if the seat is open—it will avoid embarrassment later if the person holding the reservation happens to return.
- Arrange for dining-car reservations on long-distance trains soon after boarding. Inquire with the guard (train conductor). If he or she cannot make them for you, a member of the dining-car crew will do so. Generally, they pass through the train before the first seating for that purpose. There are usually two seatings, so be prepared to select the one to your liking. You can also inquire about the menu at the same time. The second seating is scheduled so that the dining-car crew has time to tidy up before the train reaches its destination. Therefore, the first seating is preferred by many because it does not seem to be as rushed.
- If you plan an overnight journey on a sleeper, ask the attendant to explain how the equipment in your compartment operates. For example, many sleeping cars have electric shades. A push of the button and they open; another push of the same button and they close. If you did not know the button's function, you just might try pushing the button while the train is standing in a station and you are not dressed for the occasion! Tip attendants for their services; the proper time to do so is when they serve breakfast.

Safety Tips

Picking pockets is an art that is practiced seemingly throughout the world. Don't carry anything valuable in hip pockets. Money belts, holster wallets, or pouches that can be hidden are the safest way to carry cash and other valuables.

A concealable money belt or pouch is a good investment. Also, women should place the straps of their purses across their chests and carry the purses in front, not on the side with the straps only on the shoulder. Be mindful of the placement of your passport and money in backpack-style purses as well. Thieves on motorcycles can grab the purse from your shoulder very easily. You can modify the inside pocket of a coat or jacket with a zipper or Velcro. Or sew a medium-size button both above and below the pocket opening. Loop a piece of shoestring or other strong string around the buttons when carrying valuables.

Don't leave cash, cameras, or other valuables in the hotel room or locked up in a suitcase. Take them with you, or leave them in the hotel safe. We advocate leaving expensive jewelry at home, but if you must take it with you, leave it in the hotel safe when you're not wearing it.

Don't dangle your camera from around your neck or wrist; keep it in an inexpensive-looking camera bag.

Don't designate one individual to carry everyone's passports or other valuables, and don't carry all of your own valuables in one place. Split up documents and money in various safe holding locations.

Stay alert. Pickpocketing most commonly occurs in crowded public areas. Be leery of being bumped or someone causing a distracting incident. For all that, don't be alarmed—just be aware and take proper precautions.

For further peace of mind, we suggest reviewing the Web pages at www.travel.state.gov/travel/tips/safety/safety_1180.html for insightful tips and suggestions for "A Safe Trip Abroad." This site contains ideas on what to bring and leave behind and what to learn and arrange before you go, and it also contains helpful tips for public transport safety.

Remember, visitors are always subject to the law of the land; therefore, it may be helpful to pay attention to media reports and research some of the local laws and customs before departing for a foreign country. Also consider visiting the U.S. State Department's Internet site, www.state.gov, which contains up-to-date information on foreign affairs. You can contact the U.S. Department of State Consular's Office for information on travel warnings and public announcements by calling (202) 647-5225, faxing (202) 647-3000, or visiting www.travel.state.gov.

ARRIVING IN BRITAIN

That big moment is about to happen. Years of dreaming, months of planning, and weeks of anticipation are about to become a reality. The FASTEN SEAT BELTS sign has been illuminated, and the cabin attendants advise that the aircraft will be landing at your destination in just a few minutes.

For most of us, there is an unexplainable thrill about arriving in a foreign country. Enjoy the emotion; it's part of the reason for your journey—to experience the adventure of travel, to probe beyond the normal confines of your familiar environment, to meet other people, and to enjoy a bit more of the world than you had before the FASTEN SEAT BELTS sign came on.

The Airports

Within Britain, there are seven international airports servicing traffic from the United States: Gatwick, Heathrow, and Stansted in the London area, Birmingham and Manchester in central England, and Edinburgh and Glasgow in Scotland. For more information, visit www.baa.com.

Gatwick–London: There are two terminals: the North Terminal and the South Terminal. *Tel:* (0844) 335 1802. The fastest and easiest way from the Gatwick/London airport to central London is the Gatwick Express Rail Service. The Gatwick Express (www.gatwickexpress.com) dedicated rail service departs every fifteen minutes from 0550 to 0035 from the South Terminal for London's Victoria Station and runs to Gatwick/London Airport from 0500 to 2345. Approximate journey time is thirty minutes. Gatwick Express Information: 0845 850 1530 (Internationally 44 208 528 2900; Express-Class Fare: £17.90 one way; £30.80 round-trip. www.gatwickexpress.com offers a 10 percent discount when you book online.

Heathrow–London: There are five terminals—Terminals 1, 2, 3, 4, and 5—with courtesy coaches operating between the terminals on a regular basis. The fastest and easiest way from the Heathrow/London Airport to Central/London is to take the Heathrow Express. The high-speed Heathrow Express service departs every fifteen minutes from the airport, reaching London Paddington Station in only fifteen minutes (eight minutes more from Terminals 4 and 5), and runs from 0510 to 2352 Monday–Saturday, 0503 to 2351 Sunday. Express-Class Fare: £16.50 one way; £26.00 round-trip. These prices are only available online; there is a surcharge for tickets on the train (£23.00; £26.00 total). For further information, call the Care Line at (0845) 600 1515 or visit www.heathrowexpress.com.

Underground trains (the Piccadilly Line) operate every ten minutes into central London with a journey time of approximately fifty to sixty minutes; fare is about £5.

National Express coach services run between Heathrow's central bus station and Victoria Coach Station in London from 0417 to 2338. Standard fare: £4 one way; £8 round-trip.

London taxis are available outside each terminal. The cost to central London is £50–£55 and journey time is approximately thirty minutes to one hour, depending on traffic and destination.

Pick up the free guide *Central London by Tube,* which is available at the travel information centers and Tube stations at Heathrow Airport. The guide is full of information on the Underground network, shopping in the West End, and train connections to other towns and cities within Britain.

Stansted: Travelers could also arrive at London's Stansted Airport. Stansted Express rail station is located beneath the terminal. Trains run to the Tottenham Hale Sation, with connections available to the Underground there. Coaches run to London's Liverpool Street Station every fifteen minutes from 0600 to 0030 weekdays and 0530 to 0030 on the weekends. Journey time is about forty-five minutes. Express-class one-way fare is £20; round-trip is £27.20. *Tel:* (0845) 850 0150; www.stanstedexpress.com.

Terravision Express Shuttle service is nonstop to London's Victoria Station half hourly during the day and at night. Fare: £9.00 one way; £14.00 round-trip. Journey time: about seventy-five minutes. *Tel:* 39 0697 610 632 (from the U.S.); www.terravision.eu.

For more detailed information on Gatwick, Heathrow, and Stansted Airports, please consult the chapter on London.

Birmingham: Birmingham International Station is right next to the airport and offers direct service to London (Euston Station, about one hour, fifty minutes), Brighton, Edinburgh, Glasgow, Leeds, Liverpool, Manchester, Oxford, and York. *Tel:* (0121) 767 5511.

Manchester: There are three terminals: Terminal 1 Domestic, Terminal 1 International, and Terminal 2. *Tel:* (0161) 489 3000. The airport rail station is linked to Terminal 1 by a covered escalator and to Terminal 2 by a twenty-four-hour shuttle bus service. Up to six trains per hour depart from the airport station for Manchester Piccadilly railway station (twenty to twenty-five minutes).

Glasgow: One terminal, no rail connection at the airport, direct coach service connects with Paisley Gilmor Street Station (2 miles from the airport). *Tel:* (0141) 997 1111. Scottish Citylink service 905 operates from Glasgow Airport to the Buchanan Bus Station in the city center about every fifteen to twenty-five minutes. Taxi fare to Glasgow city center is about £18–£20. *Tel:* (0870) 550 5050; www.citylink.co.uk.

Clearing Customs

The customs-information cards given to you by the flight attendants before landing will expedite your clearance through arrival formalities. Actually, you will go through two processes—customs and immigration—although they appear to be integrated. Immigration officials will want to examine your passport, usually at a barrier gate en route to the baggage-claim area in the airport. After collecting the checked baggage, you should proceed to the customs-inspection area, where you will find two color-coded lanes: green for NOTHING TO DECLARE and red for TO DECLARE.

Everyone has some apprehension about passing through customs. For the most part, the apprehension is based on the question "Am I doing it properly?" In Britain this consists of going straight through the NOTHING TO DECLARE channel (unless you are asked to stop by an officer) and moving through into the airport's general-assembly area.

If customs officials want to examine your luggage, they will indicate so as you approach them. Don't go through the TO DECLARE lane unless you have brought amounts of tobacco or liquor that exceed the allowable limits or have purchased a gift with a value exceeding £145 (£75 for gifts bought in the EU) that you will be leaving in Britain.

The type and amount of duty-free goods that you may bring into Britain vary with your point of departure—a European Common Market country or otherwise. For transatlantic passengers, the limit is 200 cigarettes or 50 cigars; a liter bottle of liquor or two bottles of sparkling wine or two bottles of still wine; and 60 ml of perfume or 250 ml of toilet water. You will have plenty of advance advice on duty-free imports posted in your departing airport, and you can check with the cabin attendants on the airplane as well. Customs prohibits and regulates pornography, firearms, drugs, plants, fruits, and goods made from protected species. Know before you go, and the clearing procedures in Britain will present no problem.

This also applies to your return to North America. The U.S. Treasury Department publishes an informative booklet containing customs hints for returning residents. Write to the Department of the Treasury, Washington, DC 20229 for the *Know Before You Go* booklet. For U.S. Customs information while in London, telephone the American embassy at (020) 7499 9000; *Fax:* (020) 7499 1212; www.usembassy.org.uk.

British Currency

British currency is based on the pound sterling. The pound (£) is divided into one hundred pence (p), just as the U.S. dollar is divided into one hundred cents. Paper notes are issued in values of £50, £20, £10, and £5. Coins are issued in values of £2, £1, 50p, 20p, 10p, 5p, 2p, and 1p. The British pound sterling is used in England, Scotland, and Wales. Scottish currency is also legal tender in England and Wales. If you encounter problems using it there, the banks will exchange it free of charge.

Banks in Britain are usually open Monday through Friday from 0930 to 1700, with some operating Saturday mornings as well from 0930 to 1200. Check the Appendix for bank holiday closings.

British paper notes, like the majority of world currencies, vary in size according to their value, and a variety of them can wreak havoc on the orderliness of a North American's wallet. Certain notes, the £10 and £20 in particular, will require folding before they will fit into a wallet designed to hold dollars. Use discretion when engaged in this folding process, especially in public.

We proudly pointed out to one of our British friends how neatly organized our American wallets are because the U.S. dollar is the same size whether it's a $100 note or a $1 note. "Yes, that's quite neat," she stated, "but what do your blind people do?"

Although the European Union maintains that Europe is now one market, sort of the "United States of Europe," the British are not fond of relinquishing their pounds sterling to the "one-Europe" currency, the eurodollar or euro. At press time the United Kingdom still uses the pound sterling. For more information on the euro, visit http://ec.europa.eu/euro/.

British Telephones

The public coin-box telephones are simple—with a bit of explanation, that is. Basic differences still exist between British telephones and ours, particularly in the signals they make. A ringing signal is two short rings, followed by a pause. The busy signal sounds the same—only busier. An all-circuits-busy signal is a rapid series of high-low tones, but when you have reached a telephone number not in use, a high-pitched continuous tone is heard.

Public coin-operated telephones are identified by a red stripe across the phone booth door; some of the traditional solid red booths may still be found in smaller towns. They operate much like ours, except that a series of rapid pips will signal more coins must be deposited or your call will be terminated. Keep an eye on the window at the top of the phone box that displays the amount you deposited. The amount decreases as time passes during your call. Have more coins ready so you won't lose your connection midconversation.

Phone card pay phones are identified by a green stripe across the door. They require the use of a credit card or a prepaid phone card. The cards are sold at post offices and wherever the distinctive green British Telecom (BT) phone card sign is displayed. If you are planning on doing a bit of telephoning, it pays to shop around for the best rates of phone cards. Instructions for the use of phone cards are posted inside each booth, or you can ask an information office for the pamphlet How to Call Home from the UK.

When dialing Britain from the United States, use the international calling code **011** followed by the country code **44.** Useful phone numbers are listed in the Appendix. All area codes within Britain begin with 0, which is dropped when calling from the United States. If you need assistance telephoning while in Britain, the national directory is 192, international directory is 153, and for an emergency of any kind dial 999. Free calls within Britain begin with 0800 or 0808; the exchange 0845 is charged as a local call anywhere within Britain. Following are the exchanges for the base cities mentioned in this book: London (inner), (020) 7xxx xxxx; London (outer), (020) 8xxx xxxx; Edinburgh, (0131); Glasgow, (0141); Cardiff, (029) 20xx xxxx.

British Traditions

Some visitors entering Britain for the first time may find some of the British traditions, customs, and way of life a little difficult to understand. Perhaps what follows may assist in the transition.

If an Englishman from London, a Scot from Edinburgh, and a Welshman from Cardiff were traveling together in North America, they would describe themselves as being "British" or "Brits." But among themselves, they would be English, Scottish, and Welsh. These three nationalities, joined by the Ulstermen of Northern Ireland, make up what we refer to as the United Kingdom. Since the BritRail Pass is not accepted for rail travel in Northern Ireland, references in this book are to Britain rather than the United Kingdom, and the term British refers to the peoples of England, Scotland, and Wales.

Those who plan to add Northern Ireland and the Republic of Ireland to their rail itinerary should consider the BritRail Pass + Ireland (see Appendix for pass prices).

The British character will wear well on you after a few days. They are generally a well-disciplined and polite people. If anyone is at fault, more than likely it is the visitor, not the host. Visitors are not advised to get into controversial conversations of opinion—especially in a pub! Although the British can face crises and keep their cool, most maintain a fierce loyalty to Her Majesty, Queen Elizabeth II. You'll also learn very quickly that the British queue is the quintessence of "first-come, first-served."

On the surface Britons may seem reserved, even humorless. In fact, many Britons enjoy some very bold and bawdy humor, as their tabloids will attest. Once their facade is penetrated, you will find them capable of the highest mark of humor—they can laugh at themselves. This becomes most evident in their observations regarding their weather. "The way to ensure summer in England," snapped Horace Walpole, "is to have it framed and glazed in a comfortable room." Byron's observation was perhaps terser: "The English winter—ending in July to recommence in August." Britain does have a tendency to be damp at times. You won't regret taking a small folding umbrella or a rain hat or purchasing authentic British ones once there.

The Language Barrier

George Bernard Shaw once said America and Britain are "two nations divided by a common language." Terminology, more so than pronunciation, appears to be the problem whenever an American and a Briton cannot communicate effectively. *Bum Bags and Fanny Packs: A British-American American-British Dictionary,* by Jeremy Smith (2006, Basic Books), or *Divided by a Common Language,* by Christopher Davies (2007, Houghton Mifflin Harcourt), can be most helpful during an initial visit to Britain.

Reading daily newspapers, listening to the British Broadcasting Corporation (BBC), or watching the telly (television) are quick remedial methods for learning the language (try BBC America). These media communicate through a more or less middle-of-the-road lexicon.

Regional and local dialects can be extremely difficult to comprehend on occasion; even the Brits admit they sometimes have difficulty understanding each other. It has been said that if a Glaswegian (resident of Glasgow) and a Cockney (Londoner) were locked together in the same room, neither would be able to converse with the other—even after being properly introduced.

One of the first things a visitor from "the Colonies" (America) will notice is the manner in which directions are given. Americans geographically locate a point within a city by referring to the number of blocks distant from the point of inquiry, for example, "two blocks down the street." Britain's early road builders, however, never thought too much about a grid system and permitted their streets to wander along the easiest gradient. Consequently, directions given by a constable or someone on the street will usually be linear, that is, "Straight away for 100 meters," "A kilometer or two," and so on. Visual objects are employed as well: "Straight away to the pub," "Keep walking till you come to the third traffic light," and the like. Cabbies (taxi drivers) are good sources for directional information and advice. Every cabby carries a street map in his taxi and usually will be glad to assist you.

Nuances in the American/British vocabulary can sometimes lead to trouble. In a public place, such as a train station, those in search of toilet facilities will do well to employ the term *lavatory* in their quest. The WC (water closet) seems to be losing its effectiveness in Britain, although it still brings direct results when used in continental Europe. However, if you want to be up on British expressions, you might ask for the *loo*—that's where those in the know go to "spend a penny." (Many public loos charge a few pence for admission.) Requesting directions to the *bathroom,* particularly in a train station, might lead you to the public showers. So take our advice and stick with *lavatory* or *loo*.

When a Brit asks you for a *rubber,* don't be offended; just hand him an eraser. If you want a cookie, ask for a *biscuit;* french fries are *chips,* and potato chips are called *crisps.*

Terminology in a train station should not present much of a problem. The baggage room is *left luggage,* and *lost property* translates easily into lost and found. Elevators are labeled *lifts,* but *subway* means a pedestrian underground street crossing. The *Underground,* or *Tube,* is the British version of our subway.

A *carriage* is a (rail) coach, and a *coach* is a long-distance bus. Should you hear the term *goods wagon* or *goods train,* that translates to a freight car or a freight train in American. Aboard a train the conductor usually is referred to as the *guard;* the engineer becomes the train *driver.*

The British measure body weight in stones—a stone being a unit of fourteen pounds. A person weighing fourteen stone six pounds would be 202 pounds avoirdupois. A popular measurement of time is a fortnight, meaning fourteen days or two weeks. Britain's conversion to a decimal currency system has not changed the slang for the pound sterling—it's still a quid—and then there's the guinea. Anyway, before long you'll notice yourself picking up a few words or phrases along the way. Cheerio!

British Pubs

The pub is a uniquely British phenomenon. The ingredient that makes a true "public house" is not its construction, architecture, furniture, or the spirits it dispenses—it is the clientele. The term *public house* means just that. Everyone is welcome, even Americans and Australians.

The *local,* as most British pubs are lovingly referred to, is an organic part of the community, ranking in importance along with the local postal office and the town hall—perhaps even higher. The locals who support it generally prefer to stand when they imbibe, for pub etiquette must be observed at all times. Pub etiquette dictates you pay for the "round" when served and if you accept a drink, you are expected to buy a round in return.

To accommodate differences in the drinking etiquette of their visitors, most pubs have a second bar area, identified as a lounge or a saloon. There are more seats, and usually the drinks cost a bit more.

When are the pubs open? British pubs may now be open 24 hours a day, although in practice, most have stayed with the traditional hours. You must be age eighteen or older to buy or consume alcoholic beverages in a pub. Children age fourteen and older may be admitted legally and may consume nonalcoholic drinks. Children of all ages are usually admitted to licensed restaurants; they are also admitted to "beer gardens" and family rooms, which many pubs have.

A pub is usually rated by the congeniality of its owner, and unless "on holiday," he or she is usually found on the premises during operating hours. An entrepreneurial lot, many owners offer "pub grub" in their establishments. Visitors find it a good alternative to Wendy's or McDonald's for a snack or a lunch because a Frosty can never really compete with a good pint of ale or porter.

The personality of a pub greets you at the door. You can tell in an instant whether it's your kind of place. If its ambience reaches out to you, enter. No doubt a local or two will note your entrance with a friendly nod as the bartender beams at you and asks, "What'll you have?" When advised, the bartender will then indicate with a slight directional nod that it will be served in the lounge area. Pay when served. Never tip the owner if he or she brings the drinks to the table to bid you welcome. The owner is the host; you are the guest. Later, you might join the locals at the bar; but remember, remain standing and pay for a round when it's your turn to buy. Who knows, the locals might suggest you drop 'round again.

BRITISH PASSENGER TRAINS

The British rail network has come a long way—with yet longer to go. There is still a discernible difference between the operating speeds and passenger comforts of the trains of continental Europe and those of Britain. With privatization, the once cumbersome and bureaucratic British Rail was split into twenty-six train-operating companies that run the passenger services in specific regions. (See the Appendix for a list of the train-operating companies.) Network Rail is responsible for maintaining and improving Britain's rail infrastructure. www.networkrail.co.uk.

The light at the end of the tunnel appears to be growing brighter. Network Rail plans to spend £10 billion on rail network improvements during this decade. Thameslink 2000, the massive five-year project to improve London's existing railway infrastructure, will increase the number of trains passing through central London from eight trains per hour to twenty-four per hour in each direction during peak times and eighteen in off-peak times. Construction work began in 2007. The new cross-London services will greatly improve access to the Southeast of England. The longer twelve-car trains will increase seating capacity, and the new Channel Tunnel Rail Link Station adjacent to the existing St. Pancras Station provides easy interchange for Eurostar services.

InterCity 125 trains provide the majority of long-distance services, and they are shrinking journey times on many of the main routes out of London. From King's Cross Station, for example, the InterCity 125 covers the 393 miles between London and Edinburgh in four hours flat—an average of 98 miles per hour—and that includes a station stop at York and Newcastle in England before crossing into Scotland. The trains are powered by two 2,250-horsepower diesel-electric engines, one at each end of the train. The coaches are identified by letter (A, B, C, etc.), and the stations they serve have the platform positions marked accordingly. By InterCity 125 service from London, you can reach Cardiff, Wales, in only one hour and fifty-five minutes and Glasgow, Scotland, in only five hours, seventeen minutes.

A few older trains still in service on many of Britain's intermediate rail routes show more than a fair amount of wear and tear. Some of the train-operating companies are refurbishing the rail carriages, and others, such as Virgin, have built brand-new ones.

Virgin Trains operates 334 new high-speed tilting Voyager, Super Voyager, and Pendolino trains serving 135 stations and more than 94,500 passengers daily. Pendolino first-class travelers can enjoy at-seat catering and audio entertainment. There are also power points for laptop computers and cell phones.

First-class sleeping cars have single-berth compartments; standard-class sleepers have two-berth compartments. The sleeping cars are equipped with fresh bedding, washing basins with soap and towels, and a shaver outlet. Sleeping-car passengers are served morning tea or coffee and biscuits free of charge, and they generally can remain in the sleeping cars at their destination for an hour after arrival. The charge is standard for all destinations regardless of the distance.

Consider the sleeping cars for excursions from London to Inverness, Penzance, and Plymouth; available daily, except Saturday. Sleeper services also operate between London and Aberdeen, Edinburgh, Glasgow, and Fort William. Reservations for sleeper accommodations need to be made at the rail stations in Britain.

An overnight service is available on Caledonian Sleepers between London's Euston Station and Aberdeen, Edinburgh, Fort William, Glasgow, and Inverness. This "seated coach," as ScotRail terms it, provides comfortable reclining seats with footrests, tray table, individual reading lights, and air-conditioning. You can snooze in your comfortable recliner or get up and stretch your legs by going to the buffet car to buy drinks and snacks. Sweet dreams!

Most long-distance trains haul restaurant cars. If not, there usually is a buffet car where you can obtain snacks and beverages. Aboard the InterCity fleet, restaurant cars offer a wide range of freshly prepared traditional dishes. Silver Standard restaurant service is available on many 125s and on selected "business" trains. Passengers holding first-class tickets who wish to take meals can reserve seats in the restaurant car or in adjacent coaches. Breakfast aboard British trains has always been a great attraction. It's hearty, generally very good, and, of course, comes with hot tea or coffee.

Some buffet cars offer "grill" meals, which you may enjoy either there or back at your seat. Seating in the buffet cars is not assignable, thereby providing a reasonable opportunity to be seated while you select from the bill of fare. One innovation found aboard many food-service railcars is beer and lager on draft. This, according to many railroad buffs, is an outstanding stride forward in the annals of railroad engineering!

Admittedly, dining aboard a speeding train is an unusual gastronomic experience, but it can be on the expensive side. Although food catering aboard a British train is far more economical than similar services on the trains of the Continent, those seeking less expensive food may want to utilize the food facilities found at most rail stations in Britain. They range in service from complete restaurants serving a variety of hot and cold dishes to a snack bar–type operation. Some have off-license provisions allowing you to purchase alcoholic beverages for consumption elsewhere, but all bars operating in the stations, unlike those on the trains, must observe the local licensing hours for drinks.

The most economical food you may enjoy on a train in Britain is, of course, that which you bring aboard yourself. Many of the station restaurants will prepare box lunches for you to take on your trip. Ask for the "buffet-pack" service. Your hotel or bed-and-breakfast probably can provide similar service with advance notice. Or purchase easy traveling snacks from a convenience store to pack in your bag. Purchase bottled water before you board or from the buffet car. Water from the taps in lavatories aboard trains is not potable.

First Class, Standard Class?

On most British trains you have a choice of first- or standard-class travel. More and more routes are offering strictly standard class or very few first-class carriages. BritRail Passes and Flexipasses are sold for both classes. First-class seats are wider and more spacious. If that is the sort of accommodations you want, then it is worth paying the extra price. Standard class is, however, an excellent standard. All the facilities aboard the trains, such as restaurant and buffet services, are available for both first- and standard-class travelers.

The average British citizen usually travels by standard-class carriage (coach). In fact, it is so much the custom that if you want to purchase a first-class ticket, you must specifically state "first class"; otherwise, you will automatically receive a standard-class ticket.

First class offers extra comfort and is less crowded. First-class accommodations for weekend and holiday travel are particularly desirable. Seats may be reserved in both classes, which is a wise move if your journey is a "must" and the distance is great. "Riding the cases" (sitting on your suitcase for lack of a seat) is not comfortable!

Seat reservations may be made in any major train terminal throughout Britain. Some train-operating companies in Britain offer free seat reservations, some charge a £1 to £2 fee, and some do not accept seat reservations at all due to frequency of service. Birmingham, Cardiff, Gatwick, Glasgow, Heathrow, Manchester, and Stansted Airports have rail ticket booths where you may make reservations immediately after your arrival. You may obtain advance reservations for treks of more than two and a half hours before arriving in Britain, but it is far more economical to make them once on British soil.

Travelers holding first-class BritRail Passes may travel in either first- or standard-class carriages, which is a nice option if the good-looking person you've been yearning to chat with boards the standard-class section. It's a disaster, however, if he or she moves to the first-class section while you're holding a standard-class rail pass.

You will find some single-class trains operating on branch lines. This means that the first-class accommodations are not available aboard that particular train. It is the politely British way of avoiding the somewhat unrefined term, *second class only*.

Similar to those on the Continent, first-class British railcars are marked distinctively by a yellow band running the length of each car above its doors and windows. On other-than-mainline service, where both first- and standard-class accommodations may be provided in the same car, a yellow band will be shown for only the first-class portion of the car. Restaurant cars, buffets, and cars containing other forms of food-catering facilities are identified by a red band above their doors and windows.

Except for those of the InterCity 125s and 225s, it is difficult to determine exactly where the first-class coaches will halt during an en route station stop. The non–English-speaking nations of Europe generally provide a diagram of each train's composition and where it will stop in the station. Not always so in Britain. According to the equipment in use, the first-class section of a British train can be at the head, the rear, or the middle of the train. Through experience, we have devised a system that is relatively effective in determining where the yellow-striped cars will stop.

Position yourself midway on the platform and scan for the yellow band as the train enters the station. Should it pass you, take off to the head of the train; if it doesn't, head in the other direction. Should the yellow-striped car stop directly in front of you, fate has been kind to you this day, but you can bet it won't happen again soon.

All British trains are now nonsmoking, reflecting the noticeable change in the public attitude toward smoking. There is a stiff fine for violating the rule. So if you are a smoker, keep your eyes alert for the red nonsmoking signs and smoke only in the (limited) station areas so designated.

Train Schedules

British timetables are shown in the twenty-four-hour format, and they are generally divided into sections according to the pattern of services provided. A typical two-part division is "Monday to Saturday" and "Sunday." You may run across a mix, however, including "Monday to Friday," "Monday to Saturday," or "Saturday and Sunday." All days stated are inclusive. In other words, "Monday to Saturday" includes all six days. (The schedules appearing in *Britain by BritRail* are noted as to days of operation.)

Always be certain that you look at the correct part of the schedule for the particular day of the week on which you wish to travel, and always double-check departure times and the platform number of the next train you wish to take when you arrive in a station. Sometimes alterations are necessary. Another caution: Services may be modified on days preceding and immediately following bank holidays. The best bet for a "must" trip, a late night return, or an early morning departure is to check your plans with the rail personnel in the station travel centers. Extensive engineering work is often conducted on the rail system on weekends, which frequently affects passengers' schedules. You can also telephone the National Rail Enquiries office at (0845) 748 4950.

You should experience little difficulty in verifying the departure time of your selected train or locating the platform from which it departs once you've made it to the station—providing that in London you've gone to the proper station.

Airport-style digital displays are the usual source for train schedules in most British stations. You will find them in the main station halls and also on the train platforms in many stations. Even the old-fashioned train bulletin boards can still provide the needed information. Augmenting displayed train-departure information are the usual vocal announcements in the station halls and on the platforms. For the most part, they differ from those made by Amtrak because you can understand them. Perhaps it's the accent that makes it possible.

Ask the Guard

Almost all British passenger trains travel with a conductor aboard. As previously explained, his or her official title is *guard*. This person carries with him (or her), in either his handbook or his head, a potpourri of valuable information. If you are required to change trains in order to arrive at your final destination, talk to the guard.

Perhaps en route you learn that the train you are traveling on will be passing a famous British landmark, such as one of the many castles. On which side of the train will it pass? If you are a castle buff, maybe you would like to come back on another day to visit the castle. Is there a local train station near the castle? Is there a local bus to take you there if the castle is beyond walking distance? Is there a pub or inn in the vicinity? You'll probably get responses to all of the above plus a condensed history lesson on the castle and its surroundings—all from the guard.

CROSSING THE ENGLISH CHANNEL

The newest method of crossing the English Channel is to go under it via the tunnel (affectionately known as the "Chunnel") connecting England with France and the rest of Europe. Direct rail service from London to Paris or Brussels takes you from city center to city center in only two hours, fifteen minutes to Paris and in only one hour, fifty-one minutes to Brussels. With the opening of the new St. Pancras International station and associated high-speed lines in England, the International Service is generally faster, less expensive, and more convenient than flying between London and Paris. Trains taking the "Chunnel" are also scheduled to allow easy transfers to other services on either end.

Other convenient ways of crossing the English Channel between England and France or Spain are via the water by Brittany Ferries, P&O Ferries, and SeaFrance. For detailed information about these services, visit the Ferry View pages at the Web site **www.seaview.co.uk.** Since there are various ways of crossing the English Channel and the North Sea en route to Europe, which one should you select? The fastest route from London to Paris or Brussels is through the tunnel under the Channel, utilizing the Eurostar passenger services departing London's St. Pancras International Eurostar Terminal.

The "Chunnel" and Eurostar Trains

In 1888 Louis Figuier proclaimed that "linking France and England will meet one of the present-day needs of civilization." On May 6, 1994, England's Queen Elizabeth II and France's President François Mitterrand brought Figuier's words to life and inaugurated a new era in European train travel: the linking of England and France via a 31-mile tunnel that runs underground and beneath the English Channel. More than 17 million tons of earth were moved to build the two rail tunnels (one for northbound and one for southbound traffic) and one service tunnel.

Three different types of trains utilize the Eurotunnel. Eurotunnel's own trains convey cars, trucks, and buses between the terminals at Folkestone and Calais. Eurostar is the high-speed passenger rail service linking the three capitals of London, Paris, and Brussels, operated by the national railways of Belgium and France and by Eurostar (U.K.) Limited.

Travel times from London to Paris are reduced from as much as nine and a half hours to two hours, fifteen minutes; Brussels is only one hour, fifty-one minutes away, thus making a European Capitals tour nothing more than an exciting day excursion. Trains arrive and depart from St. Pancras International Station in London, Gare du Nord in Paris, and the Brussels Midi terminal. Connecting services link Eurostar trains to more than one hundred destinations throughout Europe. For the most up-to-date information and new timetables, please see the Web site www.eurostar.com.

The sleek Eurostar trains offer three classes of service:

- **Standard class:** Comfort for value. Snacks and refreshments are available at reasonable prices in the bar car, or you can select from the roving trolley cart as it rolls right to your seat.
- **First class:** Relax and recline in your first-class seat as you imbibe complimentary food and beverages. Complimentary newspapers are available upon request.
- **Premium class** (available London–Paris route only): At a step above first class, this is the ultimate in Eurostar comfort and service. It includes fast check-in service at St. Pancras International Station in London/Gare du Nord Station in Paris, use of the Eurostar executive lounges (the Business Premier Lounge in St. Pancras and Ashford and Salon Eurostar in Gare du Nord and Brussels Midi/Zuid), a four-course meal (choice of two main dishes) with complimentary wines, and champagne (on trains departing between 1100 and 1700; breakfast is served on trains departing up to 1100). You can also obtain a voucher to reserve a complimentary taxi/executive car transfer upon arrival at your destination station. Make your reservation at the departure station's Eurostar executive lounge. (This service is not available at Ashford International Station.)

Each train can carry 766 passengers (182 in first class and 560 in standard class, plus 24 premium first-class seats) and reach speeds of 186 miles per hour in Europe, with speeds of 100 miles per hour through the Chunnel. Eurostar zooms through the channel tunnel in only nineteen minutes. The train is based primarily on the TGV (Train à Grande Vitesse) but was redesigned to accommodate the three different voltage types encountered en route. The trains are accessible to disabled passengers and those with special needs. Arrangements must be made forty-eight hours before departure by calling Eurostar Complimentary Assistance Service, (020) 7928 0660; *Fax:* (020) 7922 6018. Sufficient storage for luggage is provided.

Those taking advantage of a trip to Paris or Brussels from London on a Eurostar train are in for a treat. The trains offer the comfort and amenities comparable to few trains in the world. From the moment of departure, you're in for a smooth, quiet ride, and even when you enter the tunnel, the only noticeable change is the sudden darkness outside the windows. Those concerned with changes in air pressure needn't worry. Air flow through the tunnel is regulated to minimize changes in pressure, and few, if any, passengers are uncomfortable.

Families traveling with children may opt for coaches 1 or 18, where baby-changing facilities are offered and flip-up seats allow more room for kids. Ask the train manager for a children's pack of things to do while traveling.

Eurostar staff members are multilingual and are available to provide assistance from the minute you enter the terminal to the minute you exit the platform. You'll notice them right away, with their stylish dark gray uniforms with yellow accents. If you have any questions, don't be shy—they're there to serve you, and serve you they do.

Given the frequency of rail service and the speed of travel, it's easy to see how a "quick trip" to Paris, Brussels, or any continental destination can be accomplished. See the schedule for Eurostar trains running between London and Paris, and between London and Brussels.

Eurostar has won the "World's Leading Rail Service" award at the annual World Travel Awards every year since 1998. In 2006 Eurostar teamed up with Columbia Pictures, producers of the film *The Da Vinci Code*. A Eurostar train was named *The Da Vinci Code* and carried the entire cast and filmmakers from London's Waterloo International Station to Cannes, France, for the global premiere of *The Da Vinci Code* at the Cannes Film Festival on May 17, 2006.

Notes

- Reservations are mandatory.
- Be certain to check in at your departure station at least twenty minutes before departure.
- Holders of BritRail Pass, Eurail pass, France Rail pass, and Benelux Tourrail Pass receive discounts on Eurostar services.
- BritRail Passes cannot be used for rail travel in continental Europe.
- Smokers take note: All Eurostar trains are nonsmoking.

To purchase one-way or round-trip Eurostar tickets or for scheduling information on trains to other cities, visit **www.eurostar.com.**

EUROSTAR SCHEDULES

DEPART London St. Pancras International	ARRIVE Paris Gare du Nord	TRAIN NUMBER	NOTES
0525	0850	9078	M–F
0653	1017	9004	M–Sa
0722	1047	9006	M–Sa
0802	1117	9008	M–Sa
0826	1147	9010	Su
1025	1347	9018	Daily
1228	1550	9024	Daily
1402	1723	9030	Daily
1602	1917	9038	M–F
1622	1947	9040	Daily
1732	2047	9044	M–F
1732	2047	9046	Daily
1902	2217	9050	Daily
2002	2317	9054	Daily

DEPART Paris Gare du Nord	ARRIVE London St. Pancras International	TRAIN NUMBER	NOTES
0643	0759	9005	M–F
0713	0828	9007	M–Sa
0813	0937	9011	Daily
0913	1034	9015	Daily
1013	1128	9019	Daily
1113	1229	9023	Daily
1304	1431	9031	Daily
1513	1637	9039	Daily
1613	1734	9043	Daily
1713	1829	9047	Daily
1813	1929	9051	Exc. Sa
1913	2034	9055	Daily
2013	2129 (2138 Sa, Su)	9059	Daily
2113	2234	9063	Daily

Note: Arrival and departure times are local; continental Europe is one hour ahead of the United Kingdom.

EUROSTAR SCHEDULES

DEPART London St. Pancras International	ARRIVE Brussels Midi	TRAIN NUMBER	NOTES
0619	0942	9108	M–F
0658	1008	9110	Sa Only
0734	1027	9112	M–F
0827	1133	9120	M–F
0857	1203	9116	Sa, Su
1057	1412	9126	Exc. Su
1258	1603	9132	Exc. Su
1434	1733	9138	Exc. Sa
1604	1911	9144	Sa–Su
1704	2003	9148	Sa–Su
1834 (1825 Su)	2133	9154	Exc. Sa
1934	2233	9158	Daily

DEPART Brussels Midi	ARRIVE London St. Pancras International	TRAIN NUMBER	NOTES
0651	0756	9109	Exc. Su
0805 (0759 Sa)	0859	9113	Exc. Su
0929	1026	9119	Sa, Su
1129	1233	9181	Sa
1229	1333	9129	M-F
1429	1526	9139	M–F
1459	1556	9141	Su
1559	1703	9145	M–F
1649	1805	9149	Su
1759	1903	9153	Daily
1850	2003	9157	Exc. Sa
2029	2133	9163	Exc. Sa

Note: Arrival and departure times are local; continental Europe is one hour ahead of the United Kingdom.

EUROSTAR FARES

London—Paris or Brussels

Eurostar fares are provided in U.S. dollars, one-way in either direction, and are subject to change at the discretion of the railways.

Fare Type	First Class	Standard Class	Conditions
Passholder*	$165	$91	Exchangeable before travel; nonrefundable
Full Fare	$261	$225	Exchangeable and partially refundable before travel
Business Premier	$419	NA	Refundable up to 2 mo. after travel date; exchangeable
Economy	$179	$90	Min. 1 night stay
Senior	$120	$61	Age 60 and older
Youth	$142	$62	Younger than age 26 on day of travel; nonrefundable
Child	$112	$48	Age 4–11
Wheelchair Adult†	$55	NA	
Wheelchair Companion†	$55	NA	
Wheelchair Child†	$35	NA	

* Holders of Eurail, BritRail, France, and Benelux passes, and holders of the Eurail Benelux–Germany Pass. Nonrefundable; may be exchanged once prior to departure; exchange only in Europe.

† 100% refundable up to 2 months after travel date; exchangeable.

- Seat reservations are mandatory on all Eurostar trains
- Tickets issued include reservation on the same voucher (inclusive price)
- 1st class includes meal served at your seat

Other Channel Crossings to France

For those who prefer to skim over the channel to France rather than ride the Eurostar trains under it, Britain's ferry and ship operators present a delightful alternative. Contact the companies listed below for detailed sailings schedules, fares, reservations, and other information.

Brittany Ferries

Millbay, Plymouth, Devon PL1 3EW
Tel: (0871) 244 0744
www.brittany-ferries.co.uk (bookings available online)

Routes and Journey Times to France

Route	Journey Time	Frequency
Plymouth–Roscoff	6 hrs	1–3 daily
Poole–Cherbourg	4 hrs 30 min via Fast Craft 6 hrs 30 min (night)	1–3 daily Mar–Oct
Portsmouth–St. Malo	10 hrs 45 min (night)	1 daily
Portsmouth–Caen	6 hrs (day) 7 hrs (night)	2–4 daily
Portsmouth–Cherbourg	3 hrs	2 daily
Cork–Roscoff	14 hrs	Saturday only

Each of Brittany Ferries' luxury cruise-ferries offers restaurant facilities, boutiques, and cabin/berth accommodations. Check in at least 45 min. in advance.

P&O Ferries

Channel House, Channel View Road
Dover, CT17 9TJ
Tel: (0871) 664 2121
www.poferries.com (bookings available online)

Routes and Journey Times to France

Route	Journey Time	Frequency
Dover–Calais	90 min	up to 46 daily

The seven P&O superferries on the Dover–Calais route offer up to forty-six return sailings daily. Travel in standard or Club Lounge class. The superferries offer restaurants, cafes, bars, a comfortable lounge area, and shopping. Purchase tickets for the sea crossing online or at the ticket offices in London rail stations.

Both first- and standard-class accommodations are available on the boat trains between London and Dover. The BritRail Pass is accepted for the rail portion of the journey from

London to the port (seat reservations are recommended). The term boat train applies to those trains departing from London's Charing Cross Station to Dover Priory for direct sailing connections at Dover's Eastern Docks with P&O Ferries crossing to the French port of Calais. The trains traveling from London to Dover Priory are met by a courtesy bus service to the docks.

SeaFrance Limited

SeaFrance Eastern Docks
Dover, Kent CT16 1JA
Tel: (0871) 423 7119
www.seafrance.co.uk
E-mail: enquiries@seafrance.fr

Routes and Journey Times to France

Route	Journey Time	Frequency
Dover–Calais	70–90 min	12–15 daily

SeaFrance's newest ship, the Molière, has an overall length of 203 meters and carries up to 1,200 passengers at speeds of up to 25 knots. Journey time for all vessels, 90 minutes. You will find a variety of French food facilities on SeaFrance vessels: Le Brasserie with waiter service; Le Relais Gourmet, a self-serve restaurant stocked with fine French foods; an English-style pub with snacks; and Le Café.

Crossing the Channel to Other Ports

Route	Operator	Journey Time	Frequency
Harwich–Esbjerg, Denmark	DFDS	19 hrs	3/week
Harwich–Hoek van Holland	Stena Line HSS	6 hrs 30 min	2 daily

DFDS Seaways (U.K.)

Scandinavia House
Parkeston
Harwich, Essex CO12 4QG
Tel: 45 334 23 010
www.dfdsseaways.com
E-mail: incoming@dfdsseaways.dk

SeaEurope Holidays, Inc.

USA Representatives for: **DFDS Seaways, Silja Line,** and **Gota Canal Cruises**
6801 Lake Worth Road, Suite 107
Lake Worth, FL 33467
Tel: Reservations, Timetables, and Fares—(800) 533-3755, ext. 1
Brochures—(800) 533-3755, ext. 6
Tours and Cruises—(800) 533-3755, ext. 2
Fax: (561) 491-5156
www.seaeurope.com (for U.S./Canada residents, online booking available)

DFDS Seaways routes also include crossing the North Sea to connect Great Britain with Sweden, Norway, and Holland. Seven modern passenger ships traverse eight routes crossing the Channel and the North Sea.

Stena Line

PO Box 2
3150 AA Hoek Van Holland
Tel: 31 0174 389 333
Fax: 31 0174 389 389
www.stenaline.com (online booking available)

The Harwich–Hoek van Holland (Hook of Holland) via Stena Line HSS (High-Speed Service) is the most direct sea link between London and Amsterdam. Convenient connections may also be made from Hoek van Holland to Brussels, Belgium. Departure by rail from London to Harwich is from the Liverpool Street Station.

Stena HSS onboard facilities include restaurants ranging from gourmet bill of fare at Maxim's to burgers and fries at McDonald's, several bars, two movie theaters, a casino, and video games.

Notes

- BritRail Passes are *not* accepted for travel on the shipping companies operating on either the English Channel or the North Sea.
- Port-to-port tickets must be purchased for all sea voyages (check with the appropriate shipping company for any qualifying discounts).
- Point-to-point tickets must be purchased for continuing rail travel in continental Europe unless you hold a rail pass (e.g., any variety of Eurail pass or France Rail pass) valid for travel in continental Europe. In this case you may have your rail pass validated at the rail station of the European port upon arrival, then continue your rail trip without the inconvenience of having to purchase point-to-point tickets.

CROSSING THE IRISH SEA

Some of the ferry crossings on the continent of Europe involve actually loading the passenger railcars aboard the ferry. When this occurs, the passengers need not even disembark. But at all ferry ports in Britain, passengers are required to leave the train and board the ferry, then board another train after docking. You will find this change of transportation mode is no great hardship. In fact, it can be a very enjoyable experience by including drinks and dinner aboard the ferry, followed by a chat with fellow passengers. The salon of a ferry is a good place for meeting people. Everyone has a common interest in travel, and everyone is going to the same destination.

Crossing the Irish Sea is very much like crossing the English Channel by ferry, except you cannot forward your luggage on to the Republic of Ireland. What you take is what you carry. So "go lightly" when it comes to luggage. Porter service is almost nonexistent at the marine terminals, except by prearrangement. Similar to the experiences in the train stations, it is best not to expect porter service. Furthermore, the trolleys (baggage carts) found in the majority of British rail stations are missing at the piers because their use is impractical on the sloping ramps and gangways to the vessels.

When you visit Ireland, keep in mind that Northern Ireland and the Republic of Ireland are two separate political states. Northern Ireland is part of the United Kingdom, while the Republic is independent. There are no customs to contend with when arriving in Northern Ireland from England, Scotland, or Wales. On the other hand, customs formalities entering the Republic of Ireland should present no problem for the bona fide traveler. The efficient "declare" or "nothing to declare" system is used by Irish customs. The BritRail Pass + Ireland covers the complete network of trains in England, Scotland, Wales, Northern Ireland, and the Republic of Ireland. Choose five or ten days of travel to be completed within one month in first or standard class with this pass.

The pass also includes a round-trip on Stena Line between Holyhead and Dun Laoghaire by HSS (High-Speed Service), between Fishguard and Rosslare by ship or Stena's Lynx catamaran, and between Stranraer and Belfast via ship or HSS fast ferry. The HSS ferries cruise at 40 knots, twice the speed of conventional ferries. For more details, visit www.stenaline.com. For schedules and fares, contact these ferry companies:

Stena Line

PO Box 2
3150 AA Hoek Van Holland
Tel: 31 0174 389 333; *Fax:* 31 0174 389 389
www.stenaline.com

Irish Ferries U.K. Limited

Corn Exchange Building, Ground Floor
Brunswick Street
Liverpool L27 TP
Tel: 0871 730 0400; *Fax:* 44 151 236 0562
Tel: In the U.S. (772) 563-2856
www.irishferries.com
E-mail: info@scotsamerican.com

Sea Links to Ireland/Northern Ireland

Operator	Services Per Day	Approx. Crossing Time	Rail Conn. From London	Rail Journey Time	Trains/ Day
Fishguard–Rosslare					
Stena Europe Superferry	2	3 hrs 30 min	Paddington Station	4 hrs 30 min	2
Stena Lynx	2	1 hr 50 min			

Crossing to Rosslare is recommended for travelers bound for Cork, Killarney, and Shannon Airport. Train time from Rosslare Harbour into Dublin is three hours; to Limerick for connections to Shannon Airport, three hours, twenty-five minutes; and travel time from Limerick to Shannon Airport is about forty-five minutes. Food, beverages, and shopping are available on Stena vessels.

Pembroke–Rosslare					
Irish Ferries	2	4 hrs	Paddington Station	5 hrs	5

Operator	Services Per Day	Approx. Crossing Time	Rail Conn. From London	Rail Journey Time	Trains/ Day
Holyhead–Dublin Port					
Stena Adventurer Superferry	2	3 hrs 15 min	Euston Station	4 hrs 5 min	13
Stena Nordica	2	99 min			
Irish Ferries–					
Fast Ferries	2	1 hr 49 min			
Irish Ferries	2	3 hrs 15 min			

Ferry services are provided by both Stena Line and Irish Ferries (choose cruise ferry or Fast Ferry service). Arriving by train at Holyhead Station, follow the posted directions to the main port terminal. The Dublin Ferryport is about 2 miles from the city center. A shuttle bus provides transport to and from Dublin's main bus station.

Holyhead–Dun Laoghaire

Operator	Services Per Day	Approx. Crossing Time	Rail Conn. From London	Rail Journey Time	Trains/ Day
Stena HSS Fastcraft	1	2 hrs	Euston Station	4 hrs 5 min	13

Dun Laoghaire is a suburb of Dublin. Facilities on the Stena HSS (High-Speed Service) Explorer catamaran include restaurants, bars, shopping, and entertainment.

Liverpool–Dublin Port

Operator	Services Per Day	Approx. Crossing Time	Rail Conn. From London	Rail Journey Time	Trains/ Day
P&O Irish Sea	2	9 hrs	Euston Station	2 hrs 27 min	12

Stranraer, Scotland–Belfast, Northern Ireland

Operator	Services Per Day	Approx. Crossing Time	Rail Conn. From London	Rail Journey Time	Trains/ Day
Stena Line Superferry	4	3 hrs 15 min	Glasgow–Stranraer	2 hrs 8 min	4
Stena HSS	2	2 hrs			

ENGLAND

www.visitengland.com

They came, they saw, and they conquered—Celts, Romans, Anglo-Saxons, Danes, and Normans constitute the major ancestry of the modern-day Briton. From the mysterious megaliths at Stonehenge to the formidable fortress at Hastings, the ancient English proved to be a capable people. Despite the size of their island and its limited resources, the English became a nation of traders fostering not only an exchange of commodities but also of cultures, giving rise to one of the most powerful empires ever in history.

England represents about 57 percent of the total land area of the island, or 130,439 square kilometers (50,363 square miles). We normally think of England as gently rolling green countrysides, but its terrain is diversified—from mountains in the northern and western portions to a deeply indented coastline providing excellent natural harbors.

When we think of England, we automatically think of royalty. Never make the mistake of thinking that Her Royal Majesty Queen Elizabeth II is merely Queen of England; she reigns over many other countries and territories as well. In recent years the older members of the House of Windsor have been puzzled, then distressed, by the world's fascination with the goings-on of its younger generation. The titillating misadventures of Fergie and Prince Andrew as well as the very public feuding of the Prince and Princess of Wales set the stage for the almost unthinkable divorce of Prince Charles from Princess Diana.

Then one fateful evening in Paris, near the end of August 1997, the world lost Diana, "the People's Princess." Her death affected not only her family and all the British but also people everywhere, who grieved for this young, vibrant woman. Today all eyes seem to be on her sons, Princes William and Henry (Harry). We'll have to see what the future brings to these handsome young men. For more information on the British monarchy, visit www.royal.gov.uk.

Rail Travel in England

BritRail Passes are, of course, valid throughout England. (See the chapter "Planning a BritRail Trip—BritRail Passes" for an explanation of the various types of BritRail Passes.) The BritRail London Plus, however, is a special rail pass for those who are limiting their travels to making day excursions from London to the surrounding area in southeastern England. It provides for rail travel in southeastern England as far west as Salisbury and Exeter (but not via Reading), as far east as Dover, Margate, and Harwich, southward to Portsmouth, Brighton, and Hastings, and as far north as Banbury, North Hampton, and Kings Lynn.

Choose from any two or four days of rail travel within an eight-day validity period, or any seven days within a fifteen-day validity period either first class or standard class. Note that many of the trains in the southeast area are standard class only and the London Plus Pass is valid neither for travel to Bath nor on services via Reading.

BritRail London Plus Pass

(prices in U.S. dollars)	First Class	Standard Class
2 days within 8 days	$189	$125
4 days within 8 days	$265	$199
7 days within 15 days	$329	$239

BritRail England Consecutive Pass

Unlimited rail travel in England for four, eight, fifteen, or twenty-two days or one month. Includes transport to/from Gatwick, Heathrow, and Stansted Airports to London. Prices in U.S. dollars.

	Adult 1st Class	Adult Standard Class	Youth 1st Class	Youth Standard Class	Senior 1st Class
4 days	$269	$179	$229	$145	$219
8 days	$385	$259	$329	$205	$309
15 days	$579	$385	$495	$309	$465
22 days	$735	$489	$625	$389	$589
1 month	$869	$579	$739	$465	$695

BritRail England Flexipass

	Adult 1st Class	Adult Standard Class	Youth 1st Class	Youth Standard Class	Senior 1st Class
4 days	$339	$229	$289	$185	$269
8 days	$495	$329	$419	$265	$395
15 days	$745	$499	$635	$399	$595

Base City: **LONDON**

www.londontown.com
www.londononline.co.uk
www.visitlondon.com

When you visit London, you will experience a wonderful combination of ancient elegance and modern technology, of old traditions and vestiges of the past mingling with contemporary conveniences and a futuristic Ferris wheel right along the Thames River. While plumed guards mount jet-black horses in Whitehall, bankers examine computer printouts on Lombard Street. This mixture provides a provocative, fascinating atmosphere in one of the largest and most sophisticated cities in the world.

Although London is Europe's largest city, most of its historical sights are clustered in a compact area. Central London sits astride the Thames River, about 40 miles inland from its estuary on the North Sea. By strolling through the oldest section of Central London, you'll see its first-century Roman walls, the Tower Bridge and infamous Tower of London, Saint Paul's Cathedral (www.stpauls.co.uk), the second-largest cathedral dome in the world, and the city's financial center.

In the so-called newer section of Central London (it's only about 1,000 years old), you can visit such famous sites as Buckingham Palace, the Houses of Parliament, Palace of Westminster, and Westminster Abbey. This area also includes Trafalgar Square (its north side is pedestrianized), Soho, and Piccadilly Circus.

Experience London from the top of the British Airways' gigantic Ferris wheel, the "London Eye," on the South Bank of the River Thames for a spectacular view from a height of 135 meters. You'll be able to see the old sights as well as the new ones, including the ten-story IMAX theater at Waterloo and the Tate Modern's collection of international contemporary art. Use London's 335-yard-long Millennium Bridge and its two newest footbridges, Golden Jubilee bridges, for easy and enjoyable exploration of this constantly changing city on foot.

In addition to Central London, the city is composed of thirty-two other boroughs. Since the streets seem to follow no particular pattern, use postal designations appearing with the addresses on maps to identify a particular region.

The British Tourist Authority publishes a very useful monthly guide to London—***London Planner***—with extensive information on events, sightseeing, theater, shopping, where to stay, maps, and much more.

Arriving by Air

London's Heathrow and Gatwick Airports are North America's primary gateways, with Stansted International Airport as well as London City and Luton Airports primarily providing service within continental Europe and Great Britain. Visit www.baa.com.

Heathrow Airport. Information Desk: 08 44 335 1801. Heathrow, the world's busiest international airport, is connected by the **Heathrow Express** train service to Paddington Station in Central London. Journey time: fifteen minutes (eight minutes more from Terminals 4 and 5); cost: £18.00 one-way; £32.00 round-trip. Trains depart every fifteen minutes daily 0510–2325. Hop on at stations in Terminals 1, 2, 3, 4, and 5 direct to Paddington Station. In the United States tickets may be purchased in advance. Tickets are also available in the arrivals hall at Terminals 1 and 4 and in the Heathrow Express Central Station in Heathrow Airport. For more information, *Tel:* (0845) 600 1515; www.heathrowexpress.com. Paddington has full luggage transfer service to Heathrow Airport. Check-in facilities are open daily 0500–2100.

Using the **Underground** (the "Tube"), the Piccadilly Line has access to all five terminals. (Terminal 4 has a separate station.) Tube service to Piccadilly Circus and Central London runs about every four to ten minutes 0502–0109 Monday through Saturday; Sunday 0552 to about 2331. Journey time: about one hour; cost: £5. London Transport information, *Tel:* (020) 7222 1234 (twenty-four hours); www.tfl.gov.uk or www.thetube.com.

AirLinks (National Express) operates Airbus (A2) transportation between Heathrow and Central London, to and from King's Cross. Adult fare is £8 single, £15 round-trip. Departures are from all five terminals every thirty minutes; journey time, one hour, forty minutes. You can purchase tickets on board. Stops include Hyde Park, Marble Arch, Baker Street, Russell Square, and King's Cross. *Tel:* (0870) 575 7757; www.nationalexpress.com.

Travelers headed directly for London's Waterloo International Station to catch the Eurostar trains can take a bus to Woking train station, which is on the main line to London Waterloo.

Gatwick Airport, about 27 miles south of London, provides easy-to-access, efficient, and swift (thirty minutes) train service to London's Victoria Station aboard the **Gatwick Express.** The express train departs Gatwick's South Terminal rail station every fifteen minutes 0550–0035. Journey time: thirty minutes. Express-class single fares: £15.95; round-trip £27.40. First-class single fare: £23.20; round-trip £44.50. Information in London: (0845) 850 1530; www.gatwickexpress.com.

AirLinks (National Express) operates coaches to and from London's Victoria Station and Gatwick Airport. Coaches run from 0700 to 2145 every hour during the morning and afternoon. In addition, there are 1630, 2030, and 2325 departures from Victoria Station. The single fare is £7.50; round-trip £14.50. For information in the United Kingdom, call 0871 781 8178 or visit www.national express.com.

Stansted Airport, located about 37 miles northeast of London, has fast and frequent links to London via its Stansted Express (www.stanstedexpress.com) train service. From the airport to London's Liverpool Street Station takes about forty minutes, with departures every fifteen minutes Monday through Saturday 0440–2325; and replacement coach service on Sunday. Liverpool Street Station departures to Stansted Airport are every fifteen minutes daily 0510–2255. One-way express-class fare is £18.00; round-trip £26.80.

Arriving by Train

London is a hub of rail travel for the Western world and a great introduction to the wonders of European train travel. With speed, little expense, and relative comfort, you can access some of the most stimulating sights in one of the world's most beautiful cities.

London's seventeen primary rail stations provide an abundance of travel opportunities within the city, to other cities, and to the countryside and seasides. New signage, departures and arrivals screens, and printed station guides enable the traveler to easily and quickly find station facilities and services. For the readers of *Britain by BritRail,* eight of these stations are well worth knowing:

Victoria Station is an international rail terminal. It also provides easy access to the south and southeast of England. When making sea-rail connections with Belgium and France, use the International Rail Centre next to platform 2. Station facilities include shops, eateries, money exchange, and tourist information, which is located at the London Tourist Office by the main entrance to the station. To reach it, follow the corridor running from platform 15. The Gatwick Express help desk is at the entrance to platforms 13/14. *Hours:* 0700–2150 daily. *Tel:* (0990) 301530 (wheelchair assistance: 020 7922 6206). For taxi service we have found it more convenient to take the escalator to the upper-level taxi entrance at the Plaza exit in Victoria Place rather than walking to the front of Victoria Station. The entrance to the London Underground (access to the Victoria, District, and Circle Lines) is opposite platform 7.

Euston Station is closely grouped with St. Pancras and King's Cross Stations for rail services to northern England, North Wales, and Scotland. Direct trains to Glasgow and a few trains to Edinburgh base cities depart from Euston. This station also serves as the terminal for Stena Line ship and ferry services to Belfast via Stranraer and to Dublin via Holyhead. The Travel Centre is located on the west side of the concourse and is open Monday–Friday 0700–midnight, Saturday 0600–2300, and Sunday 0700–midnight. Waiting rooms, restaurants, and other conveniences are located on the far side of the station hall from the Travel Centre. For taxis, use the steps adjacent to the LRT kiosk to descend to the level beneath the station. For entrance to the London Underground (access to the Northern and Victoria Lines), head down the escalators next to the LRT kiosk.

St. Pancras Station is the departure point for *Britain by BritRail*'s day excursions to St. Albans, Nottingham, and Sheffield. The station completed renovations in the fall of 2007 and now provides regional Eurostar passenger service from Glasgow, Edinburgh, Manchester, and Birmingham to Paris and Brussels via the Channel Tunnel. Eurostar is the passenger service operated by the railways of Belgium (SNCB/NMBS) and France (SNCF) and by Eurostar (U.K.) Limited. More than fifteen passenger trains make nearly one hundred daily runs back and forth through the "Chunnel," providing tourists and business travelers with quick, efficient travel to London, Paris, Brussels, and points east. For more detailed Eurostar or channel-crossings information, please see the chapter "Crossing the English Channel." Directional signs for the Euston and King's Cross Stations, as well as the London Underground, are prominent throughout the station.

Charing Cross Station is London's rail terminal for direct train service to Folkestone, Hastings, Dover, and other ports for P&O Stena Line Sealink services to Boulogne and Calais on the Continent.

Train information can be obtained at the entrance to platforms 5 and 6. *Hours:* Monday–Saturday 0430–0048 and Sunday 0630–0048. Taxis are at the front of the station. The Underground entrance is down the stairs or escalators located on the left-hand side of the ticket office (access to Jubilee, Bakerloo, and Northern Lines).

King's Cross Station is the London terminal for InterCity 125 train service to Scotland and the northeast and east of England. The Travel Centre is open Monday–Friday 0500–0136, Saturday 0500–0036, Sunday 0530–0136. Full information, reservations, and advance ticketing services are available. A money exchange service is available in the forecourt at the front of the station. Taxis are just outside the main entrance, next to platform 1. There are three entrances to the Underground. The new Western Ticket Hall of King's Cross/St. Pancras Underground Station opened in May 2006.

Paddington Station serves the west InterCity 125 service through Plymouth and Penzance and into *Britain by BritRail*'s base city of Cardiff in Wales. It also is the London terminal for Stena Line Sealink services to Ireland via Fishguard to Rosslare. The Travel Centre is located on the concourse near the entrance to platform 1; open twenty-four hours daily. Taxis are located at the side road adjacent to platform 1.

There are two entrances to the Underground in Paddington Station. To access the Bakerloo, Circle, and District Lines, use the entrances on the main concourse near platform 11. To access the Hammersmith & City Line, follow platform 8 to the footbridge, then follow the Underground signs. Since its recent renovation,

Paddington includes lifts for improved accessibility for travelers with mobility difficulties, fourteen platforms, and a dining, shopping, and waiting area called "the Lawn."

Liverpool Street Station, one of the oldest rail terminals in London, has undergone a £150 million renovation. The main ticket/train information office is located on the main concourse. Pick up a copy of the *Station Guide,* which details station facilities. Seat reservations and bookings may be made in advance 0700–2330 daily. The taxi stand is next to platform 10.

There are four entrances to the London Underground providing access to the Central, Metropolitan, Circle, and Hammersmith & City Lines: one at the end of platform 1, one on the main concourse alongside the ticket office, one next to Thorntons, and one outside at the corner of Liverpool Street and Old Broad Street.

This station is the gateway for rail and ship traffic between London and the Netherlands, northern Germany, and Scandinavia. Trains departing Liverpool Street Station proceed to Harwich, where passengers then embark from the Parkeston Quay by ship to Hook of Holland, a small peninsula jutting out into the North Sea. There, trains wait to take them to such destinations as Amsterdam, Hamburg, Berlin, and the Scandinavian capital cities of Copenhagen, Oslo, and Stockholm.

Waterloo Station is primarily for trains to the south of England, including the Isle of Wight. The Travel Centre is opposite platforms 16 and 17 and is open twenty-four hours a day. Taxi stands are at exit 3, through the main arch, on Cab Road. London Underground entrances are located down the steps from platforms 17, 18, and 19; down the escalators near platforms 18/19; down the steps opposite platforms 5 and 14 for access to Bakerloo, Northern, and Waterloo & City Lines; and via exit 2 opposite platforms 4/5 to access the Jubilee Line.

To access the **Waterloo East Station** for travel to Southeast London, Kent, and Sussex, use the stairs, escalator, or elevator opposite platforms 11 and 12 located alongside Burger King.

The **Waterloo International Eurostar Terminal** for direct service to Paris or Brussels may be accessed next to platform 19 and occupies platforms 20–24.

Getting around in London

London is meant for walking. Charming nooks, side streets, stores, and vistas all await your discovery. Of course, time constraints may force you to consider other options. To orient yourself, first-time visitors especially will find an introductory guided bus tour helpful. London Coaches makes it convenient for you to become familiar with the various sections of the city by operating "The Original London Sightseeing Tour" (www.theoriginaltour.com). The tours run across four different routes and depart every six minutes in summer and every thirty minutes in winter around a 20-mile circular route in about two hours. They pass most of London's major historic and contemporary landmarks and provide commentary in several languages. Board the tour at Haymarket, Marble Arch, Embankment Pier, Trafalgar Square outside Charing Cross Station, Victoria, or Baker Street Underground station locations. Fare: £26 adults, £13 children age five–fifteen years (discounted fares available online).

For a more personalized, albeit more expensive, introduction to London, hail a taxi. London's taxicab drivers, known as "cabbies," are a special breed. They are not issued a taxi operator's license just because they can drive a car. An extensive knowledge of the city and its history is an important part of their taxi-licensing examination. Cabbies usually have fixed rates for such sightseeing excursions, which can add up quickly.

Another picturesque way to get acquainted with London is via **London River Services.** Tours by river provide a view of London and its surroundings from an entirely different perspective. Boat services link Central London with the North Greenwich Station. Fast Ferry Service plies between Festival Pier and Rotherhithe (Holiday Inn) and calls at several piers, including Embankment (formerly Charing Cross pier), Bankside, Canary Wharf, and London Bridge City. For more information about riverboat services, ask at the tourist offices, or call London Travel Information at (020) 7222 1234 (twenty-four hours). Visit www.tfl.gov.uk/river/. *E-mail:* travinfo@tfl.gov.uk.

After an introductory tour, you will be better able to get around on London's Underground, the Tube. Don't let the enormous size of the Tube overwhelm you—it's really very user-friendly. Composed of twelve basic lines, the Tube's train system provides an easy and fast way to get around London from 0530 until 0020 Monday–Saturday and 0700–2330 on Sunday.

If you plan to use the Tube for more than one day, consider the **London Travelcard** for three, four, or seven consecutive days. The card includes unlimited travel on buses and your choice of all zones on the Tube or the Central Zone. The All Zone Card covers all six zones of the Tube, the Docklands Light Railway, and transfers from Heathrow Airport to any part of London via the Tube. It is not, however, valid on the Heathrow Express. The Central Zone Card covers zones 1 and 2 of London's public transport system.

With a London Visitor Travelcard, you are eligible to purchase the **London Pass,** which provides free entry to more than fifty major attractions, such as Buckingham Palace (open August and September), St. Paul's Cathedral, and Windsor Castle. It also includes a 160-page ***London Pass Guide Book,*** commission-free currency exchange, free offers at several top restaurants, discounted telephone calls, and more. With the London Pass, there's no need to wait in lines to purchase entry tickets. (See the Appendix for pass prices.)

Other combination transport tickets that provide access to the Tube, trains, and buses are available from London Transport offices or tourist offices. Maps of the London Underground and some discount coupons are included with the

Travelcard and are posted in all the Underground stations, or obtain them from the BTA or any London tourist office. For more information about London's remarkable transportation system, visit **www.tfl.gov.uk** or **www.visitlondon.com/tubeguru/.** When in London, you may obtain up-to-date information on many subjects about the city by dialing London Line, (090) 6866 3344 (60 pence per minute).

The Metropolitan Office forecast for Greater London weather is (09014) 722 051. Visit www.metoffice.gov.uk.

London, At Your Service

Professional tourist offices managed by Expotel provide visitors with detailed information about hotel accommodations, points of interest around the city, and a twenty-four-hour information line on using London's extensive transportation network of the Underground, bus, and rail services. www.visitlondon.com.

London Tourist Information Centre locations at your service:

Britain and London Visitor Centre: 1 Lower Regent Street, Piccadilly Circus, SW1Y 4XT. Take the Piccadilly Line to Piccadilly Circus. *Hours:* 0930–1830 Monday, 0900–1830 Tuesday–Friday, 1000–1600 Saturday and Sunday (Saturday from June until the end of September 0900–1700). www.visitbritain.com; *E-mail:* blvcinfo@visitbritain.org.

Victoria Station: Located off the forecourt, to the left of the ticket office. *Hours:* Monday–Saturday 0715–2115, Sunday 0815–2015.

Liverpool Street Station: Located at the Underground Station Concourse. *Hours:* Monday–Saturday 0715–2115, Sunday 0815–2015.

London Visitor Centre: Located at Waterloo International Station's arrivals hall. *Tel:* (020) 7620 1550. *Hours:* 0830–2230 daily.

Heathrow Airport: Located at the "Terminal 1, 2, 3" Underground station. *Hours:* 0630–2200 daily.

Visitlondon.com also operates a telephone accommodations reservations service. *Tel:* (0845) 644 3010. From the United States, (800) 318-5369.

London Limelights

There are, of course, some "must-sees" in London, particularly if you're a first-time visitor. Even if you've been to London several times, here's an update on some basics.

Buckingham Palace, The Visitor Office, Buckingham Palace, London SW1A 1AA; for tickets and info *Tel:* (020) 7839 1377; *Fax:* (020) 7930 9625; www.royal.gov.uk; *E-mail:* buckinghampalace@royalcollection.org.uk. Take the Tube to Victoria, Green Park, or St. James's Park Station.

Tours of the **Palace State Rooms:** £14.00 adult; £8.00 children ages five to sixteen; £12.50 for those age sixty and older. Open every day July 29–September 29, 0945–1800 (last admission at 1545). Tickets, which guarantee entry to the State Rooms at a specific time, may be purchased for any day in person from the Buckingham Palace Ticket Office in Green Park (August and September only); by telephoning the credit-card hotline, (020) 7766 7300; by writing to the Visitor Office at the above address; or by e-mailing bookinginfo@royalcollection.org.

Ironically, Queen Victoria's favorite palace was originally built in 1702 on the site of a notorious brothel as the home of the Dukes of Buckingham.

You can visit nineteen of the palace's 661 rooms, including the Royal Ballroom, from early August to the end of September, when the royal family is at Balmoral in Scotland. Same-day tickets for the tour are sold on a first-come, first-served basis from a booth at the end of Green Park, which faces the plaza outside the palace. The ticket booth opens at 0900. Be prepared to stand in line for as long as two hours (unless you have the London Pass). The tour includes the prominent vaulted Picture Gallery, which houses part of the royal collection of 10,000 paintings.

The Queen's Gallery is open every day 1000–1730 except October 13–15, and December 25–26. Tickets: £9.00 adult; £4.25 child.

Changing of the Guard—a military pageantry that has taken place since medieval times—takes place with the New Guard arriving promptly at 1130 daily April–July; every other day August–March. The red-jacketed Old Guard and New Guard line up facing each other to the beat of the Band and Corps of Drums—a stunning sight to see.

Imperial War Museum, Lambeth Road, SE1 6HZ; *Tel:* (020) 7416 5320; www.iwm.org.uk. *Hours:* 1000–1800 daily, except December 24, 25, and 26. Take the Tube to Lambeth North, Waterloo, or Elephant and Castle Station. Admission is free; however, audio guides are available for £3.50 adults, £3.00 seniors.

Appropriately so, the early-nineteenth century's most famous lunatic asylum, Bedlam, houses the country's memorial to the two world wars. A rotating clock hand in the basement represents the cost of war in terms of human lives, and the body count exceeds 100 million.

Churchill Museum and Cabinet War Rooms, Clive Steps, King Charles Street, SW1A 2AQ; *Tel:* (020) 7930 6961; http://cwr.iwm.org.uk. The entrance is across from St. James's Park. Take the Tube to St. James's Park or Westminster Station. *Hours:* 0930–1800 daily, except December 24–26. Admission includes both the Churchill Museum and Cabinet War Rooms: £15.95 adult; £12.80 senior or student; free for children younger than age sixteen. Free headset with commentary.

Few Americans are aware that a memorial to President Franklin Roosevelt is in London's Grosvenor Square; perhaps even fewer are aware that the place where Prime Minister Winston Churchill of Britain held secret telephone conversations with him is open to the public.

In 1936, when the storm clouds of World War II were gathering, the British began building a communications center, or war room, beneath the government offices in Whitehall. Building a 10-foot layer of concrete above a labyrinth of wine cellars and connecting tunnels, workers toiled at night so as not to arouse suspicions of what was being constructed. The Allies' direction of the war was conducted from this virtually bombproof communications center. It is interesting to see the place where some of the most dramatic decisions in the history of humanity were made. The Map Room and Churchill's combined bedroom, office, and broadcasting room remain just as they were during the war. Located within the Cabinet War Rooms, the Churchill Museum is a permanent exhibition dedicated to "the greatest Briton ever," according to a BBC poll.

Jewish Museum, Raymond Burton House, 129–131 Albert Street, London, NW1 7NB; *Tel:* (020) 7284 1997; www.jewishmuseum.org.uk. Take the Tube to Camden Town Station, then a three-minute walk. The Jewish Museum is open Monday–Thursday 1000–1700, Friday 1000–1400, Saturday closed, Sunday 1000–1700. *Admission:* adults £7.50, senior £6.50, child £3.50.

Kensington Palace State Apartments, High Street, Kensington, W8 4PX; *Tel:* 44 (0) 203 166 6000; www.hrp.org.uk. Take the Tube to Queensway, Nottinghill Gate, or High Street Kensington Station. *Hours:* March–October 1000–1800 daily, November–February 1000–1700 daily. *Admission:* £12.50 adults; £6.25 children (Internet discounts available). Order tickets in advance via telephone or Internet. Serving as the last home of Diana, Princess of Wales, the palace has been converted into a memorial to the princess and a home for a portion of the Royal Art Collection.

London Transport Museum, Covent Garden Piazza, WC2E 7BB; *Tel:* (020) 7379 6344; www.ltmuseum.co.uk; *E-mail:* enquiry@ltmuseum.co.uk. The museum completed renovations in 2007. You can visit the newly opened Covent Shop, visit The Depot, and/or join any of the numerous tours, walks, and program events. *Hours:* Saturday–Thursday 1000–1800, Friday 1100–1800. *Admission:* £13.50 adults; £10 children.

Madame Tussaud's, Marylebone Road, NW1; *Tel:* (0870) 400 3000; www.madame-tussauds.com. *Hours:* 0930–1730 weekdays, 0900–1800 weekends. Admission including Chamber Live: £28.80 adults; £24.60 child (younger than age sixteen). Purchase tickets in advance online if possible, as there is a 10 percent discount. To get there, take the Tube to Baker Street Station.

Here's a place where you can mingle with top celebs and notorious criminals at the same time. Showing her first collection back in 1770 in Paris, Tussaud's waxworks number more than 400 lifelike figures of the famous and the notorious. The figures include the late Princess Diana, Nicolas Cage, Brad Pitt, and Whoopi Goldberg. The Queen, of course, is a mainstay. Take in the dazzling "Spirit of London" time-travel ride and the chilling "Chamber Live." (Not suitable for those younger than age twelve, pregnant, or with heart conditions.)

Museum of London, 150 London Wall, EC2Y 5HN; *Tel:* (0) 870 444 3852; www.museumoflondon.org.uk; *E-mail:* info@museumoflondon.org.uk. *Hours:* daily 1000–1800, last admission 1730. Admission is free. Take the Tube to Barbican or St. Paul's, or take the Tube/rail to Moorgate.

Visit all seven permanent galleries to trace London's history from prehistoric times up to the present day, and relive the Great Fire that destroyed London in 1666. The most comprehensive city museum in the world and one of the most imaginatively designed, the Museum of London should be on your "must-see" list.

Natural History Museum, Cromwell Road, South Kensington, SW7 5BD; *Tel:* (020) 7942 5000; www.nhm.ac.uk. *Hours:* 1000–1750 daily, last admission 1730.

London Olympics

www.london2012.com

In 2012, the Olympics will be returning to London for the first time in over 60 years, with the city having previously hosted the event in 1908 and 1948. The Games will take place between July 27 and August 12, 2012. Several sections of London are being significantly redeveloped, with major changes for the Stratford area of London, the nearby Lower Lea Valley on the Thames, and several smaller areas. There will also be substantial upgrades to some public transport lines and an Olympic-specific high-speed rail service, the Javelin, which will run only during the games.

Some events of the games will be held outside of London. Rowing events will be held at Dorney Lake in Buckinghamshire, mountain biking in Hadleigh, whitewater rafting in Hertfordshire, and sailing on the Isle of Portland. Early round football (soccer) matches will be held in various locations around the country.

Though not without controversy, the intention from the start has been to create facilities that will have long-term uses. Several venues will be moved after the Games, and others downsized, in an effort to avoid what has happened to other host cities: large, expensive, highly visible facilities that go unused.

If you happen to be in London before or after the Games, consider a walking tour of the Olympic area. You will see venues under construction (from the outside), as well as learn the history of the area and information about the Olympic bidding process. There are several tour options, but the daytime Olympic Walk starts every day at 1100, at the Bromley-by-Bow Underground station. Pre-booking is required and the tour is £9, cash only.

More than half a million *additional* visitors are expected in London during 2012. If you plan to visit during the games, reservations for almost everything are a must. Purchase event tickets and reserve airline tickets and hotel rooms as soon as you are sure you will be going. In the U.S., **CoSport** (www.cosport.com) is the only official ticking agency. They provide both official event ticketing and packages that include travel arrangements, tickets, and other amenities. Tickets are certain to be at a premium, and some will be sold at lottery. While it will no doubt be possible to purchase

Entry is free, with a small fee for special exhibits. South Kensington is the nearest Underground station (served by the Circle, District, and Piccadilly Lines), and the museum is not far from Victoria Rail Station. This museum is located directly behind the Royal Albert Hall and the Science Museum, and Victoria and Albert Museum is nearby. It houses one of the world's largest collections—more than 68 million pieces (it acquires thirty objects per minute!). The Earth Galleries is a fun interactive alternative for kids of all ages.

London Trocadero, 13 Coventry Street, W1D 7DH; *Tel:* 1959 603 6035; www.londontrocadero.com. Take the Underground to Piccadilly Circus. The Trocadero is a two-acre enclosed entertainment, shopping, and restaurant complex. Attractions

tickets both closer in time and location to the Games, this will dramatically increase their (already significant) cost and open the possibility of counterfeit tickets.

Almost all visitors to the Olympic Games are expected to use public transport, primarily trains. The Olympic specific Javelin service will provide service to Stratford International from St. Pancras International and Ebbsfleet International. Visitors arriving via EuroStar from the rest of Europe will change to this service at Ebbsfleet. Both stations also will have parking available for park and ride services, although these services will require reservations.

The **Games Travelcard** will be available for event ticket holders on the day of the event for which they have tickets. This pass entitles the holder to use the Javelin service, London Underground and Overground, Bocklands Light Rail and some buses, trams, and rail service in the central London area. Other travel cards will be available for those traveling outside of London to specific events. At press time, schedules were not yet available for Olympic services. Be sure to get an up-to-date schedule upon your arrival.

Our suggestion would be (assuming you can get tickets) to add the Olympics as a portion of your trip. Consider tickets to your favorite event (or two) and schedule your trip around visiting London for the days of these events, while seeing the rest of the country in as much of the rest of the time you can be in the U.K.! A hotel in the West End of London, close to an Underground station, would allow you to see much of London, while limiting your travel time to and from events.

If you are interested in seeing a major international sporting event, as well as the unique venues of the London games, consider the Paralympic Games, to be held between August 29 and September 9, 2012. These events allow athletes with a variety of physical disabilities to compete in 20 different sports, with many of the events being held in the same locations as the Olympic Games. It will be significantly less expensive and less crowded, while still offering the opportunity to see world-class athletes compete.

include Funland, which is Europe's largest indoor family entertainment center. Eateries at the Trocadero include Ed's Easy Diner, Yo! Sushi, Planet Hollywood, and Rainforest Cafe. The Trocadero is open daily 1000–0100.

The Royal Opera House, built in 1858 and refurbished in 1999, is located in historic Covent Garden, home to the Royal Opera and the Royal Ballet. Visit www.royalopera.org for upcoming events and updates.

Shakespeare's Globe Theatre Tour and Exhibition, 21 New Globe Walk, Bankside, London SE1 9DT; *Tel:* (020) 7902 1400; *Fax:* (020) 7902 1515; www.shakespeares-globe.org. Education Centre (for lectures, workshops, etc.) *Tel:* (020) 7902 1433. *Hours:* May–September 0900–1230 (Theatre Tour and Exhibitions) and 1300–1700 (Exhibition and visit to Rose Theatre site); October–April 1000–1700 daily. No access during matinees.

To get there, take the Underground to Mansion House, or take bus 11, 15, 17, 23, 26, or 76 to Mansion House; cross over the Thames River via Southwark Bridge. The theater is along Bankside about 500 yards to the right of the bridge.

The Globe Theatre was rebuilt as the focal point of the International Shakespeare Globe Centre, an educational, entertainment, and cultural complex. Shakespeare's Globe Exhibition was voted "Best of Europe" by the European Federation of Associations of Tourism Journalists.

If you want to know what an Elizabethan audience would have experienced, find out what a "bodger" is, or learn about "penny stinkards," check out the Education Centre and workshops. A guided tour will bring England's most important theatrical heritage to life. Theater performances are from May through September. Box office *Tel:* (020) 7401 9919; *Fax:* (020) 7902 1475. According to Mark Rylance, artistic director of Shakespeare's Globe, "The theatre you will see is, to the best of our abilities, the space in which Shakespeare wanted us to meet his plays. It is unique in the world."

Tate Modern, Bankside, SE1 9TG, is the former Bankside Power Station converted into gallery space for the Tate's collection of international contemporary art. *Tel:* (020) 7887 8000; www.tate.org.uk. *Hours:* 1000–1800 daily. No admission fee.

Tower of London, Tower Hill, EC3N 4AB; *Tel:* (0870) 756 6060; www.hrp.org.uk. *Hours:* March–October: Tuesday–Saturday 0900–1730, Sunday–Monday 1000–1730. November–February: Tuesday–Saturday 0900–1630, Sunday and Monday 1000–1630. *Admission:* £19.80 adults, £10.45 child younger than age sixteen, £17.05 student/senior (Internet discounts available). To get there, take the Tube to Southwark (Jubilee Line) or Blackfriars (District and Circle Lines).

Throughout London's history, the Tower has been a fortress, a palace, and a prison, and it is one of the top travel sites in Britain. Allow two to three hours for your visit. The oldest part of the Tower complex, the White Tower, was begun in 1076 and contains the Chapel of St. John the Evangelist, the oldest church in London. Other main attractions include the Bloody Tower (where twelve-year-old Edward V and his ten-year-old brother were incarcerated by their uncle, the future Richard III), the colorful Yeoman Warders, known as "Beefeaters," and the Jewel

House, which houses the Crown Jewels. Visit the Martin Tower's special exhibition, "Henry VIII: Dressed to Kill," a large collection of 16th century armor, much of it actually owned by Henry VIII.

Victoria and Albert Museum, Cromwell Road, South Kensington, SW7 2RL; *Tel:* (020) 7942 2000; www.vam.ac.uk. Take the Tube to South Kensington Station. *Hours:* 1000–1745 daily (until 2200 Friday). Admission is free. The famous Victoria and Albert Museum, informally called the "V&A," is considered the finest decorative-arts museum in the world and includes exquisite collections of jewelry, furniture, and oriental carpets. Principal attractions include the Photography Gallery and Art & Design galleries, with a collection of more than 400 years of European fashion.

Royal Parks. Manicured gardens and pastoral grounds within London's vast Royal Parks, once the hunting and recreational property of the Royal Family, now provide the people of London and their visitors with something few megalopolises have: peace and quiet. The lake of St. James is so serene that it is a breeding ground for birds. Boats cruise the Serpentine River in huge Hyde Park, where there is room for riding trails and open-air concerts. Visit www.royalparks.gov.uk.

Westminster Abbey, Parliament Square, SW1; *Tel:* (020) 7654 7900; www.westminster-abbey.org. Take the Tube to Westminster or St. James's Park Station. *Hours:* Monday–Friday 0930–1630 (last admission 1530), Saturday 0930–1430 (last admission 1330); closed to sightseeing on Sunday. *Admission:* £16 adults; £13 child younger than age sixteen/senior; £32 family (two adults and one child). Each additional child is £6.

Every king and queen of England since 1066 has been crowned here, and more than 3,000 of the nation's most highly valued figures are buried here. You'll see the Tomb of the Unknown Soldier; Elizabeth I's tomb; the Coronation Chair, in use since 1300; Poets' Corner, commemorating Britain's greatest writers; the Chapter House, containing examples of medieval English sculpture; the eleventh-century Pyx Chamber; and the Abbey Museum.

Shopping

Shopping can be quite traditional—even stuffy—at Harrods in Knightsbridge, where the Royals shop, but the store alone is a sight to see. It's more than 150 years old. Though Harrods does have online service (www.harrods.com), the actual experience is much more pleasurable. You will find exclusive leather goods at Asprey's and rare antiques at Sotheby's on Bond Street. Oxford Street and Regent Street shopping is the most diverse and the most crowded, featuring famous London department stores such as Marks & Spencer and traditional British fare at Aquascutum, Austin Reed, and Burberry's. For those who desire a princely wardrobe, visit Gieves & Hawkes at No.1 Savile Row, London.

For a different and memorable eclectic shopping excursion, visit the Piazza near the Covent Garden Underground Station. Replacing the Covent Garden flower and vegetable market, which was in age-old times the convent gardens of the

Abbey at St. Peter at Westminster, Covent Garden is now a boisterous compound of antiques, clothing, and craft stores amid a plethora of indoor and outdoor cafes, pubs, eateries, and clubs.

Portobello Market is one of the more popular markets. Made famous in Julia Roberts and Hugh Grant's film *Notting Hill,* the market is located in the West London suburb of the same name. It's a vital mixture of English, Jamaican, Portuguese, and rich and poor. Their Notting Hill Carnival (annually, the last weekend in August) attracts more than two million people each year.

Restaurants and Pubs

Several years ago many visitors to London might have regarded English food as overcooked and boring. Now there are more than 6,000 restaurants, thirty-one of which are Michelin starred, serving more than sixty different cuisines. A wide selection of gourmet cafes and bistros sets the trend for the Soho and West Soho areas, with Carnaby Street at its center. Both areas are bedecked with fashionable boutiques, bookstores, craft shops, and expensive private clubs.

Fans of the syndicated American TV show *Cheers* will feel right at home at the Cheers London Bar & Restaurant. It's located on the ground floor of the Café Royal at 72 Regent Street. Nearest Tube station: Piccadilly Circus. For reservations, call (020) 7494 3322; *Fax:* (020) 7494 2211; www.cheersbarlondon.com.

Rail buffs will enjoy Chez Gerard at 64 Bishopsgate. Nearest Tube station: Liverpool Street. The restaurant is decorated with lamps and luggage racks reminiscent of the golden days of the railways. For reservations, call (020) 7588 1200; *Fax:* (020) 7588 1122; www.santeonline.co.uk.

While in London, grab *Time Out* at the newsstand to check out what's happening in the heart of the city for the arts, including West End shows, films, gigs, and so on.

Day Excursions

After you've seen London, explore more of this wonderful country where, among its many advantages, everyone speaks English. Well, sort of—dialects do abound. You cannot get to know Britain without experiencing the charms of its other cities and seeing firsthand the lovely rural areas that separate them. Of course, there's no better way to view the passing scene and converse with the British themselves than aboard a train.

Like the road builders of Rome, Britain's rail builders laid their tracks leading to London—or, more properly, out of London. London serves as the center of a somewhat lopsided spiderweb, with its radials running east and south to the sea on the short side of the web and the longer extensions running west to Wales and north into Scotland. Thirty-two day excursions from London await your pleasure, with three of them (Bath, Penzance, and Plymouth) just as easily done from Cardiff.

As with any knight of old, you may want to sally forth on a short sortie or two before departing on a crusade. In that case, you will find the Greenwich, Windsor, and St. Albans day excursions to your liking. Ranging southeast out of London, Kent beckons with its towns of Canterbury, Dover, Folkestone, and Ramsgate. Southward, rail trails lead along the English Channel to the port/resort towns of Hastings, Brighton, Portsmouth, and Southampton and to the Isle of Wight.

Having whetted your appetite with those excursions, you should now be ready to venture farther afield. Almost everything you plan to see has been there for quite some time—usually at least a century or two—so relax and enjoy your longer travels throughout Britain.

West from London, excursions to Salisbury, Stonehenge, and Gloucester await the train traveler. Or journey to Liverpool, home of the Beatles. With a ticket (or rail pass) to ride, you will find great history and new attractions beckoning from this seaport town beyond the Mersey beat. Day excursions to Bath, Plymouth, and Penzance may be made from either Cardiff or London. See the chapter on Cardiff for these day excursions. Schedules from both Cardiff and London are included in the chapter on Cardiff.

In the heart of England, excursions to Birmingham, Stratford-upon-Avon, Coventry, Nottingham, Sheffield, Lincoln, and York await you. Farther west beckons Chester.

Northeast of London is East Anglia, where historic King's Lynn, Bury St. Edmunds, and Ipswich abound in museums and memories of World War II. For academic flavor, visit Cambridge or Oxford; school-tie types will appreciate Eton—a stone's throw away from Windsor—where kings are educated.

Train Connections to Other Base Cities from London

London–Cardiff

DEPART Paddington Station	ARRIVE Cardiff Central Station	NOTES
0715	0924	M–F
0745	0948	M–Sa
0815	1023	M–F
0845	1046	M–Sa
0915	1123	M–F
Then service every 30 minutes daily until 2115		
2245	0114+1	M–F (R)

London–Edinburgh

Services shown operate from London's King's Cross via the so-called eastern route to Scotland. Other service is available from London Euston Station using the western route, but most trains stop at Glasgow before continuing to Edinburgh. The eastern route provides faster service to Edinburgh.

DEPART King's Cross Station	ARRIVE Edinburgh Waverly Station	NOTES
0615	1108	M–Sa
0700	1132	M–Sa
0800	1239 (1231 Sa)	M–Sa
0900	1337 (1331 Su)	Daily
1000	1425	Daily
Daily hourly departures until 1800, then		
2350	0716+1	M–F, Sleeper (R)

R=Reservation required on sleeper trains. Arrives next morning.
+1=Arrives next day.

London–Glasgow

DEPART Euston Station	ARRIVE Glasgow Central Station	NOTES
0539	1036	M–F
0730	1201	M–Sa
0830	1301	M–Sa
0845	1401	Su
Then hourly departures at 30 minutes past the hour until 1730 M–F, 1630 Sa, 1925 Su		
2327	0720+1	Su, Sleeper (R)
2350	0720+1	M–F, Sleeper (R)

+1=Arrives next day.
R=Reservation required on sleeper trains. Arrives next morning. Vacate cabins by 0800.

Day Excursion to

Birmingham

Heart of England

Depart from Euston Station

Distance by train: 115 miles (185 km)

Average train time: 1 hour, 30 minutes

Train information and InterCity services: (0845) 748 4950

Tourist information: Tourism Centre and Ticket Shop, The Rotunda, 150 New Street, Birmingham B2 4PA; *Tel:* (0121) 202 5115; *Fax:* (0121) 202 5080

www.visitbirmingham.com

Hours: 0930–1730 Monday–Saturday, 1030–1630 Sunday/bank holidays

Notes: As you exit the main entrance of New Street Station, follow the left-hand path in the direction of the city center. The Tourism Centre and Ticket Shop is on your left, at the base of the tall building in front of you, the Rotunda, next to Bullring Shopping Centre.

Birmingham has more canals than Venice. This is rather unusual because Birmingham claims to be Britain's "city at the center." Although it is in the approximate geographic midpoint of the British Isles, it was once the hub of England's waterways, which carried most of the nation's industrial traffic. With the development of other forms of transportation, particularly rail, canal transportation dissipated. Most of the canals were developed into recreation areas with walks, pubs, and restored buildings alongside their rights-of-way.

For decades Birmingham was known internationally as one of the world's great industrial cities. Along with that recognition came the image of a smoke-filled, grimy Victorian sprawl of a city. Since World War II Birmingham has made spectacular progress in developing a beautiful residential city. The center of the city has been completely rebuilt.

One of the best ways to see Birmingham is on foot. Begin a self-guided tour at **Brindley Place,** the main canalside development situated at the rear of the International Convention Centre. You'll see the old, original canal locks, as well as the newer **Water's Edge.** Your walk will lead you to the **National Sealife Centre,** restaurants of all nationalities, and the **Ikon Gallery.** If you prefer to experience the canals on water, barge trips are available at the rear of the Convention Centre.

Birmingham is said to have several haunted pubs—with plenty of ale flowing. Sample a pint when you join the **Ghost Trail tour.** You'll just die to get on this next tour—the **Graveyard Walk,** guided by Birmingham's most popular corpse, John Baskerville. Prices: £8 adults, £5 children age eight to fourteen. For more details or to sign up for any of the tours, log on to www.birminghamboxoffice.co.uk or call (0121) 245 4455.

London–Birmingham–London

Direct service from London Euston Station only; other service is available from Paddington Station via Reading and Oxford.

DEPART Euston Station	ARRIVE New Street Station	NOTES
0643	0808	M–F
0703	0827	M–Sa
0743	0908	M–Sa
0843	1008	M–Sa
0850	1047	Su

M–F service continues at 23 and 43 minutes past the hour until 2143, then hourly until 2330; Sa service continues at half-hour intervals until 2039, then 2103 and 2143. Su service is hourly from 0830 until 1638, then every 30 minutes until 2054, then 2225 and 2325.

DEPART New Street Station	ARRIVE Euston Station	NOTES

M–Sa service departs at half-hour intervals from 0550 to 1920, then 1930, 2050, 2133, and 2310 M–F; then 2010, 2110, and 2130 Sa.

Sunday service continues hourly 0810–1210, then every half hour 1400–1900, with final departure at 2300.

One of the most striking landmarks marking the city center is the **Rotunda,** a 250-foot tower. Beneath the tower is the world's first under-one-roof shopping complex, which includes the Bullring, the Palisades, the Pavilions, and the City Plaza. The redevelopment of the forty-acre Bullring site has transformed Birmingham into a world-class retail capital with department stores for Debenhams and Selfridges and more than 140 shops, cafes, and restaurants. There's a five-ton bronze bull standing in front—you can't miss it. Visit www.bullring.co.uk. *Hours:* 0930– 2000 Monday–Friday, 0900–2000 Saturday, 1100–1700 Sunday.

Birmingham's National Exhibition Centre is a modern exhibition-and-conference center on a 310-acre site readily accessible by rail through the New Street Station on any trains departing in the direction of London. The stop, Birmingham International, is a seventeen- to twenty-minute ride. Details are available from the tourist centers. With 1.2 million square feet of air-conditioned exhibition space in twelve halls, it is by far the largest complex in Britain, and it's still growing. Visit www.necgroup.co.uk.

Located in the Victoria Square vicinity and noteworthy for its classic elegance and Victorian style is the **Town Hall.** It was designed by Joseph Hansom, the inventor of the Hansom cab, and is the concert hall in which Mendelssohn conducted the first performance of *Elijah* in 1846. Many distinguished musicians have appeared there since it opened in 1834, including Sir Edward Elgar.

Sarehole Mill, on Cole Bank Road (served by Hall Green Station), is an 18th-century water mill restored to working order and would be an exciting adventure for J.R.R. Tolkien fans. So inspired by this mill was Tolkien that he chose it as the setting for his *Middle-Earth*. The mill is open 1200 to 1600 Tuesday through Sunday between April and October. This particular area of Birmingham was where Tolkien, author of *The Hobbit* and the *Lord of the Rings* trilogy, spent his childhood. His family's home, Gracewell, is now privately owned, but you can visit Edgbaston, a house he often used for holiday lodging. For a beautiful view of the hills and trees where Tolkien may have seen his first hobbit, stop at **Lickey Hills** in Rednal, just outside Birmingham. Visit www.birmingham.gov.uk/sarehole.

Blakesley Hall, Blakesley Road, Yardley (Stechford Station), is a delightful sixteenth-century timber-framed yeoman's house, furnished in period style, with a garden, barn, and historical vehicles. *Hours:* Easter–October, 1200–1600 Tuesday–Sunday. Two and a half miles north of the city center on Trinity Road is a seventeenth-century gem, **Aston Hall** (Witton Station). The Jacobean mansion was begun in 1618 and took seventeen years to complete. *Admission:* £4 adults, £3 students and seniors, children under sixteen are free.

For rail buffs a visit to the **Birmingham Railway Museum** is a must. It houses the world's oldest steam engine, which was built in 1784, along with displays of early machinery, steam engines, and the Tyseley Locomotive Works. You can even learn to drive a main-line express. Visit www.vintagetrains.co.uk.

Birmingham's Civic Centre is a modern contribution to the city's skyline. It includes a repertory theater and one of the largest and best-stocked libraries in Europe, featuring a comprehensive Shakespeare collection. The city's **Central Museum and Art Gallery** houses works by Van Gogh, Botticelli, and Gainsborough. Its pre-Raphaelite painting collection is the best. Visit www.bmag.org.uk.

After all the sightseeing, you may develop a thirst. Well, you came to the right city. Birmingham has long been one of Britain's major brewing centers, and its beer is recommended highly by both locals and visitors. There are plenty of pubs in which to conduct your own taste tests.

Birmingham is justly proud of its restaurants, which cater to every palate and purse. The city has stylish theater-restaurants with entertainment by international cabaret stars, as well as a wide selection of eateries providing French, Italian, Spanish, Greek, "Balti" (from northern India), Chinese, and traditional English cuisine.

Having undergone many structural changes in recent years, Birmingham undoubtedly is becoming one of Europe's outstanding cities. Enjoy!

Day Excursion to

Brighton

Colorful Seaside City

Depart from Victoria Station

Distance by train: 51 miles (82 km)

Average train time: 49 minutes

Train information and InterCity services: (0845) 748 4950

Tourist information: Brighton Visitor Information Centre, Royal Pavilion Shop, Royal Pavilion, 4–5 Pavilion Buildings, Brighton, East Sussex BN1 1EE; *Tel:* (0127) 329 0337; *Fax:* (01273) 292594

www.visitbrighton.com

E-mail: visitor.info@visitbrighton.com

Hours: Monday–Saturday 1000–1700; Sunday 1000–1600

Notes: Brighton's visitor information center is located in the Royal Pavilion, about a 1-mile walk from Brighton's rail station. Walk directly out of the rail station down Queens Road. Turn left onto North Street. Turn left again onto Pavilion, and proceed to the Royal Pavilion visitor information center.

Brighton is, and always has been, much more than a traditional seaside destination. Since the earliest days of travel, visitors have been attracted by the destination's unique sense of style and architectural splendor. Having merged with its neighbor, Hove, in 1997, the city's special qualities are as strong as ever. But they are only part of a continuing success story that secures Brighton's position as Britain's liveliest seaside city.

Perhaps Brighton would have remained a tiny, humble fishing village originally known as Brighthelmstone were it not for the efforts of Dr. Richard Russell and the Prince Regent who later became King George IV. In 1750 Dr. Russell, a Brighton resident, published a book extolling the magical effects of sea air and salt water. This started a fashionable trend that brought royalty and commoner alike to Brighton. The good doctor prescribed bathing in the sea and drinking a pint and a half of seawater daily as a cure for glandular diseases. Such a prescription, incredible as it seems, must have initiated a whole new series of maladies. Chronicles of that period, however, have failed to note them.

The gifted and wayward Prince Regent first visited Brighton in 1783. Enamored by it all (and well heeled with royal funds), he ordered his Royal Pavilion constructed there. Completed in 1822 from an architectural style taken somewhere east of the Suez, it has been termed one of the most bizarre and exotic palaces in all Europe. The **Royal Pavilion**'s ostentatious onion-domed exterior, looking very much like a series of hot-air balloons about to ascend, is only surpassed by its even more amazing interior. Fully furnished in its original style, it is open to the public daily 0930–1745 April–September; 1000–1715 October–March. *Tel:* (03000) 290900.

Guided tours are daily at 1130 and 1430 (£1.50 in addition to admission fee: £9.80 adult, £5.60 child). Visit www.royalpavilion.org.uk. To book a guided tour: *Tel:* (03000) 290901.

Visit **The Lanes,** where you step backward into the old fishing-village days. The buildings in these narrow, twisting passages were fishermen's cottages in the seventeenth century. Today they house quaint and fascinating antiques, jewelry, high-fashion shops, pubs, and cafes.

Part of the changing scene in Brighton has been the introduction of English-language schools, which attract international students from a score of foreign lands. With the resident student population from Sussex and Brighton Universities, this youthful input has made it one of the most vibrant destinations in Britain.

In English-style directions, had you denied yourself the turning at Grand Junction, you would have come quickly upon the gates of the **Brighton Pier,** which extends out into the English Channel like a silent sentinel. Constructed in 1899, the pier has been restored, illuminated with 13,000 lightbulbs, and features free entrance, free deck chairs, and free entertainment. It opens daily at 1000. www.brightonpier.co.uk.

For a guided walking tour of Brighton's "Old Town," obtain details from the visitor information center. From April through mid-September, the tours start at the tourist information center. Or you can pick up the *Brighton and Hove City Guide* at the information center. The town plan in the guide shows the best of where to go, what to see, and where to shop.

Attention, shoppers: The £90 million indoor shopping center, Churchill Square, is unique to southern England and only minutes from the seafront. Swank designer shops can be found in Brighton's east side and the adjoining **Regent Arcade.** For the more bizarre, shop the **Upper Gardner Street Junk Market** on Saturday mornings and the station car park's "carboot" (junk and antiques) sale on Sunday mornings. A visit to the North Lane's quirky shops is a must for a real mix of the ethnic, offbeat, and downright funky.

Because of the city's number and variety of shopping areas, Brighton is often referred to as "London by the Sea." New bars, cafes, and restaurants in the Victorian seafront arches offer an uninterrupted view of the sea along the beachfront and boardwalk. While exploring, try not to miss the **Artists' Quarter** or the **Fishing Museum.** Farther along the revamped beachfront, you'll find beach volleyball and basketball courts, a children's play area, and lots of bold works of art. The kids will love the **Sea Life Centre** and the rides on Brighton Pier.

Young and old alike should take a ride along the seafront on the **Volks Railway,** Britain's first public electric railway. Open between Easter and Labor Day, Monday, Wednesday, and Thursday 1015–1700, Tuesday and Friday 1115–1700, Saturday and Sunday 1015–1800, the railway travels along the beach on Madeira Drive to Black Rock. Lacking the speed of the InterCity 125s, the Volks Railway makes up for it with its nostalgia.

London–Brighton–London

Services shown are from London Victoria Station; other service available from London Blackfriars and London Bridge Stations.

DEPART Victoria Station	ARRIVE Brighton Station	NOTES
0630	0733	Daily
0721	0822	M–F
0807	0906	M–Sa
0836 (0832 Su)	0928 (0927 Sa, 0950 Su)	Daily
0906	0958	M–Sa
0936	1027	Daily

M–Sa service continues at half-hour intervals to 2332; Su service continues at hourly intervals until 2332.

DEPART Brighton Station	ARRIVE Victoria Station	NOTES
1619	1710	M–Sa
1649 (1640 Su)	1740 (1733 Su)	Daily
1719	1814	M–Sa
1749 (1754 Su)	1840 (1854 Su)	Daily

M–Sa service is every half hour at 19 and 49 minutes past the hour until 2219, then 2302. Su service is on the hour and 40 minutes past the hour until 2000, then 2100, 2204, and 2302.

Brighton's **Marina** is one of the largest in Europe. Whether you are a boating enthusiast or not, a visit there is well in order. A complete village is now the centerpiece of the marina, with an eight-screen movie theater, elegant shops, quayside restaurants, bowling complex, and, of course, traditional British pubs on the waterfront. The marina also stages many colorful events, such as boat shows and sailing regattas throughout July and August. Visit the £3 million casino complex and the Walk of Fame, a Hollywood-style route of Brighton's famous people, both past and present.

Time permitting, we suggest a stroll along the Hove promenade with its elegant Regency squares and crescents, or stop by the **Brunswick Town House** for a fascinating insight into Regency lifestyle. For steam enthusiasts, do *not* miss the **British Engineerium.**

Brighton has more than 400 restaurants, pre–West End theater, superb sports, and year-round event programs of fun and festivities. Annually in May, the Brighton Festival takes over the city with the biggest arts festival in England. So, if you're caught up in Brighton's buoyancy, check with the visitor information center for hotel accommodations, and catch a morning train back to London. Hove also has its own train station, with regular service to London. For those flying into or out of Gatwick Airport, Brighton is only thirty fast-train minutes away—the perfect starting point or destination.

Day Excursion to

Bury St. Edmunds

Magna Carta

Depart from Liverpool Street Station

Distance by train: 95 miles (153 km)

Average train time: 2 hours

Train information and InterCity services: (0845) 748 4950

Tourist information: Tourist Information Centre, 6 Angel Hill, Bury St. Edmunds, Suffolk IP33 1UZ; *Tel:* (01284) 764667; *Fax:* (01284) 757084

Minicom: (01284) 757083

www.stedmundsbury.gov.uk

E-mail: tic@stedsbc.gov.uk

Hours: Easter–end of October: Monday–Saturday 0930–1700, Sunday and bank holidays 1000–1500; November–Easter: Monday–Friday 1000–1600, Saturday 1000–1300, Sunday 1000–1500

Notes: Follow the pedestrian signs to the Tourist Information Centre, located immediately opposite the Abbey Gate entrance to the ruins of the Abbey of St. Edmund, approximately 1 mile from the train station. A city map is displayed in the station (map dispensers available also), or station personnel will gladly provide directions. Taxi stand is located outside.

In his *Pickwick Papers,* Charles Dickens described Bury St. Edmunds as "a handsome little town of thriving and cleanly appearance." So it remains today.

A Christian community was founded on the current site of Bury St. Edmunds in AD 633. In 903, thirty-four years after King Edmund of East Anglia was killed by the Danes at Hoxne, his body was brought to the town and consecrated around 905. Thus, the town became known as Bury St. Edmunds (the place of St. Edmund). The abbey church was built soon afterward to honor the memory of the king. It is said that in 1214, barons gathered at the high altar of the abbey to take a solemn oath to force King John to grant a charter of liberties, one of the events leading to the granting of the Magna Carta in 1215.

The town center is most notable for its pleasant Georgian atmosphere; the town is still a leading social center within East Anglia. The great **Abbey of St. Edmund** was one of the largest in Europe during medieval times. Sacked in 1327 by townspeople protesting monastic control, and again in 1381 during the Peasants' Revolt, the

Abbey Gate was severely damaged, and many monks were killed. In 1465 a severe fire damaged the church, and it had to be extensively repaired. A placard on the Abbey Gate indicates that the gate was destroyed and the abbey badly damaged by the townspeople in 1327 but was rebuilt on a spot adjacent to the old one in 1347. The dissolution of the monasteries in 1539 brought about the closure of the abbey. The stone and other material was then sold off to the locals and used in other buildings.

Across from the Abbey Gate is the **Angel Hotel,** more than 500 years old, known for its association with Charles Dickens. His room, No. 15, is preserved exactly as it was more than a century ago. The site has seen three East Anglian inns over the years. Unique attractions of the Angel Hotel include its tavern room, dating from 1433—fifty-nine years before Columbus discovered America—and the restaurant located in the medieval vaults of the structure.

During World War II, Bury St. Edmunds was ringed with American air bases. Today the U.S. Air Force European Command operates a base at Mildenhall and Lakenheath, west of Bury St. Edmunds. Visitors are welcome there if they have contacted the base information office or its community relations adviser before going. The information center can provide details.

The highlight in Bury St. Edmunds is the abbey ruins and gardens. **St. Mary's Church,** the southern boundary of the abbey precinct, is also popular. The **Borough Council's Museum of Local History** is housed in Moyse's Hall in the town center. It has been renovated and now includes the Suffolk Regiment Collection. Constructed in the latter part of the twelfth century, it is a fine example of Norman domestic architecture and houses eclectic collections from archaeology to crime and punishment. The **Manor House Museum** faces the great churchyard. This restored Georgian mansion houses clocks, paintings, and costumes from the seventeenth to the twentieth centuries.

There are two distinct parts to the town. As was customary in most medieval towns with a monastic foundation, there was a division between the monastery and the townspeople—possibly the first example of separation of church and state. This division resulted in the business section and public buildings standing on a hill only 100 meters away to the west of the abbey ruins today.

The **Theatre Royal,** one of three surviving Georgian playhouses in Britain, was built in Bury St. Edmunds during 1819 by English architect William Wilkins. He also designed Downing College at Cambridge University. Almost a miniature version of the West End London Theatre (seating only 352 people), the historical Theatre Royal's architecture displays, in elegant fashion, the style and form for which the Georgian architects were famous. The repertoire features a broad range of entertainment, plays, dance, opera, and every form of music from classical to jazz and rock. In 1892 the Theatre Royal made international headlines by presenting the world premiere of *Charlie's Aunt,* a comedy that is still performed in every major language throughout the world.

Bypassed by time, Bury St. Edmunds is essentially a country town that was spared the industrial expansion of the Victorian Age. But the town stands tall in history. The principles of the Magna Carta, which had their foundation in Bury St. Edmunds and were developed over the centuries into English common law, have become the heritage not only of the British Isles but also of countless millions throughout the world. As history records, the signing of the Magna Carta by King John is the basic source of the constitutional liberties of English-speaking peoples.

One of Bury St. Edmunds's local products is ale. Try Abbot Ale and St. Edmund Ale for great local flavor. We suggest that you sample a pint in the **Nutshell,** the smallest pub in England. Its single barroom measures only 12 feet by 7 feet.

Ask at the Tourist Information Centre about tours of Bury St. Edmunds. Modestly priced, all are guaranteed to be enjoyable and educational. Audiotapes may be picked up at the center, allowing you to be led through the sites by the historical voices of Brother Jocelin, Henry Lomax, and other town notables.

London–Bury St. Edmunds–London

Service shown is from London Liverpool Street Station via Ipswich and requires a change of trains in Ipswich; other service is available via Cambridge, with a change of trains necessary in Cambridge, with service from both London King's Cross and Liverpool Street Stations.

DEPART Liverpool Street Station	ARRIVE Bury St. Edmunds Station	NOTES
0800	0919	M–Sa (1)
0830	0955	Su (1)
1000	1119	M–Sa (1)
1100	1219	M–Sa (1)
1300	1454	M–Sa (1)

Departures every half hour M–F beginning at 0625; 0630 Sa; Su departures every hour beginning at 0830.

DEPART Bury St. Edmunds Station	ARRIVE Liverpool Street Station	NOTES
1457	1655	M–Sa (1)
1523	1719	M–Sa (1)
1657	1849 (1901 Su)	Daily
1725	1917	M–Sa (1)
1825	2017	M–Sa (1)
1857	2055	M–Sa (1)
1923	2117	M–Sa (1)
2055 (2047 Su)	2246 (2301 Su)	Daily (1)
2123	2223	M–Sa (1)

(1) Change trains in Ipswich.

Day Excursion to

Cambridge

University City

Depart from King's Cross Station
Distance by train: 56 miles (90 km)
Average train time: 1 hour
Train information and InterCity services: (0845) 748 4950
Tourist information: Tourist Information Centre, Peashill, Cambridge, CB2 3AD; *Tel:* (0871) 226 8006; Guided Tours: (01223) 457574; *Fax:* (01223) 457588
www.visitcambridge.org
E-mail: info@visitcambridge.org
Hours: Monday–Friday 1000–1700, Saturday 1000–1700, Sunday 1100–1500

Oxford graduates often refer to Cambridge as "the other place." Both universities hold one thing in common: Organized along the classic federal structure, they house a number of largely autonomous colleges. Comparisons stop here. Cambridge is Britain's "University City." It is said that if you visit only one other English city besides London, it should be Cambridge.

Cambridge is a complex blend of market town, regional center, tourist attraction, and university. It is situated on the River Cam around the original bridge over which all trade and communications passed between central England, East Anglia, and continental Europe 1,000 years ago. It was a natural spot for travelers to pause to exchange news and opinions, thereby preparing the area for a center of learning.

Several religious orders, including the Franciscans and Dominicans, established monasteries and affiliated schools in Cambridge early in the twelfth century. Students from the University of Oxford and the University of Paris left to study in Cambridge during the thirteenth century. The present-day colleges originated at that time, when students began residing in hostels and halls.

Daily walking tours with guides can tell you about the university and its colleges. Schedules may be obtained from the Tourist Information Centre. The main colleges are closed to visitors from mid-April until the end of June. A note of academic etiquette: College members are happy to welcome you to the grounds and their historic buildings, but they ask you to respect their need for quiet and privacy.

Ask at the tourist office for the *Cambridge Where to Go–What to See* pamphlet (nominal fee). It provides basic information about the colleges and museums and includes a street plan of the city.

King's College Chapel is regarded universally as one of Cambridge's finest architectural structures. It was constructed in stages over a period of nearly seventy years and was completed in 1536. The chapel (admission £6.50 adults; £4.50 children/students) displays the carved coats of arms of Henry VIII. His initials, along with those of Anne Boleyn, can be seen on the screen. The chapel's stained-glass windows depict stories from the Old Testament and the New Testament. Rubens's *Adoration of the Magi* is the altarpiece. Visit www.kings.cam.ac.uk/chapel.

Trinity College's great court is one of the largest collegiate quadrangles in England. It's so large that much of its detail goes unnoticed. It is said that, taking advantage of this situation, Byron bathed nude in the fountain and shared his room with a pet bear, which he claimed he kept for the purpose of taking examinations. Sir Isaac Newton first measured the speed of sound in the great court by stamping his foot in the cloister along the north side.The admission qualifications to the University of Cambridge are exceptionally demanding. Each year, approximately 8,000 students apply for admission, but only about 20 percent are admitted.

The Cam River, the source of Cambridge's being and delightful in any season, deserves a portion of your visit. A tour of the city by boat along the "backs," as the placid stretch of the river is called, is an experience not to be missed. You can hire a punt, rowboat, or canoe to boat along the backs. If your selection is the punt—which is propelled with long wooden poles—be aware that these poles frequently stick in the mud and have been known to vault a punter into the river. A "chauffeured punt" service is also available.

London–Cambridge–London

Frequent service with departures from both King's Cross and Liverpool Street Stations. Trains that take 61 minutes or less depart from London King's Cross Station; trains from Liverpool Street Station take 75 to 90 minutes.

LONDON KING'S CROSS TO CAMBRIDGE

M–F	Depart at 0545, 0645, 0715, 0745, and every half hour until 2015, then at 15 and 52 minutes after the hour until 2315.
Sa	Depart at 0545 and 0645, then at 15 and 45 minutes after the hour until 1845, then hourly until 2315.
Su	Depart at 0638 and 0704, then at 15 and 52 minutes after the hour until 2215, then 2315.

CAMBRIDGE TO LONDON KING'S CROSS

M–F	Depart Cambridge at 0545, 0615, 0645, and every half hour until 1945, then 2028, 2118, 2228, and 2315.
Sa	Depart Cambridge at 0645, then at 15 and 45 minutes after the hour until 1928, then hourly until 2228.
Su	Depart Cambridge at 0628 and 0728, then hourly until 2220, then 2314.

Visitors have a large selection of museums covering a wide range of interests. The **Fitzwilliam Museum** on Trumpington Street features Greek and Roman artifacts and a famous collection of paintings. Visit www.fitzmuseum.cam.ac.uk. The

Folk Museum on Castle Street contains a vast array of domestic articles. Another point of interest is **Kettles Yard Art Gallery** at Castle Street on Northampton, with its fine collection of modern paintings and sculpture.

Steeped in history, Cambridge has a reminder of a more recent historical event. **Duxford Airfield,** located 8 miles south of the city, houses a fabulous collection of aircraft owned by the Imperial War Museum (headquartered in London). Visitors can also walk through several hangars to view the aircraft being restored. Another very interesting part is the Imperial War Museum's Land Warfare Hall with displays of military vehicles and other wartime equipment. During World War II Allied aircraft flew raids from Duxford to continental Europe.

The **American Military Cemetery,** 4 miles from Cambridge, contains the graves of 3,811 American airmen who operated from bases in Britain. The cemetery and the museum may be reached by bus. For some preliminary knowledge, visit the Imperial War Museum's Web site at www.iwm.org.uk.

Day Excursion to

Canterbury

and the Cathedral

Depart from Victoria Station
Distance by train: 62 miles (99 km)
Average train time: 1 hour, 25 minutes
Train information and InterCity services: (0845) 748 4950
Tourist information: Canterbury Information Centre, 12–13 Sun Street, The Buttermarket, Canterbury, Kent CT1 2HX; *Tel:* (01227) 378100; *Fax:* (01227) 378101
Accommodations: (01227) 378188
Theater and concert bookings: (01227) 455600
www.canterbury.co.uk
E-mail: canterburyinformation@canterbury.gov.uk
Hours: Monday–Saturday 0930–1700, Sunday 0930–1630
Notes: Canterbury has two railway stations: West Station and East Station. There's a taxi queue just outside the station entrances, or you may walk to the city center and the cathedral in about fifteen minutes.

Canterbury, the Metropolitan City of the Anglican Communion, has a history going back to prehistoric times. It was once a Roman settlement and the Saxon stronghold of the men of Kent. It was here in AD 597 that St. Augustine began the conversion of the English to Christianity, where Ethelbert, king of Kent, was baptized.

Only ruins remain of the Benedictine **St. Augustine's Abbey,** the burial place of the Jutish kings of Kent, but **St. Martin's Church,** on the eastern outskirts of the city, is still in use. This church is said to have been the place of worship of Queen Bertha, the Christian wife of King Ethelbert, before the arrival of St. Augustine.

In 1170 the rivalry of church and state culminated in the murder in Canterbury Cathedral, by Henry II's knights, of Archbishop Thomas à Becket. His shrine became a great center of pilgrimage, as described by Chaucer in his *Canterbury Tales*. After the Reformation the pilgrimage ceased, but the prosperity of the city was strengthened by an influx of Huguenot refugees from the Continent, who introduced weaving.

Trains departing London's Charing Cross and Waterloo Stations arrive at Canterbury West. Those departing London's Victoria Station arrive at Canterbury East. For simplicity, day-excursion schedules are given for Victoria and Canterbury East Stations only.

Arriving in Canterbury East Station, use the pedestrian bridge to reach the city walls. **The Cathedral,** with architecture ranging from the eleventh to the fifteenth century, is world famous. Modern pilgrims are attracted particularly to the **Martyrdom,** the **Black Prince's Tomb,** the **Warriors' Chapel,** and the many examples of medieval stained glass. The medieval city walls are built on Roman foundations, and the fourteenth-century **West Gate** is one of the finest buildings of its kind in the country.

From the station entrance, you'll see a sign across the street that says CITY CENTRE—MARLOWE THEATRE—CATHEDRAL. A blue sign showing a person walking indicates where to cross the highway. Proceed along the city's old Roman walls, which enclose Dane John Gardens. Climb the mound in the gardens for a view of the town and the cathedral. Farther along you'll come to the city bus station. Descend from the wall at this point onto St. George's Street. Turn left, and walk until the cathedral is in view on your right through the Christ Church Gate. Passing through the gate will bring you onto the cathedral grounds.

The poet and playwright Christopher Marlowe was born and reared in Canterbury, and there are also literary associations with Defoe, Dickens, Joseph Conrad, and Somerset Maugham. The *Mayflower* was provisioned in Canterbury before setting sail for Plymouth and its historic journey to America.

During World War II Canterbury suffered a severe bombing raid, and parts of the city center have been rebuilt. Modern-day Canterbury has a wide range of quality shops and comfortable hotels, many of these small, family-run businesses. The 1,000-seat **Marlowe Theatre** offers first-class plays, operas, musicals, and one-night shows. Each autumn, Canterbury celebrates the **International Arts Festival.**

Not far from the Christ Church Gate is the Longmarket, a paved pedestrian area beginning at the intersection of Rose Lane and St. George's Street. Walking directly away from the Christ Church Gate on St. Margaret's Street will bring you to the Canterbury Information Centre. City tours depart from this point.

London–Canterbury–London

Service shown is from London Victoria Station to Canterbury East Station; other services available are from London Charing Cross Station and Waterloo East Station to Canterbury West Station. Passengers should be aware that trains may be split at Faversham, some coaches going to Canterbury East and others going elsewhere; passengers should be sure they are in a coach going to Canterbury before the train reaches Faversham. Consult the conductor if you are unsure.

DEPART Victoria Station	ARRIVE Canterbury East Station	NOTES
0645	0826	M–F
0752	0929	M–Sa
0822	0959	M–Sa
0852	1029	M–Sa
0933	1100	Daily

M–Sa service continues at half-hour intervals until 2022, then 2122 and 2222; Su service 0805, then hourly, with last train at 2205.

DEPART Canterbury East Station	ARRIVE Victoria Station	NOTES
1532	1707	M–Sa
1632	1807	M–Sa
1732	1907	M–Sa
1801	1929	Su
1832	2107	M–Sa
1901	2029	Su
1932	2107	M–Sa
1957	2137	M–Sa
2001	2129	Su
2132	2307	M–Sa
2202	2337	Daily

From High Street, where it intersects St. Margaret's Street, walk down until you pass over a narrow bridge on the River Stour. On the far right of the bridge you will see the **Old Weaver's House,** which was built in 1500 and now houses a restaurant and is a starting point for river tours. Canterbury was the background for Dickens's *David Copperfield,* so let your imagination take over for a few fleeting moments and transport you back into English history and literature.

Following World War II, Canterbury became a great educational center. In 1962 Christ Church College was opened adjacent to St. Augustine's College. More recently the University of Kent was established on a hill overlooking the cathedral and city from the west. Its buildings are modern in design, emphasizing artistic and cultural development.

A Friday market takes place in addition to the traditional Wednesday Market in the city center. Beach bums will want to take the seafront trek to **Whitstable,** world famous for its oysters. The annual Oyster Festival takes place at the end of July. Or visit Herne Bay, especially around the first two weeks of August when the annual **Herne Bay Festival** is held—family events, fireworks, live music, and more. The annual two-week **Canterbury Festival** is held every October.

We suggest taking in the award-winning **Canterbury Tales Visitor Attraction** as well; or make a night of it and take the **Ghost Tour of Canterbury.** This street-theater spook shows Canterbury in a whole new light and runs every Friday and Saturday all year, starting at 2000: £9.00 adult, £7.00 child, £8.00 senior.

Canterbury, proud of its historical past, is nonetheless eager to respond to the demands of modern "pilgrims"—visitors who come to see the cathedral, the other historical landmarks, and new sites. The city of Canterbury has done an excellent job by exhibiting its history as a living part of a modern community.

Visitors who wish to extend their visit may inquire at the **Magnolia House,** a lovely bed-and-breakfast. It's located at 36 St. Dunstans Terrace (*Tel/Fax:* [01227] 765121; www.magnoliahousecanterbury.co.uk; *E-mail:* info@magnoliahousecanterbury.co.uk). Phone, fax, or e-mail for nightly rates, which vary according to type of room and length of stay. All rooms include private bath/shower and toilet facilities, and all are nonsmoking.

Day Excursion to

Chester

A Modern "Medieval" City

Depart from Euston Station

Distance by train: 178 miles (287 km)

Average train time: 2 hours, 30 minutes

Train information and InterCity services: (0845) 748 4950

Tourist information: Visitor and Craft Centre, Vicar's Lane, Chester, Cheshire CH1 1QX; *Tel:* (01244) 351609; *Fax:* (01244) 403188. Town Hall tourist information: *Tel:* (01244) 402111; *Fax:* (01244) 400420

www.chester.gov.uk

E-mail: tis@chester.gov.uk

Hours: 1000–1600 daily

Notes: The railway station in Chester is about a fifteen-minute walk from the city's center. City Road, at the front of the station, will get you started in the right direction. Change at the pedestrian underpass onto Foregate Street, which turns into Eastgate Street and brings you to the center of the city's historic area. Or board a bus outside the station. The bus arrives at Town Hall in about ten minutes for a charge of 45 pence. Taxi meters click off around £3.

"All's well" in Chester, but don't take our word for it. Check personally with Chester's Town Crier. He appears at noon (Tuesday through Saturday, May through August) in the center of the city to announce that fact. Chester is one of the few cities in England with its encircling walls completely intact—a splendid example of a fortified medieval town.

The center of Chester, known as the Cross, takes its name from the stone "High Cross" standing in front of **St. Peter's Church.** From this point you may view Chester's distinctive landmark, the **Rows**—two tiers of shops (one at ground level, the other immediately above), each with its own walkway.

Developed in the thirteenth century, the Rows are unique and justly world famous. The upper levels are great for people-watchers who like to linger undisturbed while observing the stream of passersby in the streets below. The true origin of the Rows has never been satisfactorily explained, but they far exceed any modern-day shopping center in utility and beauty. One opinion is that they served as a means of defense against the incursions of the Welsh raiders, who came to plunder their richer English neighbors.

The Romans gave Chester its street plan. Walk today along the four main streets within the city's walls, and you will follow the lines laid down by Roman engineers almost 2,000 years ago. Part of the Roman wall survives and is incorporated in the massive tenth-century fortifications enclosing the city. You can find out more about the city's Roman heritage at the **Deva** (pronounced "Dewa") **Roman Experience,** just off Bridge Street (*Tel:* [01978] 761264; www.romantours.uk.com). A walk on the walls provides an opportunity to enjoy the vista of the surrounding countryside.

Restoration has thrived on a large scale in Chester. Entire blocks were renovated in massive programs. The city's famous "black and white" Tudor buildings survived the ravages of time but did not escape alterations to their facades by Victorian architects. In all, however, Chester has managed to preserve its pleasant medieval appearance.

Your first call should be at the tourist information center at the town hall on Northgate Street across from the entrance to Abbey Square. The center offers a wide range of facilities, including a national room-finder service and ticket agency.

Special guided walks are also available: **History Hunter Tours** depart daily year-round at 1015; the **Ghosthunter Trail** departs at 1930 Thursday through Saturday from June through October; and the **Roman Soldier Wall Patrol** sets forth at 1400 on Wednesday, Friday, and Saturday from June through September. Other tours may be made by special arrangement. All depart from the Chester Visitor and Craft Centre. The History Hunter, Roman Soldier, and Ghosthunter Trail tours are £5.

Opposite the town hall is **Abbey Square,** an island of quiet in the center of the city. By entering the square through its massive fourteenth-century gateway, you will find various buildings constructed from the sixteenth to the nineteenth century.

London–Chester–London

DEPART Euston Station	ARRIVE Chester Station	NOTES
0636	0846	M–Sa (1)
0710	0912	M–F
0810	1009	M–Sa
0845	1127	Su (1)
0910	1109	M–F
0915	1220	Su (1)
1010	1212	M–Sa
1110	1312	M–Sa
1202	1420	Su (1)
1210	1412	M–Sa

DEPART Chester Station	ARRIVE Euston Station	NOTES
1433	1644	Su
1435	1638	M–Sa
1535 (1533 Su)	1738 (1744 Su)	Daily (1)
1635	1938	M–F
1735	1938	M–F, Su
1755	2042	M–Sa (1)
1835	2044	Su
1935	2142	M–F
1955	2222	M–Sa (1)
2050	2354	Su (1)
2017	2356	M–F (1)
2037	2354	Su

(1) Change trains in Crewe.
Note: Some trains from Crewe to Chester have standard-class service only.

Chester Cathedral is within sight of the town hall. An abbey was founded on this site in the tenth century. It remained a monastery until its dissolution in 1540, when the building was made a cathedral. The bell tower of the cathedral is a concrete structure that was finished in 1974, the first freestanding bell tower for a cathedral built since the fifteenth century.

Chester's prestigious event—the **Chester Mystery Plays**—occurs in July once every five years and last were seen in June and July 2008. This medieval tradition draws from biblical stories, and the plays are performed on carts as they originally were in the Middle Ages. Chester's Mystery Plays texts are the most complete, with the earliest surviving records dated 1546. For more information, contact the Visitor and Craft Centre at (01244) 402111 or www.chester.gov.uk/tourism.

An interesting observation point that provides a splendid view of the city, the **River Dee,** and the locks of the Chester canal is located at the north end of the city walls. A spur wall connects there with the water tower, which was built to protect the port of Chester. Another vantage point is from **Bonewaldesthorne's Tower,** about 100 feet from the water tower. If you participate in the Roman Soldier Wall Patrol tour, you will be able to enjoy this view.

Also in view at a bend in the River Dee is the **Roodee,** home of the Chester racecourse, the oldest in Britain. The main racing season is held in May and its richest prize, the Chester Cup, was first awarded in 1824. As a matter of interest to sportive North Americans, the Roodee was, before horse racing, a football field. But due to the violent nature of the football matches, the city assembly members voted to terminate the sport in 1540.

Day Excursion to

Coventry

Lady Godiva–Show & Tell

Depart from Euston Station

Distance by train: 96 miles (155 km)

Average train time: 1 hour, 10 minutes

Train information and InterCity services: (0845) 748 4950

Tourist information: Tourist Information Centre, 4 Priory Row, Coventry, West Midlands CV1 5RN; *Tel:* (024) 7622 5616; *Fax:* (024) 7622 7255

www.visitcoventry.co.uk

E-mail: tic@cvone.co.uk

Hours: Monday–Friday 1000–1700 (until 1630 in winter), Saturday–Sunday 1000–1630. It remains open on bank holidays (except Christmas) 1000–1600.

Notes: Coventry's rail station lies outside its "ringway," a circular superhighway surrounding the city. At the bus stop you'll find a city map and information regarding Coventry's information center. Buses marked "Pool Meadow" (No. 17 or 27) will take you to the center of town in five minutes along a route that requires about twenty minutes to walk. Dismount at the Broadgate stop near the shopping square by the Leofric Hotel. The Tourist Information Centre is located at Priory Row and may be found via well-placed direction signs.

This is a city of myth and magic, from St. George the Dragon Slayer to the legend of Lady Godiva. Did she actually put everything on a horse—or has this tale, retold through the ages, changed with the telling? Was there really a "Peeping Tom"? Was he late for the show? Coventry holds the answers.

Coventry is best described as a modern city with ancient roots. Among its office buildings, new streets, and attractive shops, there is a scattering of old homes and churches, Coventry's remnants of its far-reaching past. The **new cathedral,** consecrated in 1962, stands as visible proof that today's craftspeople can create memorable works of supreme beauty, as did their medieval counterparts.

London–Coventry–London

DEPART Euston Station	ARRIVE Coventry Station	NOTES
0643	0742	M–F
0743	0842	M–Sa
0843 (0850 Su)	0942 (1023 Su)	Daily
0903	1002	M–F
0943	1042	M–Sa
1003	1102	M–Sa

M–F service continues at 03 and 43 (18 and 54 Su) minutes past the hour until 2143, then hourly at 40 minutes past the hour until 2330.

Su service is hourly until 2325.

DEPART Coventry Station	ARRIVE Euston Station	NOTES
1331	1434	Daily
1411	1514	Daily
1531	1634	Daily

M–Sa service continues at 11 and 31 minutes past the hour until 1931, then hourly until 2331 M–F, 2151 Sa.

Su service hourly until 2321.

In the new cathedral you will see outstanding examples of some of the finest modern works of art, including the **Baptistery Window,** the largest piece of modern stained glass in the world. The tapestry **"Christ in Glory"** hangs behind the altar. Weighing nearly a ton, it is the largest tapestry in the world; ten men worked for three years to complete it. The cathedral is open from 0900 to 1700 Monday–Saturday, 1200–1545 Sunday; www.coventrycathedral.org.uk.

Alongside the new stands the **old Cathedral of St. Michael,** reduced to ruins by one dreadful air raid in November 1940. An altar of broken stones surmounted by a charred cross stands at the eastern end of the ruins, backed by the words "Father, forgive." In the nineteenth century John Ruskin wrote, "The sand of Coventry binds itself into stone which can be built halfway to the sky." Attesting to this, the tower and spire of the old cathedral survived intact after the bombing. Built in the fifteenth century, it is the third-highest spire in England. A visit to both cathedrals should not be missed.

Lady Godiva was the wife of Leofric, the "grim" Lord of Coventry. Evidently, she bugged him about the heavy tax burdens he had levied on the townspeople. Legend says Leofric, weary of her nagging, agreed to decrease the tax rate if Her Ladyship would increase the town's morale by riding naked through its streets. Modern historians seriously doubt that Godiva made her gallop without benefit of even a riding crop. They believe her husband challenged her to ride stripped of her finery and her jewels and to ride humbly as one of his people and in full sight of them.

Stripped of her rank—or just plain stripped—Her Ladyship did make the ride and taxes were lowered, but she commanded the people to remain indoors with windows barred. Legend says that one town resident called "Tom" unbarred his window to peep as she rode by. Before he could satisfy his gaze, he was struck blind, poor man!

In modern-day reenactments, Lady Godiva now rides her horse through Coventry wearing a body stocking—a considerable improvement over when the event was reenacted in Victorian days and she was dressed in billowing petticoats.

Oddly enough, the Godiva story was told for some 500 years before the "Peeping Tom" version was added. In any case, a stunning bronze statue perpetuates Her Ladyship's memory in **Broadgate Park** as Tom peeps out at her on the hour from the Broadgate clock. We can't help but wonder what effect Lady Godiva's ride would have on our modern-day Internal Revenue Service.

Lady Godiva's statue stands under the **Cathedral Lanes Shopping Centre**'s canopy and immediately opposite the **Leofric Hotel** near the Tourist Information Centre. Be certain to read the inscriptions on the east and west sides of the statue's pedestal. They were written by Alfred, Lord Tennyson, England's poet laureate.

Be sure to acquire *Coventry's Historic Heart, A Walking Tour* booklet from the Tourist Information Centre, containing a plan of the city's central area, along with a brief description of places of interest. It will lead you from Broadgate to a number of interesting places, including the two cathedrals. It also provides a map and key to attractions.

When ready to head back to the hotel in your base city, board the bus at the shelter directly in front of the **Holy Trinity Church,** opposite the Leofric Hotel, to return to the rail station.

Day Excursion to

Dover

On the White Cliffs

Depart from Charing Cross Station

Distance by train: 77 miles (124 km)

Average train time: 1 hour, 30 minutes

Train information and InterCity services: (0845) 748 4950

Tourist information: Dover Tourist Information Centre, Old Town Gaol, Biggin Street, Dover, Kent CT16 1DL; *Tel:* (01304) 205108; *Fax:* (01304) 245409

www.dover.gov.uk or **www.whitecliffscountry.org.uk**

E-mail: tic@doveruk.com

Hours: April, May, and September: 0900–1730 Monday–Friday, 1000–1600

Saturday–Sunday; June–August: 0900–1730 daily; October–March: 0900–1730 Monday–Friday, 1000–1600 Saturday; closed Sunday

Notes: The tourist information center is next to the Town Hall, about a five-minute walk from the rail station. Head down Folkestone Road and, at the roundabout, turn left. You will see the Town Hall on your right.

For centuries Dover has been one of Britain's major channel ports. In theory this is where England ends and the Continent begins, where countless Englishmen have been parted from, or united with, their homeland. Here stand the **White Cliffs of Dover.** Below, on the beaches, the legions of the Roman Empire stormed ashore in 55 BC, only to be repelled and to land again, successfully, at Deal. Take the time to pause to enjoy; most people pass on through. There is no other point in all of Britain more majestic than Dover—it is the very cornerstone of Britain.

Atop the cliffs broods **Dover Castle.** Initially constructed in the 1180s by Henry II to repel invaders, it has been reinforced at every threat to England's shores, including Hitler's in 1940. From its ramparts on a clear day you can look across the 21 miles of the English Channel and see France. Approaching from the sea, a dramatic panorama unfolds as the white cliffs slowly rise from the horizon.

You cannot deny it—Dover is dramatic. Brooding clouds hang over it on a rainy, windswept day; grandeur surrounds it on a clear one when Boulogne in distant France becomes discernible. Although the deafening ramjets of the World War II German "buzz bombs" were replaced by the humming vacuums of the hovercraft, the screams of the gulls and the relentless crashing of the sea continue on, unchanged by time. If you are one to "stand in history," Dover is a must visit during your stay in Great Britain. Few other places swell the imagination as do the White Cliffs of Dover.

Train service from London to Dover follows two routes. Departures from Victoria Station split destinations at Faversham. Part of the train goes to Dover, the other part to Margate and Ramsgate. As a precaution against "trainsplitting," our rail schedule is based on direct service to Dover from London's Charing Cross Station. Readers can, however, avail themselves of either route. As a suggestion, depart Charing Cross and return via Faversham to Victoria Station. This way, you will be "joined" by the Ramsgate train instead of being "split" by it.

The tourist information center is extensive, since Dover is a major debarkation point for visitors from the Continent. The center can provide information on all of Great Britain, as well as the local area. Pick up the *Days Out* brochure for White Cliffs Country for visitor vouchers to get either a free adult or child admission or a free or discounted gift from the many attractions of the area.

Ask for information on Dover Castle and how to reach it. No doubt you will also be interested in visiting the **Roman-Painted House,** Britain's buried Pompeii, discovered by an archaeological unit in 1971. Roman legions took over the structure about AD 300 for shore-defense purposes. The house gains its name from the brilliantly painted plaster of its walls, the oldest and best-preserved painted walls in Britain. Incredible as it seems, the Romans even installed an elaborate under-the-floor heating system. The house is a permanent museum, open April–September: 1000–1700 Tuesday–Saturday, 1300–1630 Sunday. *Admission:* £3 adults; £2 children. Don't miss out on viewing the more than 2,000-year-old Bronze Age vessel (found in 1992) on display in the Dover Museum.

London–Dover–London

Schedules shown are for direct trains from and to London Charing Cross Station. Other services are available from London Victoria Station and may require a change of trains.

Readers who may be planning trips from England to France by train and sea are advised that these schedules are not valid for those services. Trains shown here terminate at Dover Priory Station, which is some distance from the Dover Docks used by ferries.

DEPART Charing Cross Station	ARRIVE Dover Priory Station	NOTES
0700	0903	Sa
0710	0901	M–F
0740	0931	M–F
0800 (0808 Su)	1001	Sa–Su
0833	1031	M–F
1010	1201	M–Sa
1040	1231	M–F

M–Sa service continues after 1040 at hourly intervals until 1740 and afterward at other intervals until 2340. Note: Some departures are from Canon Street Station. Su service is hourly, at 08 past the hour 0808 until 2108, then 2238.

DEPART Dover Priory Station	ARRIVE Charing Cross Station	NOTES
1440	1631	M–F
1510	1701	M–Sa
1540 (1550 Sa)	1731 (1736 Sa)	M–Sa
1608	1801	Daily
1708	1901	Sa–Su
1741	1935	M–F

M–F service continues with departures at 1841,1910, 2110, and 2240. Sa service continues after 1708 at hourly intervals until 2210, then 2310 and 2340. Su service continues after 1708 at hourly intervals until 2208, then at 2238.

Legend has it that if Romans are left alone long enough, they will build something. Apparently this was the case in the second century, when the Roman legions constructed two lighthouse beacons on Dover's cliffs for the purpose of guiding their galleys into the sheltered anchorage below. A single lighthouse, reaching a height of more than 40 feet, is the tallest surviving Roman structure in Britain.

Dover can hardly be compared with the Continent's Riviera. Its beaches are small, tiny enclaves in the rugged face of the looming cliffs. And the height of the surf frequently becomes more than the average bather cares to contend with. Dover and its environs, however, lend themselves well to sunbathing, walking, and viewing.

During World War II Dover was subjected to long-range artillery shelling from the Pas de Calais German gun emplacements. Dover's residents dug cellars deep into the cliffs as bomb shelters. The surviving structures, most of which are now small hotels, still maintain the shelters for use as wine cellars, bars, and boutiques. In addition, the secret underground tunnels of Dover, used by the British to mastermind the evacuation from Dunkirk, were declassified and opened to the public.

Have you ever been to France? If not, now's your chance! Day trips from Dover to Calais in France via catamaran or ferry are very popular. Stock up on wine and cheese, plus a yard or so of crusty French bread during your visit, and load up with duty-free tobacco and booze on the return journey. Plan ahead by asking any train information office for information on ferry, hovercraft, or catamaran services (see "Crossing the English Channel" or the Appendix for contact information).

Day Excursion to

Folkestone

Traditional Seaside Resort

Depart from Charing Cross Station

Distance by train: 70 miles (113 km)

Average train time: 1 hour, 20 minutes

Train information and InterCity services: (0845) 748 4950. Also departs Waterloo East Station 3 minutes after Charing Cross departure time.

Tourist information: Discover Folkestone, 20 Bouverie Place Shopping Centre, Folkestone, Kent CT20 1AU; *Tel:* (0130) 325 8594; *Fax:* (0130) 325 9754

www.discoverfolkestone.co.uk

E-mail: cckirkham@gmail.com

Hours: Monday–Friday 0900–1700

Notes: Turn right out of the train station, and follow Cheriton Road, which will dead-end into Bouverie Place, then follow the tourist information signs.

Folkestone is a "multiple treat" seaside resort—enjoy a delightful day of sightseeing, shopping, and seafood; take a memorable journey across Romney Marsh on the world's smallest public train, the **Romney, Hythe and Dymchurch Railway;** or go antiques shopping in quaint English villages. With so many possibilities, we suggest that you make your way to Folkestone's tourist information center immediately upon arrival, especially if you decide to look into accommodation information and stay over for a day or two.

The opening of the Channel Tunnel in 1994, with the terminal situated on the outskirts of Folkestone, has given car travelers to France another option. Cars are driven straight onto shuttle trains and arrive at Calais in thirty-five minutes. Special arrangements for rental cars have been made with Hertz and Eurotunnel to exchange left- or right-hand-drive vehicles at the Hertz/Eurotunnel terminal in Calais. This information is also useful if you have purchased a BritRail Pass 'n Drive package. For Le Shuttle Information, call (0870) 535 3535.

Once down in the harbor area, take a stroll under the arches and imagine what life must have been like in the time of Napoleon when the smuggling of contraband was prevalent.

For beauty of location, Folkestone probably stands second to none. The Bayle area was said to be the site of a fort built around AD 659 and also the site of a castle built around 1068. The pub in the square, the **British Lion,** claims to be one of the oldest in the country and asserts that it has served ale since the fifteenth century—it was certainly frequented by Charles Dickens, who resided just around the corner on the Leas.

The Leas, Folkestone's famous mile-long cliff-top promenade, served as an inspiration for some of H. G. Wells's finest works and surveys the town's beach from a vantage point of more than 200 feet above. From there one can view the landscape from Dover to Dungeness. Stretching behind the Leas are the spacious, well-planned business and residential quarters.

The Leas is the most popular attraction for visitors to Folkestone. With its breathtaking views of the English Channel, colorful flowers, and intriguing pathways zigzagging down to the lower Coast Road, it truly is a tranquil reminder of Victorian and Edwardian elegance.

At the west end of the Leas are steps that lead down close to **Spade House,** H. G. Wells's home from 1900 to 1910. Midway along, **The Leas Cliff Hall** is one of Kent's leading entertainment centers, and a little farther down is the **Bandstand**—constructed in 1895 and still in regular use. Before leaving this delightful area, you should experience a trip on the **Cliff Lift.** The second oldest of its kind in the country, this original water-balance lift operates from the top of the Leas down to the lower end.

Sandgate, on the western outskirts of Folkestone and on the Coast Road, is one of the major antiques centers in England. Numerous antiques and curio shops beckon from narrow High Street. Also competing for shoppers' attention are several old-world inns and the **Sandgate Castle,** which has retained its English village atmosphere with friendly residents, as well as affording visitors a brisk sea-air promenade before continuing the journey toward Hythe.

A bus service operates from Folkestone, along the Coast Road and into Hythe, approximately twelve minutes from Folkestone town center. There the young—and those not so young—may board the fascinating **Romney, Hythe and Dymchurch**

Light Railroad for a delightful journey by steam traction to **New Romney,** with stops in Dymchurch and St. Mary's Bay. At New Romney there is a wonderful model

London–Folkestone–London

DEPART Charing Cross Station	ARRIVE Folkestone Central Station	NOTES
0710	0849	M–F
0740	0919	M–F
0800 (0808 Su)	0949	Sa–Su
0833 (0903 Sa)	1019	M–F
0908 (0910 Su)	1049	Sa–Su
0940	1119	M–F

M–F service continues at hourly intervals until 2340, with Sa–Su service hourly until 2210.

DEPART Folkestone Central Station	ARRIVE Charing Cross Station	NOTES
1436	1624	Daily
1536	1726	Daily
1636	1825	Daily
1736	1923	Daily

Daily service continues hourly until 2136.

railway museum. Service is generally every hour; you may pick up a timetable at the tourist information center beforehand.

Before leaving Hythe visit the crypt of **St. Leonard's Church.** Warning: This is not for the faint of heart. It houses a fascinating, macabre collection of hundreds of skulls and thousands of other bones dating from before the Norman Conquest of 1066. St. Leonard's Church, built in AD 1080, is beautiful and has several architectural features similar to those found in Canterbury Cathedral, as well as its own very special and unique Saxon, Norman, and medieval historic features. Hythe has many small specialty shops and restaurants and is renowned for its **Royal Military Canal** and **Martello Towers.**

Stop en route at **Dymchurch,** England's "children's paradise," or at **St. Mary's Bay,** where boating and fishing are two highlights of that holiday center. The RH&D Railroad terminates its service at Dungeness, another 5½ miles down the RH&D "road," where you'll find great contrast between its fishermen's shacks and its atomic plant.

Those with the use of a car should explore the peaceful flatlands of **Romney Marsh.** Hundreds of years ago this area was part of the English Channel, and ships were moored to the castle walls at Lympne. Now drained by a series of dikes, the marsh is a haven for wildlife. Dotted around the waterways, fields of sheep, and crop pastures, nestle little villages. A surprising number of old churches are here, with their own mysterious pasts steeped in smuggling tales. Each of the thirteen medieval churches dotting this land has unique features and is well worth a visit. Notices inform visitors where the church keys can be obtained: Some are kept by local homeowners, some in the nearby pubs, and some require almost an expedition in themselves to locate the ancient artifacts.

Day Excursion to

Gloucester

On the River Severn

Depart from Paddington Station

Distance by train: 114 miles (184 km)

Average train time: 1 hour, 50 minutes

Train information and InterCity services: (0845) 748 4950

Tourist information: Gloucester Tourist Office, 28 Southgate Street, Gloucester GL1 2DP; *Tel:* (01452) 396572; *Fax:* (01452) 504 273

www.gloucester.gov.uk/tourism

E-mail: tourism@gloucester.gov.uk

Hours: Monday 1000–1700, Tuesday–Saturday 0930–1700

Notes: Gloucester's Central Station is within walking distance of the city center, or you may hail a taxi or ride a city bus. To reach the tourist center on foot, walk toward the cathedral from the Central Station until you reach Northgate Street, then turn left to where it intersects Eastgate Street at the Cross. (Northgate and Eastgate Streets take their names from the ancient city routes through the Roman wall.) Continue past the Cross into Southgate Street.

Gloucester is steeped in history. First to arrive were the Romans, following their invasion of the British Isles. A legion fort was erected at the site of the current city center, and by AD 96–98, the Roman city of Glevum (now Gloucester) was established and flourishing. Little remains of the Roman presence in modern Gloucester. None of the Roman wall is now visible aboveground, but its line is still followed by the principal streets of the city.

Although Gloucester is situated some distance from the open sea, Queen Elizabeth I declared it a port in 1580. Oceangoing ships of up to 5,000-ton capacity are able to dock at Sharpness, the terminal dock of the city's port system. The entire dock complex has been given a new lease on life: An ambitious redevelopment program converted the site into a haven of recreation, education, and commerce.

The **National Waterways Museum** is the principal tourist attraction in the dock complex. Two hundred years of history, which shaped the fortunes of Britain, may be viewed there, housed in an imposing three-story building. The historic docks are also home to three other museums, shops, restaurants, pubs, and the Gloucester Antique Centre (*Hours:* 1000–1700 Monday–Saturday, 1100–1700 Sunday; www.gacl.co.uk), with more than one hundred dealers under one roof.

Gloucester's showplace is, of course, its **Cathedral,** the oldest building in the city. A Norman nucleus (1089–1260) incorporates additions in every known style of Gothic architecture. Topped by a towering fifteenth-century pinnacle rising 225 feet above ground level, Gloucester's cathedral is judged to be one of the six most beautiful buildings in Europe. If you have a limited amount of time to spend sightseeing in

London–Gloucester–London

DEPART Paddington Station	ARRIVE Gloucester Station	NOTES
0645	0850	M–F (1)
0715	0933	M–F (1)
0815	1006	Sa
0815	1033	M–F (1)
0837	1121	Su (1)
0845	1050	M–F (1)
0900	1107	Sa (1)
0948	1144	M–F
1000	1239	Su (1)
1015	1207	Sa
1045	1250	M–F (1)
1100	1303	Sa (1)
1130	1429	Su (1)

DEPART Gloucester Station	ARRIVE Paddington Station	NOTES
1354	1609	M–F (1)
1516	1707	Sa
1554	1802	M–F (1)
1615	1814	Sa (1)
1646	1839	M–F (1)
1647	1853	Su (1)
1716	1908	Sa
1754	1954	M–F (1)
1815	2014	Sa (1)
1819	2116	Su (1)
1852	2046	M–F (1)
1916	2107	Sa
1934	2156	Su (1)
2013	2214	M–F (1)
2015	2216	Sa (1)
2213	0033+1	M–F (1)

(1) Change trains at Swindon.

Gloucester, make the best use of it by concentrating on the cathedral and its surroundings.

The cathedral's origins began in AD 679, when the Saxons founded the Monastery of St. Peter on the site. In 909 Alfred the Great's daughter gave relics to the priory, making it the Church of St. Oswald. It is a magnificent example of medieval architecture with its great Norman piers still in the cathedral nave. Although craftspeople have continued to work on the structure since the fifteenth century, gracing it with an elegant exterior of later architectural designs, it remains a Norman edifice.

Sightseeing in Gloucester has been made easy by the **Via Sacra,** a walkway around the city center that follows the lines of the original city wall. Follow the pattern of dark paving placed in the sidewalk to keep visitors from going too far astray. Leaflets of the walk are available in the tourist information center.

The walking tour begins with a considerable variety of early English architecture, ranging from fifteenth-century timber-frame structures to the Tudor facades of the current county offices. You will pass **Blackfriars,** the best-preserved medieval Dominican friary in Britain. A portion is open to the public. **Greyfriars** is also on the route, but unlike Blackfriars, most of it stands in ruins.

Stopping in the city museum and art gallery affords the opportunity to examine many archaeological items, including a part of the original **Roman city wall.** The museum is open Tuesday–Saturday 1000–1700. It is also open Sunday 1000–1600 from July through September.

Just beyond the city museum, you will see the **Eastgate Shopping Centre,** which provides traffic-free areas at ground level. The tour ends at the cathedral in **St. Lucy's Garden,** the approach to the college green.

Gloucester abounds with interesting eating establishments ranging from the popular McDonald's to such ancient eateries as the **New Inn** on Northgate Street. Don't let the name fool you. The New Inn was built by St. Peter's Abbey to accommodate pilgrims in 1450. The inn courtyard was used for staging plays during the time of Queen Elizabeth I, and in the eighteenth century the inn became renowned for its association with traveling menageries and exhibitions of "curiosities." Said to be the finest medieval open-gallery inn in England, the food served there today matches the excellence of its medieval decor.

Day Excursion to

Greenwich

It's Time to Make a Difference

Depart from Charing Cross Station

Distance by train: 7 miles (11 km)

Average train time: 15 minutes

Train information and InterCity services: (0845) 748 4950

Tourist information: Tourist Information Centre, Pepys House, 2 Cutty Sark Gardens, Greenwich SE10 9LW; *Tel:* (0870) 608 2000; *Fax:* (020) 8853 4607

www.greenwich.gov.uk

E-mail: tic@greenwich.gov.uk

Hours: 1000–1700 daily

Notes: Upon arrival in the Greenwich railway station, use the pedestrian subway (underpass) to the main station and the street. Turn left, and walk along the road into town. Follow the signs guiding you to the National Maritime Museum and the *Cutty Sark*. Where they split, continue to follow the *Cutty Sark* signs until the ship's masts come into view. The local Greenwich Tourist Information Centre is at the entrance of the *Cutty Sark* Gardens. Or, if you prefer, take the Historic Greenwich Shuttle Bus from the pier gates to visit all the principal sites. Guided walking tours leave from the tourist center daily at 1215 and 1415. *Admission:* £6 adult, free for children younger than fourteen.

A visit to Greenwich reveals the town known as the cradle of Britain's maritime history. Queen Elizabeth II knighted Sir Frances Chichester for his solo circumnavigation of the world at a public ceremony at the Royal Naval College, which now stands on the site of the Royal Palace of Greenwich, where both Henry VIII and Elizabeth I were born.

The *Cutty Sark*, launched in 1869 as one of the fastest sailing ships, now lies in dry dock at Greenwich. The clipper served in the China tea trade as well as the Australian wool trade. Her curious name, which means "short chemise," originated in "Tam O' Shanter," a poem by Robert Burns in which the witch, Nanny, appeared in a cutty sark. The ship's figurehead represents Nanny. At press time, visitors cannot board the vessel due to a fire that caused substantial damage in May 2007; the *Cutty Sark* will re-open sometime in the spring of 2012. For current information and to make donations to the *Cutty Sark* renovation project, visit the Web site www.cuttysark.org.uk.

A few yards beyond the *Cutty Sark*'s stern is the entrance to the former Royal Naval College. Built during the seventeenth-century reign of William and Mary, the current buildings were used as a hospital for disabled and aged naval pensioners. In 1873 it became the Royal Naval College to provide for the higher education of naval officers. The Royal Navy left Greenwich in 1999, and the buildings are now occupied by the University of Greenwich and Trinity College of Music.

Visitors are admitted to the old Royal Naval College's **Painted Hall and Chapel** 1000–1700 daily. Admission is free with guided tours costing £6. *Tel:* 0208 269

4747; www.oldroyalnavalcollege.org. After the Battle of Trafalgar, the body of Lord Nelson lay in state in the Upper Hall. The interior decorating, by Sir James Thornhill, took nineteen years to complete. (You'll find out why when you see it.) Benjamin West's painting of the shipwrecked *St. Paul* in the college chapel is one of the highlights of this beautiful structure.

Pay a visit to the world's largest maritime museum, the **National Maritime Museum of Greenwich** (www.nmm.ac.uk). It houses more than two million items relating to Britain's maritime history. To get there, walk along the east side of the Dreadnought Library (on the Old Royal Naval College grounds), and cross Romney Road. The museum entrance is ahead, slightly to the left. Sixteen galleries lie beneath a spectacular free-span glass roof. On a tour of the galleries, you will see historic vessels such as *Miss Britain III,* the first boat to travel at 100 mph on open water, and the elaborately carved royal barge made for Frederick, Prince of Wales, in 1732. The museum is open daily 1000–1700, and admission is free.

London–Greenwich–London

FROM CENTRAL LONDON TO GREENWICH:

1. Via the Tube, take the Jubilee Line to the Underground station in North Greenwich. From Waterloo journey time is about 12 minutes; from Charing Cross, about 14 minutes. There are twenty-four trains per hour in each direction.

2. City cruises operate on the Thames River from Westminster to Greenwich; journey time, 45 minutes. All services shown below operate from London Charing Cross Station and also stop at London Waterloo East Station approximately 3 minutes from Charing Cross and London Bridge.

DEPART Charing Cross Station	ARRIVE Greenwich Station	NOTES
0739	0759	M–F
0730	0746	Su
0756	0812	Sa
0811	0829	M–F
0830	0846	Su
0839	0859	Sa
0841	0859	M–F
0911	0929	M–Sa

M–F service continues after 0920 at half-hour intervals until midafternoon, more frequently afterward, until 2326; Sa service continues after 0911 at half-hour intervals until 1709, then 1939 and at half-hour intervals until 2356; Su service continues every half hour until 2330.

DEPART Greenwich Station	ARRIVE Charing Cross Station	NOTES
1345	1412	Su
1422	1443	M–Sa
1415	1544	Su
1454	1513	M–Sa

M–F service continues after 1454 at half-hour intervals until 2217, then 2302 and 2332. Sa service continues after 1440 at approximately half-hour intervals until 2332. Su service continues after 1425 at half-hour intervals until the last train at 2245.

The museum has an amazing display of old ship models and a gallery devoted entirely to the life and loves of Admiral Lord Nelson. Its library and archives, which can be accessed by computer, hold historic ships' draughts, transportation documents, and a collection of some 4,000 paintings.

Linked by a colonnade to the National Maritime Museum, the **Queen's House** is the first example of a classical domestic house in England. Designed in the Palladian style in 1616 for Anne of Denmark, the Queen's House is an architectural delight. The rooms have changing themed displays.

The **Royal Observatory,** on the hill in Greenwich Park, south of the museum and the Queen's House, is an integral part of the complex. The world's prime meridian—longitude 0—passes across the courtyard, and it is from here that GMT (Greenwich Mean Time) was first calculated. The chronometers, which enabled John Harrison to resolve the problem of how to measure longitude, are on display in the house designed by Christopher Wren in 1675 for John Flamsteed, the first Astronomer Royal.

Admission to the National Maritime Museum, the Queen's House, and the Royal Observatory is free; however, an admission charge may apply to special exhibitions or events. *Hours:* 1000–1700 daily.

The Greenwich and Docklands International Festival is held annually at the beginning of July and presents the finest in music, dance, literature, theater, and visual arts from around the world. A full program of events is available from the tourist office, or check out the festival Web site, www.festival.org.

Greenwich has no shortage of eating establishments—choose from more than sixty restaurants offering a wide variety of cuisine ranging from traditional English cooking to French haute cuisine or exotic Asian. Try the historic riverside **Trafalgar Tavern.** Located in a beautiful setting beside the Old Royal Naval College, the Trafalgar has been providing traditional ales and fine foods since 1837. *Tel:* (020) 8858 2909.

Day Excursion to

Hastings

Famous Battle Site

Depart from Charing Cross Station
Distance by train: 60 miles (87 km)
Average train time: 1 hour, 30 minutes
Train information and InterCity services: (0845) 748 4950
Tourist information: Hastings Tourist Office, Queens Square, Priory Meadow, Hastings,

East Sussex TN34 1TL; *Tel:* (0142) 445 1111; *Fax:* (0142) 478 1186
www.visithastings.com
E-mail: hic@hastings.gov.uk
Hours: Monday–Friday 0830–1815, Saturday 0900–1700, and Sunday 1030–1600
Notes: Exit the station through the car park, and go straight on Devonshire Road. The office is on the right side, across from Mr. Bean's Coffee. To get to the office at Queens Square from the rail station, proceed down Havalock Road. At the end, turn left onto Queens Road, then turn left at the Town Hall onto Queens Square, where you will find the information center.

Undoubtedly, 1066 is one of the most well-known dates in history. When dusk fell near Hastings on October 14, 1066, William the Conqueror, the duke of Normandy, had defeated the Saxon army of slain King Harold and had become the new king of England.

Contrary to popular belief, the actual battle was not fought in Hastings. After landing at Pevensey, the Norman troops marched to Hastings, then northward about 5 miles to Senlac Hill, where they engaged the Saxons in battle. The castle, formerly a timber form, was converted to stone in 1067, one year after the battle. Hastings holds the lore of the Battle of Hastings plus the lure of its ancient fishing village and Norman castle.

Harold's troops were not pushovers. Nineteen days before the Battle of Hastings, his men had put a Norse army to rout at Stamford Bridge near York. In the initial onslaught at Senlac, the Normans retreated with the Saxons in hot pursuit. In so doing, the Saxons had to break the tight formation of their Saxon wall of shields, and the Norman cavalry quickly took advantage of the hole opening up in the line and inflicted heavy losses upon the Saxons. This tactic was twice repeated, and the conflict ended. Today's Super Bowl tactics may have developed in Hastings. To go sightseeing at the battleground, board any "Battle Abbey" bus.

During the Roman occupation Hastings was one of the famous Cinque (five) Ports where the Caesars moored their galleys. Later the harbor was silted up by a series of violent storms, culminating with the great tempest in 1287. As a result, Hastings was reduced to the status of a small fishing community during the following four centuries.

The tourist information center has an excellent brochure titled *Discover Hastings.* With it in hand, you can easily visit the Norman Castle via the West Hill lift. After visiting the castle, venture a few more paces to St. Clement's Caves for the Smugglers' Adventure. Set in a labyrinth of caverns and secret passageways beneath West Hill, the smugglers are brought to life.

Hastings is home to Britain's largest fleet of beach-launched boats, which continue to operate in the traditional manner. In addition to its rich historical heritage and fishing industry, Hastings has been an attractive seaside resort since the mid-eighteenth century, when London physicians began prescribing sea air and salt water as a panacea for all their patients' ills. Three miles of promenades line its beaches, many of them two-tiered with sun-trapped shelters overlooking the

English Channel. Sun is more sought after than surf in Hastings because the water is very cold. Examine any photo of an English seaside resort, and you'll see that the majority of bathers are on the beach, not in the sea.

London–Hastings–London

DEPART Charing Cross Station	ARRIVE Hastings Station	NOTES
0745	0929	Sa
0817	0957	M–F
0823	1003	Su
0945	1117	M–Sa

M–Sa service continues after 0945 at half-hour intervals until 2045, then hourly until 2345. Su service after 0823 is hourly until 2323.

DEPART Hastings Station	ARRIVE Charing Cross Station	NOTES
1331	1503	M–Sa
1408	1537	Su
1431	1603	M–Sa
1550	1733	Sa
1619	1806	M–F
1719	1904	M–F
1846	2033	M–F

Plus other frequent service until 2210 M–Sa; 27 minutes past the hour until 2127 Su.

After drinking in the panoramic sights from atop the hill, you can drift back toward the sea and Hastings's "Old Town." On Hill Street, observe the two cannonballs on either side of **St. Clement's Church** belfry. The right one was shot into the tower by the French; the one on the left was added by the locals to balance things off.

The French artillery attack in 1337 also leveled the **All Saints Church** in the Old Town. Undaunted by the shelling, the locals got busy and reerected the church in 1436. The interior contains a well-preserved fifteenth-century mural depicting the *Last Judgment,* with the devil casting souls into hell. The mural was intended to portray a lesson in morality for illiterate people of the Middle Ages.

You'll pass many interesting points on your walk. Stop for a closer examination of the **Old Town Hall** on High Street, which is now a museum. Drop by the **Stables Theatre** opposite the Old Town Hall. It originally served as the stables for the Old Hastings House, which was spared demolition by being converted into a cultural center.

Your next stop should be **Shovells,** circa 1450, reputedly the oldest house in town. If you're desperate for a libation, you might try the **Stag Inn** opposite Shovells, where remains of mummified cats and rats decorate the bar. Nearing the end of the Old Town walk, you will pass an unusual wedge-shaped house called the "piece of cheese," no doubt the funniest house in town. If time permits, head out on Rock-A-Nore Road to the **Blue Reef Aquarium** and take an incredible 3-D voyage from outer space to the depths of the earth's seas; www.bluereefaquarium.co.uk.

Don't miss the 243-foot embroidery in **Sussex Hall, White Rock Theatre.** It depicts eighty-one of the greatest events of British history since 1066, including the Battle of Hastings, the Boston Tea Party, and the first television broadcast.

The city of Hastings celebrates the famous 1066 battle every year by staging a program of events and attractions over a full week, encompassing the famed fourteenth day of October.

Day Excursion to

Ipswich

Chartered in AD 1200

Depart from Liverpool Street Station

Distance by train: 69 miles (111 km)

Average train time: 1 hour, 10 minutes

Train information and InterCity services: (0845) 748 4950

Tourist information: Tourist Information Centre, St. Stephen's Church, St. Stephen's Lane, Ipswich, Suffolk IP1 1DP; *Tel:* (0147) 325 8070; *Fax:* (0147) 343 2017

www.ipswich.gov.uk or **www.visit-ipswich.com**

E-mail: tourist@ipswich.gov.uk

Hours: Monday–Saturday 0900–1700; closed Sunday

Notes: The tourist information center is easy to reach. Departing the rail station, proceed straight ahead down Princes Street to Friars Street, and turn right. Friars Street curves and turns into Falcon Street. St. Stephen's Church will be on your left. If the weather is inclement, catch the "City Centre" bus, or hail a taxi immediately in front of the station.

The architecture of Ipswich reflects its history. Bypassed by the Romans, this town does not display the former grandeur of Rome. A seafaring community long before King John granted the town's first charter in 1200, Ipswich has always been engaged in commerce and has risen or declined along with the fortunes of its citizens' enterprises. The lack of Georgian buildings in Ipswich is evidence of the town's decline during that period, caused by the loss of its famous Suffolk cloth trade. A revitalization of its harbor by the mid-nineteenth century brought new prosperity to Ipswich and accounts for the number of splendid public buildings erected then, as well as the Victorian architecture of its homes.

Ipswich has withstood the onslaughts of the Vikings and other seaborne raiders through the ages. Starting with World War I, the town's docks became the targets of a new type of raider coming from the sky rather than from the sea. From 1915 to the end of the conflict, there were a number of zeppelin attacks, but damage was light. During the years 1943–1945, Ipswich was rimmed by no fewer than sixty-five air bases of the U.S. Eighth Air Force, from which were launched a staggering 3,000-plus bomber assaults against the Third Reich.

Today, with a population of 120,000, Ipswich has a developing port and is an important industrial and commercial center with fine shopping, sports, and entertainment facilities. Ipswich considers its **Tudor Christchurch Mansion,** set on sixty-five acres of parkland only a five-minute walk from the center of town, to be its finest attraction. The information office will gladly point out the way to you. Obtain a map there before going off to explore the endless streets and enticing alleyways leading off Ipswich's **Cornhill.**

London–Ipswich–London

DEPART Liverpool Street Station	ARRIVE Ipswich Station	NOTES
0730	0843	M–Sa
0800	0906	M–Sa
0830	0943	Daily
0900	1007	M–Sa
0930	1043	Daily
1000	1107	M–Sa

Daily service continues every half hour until 2030, then hourly until 2230.

DEPART Ipswich Station	ARRIVE Liverpool Street Station	NOTES
1709	1817	M–Sa
1743	1855	Daily
1813	1917	M–Sa
1843	1955	Daily
1909	2017	M–Sa
1943	2055 (2101 Su)	Daily
2043	2155	Daily

Daily service at 2 and 30 minutes past the hour, followed by schedule above, then frequent service with last trains out at 2243.

The town's Leisure Services Department has devised an excellent series of brochures (*Ipswich Historic Churches Trail, Wet Dock Maritime Trail,* and *Ipswich Street Map*) available for a nominal charge. The trails are marked with black-and-white signs that are numbered to correspond with the descriptions in the brochures. No doubt the trail was laid out for British walkers, for it is much too ambitious a course for the average Yank to complete within the prescribed period of one hour—at least it was for us! The route is circular, so you can join (or leave) at any point.

Places along the trails that may be of interest to you include the junction of Butter Market, St. Stephen's Lane, and Dial Lane. As you can probably guess, the **Butter Market** was once a marketplace for many products, including butter. The **Ancient House** in the Butter Market will remind you of the market's age (more than 500 years old), for its windows represent the known world during its time—and Australia is missing because it had not yet been discovered by Europeans. A seventeenth-century merchant, Robert Sparrow, added the exquisite, ornate plasterwork to the exterior.

Dial Lane is a traffic-free pedestrian area named for a clock that was once on the St. Lawrence Church. Although most of the church dates from the fifteenth and early-sixteenth centuries, its tower was rebuilt in 1882 to reflect its original design.

By passing the church and turning left onto St. Lawrence Street and then right onto Tavern Street, you'll come upon the **Great White Horse Hotel.** It is the only surviving inn that can be traced in the city records before 1571. Completed in 1818, its Georgian brick facade covers a basically timber-frame structure from the sixteenth century. A young London news reporter, sent to Ipswich to cover an election, stayed in the Great White Horse and later wrote his recollections in a comic novel that changed the course of his life. The reporter was Charles Dickens; the novel, *The Pickwick Papers*. Today the original courtyard still remains but the inn is no longer open.

Near the end of your walking tour, take time to pause at the junction of Tavern Street and Dial Lane. The view down Dial Lane to the Ancient House is one of the most photographed areas in Ipswich. The Tudor-style buildings reflect the detail and attention of the city's craftsmen. From this point a left turn will take you to the Cornhill, the end of your Tourist Town Trail walk.

As you stand at Cornhill, it is sobering to consider that only 400 years ago, nine people were burned at the stake on this hill for heresy. Before becoming too sober, however, visit one of the bars in the Great White Horse Hotel. Distinguished visitors of the past, besides Charles Dickens, include such notables as King George II, Louis XVIII, and Lord Nelson, who quaffed many a draft there. A toast to these gentlemen would seem only proper. So have a go at it, mate, if you can get there before they call "time."

Day Excursion to

Isle of Wight

The Holiday Island

Depart from Waterloo Station

Distance by train: 88 miles (142 km)

Average journey time to Ryde: Train approx. 1 hour, 30 minutes; catamaran ferry, 14 minutes

Train information and InterCity services: (0845) 748 4950

Tourist information: Isle of Wight Tourism, *Tel:* (01983) 813813; *Fax:* (01983) 823031

www.islandbreaks.co.uk

E-mail: info@islandbreaks.co.uk

Hours: 0930–1700 Monday–Saturday, 1000–1530 Sunday

Notes: There are seven tourist information centers on the island: Ryde, Sandown, Shanklin, Cowes, Newport, Yarmouth, and Ventnor. All except the Ventnor office are open year-round. The one at Ryde is on the Western Esplanade opposite the pier.

"Britain's Miniature" is a term often employed to describe the Isle of Wight. Shaped like a diamond, the island is a veritable jewel, with every feature of the mainland condensed into a mere 147 square miles. It is dotted with historic spots, sandy beaches, thatched villages, rolling countryside—and discotheques, if that's your pleasure. There is fun for everyone, and getting there can be fun as well.

The majority of trains departing Waterloo Station in London for Portsmouth Harbour are InterCity trains. As they glide through the scenery of southern England bound for the coast, you'll be treated to a delightful kaleidoscope of England's landscape from the wide-vision train windows. Stay aboard when the train halts briefly in the Portsmouth and Southsea Station. Your destination is the Portsmouth Harbour Station, five minutes farther on.

Board the Portsmouth-Ryde catamaran at the end of the harbor station (www.wightlink.co.uk). Your BritRail Pass does not cover the passage. The day-return fare is £12.30 (until 0430 next day), standard-return fare is £16.60, and the crossing takes only about fourteen minutes.

After the boat docks at the Ryde pier head, you have three options for sightseeing on the island by train. The trains, by the way, run right onto the pier and look every bit like those of the Bakerloo Underground Line in London. The three options? They are Ryde, Sandown, and Shanklin. All three lie along the 9 miles of track extending from the Ryde pier head to the terminal in Shanklin.

Ryde is the Isle of Wight's gateway. Set picturesquely on a hillside, it becomes a wonderful grandstand from which to watch the great ships of the world sailing by. The pier at Ryde is more than 2,300 feet long, so board the train after disembarking from the passenger ferry and ride the train to its first stop, **Ryde Esplanade,** where you will find the Tourist Information Centre ready to assist. Ryde has 6 miles of sandy beach backed by pleasant, wooded gardens. The town is also noted for its Regency and Victorian buildings and for its **Royal Victoria Arcade** shopping center.

Sandown is the next railway stop after passing the Brading Station. It has all the facilities for a summer holiday, including a modern pier complex that offers licensed bars, cafes, and a restaurant, amusements, plus adventure golf, "super-bowl," and Dodgems (bumper cars). The sheltered **Sandown Bay** has more than 5 miles of attractive sandy beaches, where you may find such diversions as miniature golf and a canoe lake. Visit Dinosaur Isle, the exciting Geological Exhibition Centre, and the Tiger and Big Cat Sanctuary. Check at the Tourist Information Centre on High Street for details of all local attractions.

London–Isle of Wight–London

DEPART FROM WATERLOO STATION

All service to Isle of Wight is by frequent train service approximately every 20–30 minutes M–Sa and hourly on Sunday to Portsmouth Harbour Station, frequent fast-ferry service to Ryde Head Pier on the Isle of Wight, and train from Ryde Head Pier to Shanklin; the return route is the reverse.

Schedules shown here are for trains that depart from London Waterloo Station and travel via Woking, Guildford, and Portsmouth and Southsea Stations. Other services are possible from London Victoria Station via Gatwick Airport Station and/or Brighton; these may also require a change of trains at Portsmouth and Southsea Station to reach Portsmouth Harbour Station.

DEPART Waterloo Station	ARRIVE Portsmouth Harbour	NOTES
0645	0848	M–Sa
0730	0907	M–Sa
0800	0937 (1004 Su)	Daily
0830	1007 (1011 Su)	Daily
0900	1033 (1104 Su)	Daily
0930	1107	Daily

Departures continue every half hour until 2230.

DEPART Portsmouth Harbour	ARRIVE Waterloo Station	NOTES
1515 (1532 Su)	1651 (1714 Su)	Daily
1615	1754	M–Sa
1645 (1648 Su)	1843	Daily
1718	1913	M–Sa
1745 (1748 Su)	1929 (1944 Su)	Daily
1815 (1832 Su)	1959	Daily

M–Sa service continues until 2218; Su service continues until 2232.

Sandown and Shanklin are considered twin resorts on the Isle of Wight. The distance between the two stations is only 2 miles. Select one or both for your day excursion. There is much to see and do in either resort.

Shanklin frequently holds the British annual sunshine record. Built on a cliff with a sheltered mile-long beach lying below, it is the end of the line for rail travel. It is easy, however, to transfer to the buses operated by the island's bus company, Southern Vectis, for farther points such as Ventnor, Newport, and Cowes. Check with the Southern Vectis Travel Office on Regent Street, 2 blocks from Shanklin's train station, or at the Tourist Information Centre in Shanklin at 67 High Street. To reach it, as you leave the station, walk straight to Regent Street, then turn right onto High Street. The center is on the right just up the hill—about a ten-minute walk from Shanklin Station. Taxi service is available.

Our personal selection of the Isle's options would be Shanklin, as it certainly is one of the prettiest towns in Britain. Shanklin's Old Village on Ventnor Road is world-famous for its quiet beauty. From there, you may descend to Shanklin's beach esplanade via a walk through **Shanklin's Chine,** a cleft in the town's cliff with overhanging trees, plants, ferns, and a cascading stream. There is a small charge to walk through the Chine, which also has an exhibition of PLUTO memorabilia. PLUTO is the pipeline under the ocean, through which fuel was piped to France for the D-Day invasion and the weeks thereafter.

John Keats, one of the most gifted and appealing of England's nineteenth-century poets, found Shanklin's climate congenial to his health and the town's scenic beauty so inspiring that he resided there for a long period. **Keats Green,** a spacious promenade on the cliff top of Shanklin, commemorates his association with the town.

Queen Victoria spent her holidays on the Isle of Wight and died there in **Osborne House** in 1901. This house, built by order of the queen in 1845, is maintained in good order, with the queen's furniture still in place. In a shed on the property, you can see the gardening tools of the royal children from more than a century ago. Each tool and wheelbarrow is marked with the small owner's initials.

The queen and Prince Albert used Osborne as a country residence, and it is said that the prince had a considerable influence on the design of the residence. The main rooms and many of the private apartments are open to the public between Easter Monday and the end of October. Situated at East Cowes, in the north of the island on the east side of the Medina estuary (the island's central river), Osborne House can be reached by bus from Ryde Esplanade Station. On the opposite bank is Cowes, the world-famous home of yachting.

Day Excursion to

King's Lynn

Rich in Architecture

Depart from King's Cross Station
Distance by train: 97 miles (156 km)
Average train time: 1 hour, 35 minutes
Train information and InterCity services: (0845) 748 4950
Tourist information: Tourist Information Centre, The Custom House, Purfleet Quay, King's Lynn, Norfolk PE30 1HP; *Tel:* (0155) 376 3044; *Fax:* (0155) 381 9441
www.west-norfolk.gov.uk
E-mail: kings-lynn.tic@west-norfolk.gov.uk
Hours: 1030–1600 Monday–Saturday, 1200–1600 Sunday
Notes: To reach the Tourist Information Centre, walk directly away from the front of the train station (which faces the west) down Waterloo Street. The street undergoes a name change at every intersection—Market, Paradise, New Conduit, Purfleet. The Tourist Information Centre is straight ahead in the Custom House.

King's Lynn, once "Bishop's Lynn" and renamed when Henry VIII took over the bishop's manor, is one of the most historic towns in England. The old section still seems medieval, complete with narrow streets, guildhalls, and riverside quays, where the gulls reel and scream overhead. The town's former prosperity has left it with a rich heritage of architecture. Set along the east bank of the wide and muddy Ouse River, King's Lynn is the northern terminal of the London-Cambridge-Ely rail line.

King's Lynn came into being during the eleventh century and is situated on the middle of three islands, where four streams ran into the Ouse River. Water highways became vital to the commerce of the town. With waterway connections to the English Midlands, the town of Lynn became an important trading port, bustling with the romance of exotic cargoes, sailing ships, and foreign accents. By the thirteenth century, the town found prosperity in the wool trade between England and the Continent. This aura of a wealthy medieval town still prevails. Today the town is a thriving, modern port, an essential link between Britain and the rest of the Common Market.

Streets and alleyways in King's Lynn twist and wind about on a grand scale, so a town map will be an invaluable aid. Immediately make your way from the train station to the tourist information center located in the Custom House, about a ten-minute walk. Nearby, the town boasts England's oldest surviving **Hanseatic Warehouse.** The surrounding riverside area was restored in 2000. Visit the Green Quay environmental exhibition located in Marriott's Warehouse, a refurbished sixteenth-century barn.

You will be tempted to wander about in **Queen Street** with its lovely merchants' houses, each with a character all its own. At the information center equip yourself with a copy of the *King's Lynn Town Walk* booklet. This is a masterpiece of simplicity and is packed with facts about the town and its buildings. The trail follows a circular route, so you may start and finish wherever it is most convenient for you. We suggest starting at the Town Hall. Rebuilt in 1421 after a fire, it houses the "Tales of the Old Gaol House" exhibition, as well as King's Lynn regalia, including the magnificent King John Cup and the *Red Register,* purported to be one of the oldest books in the world.

A focal point in King's Lynn is the **Tuesday Market Place,** into which King Street leads. True to tradition, a country market is conducted there every Tuesday in the shadow of the **Duke's Head Hotel,** a most impressive seventeenth-century structure. The market is everything that one would expect it to be—stalls packed with the agricultural and manufacturing products of the area, augmented by absolutely free entertainment as the hucksters bid for attention. Another impressive structure in

London–King's Lynn–London

DEPART King's Cross Station	ARRIVE King's Lynn Station	NOTES
0645	0822	M–Sa
0715	0853	M–Sa
0745	0925 (0920 Sa)	M–Sa
0845	1025	M–Sa
0945	1123	M–Sa
1015	1151	Su
1045	1220	M–Sa
1145	1320	M–Sa (1)
1215	1351	Su
1415	1551	Su (2)

(1) Then hourly until 2045, then 2115 and 2215 M–Sa, with an additional train at 2315 Fr–Sa.
(2) Then hourly until 2215.

DEPART King's Lynn Station	ARRIVE King's Cross Station	NOTES
1356	1534	M–Sa
1428	1608	Su (3)
1456	1634	M–Sa
1556	1734	M–Sa
1635	1832	M–F
1656	1835	Sa
1735	1935	M–F
1756	1934	Sa
1835	2032	M–Sa
1936	2132	M–Sa
2036	2230	M–Sa
2136	2331	M–Sa
2228	0042+1	M–F

(3) Then hourly until 2028, then 2228.

the Tuesday Market Place is the magnificently restored **Corn Exchange,** now a popular concert hall and entertainment center.

If you miss the Tuesday market, there's another one on Saturday at a location appropriately named the **Saturday Market Place,** just opposite the Town Hall. A newer shopping center in the center of town is on the site of the former cattle market.

Visit **St. George's Guildhall** at 27 King Street—the largest surviving medieval guildhall. It is open 0930–1700 Monday through Saturday. Built about 1410, it has been used as a theater, a courthouse, and an armory. It is now a cultural center housing a theater and an art gallery.

King John, who ruled England between 1199 and 1216, granted the town its charter in 1204. The king came to Lynn in October 1215 in pursuit of rebellious barons. One story relates that after he was wined and dined by the burghers of Lynn, the king and his entourage set off in hot pursuit of the baronial rebels. Heading west out of King's Lynn toward Newark, the king and his entourage crossed the Norfolk tidal flats, where the River Ouse empties into **The Wash,** a shallow bay known for the treachery of its tides. During the crossing, a high tide from the Wash wiped out the king's baggage train. King John reached the safety of higher shores, but he lost the crown jewels and everything else that went with such a collection in those days. King John contracted dysentery (a bad "burger," perhaps?) and died a few days later. No one questioned the burghers as to exactly what they fed the king before he left Lynn. We have our suspicions, however, because reportedly all of the burghers felt fine the following morning.

Somewhere near King's Lynn, buried under centuries of silt, lies King John's lost treasure. None of it has been recovered, and no one knows where to look for it.

Day Excursion to

Lincoln

Hilltop Cathedral

Depart from King's Cross Station

Distance by train: 135 miles (217 km)

Average train time: 2 hours, 10 minutes

Train information and InterCity services: (0845) 748 4950

Tourist information: Lincoln Tourist Information Centre, 9 Castle Hill, Lincoln, Lincolnshire LN1 3AA; *Tel:* (01522) 545 5458; *Fax:* (01522) 541452

www.visitlincolnshire.com

E-mail: info@lincolnshiretourism.com

Hours: Monday–Thursday 0830–1700, Friday 0930–1700, Saturday–Sunday 1000–1700

Notes: On arrival in Lincoln's Central Station, go to the city bus station, which is in front and to the right of the main station entrance (use the designated pedestrian walkways, because the vehicular traffic can be heavy at times). From the bus station take city bus 1, 7, or 8 up the hill to the cathedral, and ask the driver to let you off at the corner of Eastgate and Nettleham Road (next to Forte Posthouse Hotel). Walk along Eastgate until reaching the White Hart Hotel; turn left, and the center is at the top of the hill at No. 9 Castle Hill.

Lincoln Tourist Information Centre: 21 The Cornhill, LN5 3HB; *Tel:* (01522) 873800; *Fax:* (01522) 541452

Hours: Same as the center at 9 Castle Hill, except closed Sunday

Notes: Turn left from the rail station, and cross over at St. Mary La Wigford Church on High Street. The center is in The Cornhill, opposite the British Homes store.

Lincoln's greatest landmark is its cathedral, which stands on a ridge, dominating the skyline. The cathedral appears to be half church, half stronghold. Actually, there are two Lincolns—one, the cathedral and castle standing politely on the hilltop; the other, the city below girding the River Witham and buzzing with commerce. We suggest you scale the heights first and later return to the lower level by a dizzy descent down Steep Hill.

On the other hand, if you're ambitious, bear to the left when leaving the station and walk a short distance on St. Mary Street to where it intersects with High Street. Turn right at this point, and keeping the cathedral in sight, start walking in its direction up High Street. Disregard the fact that the street changes names several times. When you reach an area where a ski lift or a cable car would be most welcome, you'll be on Steep Hill—and it's appropriately named. Now gain the high ground (and your breath), and you will find yourself in Castle Square. With a right turn at the Exchequer Gate, you may enter the cathedral grounds.

Walking up the Lincoln hill from the railway station to the cathedral can give you a sense of accomplishment. It can also be hazardous to your health. Use discretion—take the bus or a taxi if there's any doubt in your mind about the climb. This is to be enjoyed, not endured.

Walking up **Steep Hill,** you will pass the Norman House, said to be the home of "Aaron the Jew," a moneylender from the twelfth century who reportedly became the richest man in England at that time. Halfway up Steep Hill, and turning off at Danesgate, your visit will be well rewarded by an inspection of the **Usher Gallery.** You can view an assortment of personal property belonging to England's poet laureate, Alfred, Lord Tennyson, born in Somersby, a Lincolnshire village, in 1809. The gallery also houses an extensive collection of paintings by Peter de Wint (1784–1849). If you arrive at Castle Square in need of lunch or a libation, seek out the **Wig & Mitre,** a licensed restaurant with a Dickensian atmosphere.

The **cathedral** is the main point of interest in Lincoln. When you view its exterior and examine the spacious areas under its roof, it becomes rather difficult to comprehend that it was built by medieval craftsmen in only twenty years. The

Normans began construction of the cathedral in 1072. In 1141 the roof was destroyed by a fire, and in 1185 the main structure crumbled into ruins as a result of an earthquake. But it survived.

Reconstruction, which began in 1186, returned the cathedral to its original configuration. Through the ensuing centuries, it was altered frequently. The central tower was completed around 1311. In more modern times, Lincoln's greatest attraction has withstood Cromwell's artillery and Hitler's bombs. If you have but a short period of time to visit in Lincoln, the cathedral must take priority over all else.

Adding to the many reasons Lincoln Cathedral is a top attraction is Sony Pictures' blockbuster movie ***The Da Vinci Code,*** starring Academy Award–winner Tom Hanks (based on Dan Brown's best-selling novel by the same title). Crucial scenes were filmed inside the cathedral. Summer hours: 0715–2000 Monday–Friday,

London–Lincoln–London

DEPART King's Cross Station	ARRIVE Lincoln Central Station	NOTES
0615	0753	M–F (4)
0620	0855	Sa (1)
0730	0959	M–F (3)
0830	1023	M–F (1)
0930	1114	M–F (1)
1030	1236	M–Sa(1)
1130	1406	M–Sa (3)

With frequent service thereafter.

DEPART Lincoln Central Station	ARRIVE King's Cross Station	NOTES
1330	1604	M–F (3)
1445	1646	M–Sa (1)
1515	1746	Su (4)
1524	1745 (1807 Sa)	M–Sa (4)
1601	1830	Sa (3)
1644	1845	M–F (1)
1818	2028	M–Sa 2)
1831	2129	M–F (2)
1925	2145	M–F (1)
1943	2230	Sa (4)
2027	2314	M–F (4)
2100	2322	Su (1)

(1) Change trains at Newark North Gate.
(2) Change trains at Doncaster.
(3) Change trains at Peterborough.
(4) Change trains at Retford.

0715–1800 Saturday–Sunday. Winter hours: 0715–1800 Monday–Saturday, 0715–1700 Sunday. Admission is £6 adults, £1 children age five to fifteen. Visit www.lincolncathedral.com.

Lincoln Castle was built by William the Conqueror in 1068 and became the Normans' military stronghold in the area. Its construction is unusual in that it has two mounds: one crowned by the twelfth-century Tower of Lucy, the other with Norman structures on which, in the nineteenth century, an observatory tower was constructed. From either of these vantage points, there are beautiful views of the cathedral and the surrounding countryside.

Today the Lincoln Castle is a huge, walled enclosure of lawns and trees. The crown courts and the old county jail are located in the castle yard. On permanent exhibition is one of only four surviving originals of King John's Magna Carta. The castle is open daily 1000–1600 October–March, 1000–1700 April–September, 1000–1800 May–August. Admission is £6 for adults and £4 for seniors and children; www.lincolnshire.gov.uk.

If you wish to visit the "other Lincoln," start by descending (or plunging down) Steep Hill with its bow-fronted shops until you again reach High Street. You will find interest in the twelfth-century **High Bridge,** which crosses the River Witham. It is the oldest one in Britain to still carry a building on its structure, in this case, a sixteenth-century timber-framed house. The route leading from the cathedral down Steep Hill is studded with other interesting structures, such as numerous public houses and restaurants. Modern Lincoln blends easily with its historical counterparts.

Day Excursion to

Liverpool

Four Lads Who Shook the World

Depart from Euston Station

Distance by train: 194 miles (312 km)

Average train time: 2 hours, 30 minutes

Train information: (0845) 748 4950

Tourist information: Merseyside Welcome Centre, 36–38 Whitechapel, Liverpool L2 6DZ; *Tel:* 0151 233 2008

www.visitliverpool.com

E-mail: 08place@liverpool.gov.uk

Hours: Monday–Saturday 1000–1700, closed Sunday, bank holidays 1000–1600

Notes: To get to the Merseyside Welcome Centre from Liverpool Lime Street Station, exit the central Lime Street exit, cross the street and head toward the Marriott Hotel. Turn left onto Hood Street, then left again onto Whitechapel. The Welcome Centre will be ahead on the left.

Throughout its fascinating 800-year history, Liverpool has been a "place to remember." Declared the European Capital of Culture in 2008, Liverpool's diversity offers something for everyone. According to *The Official Guide to the City of Liverpool,* "It only takes a few hours to fall in love with Liverpool, and a lifetime to get to know it."

Situated at the neck of the River Mersey, Liverpool has a long association with the river and the sea. In the twelfth century, King John used it as a launching pad for his forays to Ireland. By 1551 the River Mersey was a prominent gateway for transport of goods to other ports in Britain. By the eighteenth century Liverpool became an international port, trading goods with North America, Africa, and Europe; by the nineteenth century it had become one of the principal ports of the world, second only to London. With all the international trade and cultural exchanges, it is not surprising that Liverpool has its own Chinatown, the oldest Chinese community in Europe.

The cosmopolitan city of Liverpool is one of majestic architectural heritage, with more listed buildings—some 2,500 of them—than any other British city except London, and more Georgian buildings than Bath. Just across from Lime Street Station, **St. George's Hall** is an example of one of the finest neoclassical buildings in all of Europe. The tall concrete towerlike structure with the circular top is known as St. John's Beacon and houses the U.K.'s largest commercial radio station. For a dramatic panoramic view of Liverpool, take a guided tour (available on weekends) from the Queen Square Tourist Information Centre.

Dramatically dominating the city center skyline, Liverpool boasts not one, but two cathedrals—the **Anglican Cathedral** and the **Roman Catholic Metropolitan Cathedral** at opposite ends of appropriately named Hope Street. The Anglican Cathedral is the largest in the world and was completed in 1978, taking nearly seventy-five years to build. The conical-shaped Metropolitan, known as "the Cathedral of Color," uses natural light to create an astonishing atmosphere. It took only five years to build and was completed in 1967. Ironically, the architect of the Anglican Cathedral, twenty-one-year-old Giles Gilbert Scott, later Sir Giles, was Catholic, whereas Sir Frederick Gibbard, the architect of the Metropolitan Cathedral, was Protestant. Young Giles's design won the Anglican design competition. He had never designed anything of great significance before—except the famed fire-engine-red British telephone booth.

The Anglican Cathedral has the highest and heaviest bells in the world, the highest gothic arches, and the largest organ, with almost 10,000 pipes. Each stone of the cathedral is unique—no two are exactly the same, either in size or weight. After John Lennon was killed in New York, his wife, Yoko Ono, went to Liverpool to the Anglican Cathedral, where a special service was allowed for the first time to play "pop music"—a medley of John Lennon and Paul McCartney's songs.

Liverpool is also famous as the birthplace of the Beatles—John, Paul, George Harrison, and Ringo Starr, "the four lads who shook the world." Their music first captivated young people throughout the world four decades ago—and it still does so today.

There are myriad city and Beatles-related tours available, but for those who are short on time, we recommend heading to the famous Albert Dock (named after Prince Albert) and the historical waterfront area. You can check in at the Merseyside Welcome Centre at Queen Square for information and directions.

Albert Dock is a beautifully restored waterfront complex. Stop at the Albert Dock Tourist Information Centre in the Atlantic Pavilion. It's open 1000–1800 daily. At the Dock, you will find: **The Beatles Story** exhibition in the Britannia Pavilion, the **Merseyside Maritime Museum** to learn about Liverpool's interesting development as a port, the Museum of Liverpool Life, plus a fifty-minute cruise with commentary "'cross the Mersey" to take in the stunning sights of the waterfront.

London–Liverpool–London

Schedules shown below are for direct train service.

DEPART Euston Station	ARRIVE Liverpool Lime Street	NOTES
0707	0915	M–Sa
0807	1015	M–Sa
0815	1109	Su
0907	1115	M–Sa
1107	1315	M–Sa
1115	1354	Su

Hourly departures daily until 2107 M–F, 2011 Sa, and 2121 Su.

DEPART Liverpool Lime Street	ARRIVE Euston Station	NOTES
1348	1556 (1603 Su)	Daily
1448	1656	Daily
1548	1756 (1801 Su)	Daily
1648	1901 (1856 Su)	Daily
1748	2002 (1956 Sa)	Daily
1848	2105	Daily
1948	2209	M–Sa
2048	2356	M–F
2048	2354	Su

You can view Liverpool's "Three Graces"—the Liver, Cunard, and Port of Liverpool buildings. Liverpudlians are quite proud of the fact that the clocks in the towers of the lovely Liver Building are 2½ feet larger than Big Ben in London. There are two gigantic birds atop the towers. We surmise that the one facing outward toward the sea must be the female watching for sailors coming into port; the other one must be male, as he faces inward, as if to see what time the pub opens.

There is free admission to the **Tate Gallery,** named after Liverpool businessman Henry Tate, to view its extraordinary modern art collection, and there are plenty of elegant shops and excellent restaurants in the waterfront area. *Hours:*

October–June: Tuesday–Sunday 1000–1750; June–October: daily 1000–1750; www.tate.org.uk/liverpool. Thirsty? Visit the Pump House Pub. Formerly, the Pump House pumped pressurized water to provide hydraulic power. Now it pumps pressurized lager instead—great progress for lager lovers. Hungry? One of the world's most famous fish 'n' chips restaurants, Harry Ramsden's ([0151] 709 4545; www.harryramsdens.co.uk), is nearby Albert Dock at Brunswick Way, off Sefton Street.

Beatles' fans and even those who aren't (yet) will enjoy reliving "the Fab Four's" most sensational success story in the pop music world at **The Beatles Story** museum and exhibition center. The exhibition is open daily 0900–1900 April to October, 1000–1800 November to March; *Tel:* (0151) 709 1963 ext. 220; *Fax:* (0151) 708 0039. Admission is £12.95 for adults and £7.00 for children. The souvenir shop is an excellent place to pick up Beatles' memorabilia and music. www.beatlesstory.com.

Avid Beatles' fans will most certainly want to "take a ticket to ride" on the **Beatles Magical Mystery Tour.** This two-hour bus tour departs from the Albert Dock Bus Stop (just opposite the Pump House Pub) at 1430. It includes the Beatles' homes, schools, Penny Lane, Strawberry Field, and many more landmarks associated with the Beatles. Tour price is £14.95. Advance booking is highly recommended. Telephone Cavern City Tours at (0151) 236 9091 or Mersey Tourism at (0151) 233 2457 for information and booking. The tour finishes at the world-famous **Cavern Club** on Mathew Street (www.cavernclub.org). The original Cavern Club was demolished during the construction of Liverpool's Underground transport system. Fortunately, city leaders readily recognized their gross error and reconstructed the Cavern Club, using much of its original brick, a few yards from where it initially stood.

If you have the time—and the energy—to extend your visit to Liverpool, there is no shortage of exciting nightlife. Nightlife aficionados come from all over Britain to the "cream of the crop of clubs"—Cream. Live-music fans will want to "drink in" the atmosphere at the Picket, L2, Lomax, the Jacaranda Club—with a bar on three floors—and, of course, the Cavern Club. Irish music and Guinness beer, dubbed by the Irish as their "water supply," can be found at Flanagan's Apple, also located on Mathew Street. Classical music fans can take in the Royal Liverpool Philharmonic Orchestra at the Philharmonic Hall (Box Office [0151] 709 3789). Seemingly all of Liverpool is lively with all kinds of music—live bands play in pubs and clubs throughout the city. For overnight stays check out the 120-bedroom Beatles-themed hotel, the Hard Day's Night Hotel, on Mathew Street.

Liverpool is a place you'll remember. As Prince Albert succinctly put it, "I have heard of the greatness of Liverpool, but the reality far surpasses the expectation."

Day Excursion to

Nottingham

Tales of Robin Hood

Depart from St. Pancras Station

Distance by train: 127 miles (204 km)

Average train time: 2 hours

Train information and InterCity services: (0845) 748 4950

Tourist information: Nottingham Tourism Centre, 1–4 Smithy Row, Nottingham, Nottinghamshire NG1 2BY; *Tel:* (0844) 477 5678

www.visitnottingham.com

E-mail: tourist.information@nottinghamcity.gov.uk

Hours: Monday–Friday 0900–1730, Saturday 0900–1700, Sunday 1000–1600

Notes: The main tourist information office is within walking distance of the train station. But if your time is limited, hail a cab at the station and save some time as well as your shoe leather. Otherwise, take Carrington Street on your right as you leave the station. Cross Canal Street, and pass Broad Marsh Bus Station. Continue straight through Broad Marsh Shopping Centre, and exit onto Listergate–Albert Street–Exchange. Walk in the same direction toward Exchange Arcade Shopping Centre until you come to Smithy Row. The Old Market Square will be on your left. You can't miss it—but if you do, just inquire at one of the taxi queues in the area.

Nottingham is famous for many things, among them the legend of Robin Hood. Many tales of Robin and his band of merry men have been passed down through the ages by ballad and legend, though only scattered fragments remain of his origin. It appears that one Robert Fitzooth, reputed to be the Earl of Huntingdon, was born in 1160 during the reign of Henry II. Of noble birth, he squandered his inheritance at an early age; so either by necessity or by choice, he sought refuge in the forest. Here he was joined by men in similar circumstances, such as Little John, Will Scarlet, Friar Tuck, and—to add the love-interest angle to the legend—Maid Marian.

Robin Hood reigned in the forest, defying the powers of government, protecting the poor, and giving to the needy. The king's deer provided food, and the king's forest provided fuel. Other necessities were obtained through barter. Taking the king's property was, of course, illegal, and it drove the Sheriff of Nottingham "bananas," to the point where he offered a substantial reward for Robin's capture—dead or alive. Robin Hood eluded capture and supposedly lived to be eighty-seven years old. Records show his death occurred on November 18, 1247. This man, who lived in an age of feudal tyranny, endeared himself to countless generations and became the legendary hero of Nottingham. A fine statue to his memory stands in the courtyard of **Nottingham Castle.**

The castle was built as a fortress in 1068 by William the Conqueror. It was destroyed during the English civil war, rebuilt, and again destroyed by an angry mob in 1831. Following its second restoration, the castle was transformed into a museum and art gallery late in the nineteenth century. A series of underground passages run beneath the castle. Naturally, there are many tales of intrigue relating to their purpose. The castle is open to the public daily; the underground passages can be seen only on conducted tours. Don't miss the *Story of Nottingham* at the Castle Museum and Art Gallery. The museum is open Tuesday–Sunday 1000–1700 March–September, and 1000–1600 October–February; admission £5.50.

London–Nottingham–London

DEPART St. Pancras Station	ARRIVE Nottingham Station	NOTES
0730	0926	M–Sa
0830	1025	M–Sa
0900	1124	Su
0930	1125	M–Sa
1000	1222	Su
1030	1226	M–Sa
1130	1325	M–Sa

Then hourly following the same pattern until 1930 (M–Sa); then 2200 and 2315 (M–F); and hourly until 2100, then 2230 Su.

DEPART Nottingham Station	ARRIVE St. Pancras Station	NOTES
1428	1613	M–Sa
1528 (1533 Su)	1717 (1731 Su)	Daily
1628	1819	M–Sa
1728 (1732 Su)	1919 (1934 Su)	Daily
1828	2011	M–Sa

Then the same pattern until 1928; then 2102 and 2128; Su 1810, 1840, and 2112.

If your time in Nottingham is limited, no doubt you should first see the historic castle area and return another day to see modern downtown Nottingham. To visit the castle turn right as you exit the rail station onto Carrington Street. Turn left onto Canal Street, and 3 blocks farther along in the same direction, you will come to Castle Road running up the hill to your right. Following it a short distance brings you to England's oldest pub, **Ye Olde Trip to Jerusalem,** where we suggest you rest before continuing up Castle Road to the Nottingham Castle entrance, just off Castle Place. Built in 1189, a portion of the pub was dug into the almost vertical rock formation supporting Nottingham Castle above. Legend has it that Robin Hood scaled this rock in his invasions of Nottingham Castle. The pub's "grub" isn't bad—in fact, it's downright good—so you might want to arrive there about lunchtime. Books about Nottingham and the lore of Robin Hood are on sale in the Ye Olde Trip to Jerusalem pub and in Nottingham Castle (www.triptojerusalem.com).

The train trip from London's St. Pancras Station passes through England's Midlands en route to Nottingham, passing St. Albans, where Britain's first Christian martyr was executed, and Bedford, where John Bunyan wrote *Pilgrim's Progress*. For variety, you might want to return to London via Peterborough, transferring there to a train for King's Cross Station. Consult the train information office in Nottingham's station. It is open Monday–Saturday 0800–1800 and Sunday 1000–1800.

Nottingham's main tourist information center lies astride the city's two huge shopping centers—the **Victoria** and the **Broad Marsh.** Both are somewhat mind-boggling in size, and they are linked by wide pedestrian avenues as well as a bus service (No. 90) running between the two establishments every fifteen minutes throughout the day, except Sunday. The young modern shopper must not miss the **Hockley** area of shops to catch up on the latest craze, and antiques aficionados would enjoy the abundance of shops along **Derby Road.**

A site for crime and punishment fans is *"Condemned!"* at the **Galleries of Justice.** Be prepared as you visit the nineteenth-century Shire Hall to assume the identity of a criminal, experience a public trial, and be taken off to the hangman's gallows (www.galleriesofjustice.org.uk).

Meanwhile, back at the **Old Market Square,** the tourist information center has details of walking tours of Nottingham that take you, among other places, along one of the city's main thoroughfares, **Maid Marian Way.** Also inquire about the **Explorer Pass,** which gives access to five top attractions at a great price.

Day Excursion to

Oxford

Ancient City Campus

Depart from Paddington Station
Distance by train: 63 miles (102 km)
Average train time: 1 hour
Train information and InterCity services: (0845) 748 4950
Tourist information: Oxford Information Centre, 15–16 Broad Street, Oxford OX1 3AS; *Tel:* (0186) 525 2200; *Fax:* (0186) 524 0261
www.visitoxford.org
E-mail: tic@oxford.gov.uk
Hours: Monday–Saturday 0930–1700, Sunday (during summer) and bank holidays 1000–1600
Notes: The Oxford Tourist Information Centre is located behind the bus bays on Gloucester Green, a short walk from the rail station. Just follow the black and gold pedestrian signs via either Hythe Bridge Street or Park End Street.

The first glimpse of Oxford as you approach it by train from London confirms its title, "the city of dreaming spires." Towers, domes, and pinnacles soar on its skyline as an impressive preview of one of the great architectural centers of the world. For here in this small and compact city center are some 900 "listed" buildings, illustrating practically every style of architecture from the eleventh century to the present day.

Oxford is home to the oldest university in Great Britain, with its beginnings in the twelfth century. Apparently there is no single explanation as to exactly how and when the university actually began. One theory claims that it was founded by English students who were expelled from the University of Paris in 1167. Others claim it came about from a gathering of various groups of students from monastic institutions in and around the growing city. From whatever origins, by the end of the twelfth century, Oxford was the established home of the first center of learning in England.

Dating from between the thirteenth and fifteenth centuries, the university became an established national institution and now has a history of 800 years of continuous existence. The student body has doubled in the past thirty years to about 16,000 students, of which the majority are undergraduates. There is no separate campus; most of its buildings lie within the center of the city. The university is a federation of independent colleges. Visitors coming to Oxford during the summer may miss the sight of students passing between classes and student sporting activities, but the buildings alone are worth the trip.

Fewer than half the students come to Oxford University from such exclusive schools as Eton, which was founded by Henry VI in 1440. Students are required to meet their tutor only once or twice a week, either individually or with one other student. This seemingly free and easy system, which builds on individuality and confidence, is the hallmark of an Oxford education. All students live in the college for their first year and one other year before graduation. Students are usually housed in single rooms; the restrictions on coming and going or on having guests are few.

A renaissance of reconstruction and rebuilding in Oxford during the eighteenth century destroyed much of the old street system and the houses inhabited by many religious groups. From this, the city that emerged was more spacious than before. Notwithstanding this urban renewal program, Oxford still has a certain organized clutter about it that becomes readily discernible as you move from the rail station to the city center.

In addition to being a seat of learning, Oxford (unlike Cambridge) has a strong industrial background. It was here that William Morris founded his automobile empire, now Rover Group. The commercial and academic worlds have combined to create other flourishing industries such as publishing, research and development, and tourism. Oxford is also famous as the home of several distinguished hospitals.

Today the use of cars is discouraged in the city center, with visitors making the most instead of Oxford's excellent train services, supplemented by an extremely efficient Park-and-Ride system for motorists. The city leaders also urge everyone to return to the traditional Oxford method of propulsion, the bicycle. By the way, during your visit be on the lookout for bicycles propelled by students pedaling themselves to lectures or laboratories.

London–Oxford–London

Very frequent service is available from London Paddington Station to Oxford, with journeys taking from 44 to 96 minutes. Departure times given here are for trips taking 73 minutes or less.

LONDON PADDINGTON TO OXFORD

M–Sa	Depart Paddington Station at 0548, 0620, 0721, then every 30 minutes until 2320 M–F; Sa until 2150, then 2215.
Su	Depart Paddington Station at 0800, 0842, 0935, 1042 and then hourly until 2247.

OXFORD TO LONDON PADDINGTON

M–Sa	Depart Oxford Station at 1331, 1401, then every 30 minutes until 2131, then 2211, 2234, and 2305.
Su	Depart Oxford Station at 1345, then hourly until 2247.

Guided walking tours leave the information center daily throughout the year at 1100 and 1400. Adult fares range from £6.50 to £11.75; children (age six to sixteen) fares range from £3.75 to £7.50. The two-hour tours take you around the most interesting parts of the city and into those colleges open to the guides on that day.

Those with inquisitive minds may choose the **Inspector Morse Walking Tours** and follow in the footsteps of Oxford's most famous detective. Adults: £8.50; children (age six to sixteen): £5.00. Call in advance for starting times and availability.

From this beginning build your own plan of activities, perhaps to include the Oxford Story Exhibition, punting and cruising on the **Thames** or **Cherwell,** an open bus tour, or a visit to the ancient **Bodleian Library** or one of the university's five excellent museums, all of which are free.

Day Excursion to

Portsmouth

Britain's Naval Port

Depart from Waterloo Station
Distance by train: 74 miles (119 km)
Average train time: 1 hour, 30 minutes
Train information and InterCity services: (0845) 748 4950
Tourist information: Tourist Information Centre, The Hard, Portsmouth PO1 3QJ; *Tel:* (023) 9282 6722; *Fax:* (023) 9282 7519
www.visitportsmouth.co.uk
E-mail: vis@portsmouthcc.gov.uk
Hours: 0930–1715 daily
Notes: Trains call first at the Portsmouth and Southsea Station, so stay aboard to the end of the line. Then, instead of moving straight ahead to the ferry dock, exit the station on the right-hand side of the platform to the main street. The Hard is right next to the Portsmouth Naval Base and the Harbour Rail Station. The Hard Information Centre, from where you will be able to see the gate of the naval base, is to your left. Another center is located next to the Blue Reef Aquarium Portsmouth, Clarence Esplanade, Southsea.

A visit to Portsmouth requires prioritizing. The city abounds in vast quantities of history, architecture, amusements, and literature. Portsmouth has variety, contrasts, and veneration. Ask at the tourist center about the guided walks.

Old Portsmouth is for those who relish fine buildings. Lombard Street is flanked by natural harbors, east and west, and is the home of one of the world's greatest naval bases, **Portsmouth Naval Base.** The resort area, **Southsea,** offers the largest amusement complex on England's south coast plus 4 miles of beaches, promenades, and gardens that boast splendid seventeenth- and eighteenth-century houses, many with distinctive Dutch gables. On adjoining High Street, the primarily eighteenth-century motif gives way to the ultramodern "new" Portsmouth, with its traffic-free shopping precinct, **Cascades,** on Commercial Road.

New public promenades are at the heart of the Portsmouth Harbour **Millennium Project.** A waterbus network connects the sights and attractions in the harbor area, including the City Quay/Portsmouth Harbour Rail Station, Historic Dockyard, Submarine World, Gosport Esplanade, and Priddy's Hard. According to the tourist center, a visit to the **Explosion Museum of Naval Firepower** is "guaranteed to blow your socks off and leave you thinking. . . ." At **Gunwharf Quays,** you can enjoy shopping at more than eighty-five shops, eat and drink at twenty-plus restaurants and bars, or take in a movie.

The literary greats of Portsmouth—Charles Dickens, H. G. Wells, Arthur Conan Doyle, Rudyard Kipling, and Neville Shute, to name a few—have left their mark on the city in birthplaces, residences, and museums. Resting in the world's oldest dry dock in Portsmouth Dockyard is Lord Horatio Nelson's flagship, **HMS *Victory*.** Alongside the ship stands the **Royal Naval Museum** (www.historicdockyard.co.uk) with relics of England's naval hero, ship models, and an outstanding collection of marine paintings. *Hours:* April–October 1000–1800 daily, November–March 1000–1730. For priority, our first selection is HMS *Victory,* described as the proudest sight in Britain, and well it is. Meticulously preserved, it stirs the imagination as you relive the events of the Battle of Trafalgar that "made all England weep."

London–Portsmouth–London

Schedules are for direct trains that operate from and to London Waterloo Station. There are two stations in Portsmouth: the Portsmouth and Southsea Station near the center of the city, and the Portsmouth Harbour Station, which serves the Portsmouth Royal Naval Base (HMS *Victory,* the *Mary Rose,* and the other historic ships) and ferries to the Isle of Wight and is the final destination and origination station.

DEPART Waterloo Station	**ARRIVE** Portsmouth Harbour Station	**NOTES**
0730	0907	M–Sa
0800	0937 (1004 Su)	Daily
0830	1007 (1011 Su)	Daily
0900	1033	M–Sa
0930	1111	Su

M–Sa service continues on the hour and at 30 minutes after the hour until 2230, then 2315.
Su service continues after 0930 every half hour until 2330.

DEPART Portsmouth Harbour Station	**ARRIVE** Waterloo Station	**NOTES**
1445 (1448 Su)	1624 (1644 Su)	Daily
1515	1651	M–Sa
1545	1743	Daily

M–Sa service continues after 1545 at 30-minute intervals until 2045, then 2118 and 2218.
Su service continues after 1532 at 32 and 48 minutes after the hour until 2232.

Some vital statistics in history regarding HMS *Victory* may be beneficial while you are waiting to go aboard. The ship was launched on May 7, 1765. (Lord Nelson was six years old on that date.) It weighs 3,500 tons with an overall length of 226½ feet. *Victory* carried 104 guns and a complement of 850 officers and men. In 1801 the ship was rebuilt extensively and given its current appearance. Re-commissioned in April 1803, *Victory* became Nelson's flagship. On October 21, 1805, the English fleet under Nelson's command vanquished the combined fleets of France and Spain off Cape Trafalgar. Lord Nelson was killed aboard *Victory* in the final moments of what has been called the most decisive battle ever fought at sea.

Portsmouth also features the Victorian ironclad HMS *Warrior 1860*. Launched in 1860, it was the largest, fastest, and best-armored warship of the time. The ship has been restored throughout to its appearance during its first commission of 1861–1864; when you step aboard, you catch a unique glimpse of life as it was experienced on a nineteenth-century British warship. The Royal Naval Museum supports these famous ships with displays that set them in their historic context and continues the story of the British navy into the twentieth century, up to the Falklands Campaign of 1982.

In the resort department, Portsmouth offers the **Pyramids Centre,** a giant leisure attraction built by the sea next to King Henry VIII's **Southsea Castle.** A true tropical paradise, where the temperature never drops below 84°F, the center features four areas of entertainment, ranging from swimming pools, top-name entertainment, and a patio bar to a supervised "Fun Factory" where Mom and Dad can park the kids. Another great place for the family is the **Blue Reef Aquarium,** featuring marine life found along the South Coast. The touch pools provide close-up encounters with many marine marvels.

Close by the Southsea Castle and the Pyramids Centre, Portsmouth's **D-Day Museum** and **Overlord Embroidery** tell the story of that historic event through pictures, plans, and the re-creation of wartime scenes, along with exhibits of various weapons and vehicles. A special audiovisual presentation relates the events leading to the recapture of Normandy. More history unfolds in the castle, where an audiovisual show reconstructs scenes of "Life in the Castle."

Day Excursion to

Ramsgate

Seaside Resort

Depart from Victoria Station

Distance by train: 79 miles (128 km)

Average train time: 1 hour, 50 minutes

Train information and InterCity services: (0845) 748 4950

Tourist information: Margate Information Centre, Droit House, The Pier, Margate, Kent, CT9 1JD; Call Centre for all three information centers: *Tel:* 0184 357 7577; *Fax:* (01843) 585353

www.visitthanet.co.uk

E-mail: visitorinformation@thanet.gov.uk

Hours: All three visitor information centers (Ramsgate, Margate, and Broadstairs) operate on similar schedules: November to March 1000–1700 Tuesday to Saturday; April to October 1000–1700 daily. There are tourist information centers in all three Thanet towns touched by rail service—Margate, Broadstairs, and Ramsgate.

Notes: The Margate Visitor Information Centre is northeast of the railway station near the harbor at 12–13 The Parade; *Fax:* (01843) 230099. The Broadstairs Visitor Information Centre is near the railway station at the foot of the hill at 6B High Street; *Tel:* (01843)

583333; *Fax:* (01843) 868373; www.broadstairs.gov.uk. The Ramsgate Visitor Information Centre is some distance from the railway station in the town center on York Street. Buses from the station will take you near there, or hail a taxi.

Although the sea inlets have almost been drained, Thanet still bears the semblance of an island with clusters of seaside towns—Margate, Broadstairs, and Ramsgate, each with its own unique character. Londoners were attracted to Thanet early in the nineteenth century, and it has been a thriving resort area ever since. The attractive sandy beaches, miles of coastline for swimming under the watchful eyes of fully trained lifeguards, entertainment, and a diverse cultural heritage are among the assets the area has to offer.

Ramsgate has been selected as the primary point for the day excursion, for it is the terminal stop for trains departing London's Victoria Station on the North Kent Line. En route stops at other Thanet towns are made on this rail line at Margate and Broadstairs. It should be noted that it is possible to return to Victoria Station via another rail route from Ramsgate through Ashford, or yet another route calling at Dover and Folkestone. With so many possibilities, you should consult the timetables posted in all three of the Thanet towns for possible variations of your own itinerary. The train schedule shown here gives details for the London Victoria Station–Chatham–Faversham–Margate–Ramsgate rail line only.

This frequent train service departs from the first bay (platforms 1–8) of London's Victoria Station. A word of caution: The first cars (usually four) closest to the ticket barrier will go to Dover. The balance of the cars (usually eight) at the head of the train will terminate in Ramsgate. The train "splits" at Faversham. You will be reminded of this by a train announcement when the train stops briefly in the Bromley South Station after leaving Victoria Station and crossing the Thames. Stay alert and board one of the proper cars.

London–Ramsgate–London

Note: Some trains on this route split at Faversham, part of the train continuing to Ramsgate and other cars going to Dover.

DEPART Victoria Station	ARRIVE Ramsgate Station	NOTES
0722	0929	M–Sa (1)
0752 (0805 Su)	0951 (1000 Su)	Daily
0822	1026	M–Sa (1)
0852 (0905 Su)	1051 (1100 Su)	Daily
0922	1126	M–Sa (1)

(1) M–Sa service continues after 0922 at 22 and 52 minutes after the hour until 1622, with frequent service until 2322. Su service is hourly at 5 minutes after the hour until 2305.

DEPART Ramsgate Station	ARRIVE Victoria Station	NOTES
1604	1807	M–Sa
1634 (1640 Sa)	1837	M–Sa
1704	1907	M–Sa
1734	1929	Su
1804	2007	M–Sa
1904	2107	M–Sa
1924	2137	M–F
2004	2207	M–Sa
2104	2307	M–Sa
2204	0007+1	M–F
2234	0029+1	Su

+1=Arrives next day

Ramsgate, being strong on regency flavor, centers its activities on the **Royal Harbour and Marina.** Annual events include the May Spring Festival, the July Ships Open Days Weekend, August Harbour Heritage Festival, and September Model Ship Rally. The harbor is a source of constant interest, as is the model village at **West Cliff,** a charming miniature of England's Tudor countryside.

Permanently moored on the cliff tops at **Pegwell Bay** in Ramsgate is a Viking ship commemorating the original Viking landing in AD 449. Ramsgate Harbour has seen Wellington's troops embark for the Continent, where they continued on to defeat Napoleon at Waterloo. The harbor also received thousands of battered British troops during the evacuation from Dunkirk in 1940.

Many recall memories of their travels through their senses of sight and sound. In the case of Ramsgate, we recall our visits there by our sense of taste. Most memorable was a dining experience at **Atlantis,** located at 66 Harbour Parade. Walk down to the harbor area—you can't miss it. Seafood is the house specialty. Reservations are recommended; call (01843) 581582.

Margate is the Thanet town that has been conjuring up visions of holidays for years. Its biggest drawing card is the area's beaches. The municipality of Margate owns 9 miles of seafront with sandy beaches and promenades running practically its full distance. The atmosphere of the area differs somewhat from that of England's south coast in that it is more sedate in mood and tempo. Perhaps the presence of the North Sea is one of the contributing factors.

When you arrive at Margate Station, the first sight to greet you is the golden sand of the beach. The **promenade** paralleling the beach is a length of souvenir shops, restaurants, confectioneries, and amusement halls. Beyond lies Margate's main shopping center, where courteous Kentish clerks are most eager to assist you in your shopping. Extending from the promenade, Margate's **Old Town** of narrow streets and houses clusters around the town's harbor.

Broadstairs, known as "Kent's Best-Kept Secret," has a Victorian atmosphere about it and became a fashionable watering hole during the regency of King George IV. Victorians, one of the most eminent being Charles Dickens, favored holidays in

Broadstairs. A leaflet from the information center will permit you to follow in his footsteps and see many interesting points within the town. Every June townspeople remember Dickens by appearing in costume while attending a series of plays, readings, parades, and parties set against the backdrop of Victorian Broadstairs.

Day Excursion to

St. Albans

From Romans to Roses

Depart from St. Pancras International
Distance by train: 20 miles (32 km)
Average train time: 25 minutes
Train information and InterCity services: (0845) 748 4950
Tourist information: St. Albans Tourist Information Centre, Town Hall, The Market Place, St. Albans, Hertfordshire AL3 5DJ; *Tel:* (0172) 786 4511; *Fax:* (0172) 786 3533
www.stalbans.gov.uk/tourism
E-mail: tic@stalbans.gov.uk
Hours: Monday–Friday 1000–1630 and Saturday 1000–1700
Notes: Arriving in St. Albans, leave the train station and walk uphill toward the city center on Victoria Street. The uphill walk takes about fifteen minutes. At the junction of St. Peter and Chequer Streets, the tourist information center can be seen opposite, in the Town Hall. The alternative is city bus transportation, which departs from a bus shelter in the station area. The bus stop for returning to the station is at the top of Victoria Street.

St. Albans takes its name from Britain's first Christian martyr, a Romano-British citizen who was beheaded for his faith on a hilltop outside Verulamium, one of the most important towns at that time in the western Roman Empire. A magnificent fifteenth-century Norman cathedral now stands on the hilltop, and Verulamium has become a parkland on the western side of the city.

St. Albans has much to offer its visitors. Tucked away in various corners of the city are old coach inns, many with a fascinating history. **The White Hart Inn,** built in the fifteenth century, was restored in 1930. The **Fleur-de-Lys Inn** on French Row was erected between 1420 and 1440 on the site where King John of France was held prisoner after the Battle of Poitiers. Another inn, the **Fighting Cocks,** claims to be the oldest licensed house in England, deriving its name from the cockfights that were held there for many years. All three of these ancient "watering holes" are open to the public during licensed hours. St. Albans has always had an open mind concerning alcoholic beverages; Elizabeth I granted the city permission to issue wine licenses in 1560.

French Row in St. Albans, a narrow street of medieval appearance, is fronted by a clock tower built between 1402 and 1411 from the flint and rubble of Verulamium. Its original curfew bell was cast in 1335. Across from the bell tower stands the **Wax House Gate,** where candles and tapers were made and sold to pilgrims visiting the shrine of St. Albans. The path through the gate is still the shortest route for pedestrians en route to the cathedral, proving that the ancients had a sharp eye for customer traffic flow. **St. Albans Cathedral** contains traces of an eighth-century Saxon church and has one of the largest Gothic naves in Europe. The tower was built largely of stone from Verulamium. Visit www.stalbanscathedral.org.uk.

Many of the points of interest in St. Albans must be reached on foot. The information center has a pamphlet describing a walking tour, **St. Albans's Town Trail,** which includes the cathedral and the abbey. The tour (2½ miles) may prove a bit too ambitious for the less-experienced, less-conditioned walker, but paths lead past one or more of the previously described inns, where a libation will probably instill a desire to press on—or stay at the inn until closing. Check your rail schedules if doing so, or book a room at one of the old coach inns.

Helpful publications to take on the trails are *A Historical Map of St. Albans and Mini Guide.* The center has them available for a small fee. The information center is close to the marketplace. Markets are held in St. Albans every Wednesday and Saturday. If you are in town on these days, be sure to "go to market" and enjoy watching the locals barter back and forth with the vendors. Everything from apples to zinnias, including the weather and current prices, will become subjects of discussion.

The Roman city of **Verulamium** is engrossing. You can spend an entire day at the site visiting its 200-acre grounds, which include a temple, forum, museum, hypocaust, and theater. The museum houses an impressive collection of Roman antiquities. From the center of St. Albans, you can reach Verulamium in about twenty minutes on foot, or you can opt for a local bus. The tourist information office will give you the directions.

At the **Verulamium Museum,** artifacts taken from the ruins are displayed in an environment of natural surroundings. The small items from the houses and shops range from iron hinges, latches, and locks to personal ornaments worn by the inhabitants. A full range of pottery and glassware, for both table and kitchen use, is on exhibit.

Exploratory excavations of the site have taken place from time to time, but experts estimate that only one-third of the area within the Roman town walls has been uncovered. Modern techniques such as aerial photography continue to reveal additional features.

The gardens of the Royal National Rose Society are in St. Albans. The society made its first award for a new rose in 1883 and subsequently established its own trial grounds, where you can see the future "greats" of the rose world. New varieties from all over the world are sent to St. Albans to undergo a comprehensive three-year assessment. The twelve acres of gardens are newly redesigned and reopened to the public in June 2007. They are a spectacle for the casual visitor and a total fascination to rose enthusiasts. Call 0845 833 4344 for details. www.rnrs.org.

The range of history in St. Albans extends from AD 43, with the first evidences of the Roman enclosure at Verulamium, to the moment you arrive to enjoy the vitality of this timeless city. To step over St. Albans's threshold is to step into a land of enchantment and history.

London–St. Albans–London

This is a very heavily traveled route, often crammed with commuters. Typically, on M–F there are three or four or more trains each hour in either direction. The best advice is that you make your way to the appropriate station, where you can be assured you won't have to wait more than 15 minutes for a train.

Note: The Thameslink platforms at St. Pancras International are located underneath the main station; follow the signs for Platforms A and B. Saturday and Sunday service typically leaves from Main Level platforms 1–4, with service 3–4 times per hour on Saturday, and twice per hour on Sunday.

DEPART King's Cross Thameslink	**ARRIVE** St. Albans Station	**NOTES**
0734	0754	M–F
0752	0804	M–F
0816	0836	M–F
0848	0910	M–F
0904	0925	M–F
1018	1040	M–F
1034	1055	M–F

Pattern continues with frequent service throughout the day.

DEPART St. Albans Station	**ARRIVE** King's Cross Thameslink	**NOTES**
1502	1524	M–F
1518	1540	M–F
1532	1554	M–F
1548	1610	M–F
1602	1624	M–F
1618	1640	M–F
1632	1654	M–F
1648	1710	M–F

Pattern continues with frequent service throughout the day.

Day Excursion to

Salisbury

Magna Carta Archive

Depart from Waterloo Station
Distance by train: 84 miles (135 km)
Average train time: 1 hour, 25 minutes
Train information and InterCity services: (0845) 748 4950
Tourist information: Salisbury Tourist Information Centre, Fish Row, Salisbury, Wiltshire SP1 1EJ; *Tel:* (01722) 334956; *Fax:* (01722) 422059
www.visitsalisbury.com
E-mail: visitorinfo@wiltshire.gov.uk
Hours: Monday–Saturday 0930–1730 (1000 on Wednesday). The center operates a booking service for local accommodations as well as the popular Book-a-Bed-Ahead program.
Notes: Salisbury's Tourist Information Centre is situated at the rear of the Town Guildhall where Market Square meets Fish Row. Proceed on foot down Fisherton Street, which you will find to your far left as you exit the station. After crossing the River Avon, the street will narrow and change names several times until it becomes Fish Row. The tourist information center at the rail station (platform 4) is open Easter–September, Monday–Saturday 0930–1630.

Salisbury holds the distinction of being one of the few English cities not originally founded by the Romans. The old town, Old Sarum, had been in existence since the Iron Age. The Romans fortified it, and the Saxons later developed it into an industrial town. All went well in Old Sarum until arguments between the occupants of the church and the castle caused a new church to be built in the valley below the original town site. This new location proved to be more popular than the old. Consequently, although known as Salisbury, the town's official name is New Sarum.

The center of Salisbury has traditionally been divided into two distinct areas: the cathedral and the marketplace. This tradition still exists, and the gates leading to the cathedral and the buildings in the "close" surrounding it are locked every night. Beautiful houses of medieval and Georgian architecture overlook the green.

The **marketplace** has a history all its own. In the original charter of 1227, the town was authorized to hold a Tuesday market. This got out of hand and grew into almost a daily market until protests from nearby towns resulted in a reduction of market days in Salisbury to Tuesday and Saturday only. Today Salisbury maintains those traditional market days.

Salisbury boasts a number of historic inns that have given rest and refreshment to travelers down through the centuries. The fireplaces in the **King's Arms Inn** have the same stone as that used in the construction of the cathedral. The **Haunch**

London–Salisbury–London

DEPART Waterloo Station	ARRIVE Salisbury Station	NOTES
0710	0839	M–Sa
0820	0943	M–Sa
0915	1045	Su
0920	1042	M–Sa
1015	1145	Su
1020	1142	M–Sa
1120	1242	M–Sa

Then every hour until 2220 M–Sa. Every hour until 2215 Su.

DEPART Salisbury Station	ARRIVE Waterloo Station	NOTES
1421	1549	M–Sa
1521 (1527 Su)	1649 (1659 Su)	Daily
1621 (1627 Su)	1744 (1759 Su)	Daily
1721 (1729 Su)	1845 (1859 Su)	Daily
1826 (1821 Sa)	1949 (1959 Su)	Daily
1926	2100	Daily
2026	2204	Daily
2126	2257	Daily
2226	0033+1	Daily

+1=Arrives next day

of Venison, an old English chophouse, was built about 1320. The **Red Lion Hotel,** dating from the same era, was the starting point for the Salisbury Flying Machine, the nightly horse-drawn coach to London.

In Salisbury you will find many impressive examples of architectural styles, ranging from the town's thirteenth-century cathedral to a modern pedestrian shopping district known as the Old George Mall. The most unexpected structure is the foyer of the movie theater on New Canal Street. Once the banqueting hall of the merchant John Halle, four-time mayor of Salisbury, it is now a splendid example of fifteenth-century black-and-white timbering.

From April through September you may join a daily guided **walking tour of Salisbury** at 1100 and 1800 (none at 1800 on Sunday) from in front of the information center on Fish Row. The tour lasts approximately one and a half hours. On Friday night the 1800 walking tour becomes a special ghost walk at 2000.

The cathedral has a unity of design that no doubt is attributable to the fact that, unlike most other cathedrals, which took centuries to complete, the **Salisbury Cathedral** was constructed in only thirty-eight years. In other words, it wasn't affected by several different periods of architecture. Foundation stones were laid in 1220, during the heyday of Gothic design. One of its greatest treasures is its ancient clock mechanism, which originally stood in a detached belfry and dates from 1386 as one of the oldest pieces of operating machinery in the world.

The cathedral contains a library founded at Old Sarum in 1078; seventy of the books installed in the library at that time are still there. The great treasure of the cathedral, housed in **Chapter House,** is the ***Magna Carta,*** written at Runnymede on June 15, 1215. Brought to Salisbury by William, Earl of Salisbury, he placed it in the cathedral for safekeeping, and there it remained until World War II.

Among its many historical achievements, Salisbury made its mark in the annals of medical care. Of the four hospitals currently in or near the city, the **Trinity Hospital,** on Trinity Street, has an interesting story concerning its founding in 1379 by Agnes Bottenham. Chronicles relate that Ms. Agnes ran a "house of ill repute" on the site, and when it prospered, she built a hospital and almshouse there as an act of penitence.

Visitors interested in seeing **Old Sarum,** 1½ miles north of the new town, can do so by city bus or taxi. Excavations and reconstruction have been under way for some time. Oddly enough, even after the old city was abandoned, two representatives of Parliament continued to be sent, despite the fact that the city had no inhabitants—a case of representation without taxation.

Day Excursion to

Sheffield

Trademark of Quality

Depart from St. Pancras Station

Distance by train: 165 miles (265 km)

Average train time: 2 hours, 20 minutes

Train information and InterCity services: (0845) 748 4950

Tourist information: Sheffield Tourist Information Centre, 1 Tudor Square, Sheffield, South Yorkshire S1 2LA; *Tel:* (0114) 221 1900; *Fax:* (0114) 201 1020

www.yorkshiresouth.com

E-mail: visitor@yorkshiresouth.com

Hours: Monday–Friday 1000–1700, Saturday 1000–1600

Notes: The Tourist Information Centre is about a ten-minute walk from the rail station. Cross the road by the traffic light–controlled pedestrian crossing. Pass to the left of the Sheffield Hallam University Nelson Mandela Building, and walk straight up steep Howard Street, passing the university's main entrance on your right. Cross the road straight ahead; at the other side turn right, then go up the slope on your left, on to Surrey Street. Walk past the city library and Graves Art Gallery on your right until you come to Tudor Square and the Crucible and Lyceum Theatres. Turn right on Norfolk Street, and the information center is on the corner of Norfolk Row and Norfolk Street. Taxi service is also available from the rail station.

Sheffield, England's fourth-largest city, is world famous for steelmaking, toolmaking, engineering, and cutlery. Surviving records show that cutlery was being made in

Sheffield in 1297, and Chaucer referred to a Sheffield thwitel (knife) in his Canterbury Tales. By the late nineteenth century, the area was regarded as the steel capital of the world, and in 1913 Harry Brearley made one of the great discoveries of our century, stainless steel, at Sheffield's Firth Brown Laboratories.

Forget images of smoke-belching chimneys. Present-day Sheffield is still England's greenest city. Built on seven hills and five river valleys (fast-flowing streams drove the waterwheels that powered the cutlery industry before the steam age), Sheffield has more than fifty parks and green spaces—and four trees to every person! Surrounded by open countryside, more than a third of the city lies within the beautiful Peak National Park.

The unique Heart of the City development has provided Sheffield with three new public squares and the **Millennium Galleries,** which house national exhibitions from the Victoria and Albert Museum in London, Sheffield's impressive metalware gallery, and the Ruskin Collection of the Guild of Saint George, left to the city by Victorian sage, artist, and critic John Ruskin; www.sheffieldgalleries.org.uk. The **Winter Garden** along with the Millennium Galleries form the "Heart of the City" project, which includes offices, shops, cafes, and pubs.

Sheffield has won a reputation for sporting excellence and in 1995 was the first city to be awarded the official title "National City of Sport." The country's top teams in ice hockey (Sheffield Steelers) and basketball (Sheffield Sharks) are based here, as is the national diving squad. The city has hosted more than 200 national and international sports events over the past several years.

With the **Peak National Park** nearby, outdoor sports are particularly popular. A completely unexpected attraction, set in the heart of the city, is Europe's largest artificial ski slope complex, **Sheffield Ski Village.** Just bring your gloves; you can rent everything else.

Two traditional museums, commemorating Sheffield's industrial heritage, are **Kelham Island** and **Abbeydale Industrial Hamlet.** At the former, the largest working steam engine in Europe can be seen in action. The latter museum displays scythe-producing, water-driven machinery, some of which dates from the seventeenth century. The **City Museum,** Weston Park, has excellent collections of Sheffield cutlery and Sheffield plates. Cutler's Hall, on Church Street, is the headquarters of the Cutler's Company, which was formed in 1642. The current **Cutler's Hall** dates from 1832 and houses the company's silver and cutlery collections, which can be viewed by appointment only (inquire at the Tourist Information Centre).

A heritage site is **Victoria Quays,** Sheffield's canal basin. The canal was built to ship in iron ore from Sweden and ship out steel products to England's east coast ports; now Victoria Quays is a waterside oasis in the heart of the city center, with its beautiful warehouse buildings, a cobbled waterfront, and the Waterways Cafe.

Another historic building in the city center is the **Lyceum** in Tudor Square, a magnificently restored Victorian theater that together with the modern **Crucible Theatre** forms the country's largest theatrical complex outside London.

A fifteen-minute journey from the city center on the Supertram, Britain's largest and most advanced urban light-rail transport system, will take you to one of Britain's most successful shopping malls, **Meadowhall,** with 270 shops, a food court, and cinemas.

The Tourist Information Centre offers an excellent city map. The center also offers accommodation information and advance booking services. Helpful brochures, including the ***Sheffield Mini Guide, Sheffield Visitor Guide,*** and a number of other visitor publications, are available at no cost. With one of the largest student populations in the country (more than 40,000), Sheffield has a wide variety of nightlife choices for fun-loving tourists.

Shops highlighting the local steel-crafting trade include Osbournes Silversmiths Ltd., Rivelin Cutlery Works, United Cutlers of Sheffield, George Butler Ltd., Hiram Wild Factory Shops, Mortons of Sheffield, and Don Alexander. The Tourist Information Centre can supply addresses and hours.

London–Sheffield–London

DEPART St. Pancras Station	ARRIVE Sheffield Station	NOTES
0637	0904 (0907 Sa)	M–Sa
0755	1000	M–Sa
0855	1102	M–Sa
0930	1240	Su
0955	1204	M–Sa
1030	1328	Su
1055	1304	Daily
1130	1444	Su
1155	1400	Daily

Hourly departures, at 55 minutes past the hour until 2055, then 2255 M–Sa; continue Su hourly departures half past the hour until 2130.

DEPART St. Pancras Station	ARRIVE Sheffield Station	NOTES
1427	1634	M–Sa
1527	1734 (1804 Su)	Daily
1627 (1629 Su)	1839 (1904 Su)	Daily
1727	1934	M–Sa
1729	2004	Su
1827	2034	M–Sa
1832	2127	Su
1927	2137	M–Sa
1931	2227	Su
2024	2315	Su
2039	2306	M–F

Day Excursion to

Southampton

An Imposing Heritage

Depart from Waterloo Station

Distance by train: 79 miles (127 km)

Average train time: 1 hour, 10 minutes

Train information and InterCity services: (0845) 748 4950

Tourist information: Southampton Tourist Information Centre, 9 Civic Centre Road, Southampton SO14 7FJ; *Tel:* (023) 8083 3333; *Fax:* (023) 8083 3381

www.visit-southampton.co.uk

E-mail: tourist.information@southampton.gov.uk

Hours: Monday–Saturday 0930–1700, Sunday 1000–1530

Notes: From the railway station, you can board any "City Centre"–bound bus and ask the driver to "deposit" you at the Civic Centre, next to which you will find the Tourist Information Centre. There is a map outside the Southampton railway station showing the route to the center. It's about a fifteen-minute walk.

In the minds of many, Southampton conjures visions of the great transatlantic ocean liners, for it is Britain's prime ocean-passenger port and home of many of the world's greatest passenger ships, including Britain's flagship, the ***Queen Elizabeth II (QE2).*** Many visitors, however, know little about Southampton's span of centuries, which has given it a rich heritage of England and of Europe. Southampton's museums, classic old-town area, and beautifully preserved medieval town walls help reveal this rich and interesting history.

Southampton is best seen on foot, with the assistance of a bus now and then. Pick up the free ***Southampton's Visitors Guide*** at Southampton Tourist Information Centre—it contains suggestions for sightseeing. Visitors from the United States will take special interest in the sailing of the *Mayflower* from Southampton in 1620. Persons proving descent from the original ***Mayflower*** passengers can have their names entered on the memorial. The center also can make hotel and bed-and-breakfast reservations in Southampton and its surroundings.

As mentioned in the official handbook, there are many places of interest within easy walking distance of the information center. A visit to them will gradually unfold a picture of Southampton's past. To catch Southampton's seagoing flavor, a visit to the Ocean Village or the Town Quay Marina would be in order.

Similar to the harbor renovation of Baltimore, Maryland, Southampton's **Ocean Village** has transformed some of its old docks into a cosmopolitan playground with a bevy of specialty shops, eateries, and attractions overlooking a yacht basin. Quayside at Southampton's port, you stand in history. Four hundred years before the Pilgrim fathers departed on their journey to the New World, Richard the Lion-Hearted embarked on the Third Crusade. The **Town Quay Marina** plays host to the cream of the yacht-racing world. Both areas are close to the terminal used by the QE2. Check with the information center concerning walking directions and the possibility of the QE2 being in the harbor.

Next in line is the **Tudor House Museum,** where the costumes, paintings, and furniture of centuries past are displayed against the oak beams and stone carvings of Tudor House itself. One of the few surviving examples in Southampton of a large town house from the early Tudor period, it contains a banquet hall and is surrounded by an authentic Elizabethan herb garden. Don't miss the tunnel entrance to the remains of a twelfth-century merchant's home. The kids will love it.

Next on the agenda is the **Southampton Maritime Museum,** also known as the Wool House. Once a medieval warehouse, it is now a showplace for the city's involvement with the sea. Since early times, Southampton has been an important port of call. Docks were piled high with luxuries from the Mediterranean and the East, brought there by Genoan and Venetian fleets.

With all of the rekindled global interest in the sinking of the *Titanic* on her maiden voyage, one cannot miss visiting the **"Story of the White Star Line" Exhibition.** The *Titanic*'s story is told through the voices of some of the actual survivors and the people of Southampton whose lives were affected by the tragedy. A free ***Titanic Trail*** brochure is available in the visitor center of the museum, which illustrates the various monuments and memorials dedicated to the victims of the tragedy. The walking tour begins at the Docks, the departure point of the *Titanic,* April 10, 1912.

Southampton is the place to shop in south England, with a wide choice of shopping areas and stores catering to all tastes. **West Quay** is the region's premier shopping destination, with a delightful combination of fashion and lifestyle retailers and a wide variety of restaurants and coffee shops. The Marlands Shopping Centre has an exciting mix of stores, and the Bargate Centre is an ideal shopping and leisure experience for the younger set.

Also in Southampton's repertoire is the **Hall of Aviation** on Albert Road. The museum is a memorial to R. J. Mitchell, Southampton's famous aircraft designer of the Spitfire, the fighter that valiantly defended the country during the Battle of Britain. The exhibits include a Spitfire Mark 24, possibly one of the last of 24,500 Spitfires produced by the Supermarine Aircraft Company in nearby Woolston, a quarter mile from the museum. The museum's collection also includes a Sandringham Flying Boat as well as hundreds of photographs, plans, and models connected with R. J. Mitchell and the Supermarine factory. Visit www.spitfireonline.co.uk.

The route between the museums, by the way, is dotted with historic buildings, such as the **Duke of Wellington Pub** and the **Red Lion Pub.** Pausing for a pint may provide a pleasant period for pondering Southampton's past and present.

Free guided walks through medieval Southampton depart from the Bargate at varying times throughout the year. Ask for complete details at the Tourist Information Centre.

London–Southampton–London

DEPART Waterloo Station	ARRIVE Southampton Station	NOTES
0735	0858	M–Sa
0754	0934	Su
0805	0922	M–Sa
0835	0949 (1002 Su)	Daily
0905	1022	M–Sa
0935	1049 (1102 Su)	Daily

M–Sa service continues at 5 and 35 minutes past the hour until 2305. Su service continues at 35 and 54 minutes past the hour until 2154, then 2254.

DEPART Southampton Station	ARRIVE Waterloo Station	NOTES
1400	1520	M–Sa
1430	1549	M–Sa
1455	1637	Su
1500	1620	M–Sa
1525	1649	Su
1530	1649	M–Sa

M–Sa service continues on the hour and 30 minutes past the hour until 2300. Su service continue at 25 and 55 minutes past the hour until 2055, then 2155 and 2255.

Day Excursion to

Stonehenge

Mysterious Pagan Shrine

Depart from Waterloo Station

Distance by train: 84 miles (135 km)

Average train time: 1 hour, 45 minutes

Train information and InterCity services: (0845) 748 4950

Tourist information: Stonehenge, English Heritage, First Floor Abbey Buildings, Abbey Square, Amesbury, Wiltshire SP4 7ES; *Tel:* 0870 333 1181; *Fax:* 0179 341 4926; *Information Line:* (01980) 624715

www.english-heritage.org.uk

Hours: Stonehenge is open daily April–May 31 0930–1800, June 1–August 31 0900–1900, September 1–October 15 0930–1800, October 16–March 31 0930–1600. Closed December 24–26 and January 1.

Notes: There are several ways to get to Stonehenge from the Salisbury railway station (see pages 140–141). A gift shop, refreshments, and public toilets are available at the site, and all facilities provide access for the disabled.

The poet Sir John Squire wrote about Stonehenge: "Observatory, altar, temple, tomb, erected none knows when by none knows whom, to serve strange gods or watch familiar stars . . ." Stonehenge is unmatched—truly one of the wonders of the world and one of twenty-one finalists for the "New 7 Wonders of the World." There are many opinions regarding the use and purpose of the monument. Whatever the reason for its existence, however, Stonehenge remains an awe-inspiring reminder of the past.

The landscape for a few miles around the Stonehenge monument reportedly contains more prehistoric remains than any other area of the same size in Britain. There are earthworks, burial sites, erected stones, and hill carvings. Because they belong to the prehistoric period, long before any written records were made, there are many questions about them that we shall never be able to answer. Through technology, we have been able to tell how they were made and, in some cases, *when* and by *whom.* The unanswered question is *"Why?"*

Stonehenge sits on the Salisbury plain, an almost treeless, windswept plateau. With its origins dating from about 2950 to 1600 BC, Stonehenge comprises a circular group of stones roughly 110 feet in diameter that stand in an area surrounded by a low earthen rampart and ditch approximately 330 feet in diameter. The largest stones, some weighing as much as 50 tons, were brought to the site from quarries some 20 miles distant. The stones are placed in such a manner as to reflect the position of the sun on the four main dates of the seasons, the solstices and equinoxes, possibly as an agricultural almanac or for spiritual purposes.

The monument stands on approximately 300 feet of solid chalk. Unfortunately, Stonehenge has been robbed constantly of its stone throughout the centuries. In Victorian times it was common practice for visitors to bring hammers and chisels to carve their names and other graffiti and to chip off souvenir sections of the temple stones.

Diodorus Siculus, historian to Julius Caesar, described Stonehenge as a temple to the sun god Apollo. Modern Britons have marked the area with small clumps of trees to commemorate the Battle of Trafalgar in 1805.

If time is of the essence to get to Stonehenge, a taxi can get you there in about twenty minutes. Buses, operated by Wilts & Dorset, depart from the station for Stonehenge via Salisbury and Amesbury daily, Sunday and public holidays included, *Tel:* (01980) 624715. The adult round-trip fare is £5.70; admission to the Stonehenge site is £7.50. The Wilts & Dorset bus schedule is arranged so as to connect with all express trains to and from the Waterloo Station in London. If you plan to linger at the site, this will provide you with ample time to do so.

London–Stonehenge

No train service to Stonehenge; take a bus from Salisbury. Consult the London–Salisbury timetables for train service to Salisbury.

In conjunction with Wilts & Dorset, The Stonehenge Tour Company offers a tour of Stonehenge departing from Salisbury train station for an adult fare of £14.50 which includes admission to the Stonehenge site (senior citizens and students, £13.50; children younger than age twelve, £5.00). Visit www.thestonehengetour.info for more information; fares include entrance to Stonehenge, and you are accompanied by a guide throughout the tour. Tour time is just under two hours. For complete details and bus schedules, we suggest calling ahead to the Wilts & Dorset travel office in Salisbury, (01722) 336855.

Two tour companies, AS Tours and Days Out Tours, also offer excellent one-day tours from the rail station to Stonehenge. Check with the tourist information center for details.

Time permitting, upon arriving back in Salisbury, you may want to explore the city before boarding your London-bound train. If so, stay aboard the bus returning from Stonehenge until it arrives at the Salisbury bus terminal approximately five minutes after its arrival at the rail station. See the day excursion to Salisbury for ideas and sites.

Do use one of the special excursion buses. If you use the regular public bus system between Salisbury and Amesbury, you will have to walk or take a taxi for the 2 miles between Amesbury and the Stonehenge site.

A sad note: Because of damage to the monument, visitors are not permitted to enter the actual stone circle, but can view it only from a distance. Visitors are required to remain behind a fence built around the Stonehenge temple to protect it. "TIME," as the announcement observes, "IS TAKING ITS TOLL."

Day Excursion to

Stratford-upon-Avon

Shakespeare Country

Depart from Marylebone Station

Distance by train: 121 miles (195 km)

Average train time: 2 hours, 12 minutes

Train information and InterCity services: (0845) 748 4950 or (0121) 643 2711

Tourist information: Stratford-upon-Avon Centre, 62 Henley Street, Stratford-upon-Avon, Warwickshire CV37 6PT; *Tel:* 1789 264 293; *Fax:* (01789) 295262

www.stratford-upon-avon.co.uk or **www.shakespeare-country.co.uk**

E-mail: tic@discover-stratford.com

Hours: March–October 1000–1700 daily, November–February 1000–1600 daily

Notes: The tourist center is a short walk from the station. Turn left out of the station onto Alcester Street, and follow it until Meer Street goes off to your left. Follow Meer Street to Henley Street, and turn right onto Henley Street.

William Shakespeare, the English poet and playwright recognized universally as the greatest of all dramatists, was born in Stratford-upon-Avon in 1564. His mother was the daughter of a local farmer; his father was a glove maker and a wool merchant who entered politics to become mayor of Stratford. Although Shakespeare lived throughout his professional career in London, he kept his home ties with Stratford. In 1597 he purchased New Place, one of Stratford's largest houses. He died there in 1616 and was buried in Stratford's parish church.

Rail travelers can go from London's Marylebone Station to Stratford-upon-Avon via Chiltern Railways trains. Trains depart from Marylebone at regular intervals throughout the day, Monday through Friday. There is direct return service from Stratford-upon-Avon to London, including a late train especially for theatergoers. For more detailed information on rail services, call (0845) 600 5165, or visit the Web site at www.chilternrailways.co.uk. Saturday and Sunday departures on this route are limited. Local train services also are available to Leamington Spa and Warwick from London's Marylebone Station, with connecting services to Stratford; call (01788) 560116 or (0121) 643 2711.

When visiting Shakespeare Country from London, you can take advantage of the one- or three-day Shakespeare Country Explorer tickets. They provide for travel to Stratford-upon-Avon, Leamington Spa, Warwick, and Warwick Parkway from London Marylebone Station, plus unlimited train travel between these stations and others within the Stratford-upon-Avon zone. One-day fare: £30.00 adults, £22.00 seniors, and £15.00 children. Four-day fare: £45.00 adults, £33.00 seniors, and £22.50 children.

Advance booking is not necessary. Simply purchase your ticket on departure from London Marylebone. If you do wish to purchase in advance, call 0845 600 5165.

London–Stratford-upon-Avon–London

Schedules shown are for direct trains from and to London Marylebone Station. Other service is possible from Paddington Station by changing trains in Leamington Spa.

DEPART Marylebone	ARRIVE Stratford-upon-Avon
0715	0940
0924	1133
1024	1232
1254	1509
1520	1731

DEPART Stratford-upon-Avon	ARRIVE Marylebone
1436	1656
1740	1928
1948	2223

Daily service.

Our advice is to take a guided tour of Stratford-upon-Avon. The popular **Stratford and Shakespeare Story Tour** is operated by City Sightseeing Tours. The open-top bus tours stop at each of the Shakespearean properties: the newly refurbished **Shakespeare's Birthplace** on Henley Street; **Anne Hathaway's Cottage; Mary Arden's House,** where Shakespeare's mother grew up; **New Place/Nash's House,** in which Shakespeare spent his retirement years before his death in 1616; and **Hall's Croft,** home of Shakespeare's daughter, Susanna. Visitors may get on and off the bus as frequently as they wish since the ticket is valid all day.

From May to September tours depart every twenty minutes; March to mid-May and October to November, every half hour; December and January, every hour. You can join the tours at any of the Shakespearean properties, as well as outside the tourist center at Bridgefoot, Evesham Place, or on Windsor or Meer Streets. City Sightseeing Bus Tour tickets are £11.00 adults, £6.00 children, £28.00 family, and £9.00 senior citizens and students.

Other tour highlights include the **Royal Shakespeare Theatre** and the **Swan** and **Other Place Theatres;** the **Holy Trinity Church,** where Shakespeare is buried and protected by a purportedly cursed tombstone; the **Old Fifteenth-Century Grammar School,** which he attended; and **Harvard House,** home of Katherine Rogers, whose son founded the library in the United States that became Harvard University.

A visit to see a performance by the Royal Shakespeare Company at one of its three theaters in Stratford is a must. Reserve theater seats as far in advance as possible. Telephone 0844 800 1110 for twenty-four-hour information on program and seat availability. To book seats telephone the theater box office: (0844) 800 1110. Advance tickets may also be purchased in the United States through Global Tickets in New York at (800) 223-6108. For backstage tours telephone 0844 800 1110. The theater has several restaurant/bar facilities. Telephone 0844 800 1110 for more information and reservations for special restaurant/theater packages. Also visit www.rsc.org.uk.

The **Box Tree,** a luxuriously appointed restaurant overlooking the Avon River, serves classic cuisine (closed on Sunday). The **River Terrace** is a modern restaurant/coffee shop/wine bar serving light international dishes. You can even "Pick-up-a-Picnic" here by placing your order with the cashier two hours in advance.

Day Excursion to

Windsor

The Royal Castle

Depart from Waterloo Station

Distance by train: 25 miles (41 km)

Average train time: 50 minutes

Train information and InterCity services: (0845) 748 4950

Tourist information: Royal Windsor Information Centre, 24 High Street, Windsor SL4 1LH; *Tel:* (01753) 743 900; *Fax:* (01753) 743 929; **Accommodations:** (01753) 743 907

www.windsor.gov.uk

E-mail: windsor.tic@rbwm.gov.uk

Hours: May–August: Monday–Friday 0930–1730, Saturday 0930–1700, Sunday 1000–1600; September–April: Monday–Saturday 1000–1700, Sunday 1000–1600

Notes: The traditional "i" will lead the way to the tourist information center from either arrival point, Windsor Riverside Station or Windsor Central Station. The grounds of Windsor Castle are immediately across the street from the information center.

You have a choice of two rail routes from London to Windsor. For the schedule here we have selected the route from Waterloo Station in London to Windsor Riverside Station. This line does not require changing trains en route. The alternate route, which departs Paddington Station in London, requires a change at Slough to a shuttle train before arriving at Windsor Central Station. If you take the Paddington–Slough route, the shuttle train arrives and departs in Slough from track 1. Either route gives you a magnificent view approaching Windsor Castle. On either train sit on the left-hand side (outbound) to take full advantage of the scenery. Be sure to purchase an illustrated guidebook on Windsor Castle—it will become a fond reminder of your visit.

Historic **Windsor Castle** is the official home of English royalty, and it is the largest inhabited castle in the world. *Tel:* (0207) 776 7304; *Fax:* (0207) 930 9625; www.royalcollection.org.uk; *E-mail:* windsorcastle@royalcollection.org.uk. William the Conqueror built the first structure on this site, a wooden fort that doubled as a royal hunting lodge. Other English kings added to the castle during their reigns, but despite the multiplicity of royalty and architects, the castle has managed to retain a unity of style all its own.

Queen Elizabeth II uses the castle far more than any of her predecessors, usually on weekends. When she is in residence, her Royal Standard will be flying atop the Round Tower's flagpole. Chances of seeing Her Majesty, should she be in residence, are very slim, since she has her own private rooms. Nevertheless, during that time you may find Prince Philip watching his son Charles, the Prince of Wales, and his polo team bashing about in **Windsor Great Park.**

The £50 million restoration effort after the devastating fire in the castle on November 20, 1992, was completed in 1998. Refurbishment of the Queen's Private

Chapel, St. George's Hall, and the State Dining Room were painstakingly replicated and updated.

While in **St. George's Chapel,** dedicated to Britain's highest order of chivalry, the Most Noble Order of the Garter, ask the guards about the knights' shields. Some of the shields are totally covered up and the reason is . . . well, you'll find out. Perhaps they had forgotten their royal oath! The chapel is home of the ***King's Champion,*** a full-armored statue commemorating the throwing down of the gauntlet in defense of the sovereign. Directly to the right of the *King's Champion* begins the wood paneling engraved with the names of the original members of the Order. The next three walls contain a chronological listing of all those who have been knighted—including the women who have been added in recent decades.

Rare state occasions such as the Investiture of the Garter, when the queen proceeds down the walks of Windsor Castle accompanied by a full entourage of castle guards and Knights of the Garter, are difficult for the general public to view. The **changing of the castle guard,** however, is an event conducted in a manner in which the general public can participate. The new guard leaves the Victoria Barracks precisely at 1055, then marches along High Street to the castle. The guard changing takes place at 1100, and the old guard returns by the same route at 1130. By positioning yourself along High Street or Castle Hill, you will have a good view of the pageantry as it unfolds. Note that the changing of the guard does not take place during wet weather or on Sunday.

From the battlements of Windsor Castle, you may look down and across the stately River Thames onto the playing fields of **Eton College,** where "how the game is played" has always been more important than the final score. The importance of Eton lies less in what it is than in what it stands for. The schoolyard and cloisters are open 1400–1630 except during school holidays, when they are open 1330–1630. Guided tours are at 1400 and 1515 daily.

Your initial entry into the single-street town of Eton may be a bit frightening at first. You will probably find yourself surrounded by a group of young gentlemen uniformed in pin-striped trousers, white bow ties, and formal black coats with tails. These are the students of Eton College. This school for kings is one of Britain's most exclusive educational institutions and a strong reminder that the British on occasion can cling fiercely to their traditions.

Cruising on the River Thames offers a respite from pageantry and tradition during your visit. At the bottom of High Street, at its intersection with Barry Avenue, the Windsor Boat Pier offers two cruises. The first is a thirty-five-minute trip upstream, and the other is a full two-hour trip with light refreshments and a licensed bar aboard.

Kids of all ages will enjoy a visit to **Legoland Windsor,** located a mere 2 miles from the Windsor town center (www.legoland.co.uk). Take the Legoland shuttle bus from either of the Windsor rail stations. Opening and closing times vary so check the website or call 0871 222 2001 before you go. Learn to drive your own Lego car on a real road system with traffic lights and roundabouts. At the Waterworks, fire water cannons and make water flow uphill or squirt from fountains. Cruise down Fairy Tale Brook in a boat, or whirl around on the Whirly Birds Helicopter. In My Town you don't just watch the circus—you're part of the show. You can even watch airplanes being built at Legoland Airport. Tickets may be purchased at the Royal Windsor Information Centre. Admission fees are £41.40 adults, £31.20 for children age three to fifteen and for seniors (older than sixty). You can save £4 on adult tickets and £3 on children's tickets by purchasing online or by phone at (0870) 504 0404.

Windsor Guildhall, on High Street opposite the information center, was designed by Sir Christopher Wren. Legend has it that the Council Chamber insisted Wren add four internal columns to the design for safety reasons. Somewhat insulted, he did add the four internal columns, defiantly leaving them about 1 inch short of the ceiling to prove that his original design was sound. The guildhall is open to visitors on Monday 1000–1400 (on Tuesday during bank holiday weeks).

If you have not yet been introduced to the British public house (pub), there is no better time than now. **The Royal Oak,** directly across the street from Windsor Riverside Station, is highly recommended for a relaxing break before trekking uphill to the castle entrance and as a resting spot to royally reminisce before boarding the train back to London Town. No more prim a pub can you find in all of England. Its impeccable oaken interior matches the high quality of its food and service. The inn was constructed as an alehouse in 1736 and restored in 1937. Should we meet you there, we'll buy the first round!

London–Windsor–London

There are two train stations in Windsor–Eton: the Windsor & Eton Riverside Station and the Windsor & Eton Central Station. Direct service to Windsor & Eton Riverside Station is available from and to London Waterloo Station; service from and to Windsor & Eton Central Station requires a change of trains at Slough. Schedules shown here are direct trains from and to Windsor & Eton Riverside Station.

DEPART Waterloo Station	ARRIVE Windsor & Eton Riverside Station	NOTES
0728	0824	M–Sa
0744	0846	Su
0758	0851	M–Sa
0828	0921	M–Sa
0844	0946	Su
0858	0951	M–Sa
0925	1018	Su

M–Sa service continues at 30-minute intervals until 2228, then 2313; Su service continues at 30-minute intervals until 1944, then 2044, 2144, and 2244.

DEPART Windsor & Eton Riverside Station	ARRIVE Waterloo Station	NOTES
1353	1449	M–Sa
1401	1505	Su
1623	1719	M–Sa
1634	1729	Su
1653	1749	M–Sa
1723	1819	M–Sa

M–Sa service continues every 30 minutes until 2323, then 2253; Su every 30 minutes until 2101, then 2201 and 2301.

Day Excursion to

York

Fine Medieval City

Depart from King's Cross Station
Distance by train: 188 miles (302 km)
Average train time: 1 hour, 57 minutes
Train information and InterCity services: (0845) 748 4950
Tourist information: Tourist Information Centre, 1 Museum Street, York, North Yorkshire YO1 7DT; *Tel:* (01904) 550099; *Fax:* (01904) 551888
www.visityork.org
E-mail: info@visityork.org
Hours: De Grey Rooms: 0900–1730 Monday–Saturday, 1000–1700 Sunday
Notes: Check in with the Tourist Information Centre in the rail station and request the *First Stop York* free booklet that offers half-price vouchers to many attractions in the town. Then turn left leaving the train station, and proceed along the city wall toward the tower of the York Minster. After crossing the River Ouse, at the intersection of Duncombe Place and St. Leonard's Place, you will see the Minster straight ahead. York's main tourist office is nearby in Exhibition Square, just beyond Theatre Royal.

"The history of York," according to King George VI, "is the history of England." The Romans took York from a Celtic tribe, the Brigantes, in AD 71. According to legend, King Arthur captured the city sometime after the Roman legions retreated in AD 406. The Saxons took charge in the seventh century, and the Danes ran the Saxons off in 867, only to get their comeuppance from the Anglo-Saxons in 944. In 1066 York saw the fastest turnaround ever when King Harold of England defeated the King of Norway at Stamford Bridge, 6 miles from York. Nineteen days later York (and all of England, in fact) passed to the Normans when Harold was killed in the Battle of Hastings.

William the Conqueror, following his victory at Hastings, came north to quell a rebellion, which he accomplished through his version of urban renewal—the "scorched earth" policy. The ruins and rubble of the Romans, the Saxons, the Vikings, and the Anglo-Saxons, however, remain today.

Charles I, fleeing the fermenting civil war, left London in 1639 to take residence in York. Cromwell's troops finally took York in July 1644. A condition of surrender was that there would be no pillaging; thus, the fine medieval stained glass of York Minster was saved. It is estimated that the Minster contains more than half of all the medieval stained glass in England.

York, similar to Chester, has retained most of its fourteenth-century city walls. You will see part of them as you exit from York's railway station. The city of York is best explored on foot. Once armed with a map and a **York Pass** (£30 adult; £22 child) from the tourist information center, proceed on foot into the city. Although it's a ten- to fifteen-minute walk, you'll see a lot of history en route. Your York Pass provides free entry to more than thirty attractions. While at the tourist office, ask for the York City Council's parents' folder for those traveling with youngsters. York is considered to be "the child-friendly city." And if during your journey you start to think, "I wish I could spend more time in York," as is often heard by the tourist officials, inquire about overnight accommodations.

The York Association of Voluntary Guides provides excellent free tours that depart daily from Exhibition Square at 1015 throughout the year, with an additional tour at 1415 from April to the end of October and an evening tour at 1845 in June, July, and August. The tour lasts about two hours. To request special theme tours or private tours, write to The Hon. Secretary, Tourist Information Centre, 1 Museum Street, York YO1 7DT, or telephone (01904) 550099 between 0930 and 1130 Monday to Friday.

Too tired or unable to walk? A horse-and-carriage service operates outside York Minster during good weather. Hour-long, open-top bus tours depart from the rail station and travel different routes as well.

Among York's points of interest, **York Minster** draws first choice. Built between 1220 and 1472, the Minster is England's largest Gothic cathedral. As the mother church of the Church of England's northern province, it is outranked in religious importance only by Canterbury Cathedral. A superb view can be had from the tower top . . . 275 steps above! Those who make it to the top can ask for a certificate (£1 donation). No sightseeing is allowed on Sunday or other times of religious services.

Also be certain to visit the **National Railway Museum** on Leeman Road, a ten-minute walk from the York railway station. The Great Railway Show at the museum commemorates the Railway Age from the 1820s to the present day. Visitors walk down station platforms and, in imagination, become passengers on an Edwardian Express or on a boat train to Paris. The museum's National Railway Collection ranges from a lock of Robert Stephenson's hair to the splendor of the ***Royal Train.***

York's **Castle Museum** is one of the most interesting folk museums in the world. Famous streets of York have been reconstructed to depict the daily life and occupations of various periods from Tudor to Edwardian times. The museum also contains an eighteenth-century water mill that operates throughout the summer. Other sections are devoted to Yorkshire crafts, costumes, and military history; the Tea Room has 1960s decor and style of music. Whoa, flashback!

In 1992 York's impressive medieval gatehouse, Monk Bar, was converted into the **Richard III Museum.** Since many feel that historians gave King Richard a "bum rap," the exhibition puts Richard on trial for you to decide his guilt or innocence. Based on the evidence presented, you hand down the verdict. Did Richard murder his own nephews, the Princes in the Tower?

London–York–London

DEPART King's Cross Station	ARRIVE York Station	NOTES
0615	0832	M–Sa
0700	0852	M–Sa
0730	0933	M–F
0800	0951	M–Sa
0830	1033	M–Sa
0900	1052	Daily
0930	1134	Daily
1000	1152	Daily

Service continues every half hour until 2000, then 2100 and 2200 M–F; last train 2100 Sa–Su.

YORK to KING'S CROSS STATION	
M–F	Depart York Station 1429, 1456, 1529, 1555, 1629, 1655, 1730, 1755, 1829, 1910, 1929, 1934, 2003, 2034, 2116, and 2219; journey time approximately 2 hours.
Sa	Depart York Station 1530, 1555, 1629, 1655, 1755, 1829, 1855, 1901, 1929, and 2001; journey time approximately 2 hours.
Su	Depart York Station 1558, 1629, 1657, 1717, 1729, 1755, 1857, 1930, 1948, 1959, 2029, and 2133; journey time approximately 2 hours.

You'll find the narrow, winding streets of York the most fascinating of all the city's attractions. The streets developed from the original Roman street plans. In turn, each century added a bit more color—and perhaps confusion. The Vikings left their mark in the use of street names ending in "gate," such as Petergate and Castlegate. But Stonegate existed *before* the Vikings' arrival.

For purchasing fine china and crystal, pay a visit to one of the world's leading fine-china and crystal specialists, **Mulberry Hall,** on Stonegate. *Tel:* (01904) 620736; *Fax:* (01904) 620251; www.mulberryhall.co.uk; *E-mail:* mailorder@

mulberryhall.co.uk. It's only about 200 yards from York Minster. A fifteenth-century private house, Mulberry Hall has been a shop since the eighteenth century. Here you will find an incomparable stock of fine china, including Wedgwood, Spode, and Royal Doulton, as well as crystal by Waterford, Stuart, and Baccarat, which can be shipped anywhere in the world.

The medieval citizens following the Vikings gave York its winding streets. One of these streets, the **Shambles,** is reputed to be one of the best-preserved medieval streets in Europe. Originally the street was crammed with butcher shops in half-timbered overhanging buildings. The east-west line of the street kept the meat in cool shade for most of the day and now houses an interesting assortment of stores and bookshops, where the meat hooks still hang.

SCOTLAND

www.visitscotland.com

"The pipes, the pipes are calling. . . . " They are calling you to Scotland, a country where there is much more than first meets the eye. Come to Scotland with an open mind, a keen eye, and a sense of adventure. A land of contrasts—friendly, bustling towns and cities but with easy escape to solitude—Scotland has some of the least-populated parts of Europe and yet one of the largest arts festivals.

Scotland forms the northern part of the island of Great Britain and is divided into three main regions: the Southern Uplands, the Midland Valley, and the Highlands. Filled with patriotic pride, many Scots consider themselves to be the "true Brits." With more than 5,000 years of history, they predate their Anglo-Saxon cousins by several centuries. You may visit ancient towns built even before the pyramids of Egypt.

Although Scotland has been part of the United Kingdom since the formal Act of Union in 1707, it still issues its own banknotes and maintains its own legal and educational systems as well as its own culture and traditions. From bagpipes and kilts to fine Scotch whiskey and that mysterious food known as haggis, Scotland is unique.

Scotland has produced some of the world's most talented people. Alexander Graham Bell, inventor of the telephone, was originally from Scotland, as is the famous actor Sean Connery; Robert Burns, from Ayr, wrote "Auld Lang Syne"; and John Paul Jones, who established the U.S. Navy, was born in Dumfriesshire. Other famous Scots include Robert Louis Stevenson, author of *Kidnapped* and *Treasure Island;* Sir Arthur Conan Doyle, creator of the detective Sherlock Holmes; the 1970s band the Bay City Rollers; and the pop band Garbage.

If you want to visit as many places of interest as possible in Scotland, purchase a **Discovery Ticket** for free admission to The National Trust for Scotland's attractions for three nonconsecutive days or seven to fourteen consecutive days. Prices: adult three-day £17; seven-day £22; family (two adults and up to six children under age eighteen): three-day £37; seven-day £47.50; fourteen-day £58. You can order direct from the National Trust for Scotland (*Tel:* 0844 493 2100; toll free from the U.S. 866-211-7573; www.nts.org.uk; *E-mail:* information@nts.org.uk) or from many of the tourist centers.

Rail Travel in Scotland

What better way to visit a country famous for its hospitality, scenery, and history than by train? First ScotRail provides a variety of ways to discover Scotland. It operates 2,000 daily departures to 354 stations in Scotland and provides a connecting sleeper service to London. Any BritRail Pass is valid, of course, in Scotland. First ScotRail, however, also has rail passes available for travel only in Scotland.

The **BritRail Scottish Freedom Pass** is valid for travel any four days within an eight-day period or any eight days within a fifteen-day period. See the Appendix for prices.

The Freedom Pass includes unlimited standard-class rail travel on all First ScotRail and Strathclyde Passenger Transport services and all scheduled Great North Eastern Railway and Virgin Trains operating wholly within Scotland, including Carlisle and Berwick-upon-Tweed. The pass also includes all Caledonian MacBryne and Strathclyde ferry services to the islands, a discount on some P&O ferry routes, and a free packet of timetables upon validation of your pass in Scotland. The discounts are available on reclining-seat fares only and do not apply to cabins.

First ScotRail Short Breaks will help you discover Scotland's breathtaking beauty, hospitality, and some of the world's most romantic rail journeys on its famous railway lines, including the West Highland Line (Glasgow–Oban, Fort William, and Mallaig), the Kyle Line (Inverness–Kyle of Lochalsh), and the North Line (Inverness–Thurso and Wick).

We have selected the two base cities of Edinburgh, Scotland's capital, and Glasgow, Scotland's largest city. The day excursions listed can be visited from either base city, and our rail schedules include departures from both Edinburgh and Glasgow. So sit back, relax, and enjoy the ride.

Contact First ScotRail, Caledonian Chambers, 87 Union Street, Glasgow G1 3TA. Fares and train times, telephone in the United Kingdom: *Timetables:* (0845) 601 5959; *Customer Relations:* (0845) 601 5929; www.firstgroup.com/scotrail/index.php; *E-mail:* scotrail.enquiries@firstgroup.com.

Base City: **EDINBURGH**

www.edinburgh.org
E-mail: info@visitscotland.com

"This profusion of eccentricities, this dream in masonry and living rock is not a drop-scene in a theater, but a city in a world of everyday reality!"

—ROBERT LOUIS STEVENSON

There is an understandable feeling of rocklike perpetuity enveloping Edinburgh. Formed by volcanic heat and scoured and shaped by Ice-Age glaciers in a valley punctuating its skyline with upward-thrusting crags, the setting of Scotland's capital city of Edinburgh is nothing short of dramatic.

Edinburgh's exact origins are lost in antiquity. Although dissenting opinions exist, it seems that a primitive fortress was established around AD 452 by the Picts on the sloping ground leading from the great Castle Rock on which Edinburgh Castle stands today. There have been fortresses on Castle Rock since that time, each in turn razed by a challenger and then rebuilt only to be razed again. By the eleventh century, however, events around Edinburgh began to calm down, and the town got on with the task of becoming civilized and prosperous. From its earliest days Edinburgh offered a stern, almost aloof countenance to the world and inspired great individuals to great achievements.

Edinburgh is actually two cities. The Old Town, built on a rocky ledge running from Edinburgh Castle to the Royal Palace of Holyroodhouse, is steeped in ancient history. Huddled on high ground in typical medieval fear of attack, it is full of winding and cobbled off-streets, so be sure to wear comfortable walking shoes. The New Town, formed on the lower side of Nor' Loch, a lake created from a swamp and eventually drained in 1816, spreads serenely in a succession of streets and avenues, reflecting the optimism of later centuries. Conceived in 1767 when the Scottish Parliament approved an extension of the city, the Town Council lost no time in proceeding with the work. The city planning that followed made possible Edinburgh's current wide streets and spacious squares.

The two cities within a city further reflect two great attributes: on the one hand, Edinburgh's reserved exterior, and on the other, its ability to express great warmth and even, on occasion, a high degree of gaiety. Edinburgh has been called one of the most attractive capital cities in the world. As Oliver Wendell Holmes aptly put it, "Edinburgh is a city of incomparable loveliness."

From the beauty of its setting, enhanced by its architecture, to the turbulence of its history and the stalwart qualities of its citizens, Edinburgh is a city of inexhaustible delight. Edinburgh Castle, the Palace of Holyroodhouse, the Royal Mile, and Princes Street await you. Welcome to Scotland's capital.

Arriving by Air

Edinburgh has its own international airport with limited direct service to or from North America (www.edinburghairport.com). International air service is provided to Edinburgh from most European cities. Travelers arriving in Britain via London (Gatwick or Heathrow), Birmingham, or Manchester Airport may take either a connecting flight to Edinburgh or the train. From London's King's Cross Station, the Great North Eastern Railway line will get you to Edinburgh's Waverly Station in only four hours. Or sleep through your journey to Edinburgh aboard a comfortable Caledonian Sleeper train departing from London's Euston Station just before midnight.

Glasgow is a convenient port of entry for visitors arriving in Scotland from overseas. **Glasgow's International Airport** is located 10 miles west. Express train service from Glasgow's Queen Street Station to Edinburgh takes only fifty minutes; one hour, forty-five minutes by bus. The airport is situated in an area that is relatively fog-free during most of the year, for the wind moving across the Irish Sea has few natural obstructions to interrupt its flow. See the "Arriving by Air" section of the Glasgow chapter for further information. **Prestwick Airport** (29 miles southwest of Glasgow), which for years served as the international airport for the area, is the most fog-free airport on the British Isles.

Arriving by Train

Waverley Station is the main train station in Edinburgh. Some InterCity trains from London go on to Aberdeen after a brief station stop in Edinburgh. If you are aboard one of these trains, be prepared to "set down" in the Waverley Station as quickly as possible following your arrival. Edinburgh's other station, Haymarket, is where all trains halt en route to Glasgow or Aberdeen. Trains arriving from England via Newcastle and York, however, bypass Haymarket Station.

Waverley Station appears to be completely immersed in an open ravine. The area was once a swamp that was converted into a lake as a northern defense for Edinburgh Castle during the reign of King James II (1437–1460). The lake was drained in 1816 to become the site of the Princes Street Gardens, which separate the Old Town and New Town in Edinburgh.

Today's Waverley Station complex is the second largest in Britain and has twenty-one tracks strewn about in a labyrinth of steps and passageways. But there are plenty of signs, and station map/guide leaflets are available.

Basically there are three accesses to Waverley Station. The first is a set of rather steep steps, the Waverley Steps, connecting the north side of the station (the trackage runs east and west) with Princes Street, the city's main artery. The second and third approaches are ramps leading from the main floor of the station to the Waverley Bridge, which runs between the Old Town and New Town. Both ramps have pedestrian walkways. The northern ramp serves incoming vehicles; the one to the south is for outgoing vehicles.

Tracks 12 to 18 form the backbone, or center, of the Waverley Station. At the entrance to these tracks is a digital-display board for train arrivals, departures, and special announcements. If your train is departing from tracks other than 12 to 18, ask the railroad personnel at the ticket barriers for directions.

Pay special attention to multiple train departures from the same track. A line of coaches on a single train track can actually be two trains departing for two separate destinations. They are announced with red-bannered front train or rear train signs. It pays to ask questions.

The **Rail Travel Centre** (train information center) is located in the waiting-room area of the station and is open 0800–2200 daily. Covered by a huge glass dome, the waiting area contains digital arrival/departure information and a series of facilities, including restrooms, a magazine kiosk, and eateries. The principal entrance to this area is located across the main-station concourse from the stub ends of tracks 16 and 17. Train reservations may be made at any of the counters.

Money exchange (Bureau de Change) is available from the Edinburgh and Scotland Information Centre.

Hotel accommodations, including bed-and-breakfast reservations, are provided by the Edinburgh and Scotland Information Centre. For advance reservations from outside Britain, dial country code 44 + (131) 473 3800.

The Balmoral Hotel at Waverley Station is a five-star hotel that has been a landmark for Waverley Station, and the city of Edinburgh, since 1902 when it was known as the North British Hotel. The Balmoral is located between the station and Princes Street. Topped by a mammoth 200-foot Gothic clock tower, the hotel serves as a transition between the hustle of commerce on Princes Street and the bustle of the passengers arriving at and departing from the station.

The Victorian-style hotel has undergone a £23 million restoration and is exquisite throughout. We enjoyed the pampering we received during our stay. Undoubtedly, the hotel is one of Edinburgh's most familiar and elegant landmarks, commanding an important position at the east end of Princes Street. *Tel:* (0131) 556 2414; *Fax:* (0131) 557 3747; www.thebalmoralhotel.com; *E-mail:* reservationsbalmoral@roccofortecollection.com.

Edinburgh and Scotland Information Centre, 3 Princes Street EH2 2QP; *Tel:* 0845 225 5121; *Fax:* (0131) 473 3881; *Hours:* September–June 0900–1700 Monday–Saturday, 1000–1700 Sunday; July–August 0900–1900 Monday–Saturday, 1000–1900 Sunday.

The center is located on the rooftop of Waverley Station beyond the north end of Waverley Bridge at the corner of Waverley and Princes Streets. Use the pedestrian ramp on the north side of the station, turning right as you reach the Waverley Bridge level. There are several tourist information signs to help guide the way.

Many of the facilities sought by incoming passengers—such as money exchange, city information, and hotel accommodations (reservation fee, £5)—may be found in the Edinburgh and Scotland Information Centre. The first section has information on Edinburgh and all of Scotland. Go straight ahead as you enter for self-service; go to the right for counter service. For entertainment information, proceed through the shopping section, where Scottish books, maps, and posters are available at the ticket desk; *Tel:* (0131) 558 1072.

Getting around in Edinburgh

Two bus departure points serve the area surrounding the Waverley Street rail station. The first, at Waverley Bridge, is located immediately up the ramps leading out of the rail station. This departure point serves the city bus system and the sightseeing buses. Coach service for the Glasgow Airport and other main destinations utilizes the bus terminal on St. Andrew Square. To reach it, cross Princes Street where it intersects with Waverley Bridge. Then walk north 1 block to St. Andrew Square.

City Sightseeing Edinburgh, Platform 1, Waverley Railway Station; *Tel:* (0131) 220 0770; *Fax:* (0131) 557 4083; www.city-sightseeing.com and www.edinburghtour.com.

For bus tours of Edinburgh, go to the tourist information office and its selection of bus-tour brochures. You can readily recognize the City Sightseeing open-top double-decker buses. You can get on and off at your leisure. Tours depart a minimum of every fifteen minutes and include Edinburgh Castle, Palace of Holyroodhouse, Princes Street, the Royal Mile, and New Town. Purchase your tickets from the bus driver, the City Sightseeing office at platform 1 in Waverley Station, or from the tourist information center. Fares: £12 adults, £11 students/seniors, £5 children.

Follow in the footsteps of royalty—visit the **Royal Yacht *Britannia***, which has traveled more than 1 million miles and served the Royal Family and their guests for more than forty years. This is one tour you won't want to miss. To be guaranteed admission, however, purchase tickets in advance. *Note: Closed January 1 to 31, 2012. Tel:* (0131) 5555566; www.royalyachtbritannia.co.uk; *E-mail:* enquiries@tryb.co.uk. In person visit the **Edinburgh Tattoo Office,** 33–34 Market Street. Admission fees: £11 adults, £9.50 seniors, £7 children (age 5–17); family ticket (two adults and up to three children) £32.50. The Royal Yacht is berthed at the Port of Leith, about 2 miles from the city center. *Britannia* tour buses depart from Waverley Bridge.

Guided walking tours (Robin's Walking Tours) depart daily from outside the tourist information center. There are several to choose from: The Grand Tour of the City departs at 1000, then explore the Royal Mile at 1100, and at 1900 see Ghosts and Witches.

Or try the ones offered by **Mercat Tours,** Mercat House, 28 Blair Street, Edinburgh EH1 1QR. *Tel* and *Fax:* (0131) 225 5443; www.mercattours.co.uk.

Explore where the history of the old underground city meets the supernatural in the **Ghosts and Ghouls Tour,** presented by Mercat Tours and the city of Edinburgh. Dramatic guides, who are graduate historians, will lead you from the Mercat Cross, where the "entertainment" of the ages occurred (criminals hanged, flogged, tortured, and dismembered), down through the deserted, dark, and ghostly places of Old Town Edinburgh. Paranormal activity is logged on record, so don't be surprised if you happen to see or feel something from beyond. Tours depart nightly at 1900, 2000, and 2100 (April–October); 1900 and 2000 November–March. The ninety-minute tour costs £10, the extended tour (two hours including refreshment) is £13; group and family discounts are offered. Buffet, refreshment, and specialty combination tours are also available. We heard of one brave group actually spending the night among the spirits in one of the bridge caverns. Be sure to ask the guide about the most haunted pub in Edinburgh; you may need a stiff one after this tour. Other tours include the Secrets of the Royal Mile, Ghost Hunter Trail, the Vaults Tour, and the Haunted Underground Experience.

A guided tour of the **Real Mary King's Close,** 2 Warriston's Close, Writers' Court (off the Royal Mile), takes visitors beneath Edinburgh's city chambers for a fascinating step back into the seventeenth, eighteenth, and nineteenth centuries. *Hours:* November–March 1000–1700 Sunday–Thursday, 1000–2100 Friday–Saturday; April–October 1000–2100 Monday–Saturday; August 0900–2300 daily. *Tel:* 0845 070 6244; www.realmarykingsclose.com. According to the tourist board, "access may prove difficult to people with certain disabilities," and no children younger than age five are permitted. *Admission:* £11.50 adults, £10.50 seniors/students, and £6 children. Tour duration, about one hour.

For those interested in more paranormal experiences, try the **Supernatural History Tour** departing every twenty minutes on Saturday evenings 1800–2100. Tour duration is one hour. Both tours include a copy of the *Witchery Tales* book. If you're up to braving the ghosts and goblins, murders and mysteries, book your tickets in advance and meet your guide outside the Witchery Restaurant, Castlehill, Royal Mile (by Edinburgh Castle). We hope you return.

Enticing Edinburgh

Magnificent **Edinburgh Castle** is the national symbol of Scotland and one of its top attractions. The castle radiantly crowns an ancient volcanic mount above Edinburgh proper. Guided tours of Edinburgh Castle are available, or you may pick up a free headset and tour at your own pace. As you follow numbered plaques throughout the castle, your headset will provide you with its fascinating story.

Stand in the oldest building in Edinburgh, **St. Margaret's Chapel,** just as the Queen of Scotland did more than 900 years ago. A beautiful stained-glass memorial to Sir William Wallace faces the altar. You may also see the Crown Jewels of Scotland, the Scottish National War Memorial, and the Stone of Destiny.

The castle is still garrisoned, and every day (except Sunday) a cannon is fired at 1300. It makes a rather dramatic time check for unsuspecting visitors who end up doing the "One o'Clock Jump."

During the annual **Edinburgh Military Tattoo,** the castle provides a most provocative backdrop for this dazzling celebration of music, theater, dance, and traditional Scottish pipes and pipers, drums and drummers marching on the castle esplanade. Undoubtedly one of the world's greatest shows, each tattoo has overseas contingents as well as traditional Scottish, but it always closes with the moving appearance of the lone piper on the castle battlements, a very touching moment.

Originated in the seventeenth and eighteenth centuries in the Low Countries, "tattoo" was derived from the cry of the innkeepers at closing time. Local regiments would then march through the street playing fife and drums to signal a return to quarters, and the shout would go up *"Doe den tap toe"* ("Turn off the taps"). This became the basis for many marvelous massed military bands' performances given around the globe, with the Edinburgh Military Tattoo being the leader.

The Edinburgh Tattoo occurs annually in August, but you can experience the colorful history of the tattoo year-round at the Spirit of the Tattoo Visitor Centre. It is located in a 150-year-old Victorian reservoir at the top of the Royal Mile: 555 Castlehill, Royal Mile, Edinburgh EH1 2 ND; *Tel:* (0131) 225 9661; *Hours:* 0900–1630 Monday–Friday. Tickets range from £14 to £46 and may be purchased online or from The Tattoo Office, 32 Market Street, Edinburgh EH1 1QB; *Tel:* +44 0131 225 8616 (from outside the United Kingdom); *Fax:* (0131) 225 8627; *Hours:* 1000–1630 Monday–Friday; www.edintattoo.co.uk. Order tickets well in advance as this is an extremely popular event.

Amid the contrasting charms of its Old Town and New Town, Edinburgh takes its place among an elite group of European cities conspicuous for their romance and physical attributes. As more enclosures were built during the postmedieval period, the term *close* came into existence in old Edinburgh to describe the narrow passageways giving access, or right-of-way, to the buildings in the rear of others. There are more than one hundred closes in Old Town, many of which have brass tablets at their entrances to explain their historical significance.

There are many aspects of Edinburgh to see on conducted tours, but the city's real beauty is best seen by exploring it on foot at your own pace. Walk the **Royal Mile** in Old Town from Edinburgh Castle to the Palace of Holyroodhouse. For some background before traveling, visit www.edinburgh-royalmile.com. En route you'll pass a fantastic assembly of picturesque old buildings, such as Brodie's Close, the John Knox House, the Cannonball House, Anchor Close, and the Canongate Tolbooth.

Brodie's Close housed Deacon Brodie, a respectable town councillor by day and a burglar by night. Brodie's lifestyle supposedly provided the basis for Robert Louis Stevenson's *Dr. Jekyll and Mr. Hyde*. The **John Knox House** dates from the sixteenth century and is traditionally connected with both John Mossman, Keeper of the Royal Mint to Mary, Queen of Scots, and John Knox, Scotland's religious reformer. A brief video presentation amid original timber-framed galleries and oak paneling will take you back to the sixteenth century. The John Knox House is located at the halfway mark of the Royal Mile in the Netherbow Arts Centre.

The Cannonball House, dating from 1630, got its name from a cannonball lodged in its gable, ostensibly fired from the castle by an errant cannoneer during the blockade of 1745. **Anchor Close** is the site where the first edition of the *Encyclopaedia Britannica* was printed as well as the Edinburgh edition of Robert Burns's poems. Reportedly, Burns himself read the proofs on the premises. Last renovated in 1591, the **Canongate Tolbooth** has been used as the Town Council House and a prison for the ancient village of Canongate, now incorporated into the city of Edinburgh. The Canongate Tolbooth houses the People's Story Museum, which relates the life and work of ordinary folk in Edinburgh from the late eighteenth century to the present.

Although the **Palace of Holyroodhouse** originated as a guesthouse for the Abbey of Holyrood, most of the palace we see today was built for Charles II in 1671. The most famous figure associated with the palace, however, was Mary, Queen of Scots, who spent six years of her tragic reign there. On the palace grounds you may view Queen Mary's Bath House, where, according to today's Scottish tour guides, she bathed daily. The guides also explain that her cousin Queen Elizabeth I bathed once a month—whether she needed it or not.

The Royal Mile was for many centuries the center of Edinburgh life. Its citizens lived and conducted their affairs on this busy, crowded street. At the entrance to the Palace of Holyroodhouse, you will find a line of the letter S embedded in the pavement. Until 1880 it marked the limits of sanctuary extended by Holyrood Abbey. It is said that debtors were often seen running toward the line with creditors in hot pursuit and bystanders wagering on the outcome.

At the end of the Royal Mile, next to the Palace of Holyroodhouse, visit **Our Dynamic Earth** exhibition. It uses special effects and technology to dramatically tell the story of how our planet developed.

Greyfriars Bobby. On Candlemaker Row, a short distance from Edinburgh's Royal Mile, stands the statue ***Greyfriars Bobby,*** erected as a tribute to a small dog's affection and fidelity to his master. In 1858 a wee Skye terrier named Bobby followed the remains of his master, John Gray ("Auld Jock"), to Greyfriars churchyard, where the dog lingered and slept on his master's grave for fourteen years until his death in 1872.

People tried to take Bobby away. They even found a home for him in the country. Still, Bobby returned to the churchyard, where friends began bringing food to sustain him during his vigil. The story of Greyfriars Bobby spread throughout Edinburgh, and soon Bobby's tale of devotion reached Queen Victoria in London. She sent a special envoy, Lady Burdett-Coutts, to investigate this unusual story.

Bobby, in the meantime, had made friends with children in a nearby orphanage. The terrier brought joy and love to the children, particularly to Tammy, a crippled boy with whom Bobby would play by the hour. Bobby lived his own life, however, and returned nightly to his master's grave—at first secretly, for the presence of a dog in a churchyard was unthinkable in those times. But as Bobby won hearts, he gained privileges too. He even won the heart of the Lord Provost of Edinburgh, who had a collar made for the dog in 1867 and paid Bobby's licensing fee. (The collar can be seen today in the Canongate on the Royal Mile.)

Bobby never went to London to see the queen, but royal annals reflect that the queen actually was planning to pay him a visit at Greyfriars. Bobby died, however, before that honor became a reality.

The dog's body was buried alongside that of his master. Although Bobby is no longer visible, his presence is felt so strongly by the residents of the area that they frankly admit to opening their doors briefly before retiring at night, just in case. Perhaps when the door to heaven is opened for them, they will see Bobby again, running on the green pastures at the heels of his master, beside the still waters.

Bobby's statue stands close to the iron gates of Greyfriars churchyard, where Auld Jock and his faithful dog are interred. The story of Greyfriars Bobby was filmed by Walt Disney. We think it's worth your while to visit Greyfriars, just as we do each time we return to Edinburgh.

Shopping in Edinburgh. The city of Edinburgh is well known for its fine boutiques, shops, and department stores, where you may still find bargains in the famous Harris tweeds, Fair Isle sweaters, and tartan plaids. Princes Street is lined with shops displaying a variety of Scottish wares, from argyles and bagpipes to whiskey. And when you run out of stores and shops to visit on Princes Street, turn north 2 blocks to George Street and continue your shopping there. (You may need to stop by the bank on the way.)

Shoppers' havens on Princes Street include Jenners, the largest and oldest independently owned department store in the world, and C&A, both opposite the Scott Monument in the Waverley Street Station area. If you've never been in a store more than two centuries old, try Romanes & Paterson, Ltd., at 62 Princes Street. You will find traditional Scottish tweed, exquisite Edinburgh crystal, Caithness glass, knitwear from the borders, and, of course, tartans. They are everywhere, as is the whiskey.

Still not tired of shopping? The Scotch House nearby contains more than 300 tartans available by the meter, along with Shetland knitwear and original gifts. If you know a wee one, check out Hop Scotch, the Scotch House's special department for children.

Food, foam, and fun. With all that shopping, you may be ready for a snack and a libation. You don't have far to go—between and parallel to Princes Street and George Street is Rose Street, which probably has more convivial pubs to the meter than any other street in the world. In fact Edinburgh was voted Britain's "Best City for Pubs." You'll have no problem finding food, foaming pints, and fun at more than 700 pubs ranging from traditional neighborhood pubs to chic wine bars.

For historical atmosphere, fine wines, and an innovative style of Scottish cuisine, visit the Witchery by the Castle, Castlehill, Royal Mile EH1 2NF; *Tel:* (0131) 225 5613; www.thewitchery.com; *E-mail:* reservations@thewitchery.com. The Witchery is open daily 1200–1600 and 1730–2330.

Day Excursions

A baker's dozen—thirteen exciting day excursions—have been selected for our readers. All were chosen so those who prefer staying in Glasgow rather than in Edinburgh may enjoy them as well.

Scotland is known as "the land that likes to be visited." To ensure your opportunity to visit this marvelous country by rail includes seeing as many of its features as possible, we have divided the selected day excursions into Scotland's four geographic areas: the east coast, central region, west coast, and Highlands.

East coast. Along the east coast of Scotland, starting at the harbor of Dunbar near the English border, we then swing north from Edinburgh through Dundee, Montrose, and Aberdeen—not overlooking a stop en route at the golf capital of the world, St. Andrews.

Central region. In the central part of the country, we have selected excursions to two of Scotland's most historic cities—Perth and Stirling—plus a visit to Andrew Carnegie's birthplace, Dunfermline, and a visit to Linlithgow to view the palace where Mary, Queen of Scots, was born.

West coast. For our forays to the west coast, we delve deep into the heart of Robert Burns's country by a visit to Ayr, the poet's favorite town. Farther south, we call at Stranraer, the gateway to the Irish Sea and the Emerald Isle.

Highlands. North in the Highlands, Inverness serves as a gateway to explorations of Loch Ness, with its legendary monster, "Nessie," and as a base for a dash to the west to Kyle of Lochalsh and the Isle of Skye.

Train Connections to Other Base Cities from Edinburgh

Edinburgh–Cardiff

DEPART Waverley Station	ARRIVE Cardiff	NOTES
0652	1329	M–Sa
0908	1621	M–Sa
1105 (1052 Su)	1819 (1653 Su)	Daily
1252	1933	Daily
1452	2129	Daily
1652	2257	Daily

All departures require changing trains in Crewe or Birmingham. Other departures are available, but they require two or more changes.

Edinburgh–Glasgow

There are two services between Edinburgh and Glasgow. Frequent commuter trains depart from Edinburgh Waverley Station to Glasgow Queen Street Station. Average train time to Glasgow: 48–50 minutes. There is a less frequent service on the mainline between Edinburgh Waverley Station and Glasgow Central Station—service provided on mainline trains that arrive in Edinburgh from stations in England such as Carlisle, London, and York.

COMMUTER SERVICE: ARRIVES AT GLASGOW QUEEN STREET STATION

M–Sa	Departs every 15 minutes from 0700 to 1930, then every 30 minutes until 2330.
Su	Departs hourly from 0800 to 1200, then every 30 minutes until 2100, then at 2200, 2300, and 2330.

MAINLINE SERVICE: ARRIVES AT GLASGOW CENTRAL STATION

M–Sa	Departs at 0756, 0857, 1111, 1311, 1511, 1748, 1924, and 2114.
Su	Departs at 1212, 1511, 1711, 1915, and 2133.

Edinburgh–London

Average train time: 4 hours, 42 minutes.

DEPART WAVERLEY, ARRIVE KING'S CROSS STATION

M–F	Departs at 0655, 0800, 0900, 0930, 1000, and every 30 minutes thereafter until 1400, then hourly until 1700, then 1730 and 1900. Sleeper train departs at 2340; arrives London Euston Station 0643 next day. Reservations required.
Sa	Departs at 0655, 0800, 0900, and 0930, then every 30 minutes until 1300, then hourly until 1700, plus 1730.Sleeper train departs at 2340; arrives London Euston Station 0650 next day. Reservations required.
Su	Departs at 0900, 0930, 1030, 1100, and every half hour until 1800, then 1900. Sleeper train departs at 2315; arrives London Euston Station at 0646 next day. Reservations required.

Day Excursion to

Aberdeen

The Granite City

Depart from Waverley Station

Distance by train: 131 miles (211 km)

Average train time: 2 hours, 30 minutes

Train information and InterCity services: (0845) 748 4950

Tourist information: Aberdeen Visitor Information Centre, 23 Union Street, Aberdeen AB11 5BP; *Tel:* (01224) 288828; *Fax:* (01224) 252219

www.aberdeen-grampian.com

E-mail: aberdeen@visitscotland.com

Hours: September–June: Monday–Saturday 0930–1700; July–September: Monday–Saturday 0900–1830, Sunday 1000–1600; January–June: Monday–Saturday 0930–1700

Notes: Walk across the carpark at the station, cross over to the Criterion Bar, and turn right. Walk along to Market Street, and turn left up the hill. Then turn right onto Union Street; the Visitor Information Centre is at No. 23 Union Street.

Since the discovery of oil in the North Sea, Aberdeen has earned the title of "Europe's offshore oil capital." The city, however, has not been spoiled by its industry. Oil does not come ashore in Aberdeen; only occasionally can an oil rig be seen on the horizon, under tow to a new location or at anchor awaiting a new contract.

The development of North Sea oil plus the gathering strength of northeast Scotland's agriculture, fishing, and manufacturing industries have combined to give Aberdeen one of the highest growth rates of any city in Great Britain. Therefore, you will find Aberdeen a city of many moods and steeped in history. An ancient university town and thriving seaport, Aberdeen has grown very cosmopolitan, yet it remains old in grace. Above all else, the Aberdonians always have time—time to help, time to be interested, and time to talk.

Today, with more than two million roses, eleven million daffodils, and three million crocuses, Aberdeen has won the "Britain in Bloom" competition many times. Parks, gardens, and floral displays please every visitor, with the most popular being the **Winter Gardens** at the Duthie Park.

Aberdeen lies between the rivers Dee and Don with 2 miles of golden sand connecting them. But don't think of Aberdeen merely as a large city with a beach. Union Street bisects the city and provides a mile-long shopping center lined with excellent stores sure to satisfy every shopper.

Standing like a tall sentinel, the gleaming white **Girdleness Lighthouse** guarding Aberdeen's harbor will be the first welcoming sign you'll see. As you approach Scotland's third-largest city, the lighthouse becomes visible on the right as the train curves away to the left from Nigg Bay to cross the River Dee, then glides to a halt in Aberdeen's rail station.

The port of Aberdeen is the jumping-off place for adventurers bound for the Orkney Islands and Shetland Islands to the north. Don't be surprised if you see a cruise ship or two in Aberdeen's harbor. Aberdeen has attracted the cruise ships by constructing a passenger landing stage in its Victoria Dock area. By all appearances you'd believe everyone wants to visit Europe's offshore oil capital.

Aberdeen maintains tourist information in the form of a well-stocked literature stand alongside the travel center information counter in the rail station. There's also a twenty-four-hour "View Data" service—a very user-friendly computerized inquiry unit.

The information center has a wide variety of booklets, leaflets, and posters of Aberdeen and the surrounding area. Also available are the publications of the Scottish Tourist Board covering the entire country. The center is divided into three operating sections: inquiries, accommodations, and tickets. Walking-tour and bus-tour information is also available here.

Clustered around the tourist information center on Broad Street, only a short walk away, are many of Aberdeen's places of interest. In the restored **Provost Skene's House** on Broad Street, the oldest domestic dwelling in Aberdeen, dating from 1545, you will find rooms furnished in styles covering different periods in Aberdeen's history. After exploring the grandeur of the rooms, traverse upward to the top floor, where displays of Scottish social and archaeological history are to be found. The **Costume Gallery** has a marvelous collection of fascinating costumes from over the ages. Admission is free.

Aberdeen's **Maritime Museum** is housed in Provost Ross's House overlooking one of Britain's busiest harbors. Here, attractive displays not only depict the area's maritime heritage of fishing, shipbuilding, and trade but also showcase its offshore oil industry. Visitors can experience life onboard a working scale model of an oil rig or see the nineteenth-century lens assembly from the Rattray Head Lighthouse, plus much more. Admission is free. *Hours:* 1000–1700 Tuesday–Saturday, 1200–1500 Sunday. www.aagm.co.uk.

Provost Ross's House, a restored sixteenth-century dwelling, also houses a visitor center featuring audiovisual displays of National Trust for Scotland properties, a fascinating collection of more than one hundred properties representing a rich variety of castles, gardens, scenic areas, islands, and historic sights.

The **Tolbooth Museum,** housed in the seventeenth-century prison at Castlegate, explores the history of crime, punishment, and incarceration of witches, debtors, and other lawbreakers (plus some of their ingenious escapes). Originally the city seat of government, it also shows the evolution of local power, from the sixteenth century to the present day. Admission is free.

Edinburgh–Aberdeen–Edinburgh

DEPART Waverley Station	ARRIVE Aberdeen Station	NOTES
0728	0952	M–Sa
0804	1029	Su
0828	1053	M–Sa
0928	1150	M–Sa
1027	1305	M–Sa
1127	1336	M–Sa
1055	1323	Su
1228	1453	M–Sa

DEPART Aberdeen Station	ARRIVE Waverley Station	NOTES
1407	1628	M–Sa
1450	1727	M–Sa
1510	1741	Su
1601	1832	M–Sa
1707	1934	M–Sa
1710	1935	Su
1816	2048	M–Sa
1909	2132	Daily
2005	2250	M–Sa
2010	2243	Su
2106	2350	M–Sa
2128	2358	Su
2131	0005	M–Sa

+1=Arrives next day

Winston Churchill called the British Army's Gordon Highlanders "the finest regiment in the world." Therefore, an absolute must-see is the **Gordon Highlanders Museum** on Viewfield Road, which contains treasures spanning more than two centuries. *Hours:* April–September: 1000–1630 Tuesday–Saturday, 1230–1630 Sunday; October–November, January–March: 1000–1600, closed December and January. Visit www.gordonhighlanders.com.

Aberdeen is not only a cultural center but a family-friendly town as well. Those traveling with the wee ones may find the award-winning **Satrosphere** to be phenomenally fascinating. This hands-on discovery place is located at 179 Constitution Street and is the only one like it in Scotland. Exhibits allow kids to explore science and technology firsthand. Admission helps fund a registered charity and is £5.75 for adults and £4.50 for children. The Satrosphere is open daily 1000–1700. For more information, call (01224) 640340 or visit www.satrosphere.net.

The **Baxters Visitors Centre** is popular with any age. The Baxters have been making quality jams, marmalades, soups, and sauces from the finest ingredients for the upper crust for more than 130 years. Take a factory tour, then stop by the **Spey** Restaurant for a famous Fochabers Pancake. Before leaving be sure to shop in the "Best of Scotland" to find wonderful gifts or visit the Cellar to take home some of the famous goodies for which the Baxters are so well known.

Just north of the city center is **Old Aberdeen,** where you will find one of the oldest universities in Britain. **Aberdeen University** comprises Marischal College and King's College. Both are architecturally attractive yet totally different. Marischal College, one of the largest granite buildings in the world, was founded in 1593 and united with King's College in 1860 to form the University of Aberdeen. King's College, in Old Aberdeen, was founded in 1495. The ivy-covered building with its distinctive crown tower has stood for centuries as a symbol of Aberdeen. The **Zoology Museum** offers a diverse look at the animal kingdom, with a special collection of Scottish birds. For quiet and peaceful walks, visit the eleven-acre Cruickshank Botanic Garden on campus and the 400-year-old roses. Or take one of the many guided walks offered, such as the one that leads from Seaton Park to the Brig O'Balgownie across the River Don.

Day Excursion to

Ayr

Burns's Tam o' Shanter Inn

Depart from Edinburgh Waverley Station

Distance by train: 88 miles (142 km)

Average train time: 2 hours, 20 minutes

Train information and InterCity services: (0845) 748 4950

Tourist information: Ayr Tourist Information Centre, 22 Sandgate, Ayr KA7 1BW; *Tel:* (01292) 290300; *Fax:* (01292) 288686

www.ayrshire-arran.com

E-mail: ayr@visitscotland.com

Hours: January, June and October–March: Monday–Saturday 0900–1700; July–August: Monday–Saturday 0900–1800, Sunday 1000–1700; September: Monday–Saturday 0900–1700, Sunday 1000–1600

Notes: Upon leaving the station, cross the road and walk down past Burns Statue Square, following the road 'round to the right into Alloway Street. Continue straight down into the partly pedestrianized High Street. On the left-hand side, about two-thirds of the way down the street, you will come to a large building with the pavement continuing behind it. Take this route, then turn immediately left into Newmarket Street. Go straight up Newmarket Street, and when you are at the top, the Tourist Information Centre is facing you across the street. There is a pedestrian crossing here. Total walking time is approximately ten minutes.

What William Shakespeare is to England, Robert Burns is to Scotland. Ayr is the acknowledged center of "Burns Country." The town is rich in the history of

Scotland's bard. Many famous landmarks remain in Ayr today to tell the Burnsian stories.

The Tam o' Shanter Inn on High Street is where Tam began his celebrated ride. The Auld Brig (old bridge), which was the only bridge in town for 500 years, still offers a delightful passage across the River Ayr. In a conspicuous location outside the Ayr train station, a statue of Robert Burns waits to greet travelers.

In Alloway, a pleasant southern suburb of Ayr, you will find the **Burns National Heritage Park** (www.burnsheritagepark.com), where visual displays introduce you to the life of Robert Burns and acquaint you with locations in and around Ayr that you may later want to visit. A brief walk from the exhibit will bring you to **Burns' Cottage,** where the poet was born on January 25, 1759. More than 300,000 visitors pass through the park annually. The ruins of the **Alloway Auld Kirk** (old church) where Tam spied on dancing witches, also close to the center, were the inspiration for Burns's narrative poem "Tam o' Shanter." Visitors may watch an audiovisual reenactment of the epic tale.

It was from the ruins of the Auld Kirk that witches pursued Tam, but he escaped over the Auld Brig O' Doon—the bridge over the River Doon—and eluded his pursuers because, according to legend, witches were unable to cross running water. Maggie, the mare that Tam rode, was less fortunate: "Ae spring brought off her master hale, / But left behind her ain gray tail / The carlin caught her by the rump, / And left poor Maggie scarce a stump."

Ayr was a seaside resort long before the term was invented. Well-heeled Glasgow merchants came to Ayr for short vacations, liked what they saw, and built houses there. In addition to providing Scottish gentry with suburban abodes, Ayr also is a market center, for good measure. With all these assets, Ayr is assured of retaining its prosperous, bustling atmosphere even after the summer visitors have gone.

Literature on Ayr, the district surrounding it, and Scotland's famous poet, Robert Burns (who traveled extensively around Ayrshire), abounds by the pound in the information center. You can visit many places that have been developed to tell the story of Burns and his lifetime. If interested in exploring on your own or taking a bus around "Burns Country," you should gather all the details associated with the poet from the information center.

With more than 2 miles of golden, sandy beach, Ayr gets more than its fair share of the summer sun. Golf, bowling, and tennis are among the many sports activities that can be enjoyed there. The town has three golf courses, forming part of the famous 15-mile stretch of "golfing coast" you'll see from the train approaching Ayr. All the traditional seaside amusements may be enjoyed in Ayr, as well as horse racing, held at Scotland's premier **Ayr Racecourse** throughout the year.

Away from the beaches there are many beautiful parks and gardens, notably **Belleisle, Craigie,** and **Rozelle.** Rozelle is also the home of Ayr's **Maclaurin Art Gallery** and displays one of the very few Henry Moore sculptures to be seen in Scotland. Ayr's beauty has frequently brought it the coveted titles "Britain's Floral

Town" and "Scotland's Floral Town." Enjoy the Ayr Flower Show and Gardening Festival, second only to Chelsea's, if visiting the area in late August. If you delight in old houses, Ayr has many, including one that was built in 1470—twenty-two years before Columbus sailed to America!

Edinburgh–Ayr–Edinburgh

All schedules require a change of station in Glasgow, either from Queen Street to Central or the reverse. It's only a five- to ten-minute walk; such changes can also be accomplished by taxi, underground rail, or bus.

DEPART Waverley Station	ARRIVE Ayr Station	NOTES
0715	0927	M–Sa
0745	0953	M–Sa
0800	1126	Su
0815	1026	M–Sa
0915	1126	Daily
0945	1152	M–Sa

M–Sa service continues after 0945 every half hour until 2200, then 2330; Su hourly until 1930, then 2330.

DEPART Ayr Station	ARRIVE Waverley Station	NOTES
1413	1618 (1623 Su)	Daily
1443	1648	M–Sa
1513	1722	Daily
1543	1750	M–Sa
1559	1822	Su
1613	1824	M–Sa

M–Sa service continues after 1613 at half-hour intervals until 2143; Su hourly until 2104.

Day Excursion to

Dunbar

"Fort on the Point"

Depart from Edinburgh Waverley Station

Distance by train: 29 miles (46 km)

Average train time: 30 minutes

Train information and InterCity services: (0845) 748 4950

Tourist information: Dunbar Tourist Office Centre, 143 High Street, Dunbar EH4 21ES; *Tel:* (01368) 863353; *Fax:* (01368) 832 222

www.dunbar.org.uk

E-mail: info@visitscotland.com

Hours: April, May, October: Monday–Saturday 0900–1700, June & September: Monday–Saturday 0900–1700, Sunday 1100–1600; July: Monday–Saturday 0900–1900, Sunday 1100–1600; August: Monday–Saturday 0900–2000, Sunday 1100–1800; closed November–March

Notes: The tourist information center is a short walk from the railway station. Station Road runs from the front of the station to where it crosses Countess Road and becomes Abbey Road. When you reach the general post office on your right, the thoroughfare has another name change to High Street and remains so until you reach the information center, about 50 yards beyond the Town House on the same side of the street. Part of the Town House, incidentally, is a tollgate dating from the seventeenth century, when a toll road between Edinburgh and Newcastle ran through Dunbar.

Put on your walking shoes—we're going to Dunbar. The town offers two wonderful walking opportunities: one through the historic center of Old Dunbar to appreciate the great and varied wealth of its traditional Scottish buildings, the other along the cliffs brooding over the North Sea in the John Muir Country Park. Those who like a slower pace may take in Dunbar's harbor area and watch colorful fishing boats bob about on the tide. Further assurance of a pleasant outing for all is the presence of several public houses in the harbor area. Among them is the Volunteer Arms, which houses the Volunteer Bar and the Haven Lounge.

Dunbar is situated amid some of the most beautiful countryside and coastline in Scotland. There are few other places where it is possible to witness the full range of history of a Scottish east-coast fishing port and market center. Dunbar has always played an important part in Scotland's history. Because of its strategic location, the town has been a stronghold down through the centuries. Dunbar, Gaelic for "the fort on the point," had a castle fortress at least as early as AD 856. The remains of the castle stand on the promontory overlooking Dunbar's Victoria Harbour.

The **Dunbar Castle** was where Bothwell brought Mary, Queen of Scots, when he abducted her in 1567. That same year the Scottish Parliament ordered that Dunbar Castle be demolished. When Victoria Harbour was constructed in the nineteenth century, the channel leading into the harbor was cut through the rocky palisade where the ruins of the castle lay. The remains that you may inspect during your visit to Dunbar are only a fragment of the original great castle.

Edinburgh–Dunbar–Edinburgh

DEPART Waverley Station	ARRIVE Dunbar Station	NOTES
0707	0726	M–Sa
0906	0927	M–Sa
1105	1124	Daily
1211	1236	M–F
1306	1326	Daily

Frequent departures until 2100 M–F, three more trains until 1900 Sa, and four more trains until 2100 Su.

DEPART Dunbar Station	ARRIVE Waverley Station	NOTES
1341	1410	M–F
1541	1605	Daily
1739	1805	Sa–Su
1743	1807	M–F
1944	2009	M–F
2151	2216	Daily
2313	2346	Sa–Su

There are two harbors: the **Old Harbour,** extended by Oliver Cromwell, and **Victoria Harbour.** Construction on the Old Harbour began in 1655, and it was improved and extended in the eighteenth century. This harbor, now nearly deserted, still retains the old paving stones as well as a fisherman's barometer that was erected in 1856. As part of the redevelopment, the harbor areas have had cottage-type houses built since 1951 to the special design of Sir Basil Spence, the architect of the new Coventry Cathedral. Perhaps the best evidence of Dunbar's beauty is the large number of visitors walking about simply admiring the scenery.

An interesting part of Victoria Harbour is the **Lifeboat Museum,** which is well worth a visit. Lifeboats out of Dunbar have saved more than 200 lives since beginning operation in 1808.

For the town trail tour, the book *John Muir's Dunbar* details a guided walk, available May through September. The cliff-top trail is prominently marked on the local town map. The map is available at the tourist information office, as is other information on the town, including the two harbors. John Muir, regarded as the father of U.S. national parks, was born (1838) in Dunbar and emigrated to Wisconsin in the United States when he was a youth. Later, when he moved to California, he founded the Sierra Club and played a fundamental role in lobbying efforts to create Yosemite National Park.

Begin your tour at the **John Muir House** at 128 High Street, and follow the trail outlined in his book.

If you brought your walking shoes, the place to use them is the **John Muir Country Park,** which begins at Dunbar Harbour and extends to the Ravensheugh sands to the west, and on the south it approaches the Firth of Forth. The cliff-top trail has controlled public beaches below. Throughout the summer, a park ranger is normally on duty and available to answer your questions and provide directions. You may join the ranger on a ramble along the trail, but times and routes may vary; check with the tourist office. There are several horse-riding routes within the park as well.

If you are a golf nut and have not been able to obtain a tee time for the Old Course at St. Andrews, try the par 67 **Winterfield Golf Club** maintained by the town of Dunbar. *Tel:* 01368 863562.

Prefer a game of lawn bowling? There is a bowling green on the right-hand side of the Station Road as you proceed toward town. We asked an old Scot, "How can such a green be so smooth and flat?" "It's easy," he explained. "You just plant the best of grass seed and then roll it for a few hundred years."

Day Excursion to

Dundee

City of Discovery

Depart from Edinburgh Waverley Station

Distance by train: 60 miles (96 km)

Average train time: 1 hour, 30 minutes

Train information and InterCity services: (0845) 748 4950

Tourist information: VisitScotland Angus & Dundee, Discovery Point, Discovery Quay, Dundee, DD1 4XA; *Tel:* (01382) 527527; *Fax:* (01382) 527550

www.angusanddundee.co.uk

E-mail: dundee@visitscotland.com

Hours: June–September: Monday–Saturday 0900–1800, Sunday 1200–1600; October–May: Monday–Saturday 0900–1700

Notes: The Tourist Information Center is directly across from the train station, on Riverside Drive.

As your train approaches the city of Dundee, you will be able to witness a scene of railroading history—one of disaster and one of triumph. Following the station stop at Leuchars, watch as the train passes through the local station of Wormit and on to the railway bridge crossing the Firth of Tay inbound to Dundee. The bridge, a double-track structure 11,653 feet long, was opened in 1887 and was considered to be a triumph of railroad engineering. Alongside the current bridge, you will see a series of old bridge piers. These once supported a single-track bridge that was swept away during a violent storm in 1879, along with a train and seventy-five of its passengers. The River Tay and its rail and vehicular bridges are a vital part of Dundee's existence.

Dundee, the capital of Tayside, is Scotland's fourth-largest city and lies in the heart of Scotland in a magnificent setting between the Sidlaw Hills and the banks of Britain's finest salmon river, the Tay. Dundee is where the game of golf originated. The latest count reveals forty golf courses within one hour's drive of the city. Three actually lie within the city's district. In Dundee the name of the game is golf, and its citizens have proven to the world that they can construct courses that can confound and confuse but always entertain.

The cultural aspects of Dundee are enhanced by its **McManus Galleries** and the **University Botanical Gardens. Camperdown Park** and the **Wildlife Centre** are also stellar attractions for those who prefer outside activities.

Discovery Point is a state-of-the-art visitor center portraying the history of Captain Scott's Royal Research Ship *Discovery* and its Antarctic voyages. Built in Dundee, Britain's first scientific research vessel set sail on a voyage to the Antarctic in 1901. You may visit *Discovery* berthed adjacent to the visitor center. www.rrsdiscovery.com.

Verdant Works is a mill dating from 1833 that celebrates Dundee's jute industry. The Scottish industrial heritage center offers a range of audiovisual displays, computer activities, and sound and light effects along with a cafe and gift shop.

Dundee's other attractions include its four castles—Dudhope, Mains, Claypotts, and Broughty—its old steeple, and the **Mercat Cross,** which is moved about as the population center changes. The old steeple, standing at a height of 156 feet above the ground, dates from the fourteenth century. Climb to the top for a spectacular view. A replica of the old structure that was demolished in 1877, the Mercat Cross is currently located at the end of High Street.

Attention shoppers: Visit Tayside's regional shopping center, **Overgate.** From the rail station, proceed across the pedestrian bridge. Head up Union Street, and at the top turn left onto Nethergate. Cross the street to the Overgate Centre. Constructed in a curve around St. Mary's Church, its curved glass wall has the effect of bringing the outside inside. A series of balcony cafes provide respite and refreshment to weary shoppers.

The **Dundee Contemporary Arts Center,** at 152 Nethergate, contains works by artists from Scotland and from around the world. From the rail station, walk across the car parking area (or use the overpass) until you arrive at the main road called Marketgait. Turn left, and walk about 200 yards up Marketgait. Turn left onto Greenmarket, and follow the signs to SCIENCE CENTER/SEABRAES CAR PARK. *Hours:* 1100–1800 Tuesday–Saturday; 1200–1800 Sunday (open late on Thursday until 2000); admission is free; www.dca.org.uk.

Edinburgh–Dundee–Edinburgh

DEPART Waverley Station	ARRIVE Dundee Station	NOTES
0629	0813	M–Sa
0800	0922	M–Sa
0804	0918	Su
0900 (0910 Su)	1018 (1027 Su)	Daily
1000	1120	M–Sa
1027	1143	M–Sa
1055	1207	Su
1127	1236	M–Sa
1115	1248	Su

Then minimum hourly service through 2309 M–Sa; twice per hour until 1915, 2100, and 2225 Su.

DEPART Dundee Station	ARRIVE Waverley Station	NOTES
1434	1555	M–Sa
1504	1625	Su
1535 (1525 Su)	1656 (1659 Su)	Daily
1650	1822	M–Sa
1726 (1725 Su)	1849 (1900 Su)	Daily
1819	1935	Daily
1842	2009	M–Sa
1930 (1927 Su)	2048 (2036 Su)	Daily
2021	2131 (2136 Su)	Daily
2042	2216	M–Sa
2115 (2121 Su)	2250 (2243 Su)	Daily
2306 (2309 Su)	0041+1 (0036+1 Su)	Exc. Sa

+1=Arrives next day.

Adjacent to the arts center is the £5 million–plus **Dundee Science Centre** "Sensation." Award-winning Scottish architects Merrylees and Robertson effectively use natural light to convey the cathedral-like effect in Dundee's most recent attraction, touted as "a cathedral of science." www.sensation.org.uk.

Day Excursion to

Dunfermline

Andrew Carnegie's Birthplace

Depart from Edinburgh Waverley Station

Distance by train: 17 miles (27 km)

Average train time: 32 minutes

Train information and InterCity services: (0845) 748 4950

Tourist information: Tourist Information Centre, 1 High Street, Dunfermline, Fife KY12 7DL; *Tel:* (01383) 720999; *Fax:* (01383) 625807

www.dunfermlineonline.net

E-mail: admin@dunfermline.info

Hours: March 17–September 28: Monday–Saturday 0930–1700; July 7–August 30: Monday–Saturday 0930–1730, Sunday 1100–1600; October 1–March 16: Monday–Saturday 0930–1700

Notes: Cross St. Margaret's Drive in front of the station and follow the signposts to the tourist information center. Taxis queue at the front of the station. About £3.50 will see you to the city center. The bus stop is close to the station at an underpass on the left.

Dunfermline was once the capital of Scotland and holds an important position in Scottish history. The main points of interest are the Dunfermline Abbey, Abbot House, Pittencrieff Park, and Andrew Carnegie's birthplace. We suggest visiting the tourist information center first.

The walk is not too distant to the tourist information center and the main attractions in town. On foot allow about fifteen minutes to cover the ground between the train station and the center of the city.

The majestic spires of the **Dunfermline Abbey** dominate the town's skyline. Within the abbey are the graves of seven Scottish kings, including the **Tomb of Robert the Bruce.** The abbey was founded by Scotland's King David in the twelfth century as a Benedictine monastery. In the course of time, through royal gifts and other extensive endowments, it became one of the most magnificent establishments in Scotland. In its time the monastery has played host to a wide range of people, from Edward I of England to Oliver Cromwell.

The site of the Dunfermline Abbey has had continual Christian worship for about 1,500 years. In the fifth or sixth century, the first building on the site was the Culdee Church. Later it was rebuilt on a larger scale by Malcolm III, father of King David I, and was dedicated in 1072. Traces of both buildings are visible beneath gratings in the floor of the abbey's Old Nave.

From April through October the abbey church is open 1000–1630 Monday–Saturday and 1400–1630 on Sunday. Between October and April the abbey is closed, except for services. The abbey shop is open during the same hours as the church between April and October. www.dunfermlineabbey.co.uk.

Edinburgh–Dunfermline–Edinburgh

DEPART Waverley Station	ARRIVE Dunfermline Town Station	NOTES
0718	0749	M–Sa
0811	0844	M–Sa
0847	0918	M–Sa
0950 (0955 Su)	1022 (1028 Su)	Daily
1019	1050	M–Sa
1048	1119	M–Sa
1148 (1155 Su)	1219 (1231 Su)	Daily

With frequent service continuing at 18 and 49 minutes past the hour M–Sa, and alternating 15 and 55 minutes past the hour Su. Last train M–Sa at 2319, 2155 Su.

DEPART Dunfermline Town Station	ARRIVE Waverley Station	NOTES
1402	1439	M–Sa
1431	1506	M–Sa
1502	1540	M–Sa
1532 (1542 Su)	1607 (1621 Su)	Daily
1604	1638	M–Sa
1633	1708	M–Sa
1731 (1737 Su)	1808	Daily
1806	1841	M–Sa

With frequent service until 2344 M–Sa, and until 2226 Su.

The **Abbot House** is the oldest domestic building in Dunfermline and now houses the award-winning Heritage Centre, unfolding the history of Dunfermline. *Hours:* daily 0930–1630 year-round; www.abbothouse.co.uk. *Admission:* £4 adults.

Another attraction is **Pittencrieff Park,** a lovely area with its flower gardens, music pavilion, aviary, and museum. Andrew Carnegie, the Scottish-American philanthropist who was born in a humble weaver's cottage in Dunfermline in 1835, generously donated Pittencrieff Park and gave funds for its upkeep. The park has become a popular place for visitors to pause and reflect on his donations of a library, public baths, and a theater in addition to the park. During your stroll through the park, swing aboard *Old Pug* and marvel at the advances that have been made in railroading since its engine's fires were banked for the last time.

Andrew Carnegie's birthplace is open to the public daily from March through November from 1000 to 1700 (Sunday opening, 1400) and attracts thousands of visitors every year. From his humble beginnings Carnegie found his fortunes in the New World. Nevertheless, with his philanthropist attitude, he never forgot his hometown. At age thirty-three, with an annual income of $50,000, Carnegie said, "Beyond this never earn, make no effort to increase fortune, but spend the surplus each year for benevolent purposes." This he certainly did. His generosity in Dunfermline is administered today by a trust fund. A statue of the steel millionaire, erected by the citizens of Dunfermline in grateful appreciation of his many gifts to his native city, stands in the center of Pittencrieff.

When you visit Dunfermline, you will be following in the footsteps of British royalty. Both Queen Victoria and Queen Mary visited here, and in 1972 Queen Elizabeth and Prince Philip were present to dedicate a Royal Pew in celebration of the abbey's 900th anniversary. You'll find, however, that Dunfermline extends a royal welcome to all of its visitors.

An "Out-and-Back" Excursion to

Inverness

Highland Gateway

Depart from Edinburgh Waverley Station

Distance by train: 176 miles (283 km)

Average train time: 3 hours, 40 minutes

Train information and InterCity services: (0845) 748 4950; First ScotRail services: (0845) 7550 0339

Tourist information: The Highlands of Scotland Tourist Board, Castle Wynd, Inverness IV2 3BJ; *Tel:* 0845 225 5121; *Fax:* 01506 832 222

www.inverness-scotland.com or **www.visithighlands.com**

E-mail: ken.gordon@highland.gov.uk

Hours: March 31–May 25: Monday–Saturday 0900–1700, Sunday 1000–1600; May 26–June 29: Monday–Saturday 0900–1800, Sunday 0930–1600; June 30–August 31: Monday–Saturday 0900–1800, Sunday 0930–1700; September 1–September 14: Monday–Saturday 0900–1800, Sunday 0930–1600; September 15–December 31: Monday–Saturday 0900–1700, Sunday 1000–1600

Notes: For the shortest route turn left when leaving the train station, and continue until you see Marks & Spencer. Cross the street, and continue up Inglis Street, then turn right onto High Street, walking until you come to McDonald's. Cross the pedestrian walk, past the Town House and across Castle Wynd, where the tourist information center is located at the top of a short flight of stairs.

The position of Inverness at the eastern head of Loch Ness, Scotland's famous inland sea loch, earns the city its title, "Capital of the Highlands." From Inverness you may get to more places in the Highlands than from any other location in Scotland. For this reason we have termed the excursion to Inverness an "out-and-back" excursion, for you may want to use Inverness as your base for exploring the Highlands.

There is so much to do in and around Inverness that not even a series of action-packed days could absorb all of the possible activities. Here are but a few of the sightseeing possibilities in and around Inverness: Visit the castle grounds, and walk along the garden paths at the River Ness. Cruise on Loch Ness, as far away as Urquhart Castle if you like, where most of the sightings of the Loch Ness "monster" (or "beastie," as the locals call it) have occurred. Journey on the renowned railway line between Inverness and Kyle of Lochalsh along 82 miles of railroad right-of-way that involved beauty, romance, history, and endurance in its building. Forge northward to Thurso, Scotland's most northerly town, on a dramatic rail route along 162 miles of Scotland's better scenery. If you prefer the solitude of surf breaking on a shore, take a train east to Nairn, 15 miles from Inverness. Or train south a mere 30 miles to Scotland's St. Moritz, where the ski boom has transformed the town of Aviemore into a continental sports village.

Eons ago **Loch Ness** was carved out along a geological fault between two land masses in northern Scotland. The earth's forces formed a long, narrow lake of approximately 24 miles with depths of up to 750 feet, possibly 1,000 feet in some parts. To go to Inverness and not have a look at Loch Ness would be like eating one potato chip and throwing the rest of the bag away. We urge you to dip into the mystery, history, and beauty of Loch Ness.

Loch Ness is reportedly the home of **"Nessie," the Loch Ness monster,** which has often been described as one of the world's greatest mysteries. The first recorded sighting of Nessie was made by an unimpeachable witness (St. Columba, no less) in AD 565. According to the report, the monster attacked one of the members of his group. Since then, there have been too many visual and photographic sightings of the monster for it to be easily explained.

Fact or fiction, there is a continuing similarity in the descriptions of Nessie given by most of those who claim to have seen the monster over the years. Photographs also support a common description, that of a small head at the end of a long, thin neck, with an overall body length between 20 and 30 feet. Underwater evidence gathered by every means from space-age technology to yellow submarines suggests it may have four flippers. Zoologists recognize this description as a plesiosaur, a type of marine dinosaur that existed more than seventy million years ago and should be extinct.

Scientific data notwithstanding, the fact that malt whiskeys have been produced in large volumes throughout the area since the beginning of recorded time may account for many or all of the sightings!

Inverness also offers the town attractions of the **James Pringle Weavers and Clan Tartan Centre,** the **Scottish Kiltmaker Visitor Centre, Floral Hall, St. Andrew's Cathedral,** and the **Inverness Museum and Art Gallery.** Enjoy the **Castle Garrison Encounter** and the **Aquadome and Sports Centre.** Dolphin fans should not miss the **dolphin-watching boat trips.**

If your visit to Inverness is limited, you may want to try the excellent Caledonian Sleeper services. For example, you can board a sleeper one night in London and awaken the following morning in Inverness. Spend an entire day sightseeing, then board another sleeper back to London.

Going in and out of Inverness by sleeper could permit you to board the 0900 train from there to the Kyle of Lochalsh, where you arrive at 1128, then ferry to the Isle of Skye, soak in the sights, and leave Lochalsh on the 1715 to be back in Inverness by 1949 with some time to spare before boarding the sleeper again.

Departing from the Inverness Station, the journey to Kyle of Lochalsh takes about two and a half hours. The railway between Inverness and Kyle of Lochalsh has been accorded the distinction of being the premier scenic rail line in Great Britain. It offers a lovely ride through the Highland towns of Dingwall, Garve, Achnasheen, and Stromeferry before terminating on the western shores of Scotland overlooking the Isle of Skye. The rail line passes through a region of superlative natural beauty loaded with Scottish folklore. This 82-mile journey, which appears rather uninspiring in the cold prosaic type of the timetable, is in reality a rare mixture of beauty, romance, history, and endurance.

Edinburgh–Inverness–Edinburgh

DEPART Waverley Station	ARRIVE Inverness Station	NOTES
0632	1029	M–Sa (2)
0834	1154	M–Sa
0925	1309	Su
0935	1327	M–Sa (1)
1135	1506	M–Sa
1335 (1350 Su)	1705 (1738 Su)	Daily

DEPART Inverness Station	ARRIVE Waverley Station	NOTES
1247	1624	M–Sa
1325	1642	Su
1451	1825	M–Sa (1)
1615	2004	Su (2)
1653	2029	M–Sa
1830	2203	Su
1843	2219	M–Sa
2015	0009+1	M–Sa (2)

(1) Change trains in Perth.
(2) Change trains in Stirling.
+1=Arrives next day.

An "Out-and-Back" Excursion to

Kyle of Lochalsh

Scenic Journey

Tourist Information: The Highlands of Scotland Tourist Board, Tourist Information Centre, Kyle of Lochalsh: The Car Park IV40 8AQ; *Tel:* 0845 225 5121; *Fax:* (01599) 534808

www.visithighlands.com

E-mail: info@visitscotland.com

Hours: April to October: Monday–Saturday 0900–1730; mid-July to mid-August: also Sunday 0900–1800

Notes: The tourist information center is conveniently located midway between the train station and the ferry dock. To reach it use the stairs to the overpass, and then walk downhill.

When the railroad opened in 1870, the western terminal was the town of Stromeferry on the saltwater Loch Carron. Although the original intention was to build right through to Kyle of Lochalsh, construction money ran out, and Stromeferry remained the terminus for twenty-seven years. Completing the remaining 26 miles of right-of-way proved to be a formidable task of engineering, forging through solid rock and requiring cuts up to 88 feet deep. Even the area of the train terminal at Kyle required blasting and removing rock. When you reach Kyle of Lochalsh, pause to appreciate the backbreaking toil that created the train station and the right-of-way leading to it.

A bridge was built between Kyle of Lochalsh and Kyleakin on the Isle of Skye. The ruins of **Castle Moil** stand on a promontory close to the Kyleakin ferry dock. During the time of the Vikings, the castle was the home of a Norwegian princess. History relates that the princess made quite a bundle during her stay in the castle by exacting a toll from ships passing through the narrow straits. To ensure prompt payment she had a heavy chain attached between the castle and the Kyle of Lochalsh, which was drawn taut when a ship approached. The chain was probably depreciated and charged off as a business expense, for there's no evidence of its existence today.

Scottish legends leap out at you as the train plies between Inverness and Kyle. **The Castle at Dingwall** was said to have been ruled by Finlaec, the father of Macbeth. In a graveyard opposite the castle ruins, the ghost of a young girl wanders nightly in search of her faithless lover. Approaching Garve, you'll pass **Loch Garve,** where even in the dead of winter there is a small part that never freezes—attributed to the water-horse monsters who carry off local girls. The inn at Garve purveys Athole Brose, a libation of Scottish whiskey, oats, and honey, several drafts of which could produce a whole herd of water horses.

The right-of-way passes areas that stir the imagination. Departing Achnasheen en route to Stromeferry, passengers may get a fleeting glance at the **Torridon Mountains,** the oldest mountains on Earth. They are so old that geologists have been unable to find any trace of fossils, indicating the mountains were formed long before life of any description began. The range, consisting of peaks such as Liathach (3,456 feet), Beinn Eighe (3,300 feet), and Beinn Alligin (3,021 feet), has sparkling quartzite peaks, often mistaken for snow.

In the seventeenth century, Brahan Seer, the Highlands' prophet extraordinaire, said, "The day will come when every stream will have its bridge, balls of fire will pass rapidly up and down the Strath of Peffery and carriages without horses will cross the country from sea to sea." And so it came to pass: On August 10, 1870, the railroad steam engines began operating from sea to sea.

Edinburgh–Kyle of Lochalsh–Edinburgh

Note: A day trip from Edinburgh to Kyle of Lochalsh and return to Edinburgh is not possible on Sunday because the only Sunday trip from Inverness to Kyle of Lochalsh arrives in Kyle at 2029; there is no return trip from Kyle on Sunday later than 1522. A two-day weekend excursion is possible, however, by departing Edinburgh on Saturday at 0632 and returning on Sunday by departing Kyle at 1522 (change in Inverness) and arriving Edinburgh at 2205.

DEPART Waverley Station	ARRIVE Kyle Station	NOTES
0632	1326	M–Sa (1, 2)
1335	2026	M–Sa (2)

DEPART Kyle Station	ARRIVE Waverley Station	NOTES
1203	1825	M–Sa (1,2)
1522	2203	Su (2)
1715	0009+1	M–Sa (1, 2)

(1) Change trains in Stirling.
(2) Change trains in Inverness.
+1=Arrives next day.

Day Excursion to

Linlithgow

Birthplace of Mary, Queen of Scots

Depart from Edinburgh Waverley Station or Glasgow Queen Street Station

Distance by train: 18 miles (29 km)

Average train time: 21 minutes

Train information and InterCity services: (0845) 748 4950

Tourist information: County Buildings, High Street, Linlithgow, West Lothian, Scotland EH49 7EZ; *Tel:* (01506) 775 320; *Fax:* (01506) 671373

www.linlithgow.com

Hours: Monday–Thursday 0830–1700, Friday 0830–1600, Saturday 1000–1600, Sunday 1100–1500

Notes: Exit the train station main exit onto Station Road. Turn left onto High Street. Walk until you see the traffic lights and pedestrian crossing. Cross over High Street, then turn left toward the Cross. The tourist center is at the Cross, recognizable by the cross-shaped well in the center.

Linlithgow lies between Edinburgh and Glasgow and stands in the midst of Scotland's history. The town offers so many attractions that we advise going there early and planning to stay late—very late.

Linlithgow Palace, the birthplace of Mary, Queen of Scots, is the town's main attraction. It lies in what historians would describe as a splendid ruin. Nevertheless, it tells a poignant tale of Scotland's royal history in an intriguing manner. The palace was the successor to a wooden fortress that burned down in 1424. King James V, father of Mary, Queen of Scots, was born in Linlithgow Palace in 1512. Defeated by the English at the Battle of Solway Moss in November 1542, the king died on December 14 of that year, only six days after the birth of his daughter. The infant child became Mary, Queen of Scots, at six days of age.

In the years to follow, Bonnie Prince Charlie and Oliver Cromwell took brief residence in the palace. At the beginning of 1746, troops belonging to the Duke of Cumberland's army were billeted there. As they marched out on February 1, fires were left burning that soon spread throughout the building. Since then, the palace has remained unroofed and uninhabited. There has been talk about restoring Linlithgow Palace, but as it stands now, just let your imagination "restore" it. *Tel:* (01506) 842896. *Hours:* April–September: 0930–1730 daily; October–March: 0930–1630 daily. *Admission:* Adults £5.50, children £3.30, senior citizens £4.40.

A short walk westward from the palace along High Street you'll discover **"The Linlithgow Story,"** a fascinating museum telling of life in one of Scotland's most important royal burghs.

Edinburgh–Linlithgow–Edinburgh

DEPART Waverley Station	ARRIVE Linlithgow Station	NOTES
0745 (0800 Su)	0804 (0818 Su)	Daily
0803	0825	M–Sa
0815	0833	M–Sa
0831	0855	M–Sa
0845	0903	M–Sa
0903 (0900 Su)	0925 (0918 Su)	Daily
0915	0933	M–Sa
0933	0955	Daily

M–Sa service continues at 3, 15, 32, and 45 minutes past the hour; Su service continues hourly on the hour and 35 minutes past the hour. Last train at 2333 M–Sa, 2300 Su.

DEPART Linlithgow Station	ARRIVE Waverley Station	NOTES
1437	1502	Daily
1444 (1459 Su)	1505 (1521 Su)	Daily
1507	1536	M–Sa
1514	1535	M–Sa
1537	1604	Daily
1544 (1559 Su)	1607 (1623 Su)	Daily

Plus other very frequent service until 2333 with departures at 7, 13, 37, and 45 minutes past the hour M–Sa, and 29, 40, and 59 minutes past the hour Su. Last train at 2345 M–Sa, 2303 Su.

A mere 100 yards from the rail station, the Union Canal runs through the center of Linlithgow. Some 31 miles in length, it was once a major thoroughfare for taking coal from the mines in Falkirk to Edinburgh. From the Canal Basin at Manse Road, you can board the *St. Magdalene* at 1400, a diesel-powered replica of a Victorian steam packet boat, for a cruise to the Avon Aqueduct (two-and-a-half-hour cruise: £8 adults, £4 children). For shorter trips (about twenty minutes), board a steam packet boat replica, the *Victoria*. Departures are every half hour 1400–1630. Both boats operate Saturday and Sunday afternoons from Easter until the end of September; the last departure is at 1630 (£3.00 adults, £2.50 children/senior citizens); www.lucs.org.uk.

A short distance from the town, visit **the Binns,** one of the most "lived in" mansions in Scotland. It has been occupied by the Dalyell family for more than 350 years. The house dates from the sixteenth century. General Tam Dalyell (1599–1685) had some hair-raising adventures in his lifetime, including an escape from the Tower of London and military service in Russia. The house reflects the early-seventeenth-century transition from a fortified castle to a gracious, more comfortable house. Open June through September, 1400–1700, Saturday–Wednesday (£9.00 adults, £6.50 children/senior citizens, £22.00 family). www.nts.org.uk.

A short bus ride will take you to the seaport town of **Bo'ness** (www.bo-ness.org.uk) with its own attractions ranging in historical significance from Roman ruins to the Industrial Revolution. Bo'ness also has a reconstructed Victorian railway station, where you may board the **Bo'ness & Kinneil Railway** steam train for a delightfully romantic 7-mile round-trip, including a stop at the **Birkhill clay mine,** where fireclay was mined. Without fireclay, many say there could never have been an Industrial Revolution.

The Bo'ness & Kinneil Railway operates April–October on Saturday and Sunday at 1045, 1215, 1405, 1535; July–August departures are at the same times Tuesday through Sunday. Train fare: £6.00 adults, £3.00 children, £5.00 senior citizens, £15.00

family. Train and clay mine: £8.00 adults, £4.00 children, £7.50 senior citizens, £20.00 family. The Scottish Railway Exhibition is free; www.srps.org.uk/railway.

Back in Linlithgow, be sure to stop at the **Four Marys' Public House** on High Street for great atmosphere, excellent libations, and superb food. Don't miss it!

Day Excursion to

Montrose

Seaside Resort

Depart from Edinburgh Waverley Station
Distance by train: 90 miles (145 km)
Average train time: 2 hours, 8 minutes
Train information and InterCity services: (0845) 748 4950
Tourist information: Montrose Tourist Information Centre, Panmure Place, Montrose DD10 8HE; *Tel:* (01674) 673232
www.angusanddundee.co.uk
E-mail: dundee@visitscotland.com
Hours: Monday–Saturday 1000–1700
Notes: From the station turn right onto Western Road until it reaches Hume Street, where a quick left followed by a right turn 1 block away onto High Street puts you in view of the Town House and its grand piazza. Stay on the right-hand side of High Street, and walk a short distance south. Turn left onto George Street, and follow this to Panmure Place, left onto Panmure Place.

Travelers who have visited many villages, towns, and cities throughout continental Europe and the British Isles learn to "read" the history of a place through its architecture and street names. Montrose is an outstanding example of this point.

Even at first glance Montrose does not look like a typical Scottish town. High Street is wide and has many elegant houses with gabled ends on the street side. There was a time in the city's history when only Edinburgh surpassed it in prosperity and elegance. The **Town House of Montrose**—Americans would consider it the city hall—is fronted by a broad piazza. From its facade Montrose looks more like a page out of a Flemish picture book rather than a Scottish one. Great houses are surrounded by garden walls—not ordinary ones, but remarkably high garden walls. It has oddly named streets, such as "America" and "California"—another hint that the history of Montrose is different.

When Glasgow was still a village, Montrose was one of Scotland's principal ports. For centuries the merchants of Montrose traded with the Low Countries. It was only natural that they would bring back some of the things they admired on the Continent: for example, houses with gabled ends to the street side as they are constructed in the Netherlands. The wide streets? From the promenades of Europe, no doubt. And what about the street names? Almost within living memory, ships sailed from Montrose to North America carrying emigrants and returned laden with lumber.

For the last thirty years, North Sea oil has virtually pumped life back into the city's harbor, where, until the recent past, an air of sleepiness prevailed as trade with North America subsided. The first part of the civic motto of Montrose—*Mare ditat* (the sea enriches)—is again true.

Baffled by the high garden walls? More than 300 years ago, the streets of Montrose ran red with blood when a band of Highlanders raided the town. The inhabitants were defenseless as they slept without the protection of a city wall and with only low garden walls about their residences. The carnage was swift and horrible. Within months the majority of the walls within the town were built up to their current height to prevent attacks from intruders.

When you arrive in Montrose from Edinburgh, take a moment at the train station to look west, away from the town. You will see the **Montrose Basin Wildlife Centre,** where thousands of wildfowl forage for food, including the pink-footed Arctic goose during the winter. It is well worth a visit; www.montrosebasin.org.uk.

The tourist office has a wealth of information available regarding both Montrose and the area surrounding it. The *Town Guide* leaflet (free) provides information on Montrose. There is also a street map for sale that lists many points of interest. Note for shoppers: Many stores have "half-day closing" on Wednesday afternoons.

Montrose is one of Scotland's leading seaside resorts, and it can become crowded during the peak summer season. Four miles of magnificent sandy beaches attract many an inlander to the sea. Beaches also have a way of indicating their latitudes, just as places reflect their history in their names and facades. Beaches in Britain, for example, attract huge crowds in summertime, but note the distribution of the people on the beach. Except for a hardy few, the majority of holidaymakers are on the sands and not in the water.

Edinburgh–Montrose–Edinburgh

DEPART Waverley Station	ARRIVE Montrose Station	NOTES
0728	0912	M–Sa
0804	0949	Su
0928	1104	M–Sa
1027	1216	M–Sa
1055	1237	Su
1228	1407	M–Sa
1240	1424	Su

DEPART Montrose Station	ARRIVE Waverley Station	NOTES
1344	1529	M–Sa
1430	1625	Su
1530	1727	M–Sa
1548	1741	Su
1749	1934	Daily
1856	2048	M–Sa
1948	2136	Su
1951	2131	M–Sa
2048	2243	Su
2144	2350	M–Sa
2210	0005+1	M–F
2225	0041+1	Daily

+1=Arrives next day.

The city's large indoor swimming pool and two eighteen-hole golf courses, plus numerous other sports facilities, make up for the other-than-tepid temperature of the North Sea waters off Montrose. The seaside also offers something rather unusual—on the beaches beside Elephant Rock, you can search for semiprecious stones such as agates, amethysts, carnelian, and onyx.

Cultural life is not lacking in Montrose. The name of William Lamb immediately relates to the world of art in fine sculptures and etchings. This well-known artist's studio is maintained at 24 Market Street. On Panmure Place, the **Montrose Museum** houses an excellent collection of art relating to the natural and maritime history of the area. *Hours:* 1000–1700 Monday–Saturday.

If you've been waiting for us to drop the other shoe, the second part of the Montrose civic motto is *rosa decorat* (the rose adorns). If you walk in the **Mid-Links Park** on a summer day, the air is scented with the perfume of roses. Although the city's name has nothing to do with roses—it was originally called "Monros" (the mossy promontory)—there are few towns in Scotland where roses grow more abundantly.

Day Excursion to

Perth

First Capital of Scotland

Depart from Edinburgh Waverley Station

Distance by train: 58 miles (93 km)

Average train time: 1 hour, 30 minutes

Train information and InterCity services: (0845) 748 4950

Tourist information: Tourist Information Centre, Lower City Mills, West Mill Street, Perth PH3 1LQ; *Tel:* (01738) 450600; *Fax:* (01738) 444863; Activity Line: (01738) 444144

www.perthshire.co.uk

E-mail: perth@visitscotland.com

Hours: April–June: Monday–Saturday 0930–1700, Sunday 1030–1530; July–August: Monday–Saturday 0930–1800, Sunday 1000–1630; September–October: Monday–Saturday 0930–1700, Sunday 1030–1530; November–April: Monday–Saturday 1000–1600.

Notes: The tourist information center is located in the Mill buildings. From the rail station, turn left onto Leonard Street. Follow until you reach the modern A. K. Bell Library; then cross onto York Place, and go straight ahead to a small street called New Row. Follow to the end, and take a right onto West Mill Street. The Mill buildings lie ahead.

"Behold a river more mighty than the Tiber!" History relates that these words were uttered by a Roman commander as, approaching what is now the city of Perth, he caught his first glimpse of the River Tay. Beginning as a mountain stream at Ben Laoigh, the Tay trickles down the hillsides, gaining tributaries as it flows on its 120-mile journey to the sea. Perth stands astride the Tay, their history inextricably linked.

Two vehicular bridges plus a rail bridge (all with pedestrian footpaths) cross the River Tay today, but "Old Man River" Tay kept the locals quite busy in earlier years, when floods swept away the first bridge in 1210 and its successor in 1621, leaving travelers no alternative but ferries for the 150 years to follow.

Perth is often referred to as "the gateway to the Highlands." This is not its only attraction, for its prominent position in the history of Scotland has left a legacy of distinctive buildings in an area compact enough to be easily examined on foot. Perth's architecture mixes the modern with the ancient. City fathers are justly proud of Perth's sports centers, with an ice rink, swimming pools, tennis courts, and indoor bowling stadium.

Tay Street fronts the river on the city side. Without straying too far from the river, it is possible to enjoy the riverside and visit places of interest such as St. John's Kirk, the Perth Art Gallery and Museum, the Fergusson Gallery, the Lower City Mills, and the Fair Maid's House, as described in Sir Walter Scott's novel *The Fair Maid of Perth*. Turn left off Tay Street at Queen's Bridge, and proceed 2 blocks to sight St. John's to your right. One of Perth's most famous landmarks, **St. John's Kirk** is where the Protestant reformer John Knox, following his return from exile in

Geneva, preached his famous sermon against idolatry in 1559. The congregation was so taken with his sermon that they wrecked the church and then went on to create similar outrages on the monastic houses of the friars. Originally founded in 1126 and revamped over the centuries, St. John's Kirk now is a fine example of Gothic-style architecture from the mid-sixteenth century.

Returning to Tay Street, continue to walk to the Perth Bridge, where you will find the **Perth Art Gallery and Museum** on George Street close to the bridge approach. In quest of the **Fair Maid's House,** ask directions when leaving the museum to its location at North Port, a short distance away; there are several ways to reach it.

Close by the Fair Maid's House is the **North Inch,** a beautifully situated park bordered by Georgian terraces and the River Tay and overlooked by Balhousie Castle, the historic home of the **Black Watch Regimental Museum.** Across the river lies the colorful Branklyn Garden, owned by the National Trust for Scotland and said to be "the finest two acres of private garden in the country." It sits on the wooded slopes of Kinnoull Hill and offers an excellent view over the town.

Edinburgh–Perth–Edinburgh

DEPART Waverley Station	ARRIVE Perth Station	NOTES
0629	0747	M–Sa
0834	0950	M–Sa
0935 (0925 Su)	1053 (1052 Su)	Daily
1135	1253	M–Sa
1335 (1350 Su)	1453 (1512 Su)	Daily

Five more trains until 2239 M–Sa; final departure at 2234 Su.

DEPART Perth Station	ARRIVE Waverley Station	NOTES
1501	1624	M–Sa
1525	1642	Su
1700	1825	M–Sa
1909	2029	M–Sa
2102 (2046 Su)	2219 (2203 Su)	Daily
2238	0018+1	M–Sa

+1=Arrives next day.

For centuries Perth has been a prosperous market town, serving a rich agricultural hinterland and profiting from its geographical position in the heart of Scotland. The town's livestock markets flourish, with the famous Perth Bull Sales in February and October attracting buyers from all over the world. Perth's reputation as a trading center, however, rests principally with its excellent shops. Much of Perth's center is traffic free and bedecked with floral displays.

An excellent addition to Perth's city center attractions is the Fergusson Gallery in the Round House (Perth's old waterworks) at Marshall Place. Here you can view the largest and most important collection of the works of the famous Scottish colorist John Duncan Fergusson. Three specially designed galleries display rotating exhibits taken from a total collection of 6,000 items.

Scone Palace, a mile north of Perth, stands close to the historic spot where Scottish kings were crowned through 1651. The Moot Hill, which stands in front of the palace, is an artificial mound that was constructed in the Dark Ages. Traditionally, Scottish chiefs and lairds came to Scone to pledge their allegiance to the king. This they did, filling their boots before they left home with the earth of their own districts. Thus, with the earth still in their boots, they were standing on their own land when they swore allegiance to their king. Afterward they ceremoniously emptied their boots on the Moot Hill (or Boot Hill, as it is appropriately known today).

The palace is open to the public, and there is an admission charge. Take bus No. 58 from the Leonard Street Bus Station, and check with the information center for details if you plan to go. By the way, don't plan to heist the Stone of Scone—it is resting safely back in Edinburgh Castle.

Day Excursion to

St. Andrews

World's Golf Capital

Depart from Edinburgh Waverley Station

Distance by train: 57 miles (92 km)

Average train time: 1 hour

Train information and InterCity services: (0845) 748 4950

Tourist information: St. Andrews Tourist Information Centre, No. 70 Market Street, Fife KY16 9NU; *Tel:* (01334) 472021; *Fax:* (01334) 478422

www.standrews.com or **www.standrews.co.uk**

E-mail: standrews@visitscotland.com

Hours: April–June and September–October 14: Monday–Saturday 0915–1700, Sunday 1100–1600; July–August: Monday–Saturday 0915–1900, Sunday 1000–1700; October 15–March: Monday–Saturday 0930–1700

Notes: Leuchars is the rail station serving St. Andrews. From outside Leuchars Station, take the No. 95 bus (check latest bus numbers by calling 01334 474238). The trip to the town of St. Andrews is about fifteen minutes by bus. Buses run regularly from Monday to Saturday, usually every thirty minutes. Limited Sunday bus service is available. Disembark at St. Andrews Bus Station, then turn right onto City Road. Cross the street here, and take the next street on your left to Market Street. Walk down Market Street for about five minutes, and you will see an old fountain in the middle of the street. Walk another 500 yards, then cross the street to the tourist information center. Watch for the blue thistle sign. Or, if you're in a hurry, a taxi into St. Andrews costs about £10.

No town in the world is so completely identified with one game as St. Andrews is with golf. No matter where in the world they have played the game, there is nothing as exhilarating to devoted golfers as a round on the **Old Course** at St. Andrews (www.standrews.org.uk). Anyone may play the Old Course, provided he or she can produce a current, official handicap certificate, or a letter of introduction from a bona fide golf club, together with proof of identity. This rule applies only to play on the Old Course. Play on the other six courses at St. Andrews is not affected. The links belong to the townspeople and, as such, are open to all.

In summer and autumn most available tee times on the Old Course are reserved, in many instances a year in advance. Tiger Woods has increased St. Andrews' popularity even more. To be certain of obtaining a starting time for the Old Course, it is essential to apply well in advance of the date of play. Latecomers still have a chance because some starting times are retained each day for issue by a random ballot procedure. To enter your ballot, it is necessary to apply to the starter by 1400 on the previous day. (The Old Course is closed on Sunday.)

To obtain full details and reservations for golf in St. Andrews, telephone the St. Andrews Links Trust at (0133) 446 6666 or visit www.standrews.org.uk to book online as far in advance of your visit as possible (*E-mail:* reservations@standrews.org.uk). In total St. Andrews and its surrounding area list sixteen courses from which to choose. For information on courses throughout the St. Andrews area, call the St. Andrews Links Trust or the St. Andrews Tourist Information Centre.

How old is the game of golf? Apparently no one knows. Seemingly it originated on the stretches of grassland along Scotland's east coast next to the sandy beaches—the ground known in Scotland for centuries as "links." The sand dunes interspersed throughout the grasslands became the original traps or bunkers. A round of golf consisted of whatever number of holes were possible in the terrain of a particular link. For more on the history of golf, ask the tourist information center about the British Golf Museum.

At first the pastime of golf was indulged in predominantly by the Scottish aristocracy. With the advent of the inexpensive golf ball, however, golfing in Scotland soon became a mass sport. Aristocracy again moved to the fore by establishing clubhouses for the leisured gentlemen, where they could attend dinners to observe the end of matches between players.

Edinburgh–St. Andrews–Edinburgh

There is no train service to St. Andrews; the nearest station is Leuchars, 10 km from St. Andrews. A number of local bus services provide direct travel from Leuchars to St. Andrews. Consult the bus timetable in the station bus stop shelter.

DEPART Waverley Station	ARRIVE Leuchars Station	NOTES
0530	0632	M–Sa
0728	0825	M–Sa
0828	0923	M–Sa
0900 (0910 Su)	1003 (1013 Su)	Daily
1000	1104	M–Sa
1027	1128	M–Sa
1100	1203	M–Sa

Departures continue hourly on the hour until 2309; Su, every 2 hours until 2225.

DEPART Leuchars Station	ARRIVE Waverley Station	NOTES
1548	1656	M–Sa
1618	1726	M–Sa
1701 (1637 Su)	1822 (1741 Su)	Daily
1739 (1737 Su)	1849 (1900 Su)	Daily
1831	1935	Daily
1939	2101	Su
1944	2048	M–Sa

M–Sa departures continue at 2033, 2054, 2128, 2227, 2256, and 2325. Su departures continue at 2032, 2133, 2252, and 2328.

Such was the case at St. Andrews in 1754 when twenty-two "noblemen and gentlemen, being admirers of the ancient and healthful exercise of the golf," founded the Society of St. Andrews Golfers, which is now known throughout the world as the Royal and Ancient Golf Club.

St. Andrews and history go together hand in hand. Such stellar sights as the St. Andrews Castle, with its bottle dungeon and secret passage, vie for your attention along with the ruins of **St. Andrews Cathedral** (www.historicscotland.gov.uk), once the largest in Scotland. Mary, Queen of Scots, had a house in St. Andrews that you can still see. The town is the home of Scotland's oldest university, founded in 1410–1411. Long before Columbus arrived in America or Cooke disembarked in Australia, students were attending classes at **St. Andrews University.** Another attraction is **St. Mary's College** and its unique quadrangle. Founded in 1537, St. Mary's is a part of the university complex. To visit St. Andrews and to roam its streets and scenes is to establish a tangible link with the past.

Of all the places and views, we give our nod to **St. Andrews Castle** (*Tel:* [0133] 447 7196) overlooking St. Andrews Bay. Initially constructed in 1200, the castle was destroyed and rebuilt during a war between Scotland and England, only to be demolished again during the Reformation. The savagery of those times can be noted on a stone outside the castle gate where George Wishart was burned at the stake. The castle has been in ruins since the seventeenth century, when much of its stone was removed for repairing the harbor. *Admission:* £7.60 adult, £4.60 child, £6.10 senior.

St. Andrews Castle may be reached by proceeding along North Street until reaching Castle Street, where you turn left and then proceed 1 block to the castle. Continuing 1 block farther on North Street will put you in front of the ruins of St. Andrews Cathedral.

Golfer or not, you must see the **Royal and Ancient Clubhouse of St. Andrews** during your stay. Though founded in 1754, the current clubhouse was built in 1854. The Royal and Ancient Golf Club is now the ruling authority of the game, and its clubhouse is recognized as the world headquarters for the game of golf. From the castle ruins walk along the Scores until you come to Gillespie Terrace. From this point the clubhouse and the eighteenth hole of the Old Course come into view.

Day Excursion to

Stirling

Stirling Castle

Depart from Edinburgh Waverley Station

Distance by train: 37 miles (59 km)

Average train time: 50 minutes

Train information and InterCity services: (0845) 748 4950

Tourist information: Stirling Tourist Information Centre, 41 Dumbarton Road, Stirling FK8 2QQ; *Tel:* (01786) 475019; *Fax:* (01786) 450039

www.visitscottishheartlands.com

E-mail: stirlingtic@visitscotland.com

Hours: July and August: Monday–Saturday 0900–1830, Sunday 0930–1700. The center operates on more restricted hours during winter.

Notes: To get there from the train station, cross the road directly in front of the station, and follow Station Road; then make a left turn onto Murray Place, a short distance. Walk to the first traffic light to the pedestrian section of Port Street, and turn right onto Dumbarton Road, immediately opposite the city wall. Total walking time is no more than ten minutes.

All the information you might need for an enjoyable day excursion in Stirling is available at the Royal Burgh of Stirling Visitor Centre, Castle Esplanade; *Tel:*

(01786) 479901. Several publications describing walks around Stirling are available. One of particular interest is *Stirling Heritage Trail,* published by the Stirling District Council. It covers a course starting and ending at Stirling Castle and includes photographs and drawings as well as colorful text on the history of Stirling Old Town.

Stirling Castle cannot be ignored. Standing on a 250-foot rock overlooking the River Forth Valley, it offers one of the finest panoramic views in Scotland. The area surrounding the crag on which the castle sits has given up relics of early humans' presence from the Stone Age down through the Bronze Age. There is no evidence that the Romans occupied the area, but it seems implausible that they didn't "take the high ground."

Stirling Castle has witnessed endless struggles for power. Kings and queens have been crowned in its halls and great battles fought on the plain below it. Originally named Striveling, which may be translated as "a place of streams," Stirling has been the scene of strife within the Scottish nation since before the time of recorded history. The town of Stirling and its castle truly stand at the crossroads of Scotland. Its position overlooking the Forth Valley and the crossing of the River Forth at its tidal limits has contributed to its past and present importance.

The castle as seen today began to develop around 1370 with the accession of the Stuart kings, serving as a royal residence from then until the son of Mary, Queen of Scots, James VI of Scotland, departed for London in 1603 to become James I of England. Scotland's tragic queen spent the first five years of her life in and around Stirling Castle. The castle is perhaps the finest example of Renaissance architecture in Scotland, most of its buildings dating from the fifteenth and sixteenth centuries. As it was the royal Stuart residence, Scotland's kings and queens held court there, and parliaments met on its premises.

The Royal Burgh of Stirling Visitor and Tourist Information Centre just below the castle combines a multilanguage audiovisual presentation and photographic exhibition of Stirling Castle through seven centuries. A bookstore and souvenir shop are included. According to its innovators, it is the first building in Europe to be designed specifically to bring alive the history of a town.

All is bustle and noise as ships from France and the Netherlands unload their cargoes and farmers drive their cattle to market. Stirling's market, now the city's Broad Street, is lined with shops selling everything from swords to spices. Meanwhile, back at the castle, a roistering banquet is being held in the great hall, packed with honored guests.

Throughout Stirling during the summer months, the presence of flowers is always evident. You will notice this first in the railway station, and it continues all around town. Possibly Stirling developed its love for flowers from the King's Knot, an octagonal, stepped mound laid out as the royal gardens in 1627–1628 beneath the walls of Stirling Castle by an Englishman, William Watts, who was brought from London to supervise the project. The raised central portion of the Knot is thought to have originated as a Bronze Age burial mound and was probably used as an outdoor royal court for tournaments before being incorporated into the formal gardens by Mr. Watts.

There are many historic buildings in Stirling. Below the castle stands the imposing **Church of the Holy Rood.** It has witnessed great moments in history. Here, at its altar, James VI of Scotland, and subsequently James I of England, was crowned at the age of eighteen months to succeed his exiled mother. The tower of the church still bears the marks of the 1745 rebellion, when Bonnie Prince Charlie's troops attempted to capture Stirling Castle. In the overture to the Reformation, the strident voice of John Knox boomed from the church pulpit.

Stirling is indeed a historic center that has played a vital role in the making of Scotland—an atmosphere that is hard to match. Over the centuries of its involvement in historical events, Stirling has preserved its heritage.

Edinburgh–Stirling–Edinburgh

DEPART Waverley Station	**ARRIVE** Stirling Station	**NOTES**
0703	0754	M–Sa
0733	0824	M–Sa

M–Sa service continues every 30 minutes until 2033, then hourly until 2333.

0933	1029	Su
1035	1125	Su

Su service continues hourly until 2234.

DEPART Stirling Station	**ARRIVE** Waverley Station	**NOTES**
1406	1502	M–Sa
1436	1532	M–Sa

M–Sa service continues every 30 minutes until 2106, then 2206 and 2314.

1410	1504	Su
1510	1604	Su
1606	1702	Su

Su service continues hourly until 2210.

Day Excursion to

Stranraer

Gateway to Northern Ireland

Depart from Edinburgh Waverley Station

Distance by train: 147 miles (237 km)

Average train time: 3 hours, 50 minutes

Train information and InterCity services: (0845) 748 4950

Tourist information: Tourist Information Centre, Burns House, 28 Harbour Street, Stranraer DG9 7RA; *Tel:* (01776) 702595; *Fax:* (01776) 889156

www.stranraer.org

E-mail: stranraer@visitscotland.com

Hours: April–Mid June: Monday–Saturday 1000–1630; Mid June–Mid September: Monday–Saturday 1000–1700, Sunday 1200–1600; Mid September–Easter: Monday–Saturday 1000–1600

Notes: The tourist information center is located on Harbour Street to the right of the Stena Line Terminal.

Stranraer is primarily the terminal for passenger and car ferry service to Belfast in Northern Ireland. At press time, however, the BritRail Pass was not accepted for travel on trains operated by the Northern Ireland Railways. Travelers crossing from Stranraer to Belfast must purchase regular rail tickets or a BritRail Pass + Ireland option, which includes the sea crossing on Stena Line plus rail travel in England, Scotland, Wales, Northern Ireland, and the Republic of Ireland.

Arrangements for visiting Northern Ireland should be completed before departure rather than en route. One important requirement is a control ticket each passenger must have before boarding the Stranraer–Belfast ferry. These tickets are issued free of charge. Ticketing and reservations are available in the Stena Line ferry terminal, along with a comfortable passenger lounge with restrooms and refreshments.

The crossing between Stranraer and Belfast usually takes three hours by conventional ferry, but Stena Line's HSS *Fast Craft* takes only one hour and forty-five minutes. Trains are waiting at the terminals to take travelers to their final destinations. In Stranraer the train terminal is directly alongside the ferry dock. Porter service is available. The BritRail Pass + Ireland option is valid on the Stena Line.

Stranraer has direct, daytime express-train connections to London. For sleeper services to London, go to Glasgow for departures from Glasgow Central. The last train leaves Stranraer for Glasgow at 2110. Frequent train service connecting with ferries to and from Belfast is also available from Glasgow. Edinburgh passengers should use the Edinburgh–Glasgow service for the fastest connections to Stranraer.

The old section of Stranraer clusters around its port area and is entwined with interesting streets and alleyways. The Stranraer Castle, which houses a visitor center, is a relic of the sixteenth century and adds a certain attraction to the area. The information center can provide you with a map of the town and suggest various sights to see on a walking tour. The area is renowned for its golf and fishing, and there are a number of beautiful gardens, which flourish in the mild climate.

The Stranraer Castle, with the formal title of **Castle of St. John,** is known locally as the "Old Castle." Built in what is now the heart of Stranraer around 1510, it was erected on a site that gave the settlement its original name, Chapel. The name was later changed to Chapel of Stranrawer and finally shortened to Stranraer. Stranrawer was believed to have referred to a row of original houses on the strand, or beach, now buried beneath the town's streets.

An interesting hotel in Stranraer, one that you might mistake as the town's castle when you first see it, is the **North West Castle Hotel.** Its castle tower cleverly conceals two well-stocked bars. If you are anticipating a long train trip, you may want to bolster your spirits here in the quaint tower. In the lower bar there are some fossiliferous wooden beams (no, they are not former patrons), and topside in the Explorers Lounge you are treated to a fine view of the harbor.

The hotel was originally the home of Sir John Ross, the famous Arctic explorer. He gave it the name North West Castle as a reminder of his journeys to the northern and western reaches of the Arctic. Although the "castle" has been transformed into the largest hotel in southwest Scotland, its origins with Sir John have been carefully preserved. An indoor ice rink caters to curling fans, and the hotel proprietor added a swimming pool, sauna baths, and several restaurants. A brochure at the hotel desk gives the full history of this most interesting hostelry.

Stranraer lies at the southern end of Loch Ryan, known since Roman times as a safe harbor. At the point where Loch Ryan meets the Irish Sea, the granite bulk of **Ailsa Craig** stands as a sentinel guarding the enclosed waters of the loch from the ravages of the storms that sweep into the area from the Atlantic.

Edinburgh–Stranraer–Edinburgh

DEPART Waverley Station	ARRIVE Stranraer Station	NOTES
0645	1057	M–F
1030 (1000 Su)	1354	Daily

DEPART Stranraer Station	ARRIVE Waverley Station	NOTES
1440	1822	Su
1443	1824	M–Sa
1945	2320 (2324 Su)	Daily

All schedules shown require a change in Glasgow from Queen Street to Glasgow Central Station or the reverse. Schedules shown allow 15–25 minutes for this change.

Base City: **GLASGOW**

www.seeglasgow.com
E-mail: info@visitscotland.com

Glasgow has undergone a sweeping renaissance, shaking off its former image of a grim, depressed industrial city to dawn as one of Europe's foremost culture hubs. Emerging from a century or so of accumulated grime, the cleaning-up process has highlighted some of Europe's finest Victorian architecture in gleaming gold and red sandstone. Bustling city streets lined with imposing hand-carved facades pay homage to the optimism of the Victorian city fathers, as do the stunning marble staircases of the opulent City Chambers in central George Square. Glaswegians have reason to be proud of their city and cordially invite you to enjoy it.

Glasgow is Scotland's largest metropolis. As the gateway to bonnie Loch Lomond and the western Highlands, Glasgow's River Clyde flows into the Firth of Clyde, thus opening its western waterways to myriad islands and the Irish Sea. At the height of its shipbuilding boom, Glasgow was launching more than one-third of the world's shipping tonnage. The *Queen Mary,* the *Queen Elizabeth I,* and the *Queen Elizabeth II* (*QE2*) were built there. With the industry now only a shadow of its former self, the River Clyde has become a scenic waterway where you can cruise aboard luxury riverboats or the paddle-wheel steamer *Waverley.*

Glasgow abounds with sights to see, ranging from its great twelfth-century cathedral to a variety of museums and universities. It is said that Glasgow has more parks than any other European city of its size. George Square, opposite the Queen Street railway station, projects a panorama of Scottish and British history in its statues of individuals who forged the British Commonwealth through their scientific, leadership, and literary endeavors.

Direct transatlantic flights into the Glasgow Airport, only fifteen minutes from the city center, as well as regular train services from London and the south, make Glasgow an ideal "base city" for Scotland. The same day excursions from Edinburgh may just as easily be made from Glasgow. With the excellent train service between the two base cities and to all of the day excursions from either city, which one you choose as a base is your personal decision.

Arriving by Air

Along with its excellent weather, Glasgow offers travelers the opportunity of "open jaw" airline ticketing: arriving or departing on one leg of their transatlantic flight in Scotland rather than flying both in and out of the London complex of Gatwick, Stansted, or Heathrow. Glasgow Airport is the busiest of Scotland's three main international airports. www.glasgowairport.com.

The Glasgow Tourist Information Desk, located in the international arrivals concourse, provides information to incoming passengers. The office is open from 0730 to 1700 daily. Currency exchange services are available daily between 0700 and 2200.

Frequent airport bus service (No. 500) is offered between the airport and Glasgow city center 0500–2400 Monday–Saturday, 0600–2400 Sunday. *Tel:* (0844) 8004411; www.glasgowflyer.com. Journey time is approximately twenty-five minutes; the fare is £4.00. Taxi fare from the airport to Glasgow city center is about £20–£25. Taxi and frequent bus service also can transport travelers to the nearest rail station, Paisley Gilmour Street Station, just 2 miles from the airport. Direct rail service connects Paisley Gilmour Street with Glasgow Central station, Ayr, and Clyde Coast destinations.

Arriving by Train

Glasgow has two main railway stations. Trains arriving from southwestern Scotland and England terminate in the Glasgow Central Station. For train travel north and east out of Glasgow to Edinburgh, Perth, and Inverness or west to Oban and Fort William, the Glasgow Queen Street Station becomes the departure point. A convenient city bus service links the two rail stations. The twenty-minute walk between them, however, runs through some of the city's finer shopping areas, thereby offering the opportunity to walk off a few British "pounds." If you choose to walk from the Queen Street Station to the Central Station, walk past George Square and the tourist information center to St. Vincent Street. Turn right, and walk 1 block farther to Buchanan Street, a pedestrian shopping precinct. Turn left onto Buchanan Street, and walk until your path intersects with Gordon Street. The intersection is easy to locate because this section of Gordon Street is reserved for pedestrians (and shops). Turning right at this point and continuing along Gordon Street for 2 blocks will bring you to the Glasgow Central Station, on your left.

From the Central Station to the Queen Street Station, merely reverse your line of march. Those who wish to avoid running the shopper's gantlet on Buchanan Street may proceed between the two stations by traversing Queen and Argyle Streets. A map of central Glasgow is available at the tourist information center at 11 George Square.

The Interstation Bus Link provides passenger transfer service between the Central and Queen Street Stations with no stops en route. Departures are approximately every fifteen minutes.

Don't look for a kiosk or a newsstand where you can purchase tickets; you pay your fare when you get on the bus. BritRail Passes are not accepted for the bus transfer between rail stations. The time en route varies between five and ten minutes, depending on traffic conditions. For those in a hurry or heavily loaded with luggage, taxis are standing by in queues at both stations.

If you are arriving in one of Glasgow's rail stations to transfer to the Glasgow Airport at Abbotsinch, frequent bus service departs from Buchanan Bus Station. Paisley Gilmour Street Station is the closest rail terminal to the airport. Transport via taxi or local bus is located here as well to make the 2-mile journey to the airport.

Glasgow Central Station

Glasgow Central Station, transformed radically in recent years, caters to the needs of the train traveler, ranging from restrooms with bathing facilities to a grand Victorian hostelry, the Central Hotel. The station's old ticket office was transformed into a delightful array of quality shops, bars, and restaurants. Pick up a copy of *The Station Guide* leaflet for a detailed guide to station facilities.

The Glasgow Central Station provides InterCity electric services for English destinations, including Liverpool, Manchester, Birmingham, and London (Euston Station). Also provided are connections for Wales, the west of England, and destinations in south and west Scotland, which include Ayr and Stranraer (for connections to Larne and Belfast in Northern Ireland). Commuter-train service to Gourock and Wemyss Bay for connections with steamer services on the River Clyde also operate from Central Station.

Money exchange is available at Currency Express by the Gordon Street entrance. ATMs are located throughout the station.

Hotel reservations may be arranged at the **tourist information center** at 11 George Square. *Tel:* (0141) 566 0800; *Fax:* (0141) 566 0810.

Train information is displayed in the Central Station by means of a digital departures-and-arrivals board located between tracks 2 and 5. For expanded train information and reservations, visit the travel center at the Gordon Street entrance.

The taxi rank is across from the front of the station on Gordon Street.

Queen Street Station

Queen Street Station is the terminal for trains operating on the scenic West Highland Line to Oban, Fort William, and Mallaig, where steamer connections may be made to the Scottish islands. From the Queen Street Station, InterCity express trains depart for Edinburgh and connect with destinations in England, including York, Doncaster, and London (King's Cross Station).

Services for north and east Scotland, including Stirling, Perth, Dundee, Aberdeen, Inverness, and the Kyle of Lochalsh, depart from the Queen Street Station. Electric trains to Dumbarton and Balloch (for Loch Lomond cruises) also operate from this station.

Money exchange services are not available within the Queen Street Station. There are several banks in the general area, including an office of the Royal Bank of Scotland adjacent to the main entrance of the Central Station.

Hotel reservations for Glasgow and for all of Scotland may be arranged through the "Book-a-Bed-Ahead" service with the Greater Glasgow & Clyde Valley Tourist Board located at 11 George Square; *Tel:* (0141) 566 0800.

Tourist information in Glasgow is also available at the **Greater Glasgow and Clyde Valley Tourist Board.** *Hours:* June–September: Monday–Saturday 0900–1900 (2000 in July–August), Sunday 1000–1800; October–April: Monday–Saturday 0900–1800, closed on Sunday until Easter, open 1000–1800 Sunday after Easter.

The center has a wealth of Glasgow tourist information on hand. Call to request a copy of the *Greater Glasgow Quick Guide* booklet. In addition to a listing of city attractions, the booklet contains information on restaurants, pubs, events, and shopping that will be very helpful for getting to know Glasgow. There is a Bureau de Change in the center as well as an office for theater and sporting-events tickets.

Train information is available in the Rail Travel Centre located on the left-hand side of the station as you face the train platforms. Train reservations can be made in the travel center. For sleeper reservations, however, use the travel center in Central Station.

Glasgow Gazette

Glasgow's modern subway system is a circular line with trains running in both directions beneath the center of the city. A three-minute service from each of its fifteen stations is provided, achieving a circular journey in about twenty-two minutes. A separate subway, the Argyle Line, links the suburban networks. The main link with British rail services, however, is the subway station at Buchanan Street, connecting with the Queen Street Station by a moving pedestrian platform similar to those found in airports. The Scotland TravelPass allows passholders to travel the Glasgow Underground at no charge.

For travelers going to Loch Lomond, the rail route departing Glasgow is an electric-train service that departs from subterranean platform 8 in the Queen Street Station. To reach it, after entering the main hall of the station, turn left and exit the station by the side entrance, where you turn right to follow the well-marked PLATFORM 8 signs.

In the Queen Street Station's Travel Centre, you may obtain information and tickets for cruising on the River Clyde aboard the paddle steamer *Waverley*. Connecting rail services to the ship's pier originate in the Queen Street Station. The vessel offers a number of interesting cruises on the River Clyde and the Firth of Clyde, including a special upriver cruise on Saturday during the summer. Advance bookings are recommended. *Tel:* (0845) 130 4647; www.waverleyexcursions.co.uk.

Throughout the summer a two-hour bus tour of Glasgow aboard specially converted double-decker buses will take you around some of the best-known places—and some of the more-out-of-the-way places—in the city. For bus-tour schedules and rates, check with the Greater Glasgow Tourist Information Centre.

Every visitor to Glasgow, and model railroad buffs in particular, will not want to miss Glasgow's **Museum of Transport** at 100 Pointhouse Place, Glasgow G3 8RS. *Tel:* (0141) 287 2720. Open Monday through Thursday and Saturday from 1000 to 1700, Friday and Sunday between 1100 and 1700. Displays include ship models, Glasgow trams and buses, locomotives of Scottish origin, Scottish-built motorcars, fire engines, and a reconstructed subway station. There is also a section in the museum known as "The Clyde Room," where meticulously detailed models illustrate the story of shipbuilding and shipping on the River Clyde. An operating model railroad is one of the museum's highlights. Admission is free.

St. Mungo Museum of Religious Life and Art, at 2 Castle Street (in front of Glasgow Cathedral), provides an exploration of the different faiths of the world through paintings and religious artifacts. Included in the collection is Salvador Dali's *Christ of St. John of the Cross*. The museum is open Monday through Thursday and Saturday 1000–1700, Friday and Sunday 1100–1700. Admission is free.

Glasgow's Art Gallery and Museum is directly opposite Kelvin Hall. Home of Britain's finest civic collection of British and European paintings, the museum also features displays of natural history, archaeology, and collections of silver, pottery, arms, and armor. In the performing-arts sector, **Glasgow's Mayfest** (which, of course, occurs in the merry month of May) is a key international festival for theater, dance, music, and related performing arts in Europe. All of these museums can be found online at www.glasgowlife.org.uk.

Among the many superb galleries and museums throughout Glasgow is the renowned Burrell Collection in the Pollok Country Park, a unique collection of more than 8,000 *objets d'art* donated to the city by one man, Sir William Burrell.

Previously, we identified the area of the city between the two rail stations as an ideal place to "walk off a few British 'pounds.'" It is. Glasgow is a shopper's paradise. Department stores line the great pedestrian shopping districts of Argyle and Buchanan Streets. Adjacent to them, Princes Square provides some of Europe's top specialty shops blended with an exciting array of restaurants and bars. Slightly farther than a stone's throw from the square, St. Enochs indoor shopping mall offers a wide variety of stores beneath the same roof, and Argyll Victorian Arcade is the place to look for jewelry and fine gifts. Farther out, but well worth it if you are visiting Glasgow over a weekend, is the city's famous **"Barras Street Market,"** a bargain collector's delight with goods ranging from Victorian bric-a-brac to high fashion, all flavored by the antics of the stall holders.

Glasgow Connections to Day Excursions

All-day excursions described departing from Edinburgh also may be taken from Glasgow. Refer to the "Train Connections to Other Base Cities" schedules. In fact, two of the day excursions (to Ayr and Stranraer) require passing through Glasgow. For these excursions, readers residing in Glasgow need only refer to the appropriate day-excursion schedule.

Two of the day excursions—Dunbar and Dunfermline—may be reached conveniently only through Edinburgh. Consequently, readers need refer only to the Glasgow–Edinburgh shuttle-service schedule for these day excursions.

Five day excursions—Aberdeen, Dundee, Montrose, St. Andrews, and Stirling—are so situated on Scotland's rail lines that they may be reached either by direct connection from the Queen Street Station in Glasgow or through Edinburgh.

Two other day excursions—Inverness and Perth—are reached more conveniently from Glasgow by direct train service from the Queen Street Station rather than through Edinburgh.

All services shown are subject to change. Readers are advised to consult with the schedules posted in the train stations or with a British Rail Travel Centre for train information before commencing each journey.

Regardless of which city you select as your base, don't forget that the frequent train service between Glasgow and Edinburgh enables you to make a day excursion to the one you didn't select as your base. For what to see and do in Edinburgh, consult the chapter on Scotland's capital.

There are times throughout the year when one of the two cities, either Glasgow or Edinburgh, may be fully booked. This can take place in Glasgow during May when the city hosts a Mayfest, a festival focusing attention on Glasgow's many activities within its cultural sphere. On the other hand, Edinburgh can be filled to overflowing when visitors attend its world-famous Military Tattoo. When this happens, and your reservationist gives up on the city of your choice, try the other. Your chances of finding accommodations there are very good, and the ease of rail travel between Glasgow and Edinburgh will make it an "easy commute," far better than anything that the Long Island Railroad could come up with!

Glasgow Connections to Day Excursions

Excursion Destination	DEPART Queen St. Station	ARRIVE Destination	DEPART Destination	ARRIVE Queen St. Station	NOTES
Aberdeen	0556	0844	1342	1614	M–Sa
	0741	1016	1439	1718	M–Sa
	0841	1117	1533	1815	M–Sa
	0941	1233	1637	1916	M–Sa
	1041	1314	1736	2015	M–Sa
			1830	2114	M–Sa
			2042	2315	M–Sa
	0938	1235	1530	1812	Su
	1145	1423	1747	2031	Su
			1935	2215	Su

Excursion Destination	DEPART Queen St. Station	ARRIVE Destination	DEPART Destination	ARRIVE Queen St. Station	NOTES
Dundee	0741	0903	1452	1612	M–Sa
	0841	0959	1549	1718	M–Sa
	0941	1057	1647	1815	M–Sa
	1041	1159	1751	1916	M–Sa
	1141	1259	1852	2015	M–Sa
			1946	2114	M–Sa
			2057	2220	M–Sa
	0938	1112	1445	1628	Su
	1145	1310	1643	1812	Su
			1904	2031	Su
			2043	2215	Su
Inverness	0706	1029	1653	2015	M–Sa
	1011	1327	2015	2339	M–Sa
	Su schedule not conducive to day excursions.				
Montrose	0741	0937	1715	1916	M–Sa
	0841	1031	1817	2015	M–Sa
	0941	1132	1910	2114	M–Sa
	0938	1145	2013	2215	Su
Perth	0741	0840	1514	1614	M–Sa
	0841	0936	1711	1815	M–Sa
	0941 (0938 Su)	1034 (1047 Su)	1914 (1927 Su)	2015 (2031 Su)	Daily
			2118	2220	M–Sa
			2230	2339	M–Sa
St. Andrews	Train from Glasgow Queen Street Station to Dundee, first train out 0555				
	Transfer to St. Andrews bus, departing every hour on the half hour.				
Stirling	At 22, 40, and 51 minutes past each hour, last train 2305				M–Sa
	At 0938, then 1015 and every hour thereafter.				Su
	Depart Stirling at 21, 43, and 53 minutes past each hour.				M–Sa
	Depart Stirling at 1545, 1738, 1955, 2025, or 2138.				Su
	Journey time: 26 minutes				

Train Connections to Other Base Cities from Glasgow

Glasgow–Cardiff

DEPART Glasgow Central	ARRIVE Cardiff Central	NOTES
0550	1208	M–Sa (1)
0800	1427	M–Sa (1)
1000	1624	M–Sa (1)
1158	1828	Su (1)
1200	1819	M–Sa (1)
1400	2022	M–F (1)
1557	2206	Su (1)
1600	2223	M–Sa (1)
1740	0002+1	M–F (1)

+1=Arrives next day.
(1) Change trains in Crewe.

Glasgow–Edinburgh

There are two services between Glasgow and Edinburgh. Frequent commuter trains depart from Glasgow Queen Street Station to Edinburgh Waverley Station. There is a less frequent service on the mainline between Glasgow Central Station and Waverley—service provided on mainline trains that arrive in Glasgow Central from stations in England such as Carlisle, London, and York. Average train time to Edinburgh: 48–50 minutes.

COMMUTER SERVICE: DEPART GLASGOW QUEEN STREET STATION

M–Sa	Departs every 15 minutes from 0700 to 1930, then every 30 minutes until 2330.
Su	Departs hourly from 0830 to 1230, then every 30 minutes until 2130, then 2230 and 2330.

MAINLINE SERVICE: DEPART GLASGOW CENTRAL STATION

M–F	Departs at 0650, 0750, 0950, and 1150, then every 2 hours until 1950.
Sa	Departs hourly from 0650 until 1005, then at 1105, 1305, 1605, and 1850.
Su	Departs at 1050 and 1250, then 1455, 1655, and 1857.

Glasgow–London

DEPART Glasgow Central	ARRIVE London Euston Station	NOTES
0650	1246 (arrives London King's Cross)	M–Sa
0735	1212	M–F
0940	1412	M–F
1140	1603	Su
1240	1712	M–F
1440	1913	M–F
1640	2138	M–F
2315*	0646+1	Su
2340*	0637+1	M–F

*Sleeper service; reservations required.
+1=Arrives next day
Reservations recommended for above-listed trains.

WALES

www.visitwales.com
E-mail: info@visitwales.com and walesinfo@visitbritain.org

Welcome to Wales, the passionate area of Britain. You will readily notice the distinctly romantic spirit of the Welsh through their lilting language and their crooning, mellifluous voices. According to the Wales Tourist Board's brochure, "Something as simple as travel directions can become a lyrical journey, taking in history, folklore and a fair amount of local gossip." You may be dumbfounded by the language, but don't let it frighten you. Although Welsh is considered the oldest living language in Europe—it has been around for more than fourteen centuries—everyone in Wales speaks English.

The Welsh are well known for their extraordinary vocal talent, and in the towns and villages you can hear some of the finest male choirs in the world. With their gift for oratory, it is no wonder the Welsh have figured so prominently in British politics.

Wales is about 170 miles (256 kilometers) long and 60 miles (96 kilometers) wide, about the size of Massachusetts. This compact little country has an abundance of scenic natural beauty, including three national parks and beautiful rivers, streams, lakes, and mountains. Add the myth and magic of a king named Arthur, a magician named Merlin, a knight named Lancelot, and a queen named Guinevere, stir in a castle called Caerleon, and you've got Camelot. If you like castles, you can choose from more than 400 castles and monuments to visit in Wales—more castles than any other country in Europe. Take a peek at www.castlewales.com.

Wales is the home and inspiration of many performers and poets, including actress Catherine Zeta Jones; the great brooding actors Sir Anthony Hopkins and the late Richard Burton; popular singers Tom Jones, Shirley Bassey, and Charlotte Church; great bass-baritone opera singer Bryn Terfel; and one of the twentieth century's greatest English-language poets, Dylan Thomas.

South and West Wales contain the majority of the country's people as well as Cardiff, the capital of Wales and a base city for five day excursions. This region also has some of Britain's most outstanding natural beauty: the Gower Peninsula, the sandy beaches of Pembrokeshire Coast National Park, and the resort town of Tenby.

In North Wales visit a special little village with the title of longest name in Britain and the second longest name in the world—Llanfairpwllgwyngyllgogerychwyrndrobwllllantysiliogogogoch—whew! (Visit www.anglesey-history.co.uk to hear the pronunciation.) It means "Saint Mary's Church in the hollow of the white hazel near a rapid whirlpool and the Church of Saint Tysilio by the red cave." Found on the Isle of Anglesey, it is the next stop after Bangor on the North Wales Coast Line.

Or travel to "the roof of Wales" and view England, Wales, and Ireland from the summit of Snowdon, the highest peak, at 3,560 feet (1,085 meters). As Hilaire Belloc wrote: "There is no corner of Europe that I know which so moves me with awe and majesty of great things as does this mass of northern Welsh mountains."

Snowdonia National Park extends southward through Mid Wales, which also contains the smallest town in Britain—Llanwrtyd Wells—the mountainous Brecon Beacons National Park, and the spectacular showcaves of Dan-yr-Ogof, Europe's largest showcaves complex.

Wales Tourist Board, Brunel House, 2 Fitzalan Road, Cardiff CF24 OUY; *Tel:* (029) 2049 9909; *Fax:* (029) 2048 5031; www.visitwales.com. For brochures and travel information, call (800) 462-2748 (U.S. only).

Rail Travel in Wales

National Rail Enquiries: (0845) 748 4950

The Great Little Trains of Wales, LLR, Dept GLTW, Gilfach Ddu, Llanberis, Gwynedd LL55 4TY, is the joint marketing group for the narrow-gauge steam trains (some of which are more than one hundred years old) that provide a special way of seeing some of the best scenery in Britain. A Discount Ticket is valid on any of the nine-member narrow-gauge railways listed below. Tickets may be purchased online at www.gltw.co.uk; or *Tel/Fax:* (01286) 870549.

Bala Lake Railway, The Station, Llanwchllyn, Bala, Gwynedd, Wales LL23 7DD; *Tel:* (01678) 540666; *Fax:* (01678) 540535; www.bala-lake-railway.co.uk. *E-mail:* balalake@btconnect.com.

Brecon Mountain Railway, Pant Station, Merthyr Tydfil, Wales CF48 2UP; *Tel:* (01685) 722988; www.breconmountainrailway.co.uk; *E-mail:* info@breconmountainrailway.co.uk.

Ffestiniog Railway, Harbour Station, Porthmadog, Gwynedd, Wales LL49 9NF; *Tel:* (01766) 516000; *Fax:* (01766) 516005; www.festrail.co.uk; *E-mail:* enquiries@festrail.co.uk.

The Ffestiniog Railway is the oldest independent railway company in the world—having been founded in 1832. The narrow-gauge steam train travels some 13½ miles through delightful scenery from the coast at Porthmadog to the former slate mining town of Blaenau Ffestiniog.

Llanberis Lake Railway, Gilfach Ddu Llanberis, Gwynedd, Wales LL55 4TY; *Tel:* (01286) 870549; www.lake-railway.co.uk; *E-mail:* info@lake-railway.co.uk.

Talyllyn Railway, Wharf Station, Tywyn, Gwynedd, Wales LL36 9EY; *Tel:* (01654) 710472; *Fax:* (01654) 711755; www.talyllyn.co.uk; *E-mail:* enquiries@talyllyn.co.uk.

Vale of Rheidol Railway, Park Avenue, Aberystwyth, Cardiganshire, Wales SY23 1PG; *Tel:* (01970) 625819; *Fax:* (01970) 623769; www.rheidolrailway.co.uk; *E-mail:* vor@rheidolrailway.co.uk.

Welsh Highland Railway (Porthmadog), Tremadog Road, Porthmadog, Gwynedd, Wales LL49 9DY; *Tel:* (01766) 513402; www.whr.co.uk; *E-mail:* info@whr.co.uk.

Welsh Highland Railway (Caernarfon), c/o Harbour Station, Porthmadog, Gwynedd, Wales LL49 9NF; *Tel:* (01766) 516000; *Fax:* (01766) 516005; www.festrail.co.uk; *E-mail:* enquiries@festrail.co.uk.

Welshpool & Llanfair Light Railway, The Station, Llanfair Caereinion, Powys, Wales SY21 0SF; *Tel:* (01938) 810441; *Fax:* (01938) 810861; www.wllr.org.uk; *E-mail:* info@wllr.org.uk.

Base City: **CARDIFF**

www.visitcardiff.com
E-mail: visitor@cardiff.gov.uk

Want to go from the first to the twenty-first century in short order? By all means go to Cardiff. The spectacular 2,000-year-old Cardiff Castle dominates the historic city center, and the futuristic Cardiff Bay waterfront development encompasses Techniquest, the United Kingdom's leading hands-on science discovery center.

Since 1991, when the Cardiff marketing campaign was launched by the late Diana, Princess of Wales, and the then eight-year-old Prince William, Cardiff has been recognized as a world-renowned international center for business, tourism, and leisure. Undoubtedly, Cardiff is one of the friendliest capital cities in the world and is rapidly becoming the United Kingdom's fastest-growing visitor destination.

Cardiff was first developed by the Romans and then by the Normans. Both left their marks in the form of formidable fortifications. The Romans found their way into South Wales and reached the area that is now Cardiff about AD 76. At first they erected a wooden fort, but as Cardiff grew in importance as a Roman naval base, a stone fortress was erected. Following the conquest of England in 1066, the Normans arrived in Cardiff in 1091 and established a stronghold on the site of the old Roman fort. By the sixteenth century Cardiff had established itself as an important port and trading center, complete with pirates and cutthroats who were primarily responsible for Cardiff's decline over the next couple hundred years. With the arrival of the Industrial Revolution, however, Cardiff was to become the world's premier coal-exporting port, thanks to the second Marquess of Bute, who was known as the "Creator of Modern Cardiff."

Today's city is largely a creation of the nineteenth century. Cardiff cast off its grim mantle of industrialism to reveal a sparkling paradise of shopping arcades, a glistening white array of impressive neoclassical civic buildings, a cast iron and glass indoor market, a memorable museum, a transformed harbor area, and the restored (or "reinvented") Cardiff Castle.

Arriving by Air

Visitors to Wales from North America most likely will use either Heathrow or Gatwick Airport. Refer to the London chapter for information regarding these airports. Travelers wishing to avoid a trip into central London and head directly to Cardiff from Heathrow Airport can take a bus from any terminal to Reading rail station and then a train into Cardiff. All trains for Cardiff stop at Reading. Transatlantic flights also are available into Birmingham and Manchester Airports.

Cardiff International Airport, 19 kilometers from the city center, is one of the fastest-growing airports in the United Kingdom and provides direct flights to and from Amsterdam, Belfast, Brussels, Dublin, Guernsey, Isle of Man, Jersey, and Paris. A multimillion-pound expansion has provided an international departure lounge, shopping, and catering facilities. The airport's telephone number is (0144) 671 1111; www.cwlfly.com.

Arriving by Train

Hourly trains depart from London's Paddington Station and arrive in Cardiff Central Station in only about two hours. All facilities, including ATMs, train information, and lockers, are located in the main concourse.

National Rail Enquiries: (0845) 748 4950

Cardiff Gateway Visitor Centre, The Old Library, The Hayes, Cardiff CF10 1WE; *Tel:* 0292 022 7281; *Fax:* (0292) 023 9162; www.visitcardiff.com; *E-mail:* visitor@thecardiffinitiative.co.uk; *Hours:* 0930–1800 Monday–Saturday, 1000–1600 Sunday.

The Cardiff visitor center is within walking distance of the rail station. Exit the main concourse of Central Station onto Central Square. Continue past the bus station, turn right onto Wood Street, and then left onto St. Mary Street. Continue on St. Mary Street to Wharton Street, and turn right (alongside Howells Department Store). Cardiff Gateway Visitor Centre is on the left, opposite Mothercare, the building with the glass front.

Hotel and bed-and-breakfast (B&B) accommodations may be made at the visitor center. **The Townhouse Hotel** (*Tel:* [0292] 023 9399; *Fax:* [0292] 2022 3214; www.thetownhousecardiff.co.uk; *E-mail:* thetownhouse.msn.com.uk) is a beautifully restored Victorian-style B&B located at 70 Cathedral Road, within walking distance of the city center, including Cardiff Castle. The rate for single occupancy starts at £45.00; twin/doubles from £65.00 (all rooms en suite; nonsmoking; price includes full breakfast and VAT). The Townhouse is richly appointed with antiques and paintings. Breakfast is always good too. By taking a left at Sophia Close, you can walk through Bute Park and end up on Castle Street.

If the Townhouse Hotel is fully booked, try the **Lincoln House Hotel** (*Tel:* [029] 2039 5558; *Fax:* [0292] 023 0537; www.lincolnhotel.co.uk), only about 1 block farther at 118 Cathedral Road. The Lincoln House is another charming B&B.

Single room rates: £55–£65; double room rates: £85–£125. All rooms have private shower and toilet facilities, and stays include breakfast and VAT.

If you prefer to fork out the extra pounds for superior first class, you'll want to stay at the **Angel Hotel** on Castle Street, superbly located between the Millennium Stadium and Cardiff Castle. Many a beautiful bride has descended the grand staircase to her "knight in shining armor." But the prices are steep too. Room rates begin at £85 for a standard room with one double bed. Check online for special offers. *Tel:* 0800 652 8413; *Fax:* (029) 2039 6212; www.barcelo-hotels.co.uk/hotels/wales; *E-mail:* stay@barcelo-hotels.co.uk.

Getting around in Cardiff

An easy, economical way to get around in Cardiff is by bus. Cardiff's regular bus service covers the entire city and beyond—even to attractions such as Llanerch Vineyard and Castell Coch. The Central Bus Station is immediately in front of the rail station: Cardiff Bus, St. David's House, Wood Street, Cardiff CF1 1ER; *Tel:* 0870 121 1258. In the outlying areas, the train service can take you to attractions such as **Rhondda Heritage Park** (near Pontypridd) and **Methyr Tydfil,** location of Cyfarthfa Castle, the most impressive monument of the Industrial Iron Age in South Wales.

You can get a great introduction to Cardiff by booking a City Sightseeing tour. You can get on and off the double-decker sightseeing bus as you wish. The tours operate daily from April through October (weekends only the remainder of the year), and the bus departs from in front of Cardiff Castle every thirty minutes. Tickets cost £10 for adults, £8 for students and senior citizens, and £5 for children. To see an overview of the tour, go to www.city-sightseeing.com.

Capitalize on Cardiff

Begin your tour at **Cardiff Castle.** From Cardiff Central Station proceed past the bus station in front, turn right onto Wood Street, then left onto St. Mary Street, which becomes High Street. As High Street intersects with Castle Street, you will see the mighty castle right in front of you.

Cardiff Castle is a lavishly restored medieval fortress with 2,000-year-old Roman foundations, parts of which still exist today. The castle's extensive Roman walls, which were 10 feet thick, were well preserved by earthen banks until their excavation in the nineteenth century. Visit the Roman Wall exhibition area immediately behind the ticket kiosk just inside the main castle entrance.

The medieval stronghold built by invading Normans fell into ruin after the Civil War in the seventeenth century and was saved by the first Marquess of Bute in the late 1700s. The third Marquess of Bute and his pal, the eccentric architect William Burges, lavishly reconstructed Cardiff Castle to the nineteenth-century splendor we see today. The extravagant, opulent rooms are laden with an eclectic mix of decor and architectural features inspired by medieval England, Arabia, the Old

Testament, Islam, even the fairy tales of Hans Christian Andersen. Each room has a different theme.

Today the castle interior provides the setting for medieval "Welsh Nights" and private or public receptions. The castle and its grounds provide a dramatic backdrop for a series of spectacular events throughout the summer, ranging from a hot-air balloon festival to massed military bands and, in case you have the urge to say "I do" in a castle, even enchanted weddings.

The castle is open daily all year except Christmas Day, Boxing Day, and New Year's Day. *Hours:* March–October 0900–1800 (last tour/entry at 1700); November–February 0900–1700 (last tour at 1600). Admission is £11.00 for adults, £8.50 for children age five to sixteen, £9.00 for seniors and students. *Tel:* (0292) 087 8100; www.cardiffcastle.com; *E-mail:* cardiffcastle@cardiff.gov.uk.

Cardiff Civic Centre lies beyond the castle, as does the National Museum & Gallery. The **Civic Centre** is one of the most impressive buildings in Europe. Separated by wide avenues and parks, the presence in the spring of cherry blossoms and tulip beds creates a perfect setting for the white stone buildings.

The **National Museum & Gallery** in Cathays Park is unusual in that it contains a variety of exhibits, from priceless works of art to dinosaurs. *Hours:* 1000–1700 Tuesday–Sunday and bank holidays. For more information telephone (0292) 039 7951, or visit the National Museum & Gallery of Wales's Web site: www.museumwales.ac.uk. Admission is free.

Ready for shopping? Cardiff is a shopaholic's paradise. According to Cardiff Marketing Limited, Cardiff "offers the best shopping in Britain outside London," with more big-name retailers than any comparable British city. Seven Victorian shopping arcades blend well with three modern shopping areas. Cardiff claims to have had pedestrian shopping areas long before the phrase was invented. The two main shopping streets, Queen Street and St. Mary Street, form an L-shape that partially encloses Cardiff's largest shopping mall, **St. David's Centre.** For those with the "shop till you drop" philosophy, this is the place.

A visit to **Castle Welsh Crafts** is a must: 1 Castle Street, Cardiff CF1 2BS, South Glamorgan; *Tel:* (029) 2034 3038. Located across the street from Cardiff Castle, this shop has traditional Welsh crafts, including intricately hand-carved lovespoons. The tradition of the Welsh peasantry to give their loved ones a carved wooden spoon as a token of affection goes back many centuries. In fact, the English term *spooning* is almost certainly derived from this old Welsh custom.

Some people believe that the presentation and the acceptance of the lovespoon was confirmation that a courtship was about to start; others believe the lovespoon represented an early form of engagement ring. Certain designs have specific meanings. For instance, the giving of a spoon shaped as leaves or trees represents growing love, a horseshoe represents good luck and happiness, and bells indicate marriage. The lovespoon makes a perfect Welsh souvenir or gift.

To sample some contemporary Welsh dishes try the **Armless Dragon Restaurant** at 97 Wyeverne Road, about a fifteen-minute walk from Cardiff Castle. Follow Castle Street, keeping the castle on your left. At the second traffic light, turn right onto Boulevard de Nantes. At the next set of lights, turn left onto Park Place and take an almost immediate right at the lights onto Salisbury Road. Follow Salisbury Road to Wyeverne Road. Reservations are advised; *Tel:* (0292) 038 2357; www.armlessdragon.co.uk.

We enjoyed lunch at the **Hogshead Bar,** Owain Glyndwr, St. Johns Street (*Tel:* [0292] 022 1980 or [0292] 039 9303), near St. John's Church in the pedestrian shopping area. Their menu says it all: "There's ne'er a moment so sweet when the best of friends choose to meet when conversation fills the air with a jug o' ale and hearty fayre. Eat with gusto, drink with cheer good ale, good food, and good atmosphere." Hours for eating are 1200 to 1800; pub-only hours are 1800 to 2300.

Techniquest, Britain's leading science discovery center, is located in Cardiff Bay. *Tel:* (0292) 047 5475; www.techniquest.org. Admission to Techniquest is £7.00 adults, £5.00 children age four to sixteen and seniors. The area is also home to the Butte Street Maritime Museum, the Norwegian Church Arts Centre, Lightship 2000, the Point, and, last but not least, the world's most famous fish 'n' chips restaurant, **Harry Ramsden's.** *Tel:* (0292) 046 3334; *Fax:* (0292) 046 0693; www.harryramsdens.co.uk.

Since improving the harbor area is an ongoing process, new venues are rapidly being established. The **Cardiff Bay** area is definitely one of the "hot spots" of Britain. You can telephone the Cardiff Bay Visitor Centre at (0292) 087 7927 or visit www.cardiffbay.co.uk on the Internet. To get to Cardiff Bay Inner Harbour area, take Bus 1, 2, or 6. Shuttle trains operate from Queen Street Station.

The **National History Museum** at St. Fagans is one of Europe's largest open-air folk museums. *Tel:* (0292) 057 3500; www.museumwales.ac.uk; *Hours:* 1000–1700 daily. Admission is free; however, parking is £3.50. Here you can travel through time from the Celtic village of 2,000 years ago to a miner's cottage of the 1980s. "Living" buildings depicting daily Welsh life were reconstructed stone by stone. You'll see an ornate timber-framed barn originally built around 1550, a working blacksmith and bakery shop, an Elizabethan manor (St. Fagans Castle), a medieval farmhouse, and much, much more. To get there, take Bus No. 32 and 320 from Central Bus Station, Stand B3.

Waverley and *Balmoral* steamer cruises depart from Penarth Pier, 4 miles from Cardiff. Take the Valley Line train to Penarth or Bus L1, L2, P10, or P20 to Penarth Pier from the Central Bus Station. Cost varies.

The *Waverley* is the last seagoing paddle steamer in the world. Both the *Waverley* and the *Balmoral* are beautifully restored, and each can carry up to 925 passengers. An afternoon cruise affords the spectacular scenery of Bristol Channel; romantics should opt for an evening cruise. The cruises are conducted by

Waverley Excursions Ltd., *Tel:* (0845) 130 4647, or check with the tourist office; www.waverleyexcursions.co.uk.

Tredegar House is a magnificent country house set in ninety acres of parkland and gardens and was the home of one of the great Welsh families, the Morgans, for more than five centuries. See the vastly different lifestyles of those of "the manor born" and their servants. Located in Newport, it is a twenty-minute bus ride (No. 30) from Central Bus Station, Stand E2. *Tel:* (01633) 815880; *Hours:* Easter–September, Wednesday–Sunday 1100–1600; August, open daily; October, weekends only. Entrance fees: £6.25 adults; £4.65 seniors/students; children under age sixteen admitted free. After the tour, opt for a carriage ride, go boating on the lake, or visit the craft workshops.

Llanerch Vineyard is an international award-winning winery in the Vale of Glamorgan. Producing estate bottle white, rosé, and sparkling wines, it is the largest vineyard in Wales. Of course, you may sample a bit o' the juice during your tour. Take Bus 32 from Central Bus Station, Stand B1. Entrance fees: £8 adults (includes a wine tasting), £3 for children. www.llanerch-vineyard.co.uk.

Second in size only to Windsor Castle, **Caerphilly Castle** is one of the largest fortresses in Europe and is a mere fifteen-minute train ride from Cardiff's Queen Street Station. This Norman castle covers thirty acres, is remarkably well preserved, plus it's crammed with interesting things, including a tower that even Oliver Cromwell's gunpowder could not topple—at least not completely. Trains depart Queen Street Station thrice hourly, or take Bus 26 at Stand B3 from the Central Bus Station. *Hours:* April–June, September–October, and March: 0930–1700; July–August: 0930–1800; November–February: 1000–1600 Monday–Saturday, 1100–1600 Sunday. Entrance fees are £4.00 for adults; £3.60 for children age five to sixteen. *Tel:* (029) 2088 3143; www.caerphilly.gov.uk. The Caerphilly Visitor Centre at Twyn Square has a wealth of information and a fabulous gift shop. *Tel:* (0292) 088 0011.

Not satisfied being a one-castle owner, John Marquess of Bute commissioned William Burges to design a little country retreat, **Castell Coch,** which is perched on a wooded hillside just a few miles north of Cardiff at Tongwynlais. Known as the "fairy-tale castle in the woods," Castell Coch appears to have been magically removed from the pages of *Sleeping Beauty*. Unfortunately, Billy Burges died suddenly in 1881 before completing his Victorian dream of the Middle Ages. Castell Coch was completed by colleagues who remained faithful to the rich, detailed decor, grandeur, and allusion of medieval architecture. To reach Castell Coch (*Tel:*[0292] 081 0101), take Bus 26 from Cardiff Central Bus Station, Stand B3. Entrance fees are £3.60 for adults, £3.20 for children age five to sixteen.

Train Connections to Other Base Cities from Cardiff

Cardiff–Edinburgh

DEPART Cardiff Central	ARRIVE Edinburgh Waverley	NOTES
0540	1222	M–Sa (2)
0750	1422	M–Sa (2)
0930	1622	Su (2)
1055	1621	M–F (2)
1135	1822	Su (2)
1155	1822	M–Sa (2)
1340	2022	Su (2)
1355	2022	M–Sa (1)
1455	2216	M–F (1)
1545	2310	Sa (1)
1615	2222	M–F (2)

(1) Change trains at Birmingham New Street.
(2) Change trains at Crewe.

Cardiff–Glasgow

DEPART Cardiff Central	ARRIVE Glasgow Central	NOTES
0650	1317	M–Sa (1)
0830	1502	Su (1)
0850	1517	M–Sa (1)
1035	1717	Su (1)
1050	1714	M–Sa (1)
1245	1917	Su (1)
1250	1919	M–Sa (1)
1450	2117	M–Sa (1)
1645	2335	Su (1)
1650	2318	M–F (1)

(1) Change trains at Crewe.

Cardiff–London

DEPART Cardiff Central	ARRIVE London Paddington	NOTES
0555	0802	M–Sa
0624	0832	M–Sa
0655	0906	M–Sa
0725	0929	M–Sa
0755	0959 (1002 Sa)	M–Sa
0756	1027	Su
0825	1031	M–Sa
0925	1132	M–Sa
0940	1224	Su
Continuing service at 25 and 55 min past each hour until 1825, then 1925, 2025, and 2125.		M–F
Continuing service at 25 min past each hour until 2025		Sa
Continuing service at 55 min past each hour until 2055		Su

If you would rather sit and reflect on your day or daydream of days of yore, we suggest visiting one of the oldest restaurants in the area, **The Courthouse,** *Tel:* (0292) 088 8120. The view of Caerphilly Castle is spectacular; the back patio overlooks the moat, the walkway encircles the castle grounds, and the antique decor is almost as enticing as the ale. The Courthouse is on your left as you wind down the hill from the rail station toward the castle or on your right if you are ascending the incline.

Day Excursions

After you've seen Cardiff and its nearby attractions, you may want to venture farther afield. Visit Bath to learn more about Roman England, opt for visiting the most western point of England, the pirates' Penzance, or Plymouth, whose historical heritage is closely related to America. Or see the ideal Swansea and the Mumbles in South Wales. And there is always Tenby for the resort lover.

Day Excursion to

Bath

Roman England—The Original Hot Tub

From Cardiff: Depart from Cardiff Central Station
Distance by train: 53 miles (62 km)
Average train time: 1 hour, 15 minutes
From London: Depart from London's Paddington Station
Distance by train: 107 miles (172 km)
Average train time: 1 hour, 30 minutes
Train information and InterCity services: (0845) 748 4950
Tourist information: Bath Tourism Bureau, Abbey Chambers, Abbey Church Yard, Bath BA1 1LY; *Tel:* (0906) 711 2000 (50 pence per minute); outside U.K., 011 44 0844 847 5257; *Fax:* (0122) 547 7787
www.visitbath.co.uk or **www.heritagecities.com**
E-mail: tourism@bathtourism.co.uk
Hours: October–May: Monday–Saturday 0930–1700; June–September: Monday–Saturday 0930–1800; all year Sunday 1000–1600
Notes: To reach the information center on foot, proceed up Manvers Street directly in front of the Bath Spa rail station until you cross North Parade Road at the traffic light. At this point you will see the Bath Abbey tower to your left. Looking to your left, enter York Street, and proceed until reaching an open square on the right. The tourist information center will be in the building on the right of the square on the ground floor.

The **Roman Baths** (www.romanbaths.co.uk) are one of Britain's major tourist attractions and draw visitors from all points of the globe to their waters. The baths rank a close second to England's number one attraction, the Tower of London, and are well worth the short train ride from either Cardiff or London to see them and the "glory that was Rome," transposed to England.

Bath has been in the limelight as the social center "to see and be seen" during two eras of recorded history—once during the Roman occupation of Britain and again in the eighteenth century when Bath became the "gathering place" for royalty and other well-to-do folk. Development of the only hot springs in Britain is attributed to the Romans soon after Emperor Claudius invaded the land in AD 43.

Bath–Cardiff–Bath

DEPART Central Station	ARRIVE Bath Spa Station	NOTES
0730	0835	M–Sa
0805	0926	Su
0830	0934	M–Sa
0930 (0915 Su)	1035 (1028 Su)	Daily
1030 (1008 Su)	1135 (1126 Su)	Daily
1130 (1108 Su)	1235 (1221 Su)	Daily
1230 (1208 Su)	1335 (1326 Su)	Daily

DEPART Bath Spa Station	ARRIVE Central Station	NOTES
1536 (1528 Su)	1643	Daily
1636 (1628 Su)	1743	Daily
1736 (1726 Su)	1842	Daily
1836 (1827 Su)	1943	Daily
2036 (2027 Su)	2143	Daily
2136 (2128 Su)	2300	Daily
2236 (2229 Su)	2356	Daily

London–Bath–London

Direct trains from London Paddington Station only; other service is available from London Waterloo Station and may require a change of trains.

DEPART Paddington Station	ARRIVE Bath Spa Station	NOTES
0700	0824	M–Sa
0730	0855	M–Sa
0800	0928	M–Sa
0830	1000	M–Sa
0900	1023 (1040 Su)	Daily
0930	1100	M–Sa

M–F Service continues every 30 minutes until 2000, then 2045, 2145, 2215, and 2330.
Sa Service continues every 30 minutes until 2030, then 2130 and 2235.
Su Service continues every 30 minutes until 1803, then 1903, 2000, 2100, 2203, and 2337.

DEPART Bath Spa Station	ARRIVE Paddington Station	NOTES
1413	1538	M–Sa
1413	1558	Su
1443	1614	M–Sa
1513	1644	M–Sa
1513	1658	Su
1543	1714	M–Sa

M–F Service continues every 30 minutes until 1843, then 1943, 2043, 2202, and 2247.
Sa Service continues every 30 minutes until 1843, then 1943, 2046, and 2202.
Su Service continues every hour until 2222, then 2243.

To the Romans the city's name was Aquae Sulis—literally translated, it means "the waters of Sulis." By the end of the first century, the Romans had established a great bathing facility. The magnificent hot baths were said to have curative powers. There is no doubt that the only hot mineral springs in Britain played a major role in establishing Bath as the "hot spot" for socializing.

The baths made *Aquae Sulis* famous throughout the empire. Its fame lasted 400 years until the rising sea level and the fall of the Roman Empire brought the city's prosperity to an end. By the end of the seventh century, the city was described as "a ghostly ruin with crumbled masonry fallen into dark pools, overgrown and bird haunted, but still a wondrous sight."

The second revitalization of the city, a cultural one, began in 1705 with the arrival of thirty-one-year-old Richard Nash. Like the Romans, he too conquered, but not by force. Nash was Bath's first public-relations expert. It was during his "reign" that Queen Anne visited Bath, and it again became an elegant and stylish resort for the wealthy. By the time Nash died at the age of eighty-seven, he had created a kingdom of taste and etiquette over which he reigned as Beau Nash, King of Bath.

Although the hot springs were used again from the Middle Ages, the Roman ruins remained buried during most of Beau Nash's time. Finally, the gilded bronze head of Minerva was uncovered by workmen digging a sewer in 1727. The statues and columns of present-day Roman baths were added by Victorian restorers, but the original bath area still has the lead floor and limestone paving installed by the Romans.

The real restoration and melding of Bath's Roman past and of the city's two eras of fame began in 1878 when the city engineer, while investigating a water leak, came upon the Roman reservoir and the huge complex of baths that it fed. Someone finally called a plumber.

Visitors to Bath can once again bathe in the city's natural thermal waters. The Bath Spa project combined the old with the new to produce a most remarkable health and leisure complex. The Sacred Cross Bath has been restored as a working spa, and a state-of-the-art glass and stone building houses thermal pools, saunas, whirlpools, massage and treatment room, and a cafe.

Bath abounds in sightseeing opportunities. Bath Parade Guides, composed of thirty experienced, well-informed Blue Badge guides, specialize in walking tours and Jane Austen tours. *Tel:* (0122) 542 6621; *Fax:* (0122) 533 7111; www.bathparadeguides.co.uk; *Hours:* Monday–Sunday 1100–1630 year-round.

Jane Austen fans will want to visit the **Jane Austen Centre** at 40 Gay Street to discover more about the importance of Bath in the great novelist's life and works. *Hours:* April–October 0945–1730 daily; November–April 1100–1630. *Admission:* £7.45 adults, £4.25 children age six to fifteen, £5.95 students/seniors. *Tel:* (0122) 544 3000; www.janeausten.co.uk; *E-mail:* curator@janeausten.co.uk.

Those interested in fashion over the last 400 years will want to visit the **Museum of Costume and Assembly Rooms** (No. 25 on the pamphlet map), located on Bennett Street. Then, turn left onto Bennett Street and proceed to nearby **No. 1 Royal Crescent** (No. 29 on the pamphlet map) to tour the beautifully restored eighteenth-century town house designed by John Wood. www.fashionmuseum.co.uk or www.bath-preservation-trust.org.uk.

Bath has won many awards for its floral displays, and its natural beauty makes a walking tour through the city a real pleasure. The tourist information center has a wealth of information about the city and its surroundings and sells a wide range of publications to help you get the most out of your stay. We recommend pamphlet 35, *Leisure Attractions in and around Bath*. This informative piece contains a city map and lists places of interest.

If you are on a tight schedule, the best sights in the city are clustered about the Roman Baths. The baths and the abbey practically adjoin each other. Upstairs from the baths, you may visit the Pump Room, which also contains a restaurant for lunch and light refreshments. Take time to touch the worn paving, and in that moment you can recall the glory that was the empire of Rome.

Day Excursion to

Penzance

Western End of the Line

From Cardiff: Depart from Cardiff Central Station
Distance by train: 245 miles (394 km)
Average train time: 5 hours, 30 minutes
From London: Depart from Paddington Station
Distance by train: 305 miles (491 km)
Average train time: 5 hours
Train information and InterCity services: (0845) 748 4950
Tourist information: Tourist Information Centre, Station Road, Penzance, Cornwall TR18 2NF; *Tel:* (0173) 636 2207; *Fax:* (0173) 636 3600
www.penzance.co.uk
Hours: Easter–September: Monday–Friday 0900–1700, Saturday 1000–1600, Sunday 1000–1400; October–Easter: Monday–Friday 0900–1700, closed Saturday and Sunday
Notes: The tourist information center is located immediately outside the rail station. The first item of information you should collect at the center is a Penzance & District map. This graphic presentation of the peninsula will help you put the area into the proper perspective for your visit. Publications that are available in the information center will be extremely helpful.

When you arrive in Penzance, you are literally at "the end of the line" insofar as rail travel is concerned. Geographically speaking, you are also at the western end of England. A mere 10 miles more would bring you to Land's End, where a road sign pointing to the west cryptically states, AMERICA 4,000 MILES. It is difficult to find a grander coastline. This is Land's End Peninsula—the sightseeing opportunities are endless.

Once you are fully armed with the publications needed to explore this most interesting area, we are certain that you will be immediately attracted to the harbor area lying to the left just beyond the rail terminal. We suggest making it your first "port of call," since it can readily put you in the proper adventurous mood to see the rest of the area.

At harborside inspect the old warehouse and granary overlooking Battery Rocks, which has been converted to a craft center and art gallery. Next door is the **Dolphin Inn,** formerly a smugglers' hideaway and said to be haunted by an old sea captain's ghost. From there a walk up Chapel Street away from the harbor brings you to a part of Old Penzance filled with Georgian town houses, fishermen's cottages, and the **Museum of Nautical Art.** This unusual museum, in the form of an eighteenth-century battleship with gun decks and life-size figures manning muzzleloading guns, is filled with displays of actual navigational gear from former times. The museum is well worth a visit and is a delight to young and old alike.

Cardiff–Penzance–Cardiff

DEPART Central Station	ARRIVE Penzance Station	NOTES
0800	1317	M–Sa (1)
0950	1736	Su (2)
1030	1552	M–Sa (1)
1200	1824	M–F (3)
1250	2025	Su (2)

DEPART Penzance Station	ARRIVE Central Station	NOTES
0628	1143	M–Sa (1)
0741	1322	M–F (1)
0828	1343	Sa (1)
0930	1433	Su (1)
0940	1522	M–Sa (1)
1125	1634	Su (1)
1158	1818	Sa (3)
1400	2020	M–Sa (2)
1739	2256	M–Sa (1)

(1) Change trains at Bristol Temple Meads.
(2) Change trains at Reading.
(3) Change trains at Tauton.

For a unique treat visit the **Trinity House National Lighthouse Centre,** which holds probably the largest and finest collection of lighthouse equipment in the world. Located on Wharf Road (*Tel:* [0173] 636 0077, www.trinityhouse.co.uk), it is open daily 1000–1700 Easter to October. Within the center, you can relax in the audiovisual theater and enjoy your trip back in time to the first lighthouses, those lonely citadels that guarded the treacherous waters around England's shores. *Admission:* £3.50 adult, £1.50 child, £2.50 senior/student.

Termed the "Capital of the Cornish Riviera," Penzance occupies an unusually well-sheltered position on England's western coast. Because the town faces due south and is protected from all other points of the compass by a ring of hills, its climate is ideal year-round. Winter is mild and virtually without frost, followed by an early spring and a temperate summer. Botanically, Penzance is noted for its early flowers and produce.

You need not confine yourself to the limits of Penzance, although you'll find it almost impossible to get away from its magnetic attractions. Local bus service can take you to **Land's End,** and rail connections (inquire at the rail station) can be made to other equally interesting points on the peninsula, such as Falmouth, Newquay, and St. Ives. The tourist information center can give you the background on these interesting places, and you can ask the Rail Travel Centre in the train station to work out the needed schedules.

From Cardiff or London, Penzance lends itself more to an "out-and-back" excursion than to a day excursion, although it is possible to visit England's westernmost town in the course of a day and still be back in Cardiff or London that evening.

An excellent way to visit Penzance is to board the sleeper that departs from London's Paddington Station just before midnight, at 2345. You can board about an hour before departure time, have the attendant make a nightcap for you, and be well into dreamland by the time the train rolls out of London's suburbs. At 0800 you arrive in Penzance Station after being awakened by the attendant bringing your morning tea or coffee and biscuits. After a full day's sightseeing in Penzance, you can board either the sleeper departing at 2145 to return to London or the InterCity 125 at 1600 to return to London by 2121 or depart at 1737 and arrive in London at 2336 the same evening.

Penzance also offers a diversion. When you feel it's time to move on from London to the north toward Edinburgh, check out of your London accommodations and take the sleeper to Penzance. Go sightseeing in Penzance, then arrive back in London as previously described at 2121 and transfer leisurely to London's Euston Station to board a Caledonian Sleeper at 2350. You'll arrive in Edinburgh the next morning at 0728.

Sleeper reservations should be made well in advance. Don't wait until the last minute or you may be disappointed, especially during holidays and peak summer travel periods. Reservations may be made in the rail station once you are in Britain. Don't forget to check the standard-class sleeper availability if first class is filled. Sometimes if you show up on the departure platform about half an hour before the train leaves, you can pick up a berth cancellation, but don't count on it.

London–Penzance

Schedules shown are for direct service that departs from London Paddington Station. Other services are possible by changing trains in Plymouth or by departing from London Waterloo and changing at Exeter St. Davids Station.

DEPART Paddington Station	ARRIVE Penzance Station	NOTES
0730	1317	M–Sa
0800	1413	Su
1006	1512	M–Sa
1206 (1230 Su)	1712 (1847 Su)	Daily
1406	1935	M–Sa
1506 (1430 Su)	2039 (2055 Su)	Daily
1606	2131	M–Sa
1703 (1633 Su)	2229 (2253 Su)	Daily
1803 (1755 Su)	2313 (0055+1 Su)	Daily
2345	0800+1	M–F

Last train shown conveys first- and standard-class sleepers and standard-class chair cars.
Reservations required for all overnight sleeper trains.
+1=Arrives next day.

Penzance–London

DEPART Penzance Station	ARRIVE Paddington Station	NOTES
0645	1223	M–Sa
0741	1338	M–F
0844	1344 (1429 Su)	M–Sa
1000 (1013 Su)	1524 (1644 Su)	Daily
1049 (1058 Sa)	1621	M–Sa
1209	1850	Su
1400	1924	M–Sa
1415	2042	Su
1600 (1553 Sa)	2121	M–Sa
1721	0038+1	Su
1739	2350	M–Sa
2115	0505+1	Su
2145	0525 +1	M–F

Last train shown conveys first- and standard-class sleepers and standard-class chair cars. Arrival time shown is next day. Reservations required for all overnight sleeper trains. +1=Arrives next day.

Day Excursion to

Plymouth

Pilgrim's Progress Port

From Cardiff: Depart from Cardiff Central Station
Distance by train: 166 miles (267 km)
Average train time: 3 hours, 15 minutes
From London: Depart from Paddington Station
Distance by train: 226 miles (363 km)
Average train time: 3 hours
Train information and InterCity services: (0845) 748 4950
Tourist information: Plymouth Tourist Information, Plymouth Mayflower Centre, 3–5 The Barbican Plymouth, Devon PL1 2LR; *Tel:* (0175) 230 6330
www.visitplymouth.co.uk
E-mail: barbicantic@plymouth.gov.uk
Hours: Monday–Saturday 0900–1700, Sunday and bank holidays 1000–1600
Notes: You can reach the tourist information center on foot from the train station in about twenty minutes through short underground passages and a pedestrian area. Look for the streams, fountains, and gardens, which form part of an outstanding display. If you don't feel like walking, then take Bus No. 25 (the "hop-on-hop-off" service), or board any bus stopping at the shelter to the right of the station entrance. Pay your fare and ask

to be "deposited" at the Barbican. Folks who are in a real hurry can hail a taxi. There is also a taxi queue just outside of the rail station; the bus stop is a few steps beyond.

Plymouth has one of the finest natural harbors in Europe. From Plymouth Hoe (a Saxon word meaning "high place above the sea"), there are magnificent views over Plymouth Sound and the harbor. Stand on this huge brow of a hill, one of the world's finest natural promenades, and you stand in the midst of history. Sir Francis Drake continued his game of bowls here before setting out to deal with the Spanish Armada in 1588. Earlier, in 1577, he set sail from the same harbor in the *Golden Hind* on a three-year voyage around the world. Here, too, in 1620 the Pilgrims embarked on the *Mayflower* for the New World. Too few remember that the first airplane to cross the Atlantic Ocean, the U.S. Navy seaplane *NC4,* touched down in Plymouth Sound. This spot is indeed steeped in historical heritage, much of it related to America. Stand here proudly!

While at the tourist information office, ask for a copy of the pamphlet *Plymouth in Your Pocket;* it contains an easy-to-read map of things to see and do within and near Plymouth. For an introduction to Plymouth, visit the **National Marine Aquarium** or see the **Plymouth Dome.** Situated on Plymouth's famous Hoe, the Dome is one of the most up-to-date centers of its kind in Britain. Here you can take a journey through time, use high-resolution cameras to zoom the shoreline, and enjoy many other exciting activities. We guarantee you won't run out of things to do while in Plymouth.

The Plymouth of today is a city of two distinct parts: the original Elizabethan harbor area called the "Barbican" and the modern city center that rose from the devastation and debris of World War II. If your time in Plymouth is limited, concentrate on visiting the Barbican area of the city.

The Barbican section, where the old town of Plymouth is nestled, derived its name from the fact that at the entrance to the harbor stood an outpost of the ancient Plymouth Castle. According to castle phraseology, such outer fortifications were called barbicans. The Barbican was spared much of the damage that Plymouth suffered during the bombardments of World War II. Consequently, there are still many old buildings and narrow streets in this area that recapture the Elizabethan atmosphere.

One Barbican landmark of particular interest to U.S. citizens is a **memorial stone** marking the place on the harbor pier from which the *Mayflower* sailed. Historic Elizabethan buildings include the **Black Friars Distillery,** home of Plymouth Gin since 1793. The distillery is still operating in buildings formerly used as a monastery and dating from 1425. Visitors are welcome. The **Merchants House** on St. Andrews Street is the largest and finest structure remaining from the sixteenth and seventeenth centuries. Restored, it is open daily, except Monday (April–September), displaying Plymouth's history with the theme, "Tinker, Tailor, Soldier, Sailor . . . ."

The **Plymouth Mayflower Centre** is Plymouth's newest attraction, and the tourist information center is located on the ground floor. Through films, models, and interactive games and historical artifacts, you can enjoy all the stories of emigration from Plymouth in the nineteenth century and learn about the fascinating Barbican history. It's located on Barbican Quay near the Barbican Glassworks. For more details, contact the tourist information centre.

Towering over the Barbican, the **Royal Citadel,** built in the 1660s by Charles II, was erected as a warning to the citizens of Plymouth. Many of the fortress cannons still point toward the town and not out to sea, as one would normally expect them to do. They are open to the public daily between May 1 and September 30 for guided tours.

If you have ever sung a chorus or two of "The Eddystone Light," you are a likely customer for the engrossing book *The Four Eddystone Lighthouses,* by Robert Sanderson. Additional information on the lighthouses may also be found in the booklet *Smeaton's Tower and the Plymouth Breakwater*. The first Eddystone lighthouse was blown down in a storm. The second lighthouse withstood the elements but was destroyed by fire. **Smeaton's Tower** stood on the Eddystone Reef from 1759 to 1884 and subsequently was rebuilt on Plymouth Hoe.

If your urge "to go down to the sea in ships" overwhelms you, take a boat trip on **Plymouth Sound.** The information center has the details, including how to view the nearby **Royal Naval Base** at Devonport. If your call to the sea is more limited, browsing in the Barbican area will suffice if you throw an occasional glance seaward.

Cardiff–Plymouth–Cardiff

DEPART Central Station	**ARRIVE** Plymouth Station	**NOTES**
0800 (0805 Su)	1117 (1148 Su)	Daily
0930	1250	M–Sa (1)
1030	1343	M–Sa (1)
1130	1450	M–Sa (1)

DEPART Plymouth Station	**ARRIVE** Central Station	**NOTES**
1323	1643	Daily (1)
1425	1743	Daily (1)
1523	1843	Daily (1)
1625	1946	Daily (1)
1723	2045	Daily (1)
1825	2144	Daily (1)
1942	2254	M–Sa (1)
1955	2338	Su

(1) Change trains at Bristol Parkway or Temple Meads.

London–Plymouth–London

DEPART London Paddington Station	ARRIVE Plymouth Station	NOTES
0730	1117 (1121 Sa)	M–Sa
0800	1222	Su
0906	1225	M–Sa
1006	1306	M–F

DEPART Plymouth Station	ARRIVE London Paddington Station	NOTES
1500	1821	M–Sa
1600	1924	Su
1800 (1754 Sa)	2121 (2132 Sa)	M–Sa
1921	2315	Su
1942	2350	M–Sa

Day Excursion to

Swansea

The "Ugly, Lovely Town"

Depart from Cardiff Central Station
Distance by train: 46 miles (74 km)
Average train time: 50 minutes
Train information and InterCity services: (0845) 748 4950
Tourist information: Tourist Information Centre, Plymouth Street, Swansea SA1 3QG; *Tel:* (0179) 246 8321; *Fax:* (0179) 246 4602
www.visitswanseabay.com or **www.swansea.gov.uk**
E-mail: tourism@swansea.gov.uk
Hours: Monday–Saturday 0930–1730; Sunday 1000–1600 (summer only)
Notes: Take any bus from the rail station to the bus station. The tourist center is just opposite the bus station. On foot, it's a ten- to fifteen-minute walk.

Birthplace of poet and playwright Dylan Thomas (1914–1953), who once referred to Swansea as the "ugly, lovely town," Swansea is the gateway to West Wales. Now Wales's second-largest city, it boasts one of Europe's most striking and successful waterfront developments. During the eighteenth and nineteenth centuries, Swansea became an important industrial center when the port was developed to export coal and its rapidly growing copper products.

Thanks to heavy destruction in World War II, Swansea's city center was rebuilt to include pedestrianized shopping areas. In 1974 it was expanded to include the scenic sandy beaches and resort area, the Gower Peninsula, which was designated Britain's first area of "Outstanding Natural Beauty."

Enjoy a panoramic view of Swansea Bay from the **Observatory Tower** in the magnificent Maritime Quarter. There's a footpath that runs from the Maritime Quarter for about 5 miles along the seafront to the Mumbles, a charming little resort. The 900-foot Victorian **Mumbles Pier** is one of Swansea's most famous landmarks and affords an excellent view of Swansea Bay. Hungry? Along Mumbles Mile, you'll find no shortage of excellent restaurants and pubs.

The world's first **Lovespoon Gallery** opened in the Mumbles in 1987 and features more than 300 designs of the traditional hand-carved Welsh gift of love. Visit daily from 1000 to 1730. Since the seventeenth century, Welshmen have given hand-carved wooden spoons, known as "lovespoons," to their lady friends as a prelude to courtship and an indication of their serious intentions. Over the years the carved designs on the spoons became more intricate, and certain symbols took on definitive meanings. For example, intricately carved boxes with balls inside came to mean the number of children desired. Then, carved chains added to the spoon indicated the number of years together. Perhaps over the years, the original "prelude to courtship" lovespoon matured into the "ball and chain" anniversary spoon.

Cardiff–Swansea–Cardiff

DEPART Central Station	ARRIVE Swansea Station	NOTES
0758	0851	M–Sa
0904	0957	M–Sa
0948	1044	Daily
1048	1143	Daily
1148	1243	Daily
1314	1420	Daily

Then two or three departures hourly until 2104 M–Sa, then 2226 and 2315. Trains every other hour Sunday, last train 2230.

DEPART Swansea Station	ARRIVE Central Station	NOTES
1428	1522	M–Sa
1528 (1533 Su)	1622	Daily
1555	1746	Su
1629	1722	M–Sa
1655	1748	Daily
1728	1822	Daily
1828	1922	M–Sa
1929	2022	M–Sa
2028 (2040 Su)	2122	Daily
2145	2249	Daily
2232	2338	M–Sa
2330	0029+1	Su

+1=Arrives the next day.

The heart of Swansea is a square bounded by four streets: Princess Way on the east side, Westway on the west, the Kingsway along the north, and Oystermouth Road on the south side. Within the square you'll find the tourist information center, the Grand Theatre, St. David's Square, the Quadrant Centre, two shopping districts, and Swansea's famous **Covered Market,** featuring everything from antiques and books to pottery and fresh produce. Try the local delicacy, a spicy meat dish called hot faggots and peas.

Swansea's Maritime and Industrial Museum on Oystermouth Road is open daily, except December 25, 26, and January 1. Admission is free. According to Dr. Richard Bevins, the project leader for the expansion and reconstruction of the museum, "From the very beginning we wanted to build a museum for people who don't do museums." **The National Waterfront Museum,** which tells the story of industry in the sea in Wales, is located on the marina next to the old Leisure Centre building, across from Princess Way (*Tel:* 0179 263 8950, www.museumwales .ac.uk). It is housed in an amazing glass and slate building and open daily 1000–1700, with free admission.

London–Swansea–London

Schedules shown are for direct trains. Additional service is available by changing trains in Cardiff.

DEPART Paddington Station	ARRIVE Swansea Station	NOTES
0645	0945	M–F
0745	1044	M–Sa
0830	1151	Su
0845	1143	M–Sa
0945 (0930 Su)	1243	M–Sa
1045 (1037 Su)	1343	Daily

M–F hourly service continues after 1045 until 1545, then every half hour until 1915, then 2015, 2115, and 2245. Sa, Su hourly service continues until 2045 Sa, and 2137 Su.

DEPART Swansea Station	ARRIVE Paddington Station	NOTES
1428	1732	M–Sa
1528	1827	M–Sa
1555	1902	Su
1628	1932	M–Sa
1651	2011	Su
1728	2032	M–Sa
1751	2114	Su
1828	2133	M–Sa
1851	2215	Su
1929	2245	M–Sa
1959	2316	Su

Seat reservations are available for above-listed trains.

The **Abbey Woollen Mill** at the museum features the stages of manufacturing woolen products, and you can take home finished traditional Welsh woolen goods. Admission is free, and the finished products are sold at bargain factory prices, so bring your credit card. The Maritime Quarter also is home to a leisure center, theater, arts workshops, and, of course, marinas dotted with colorful boats and yachts.

Follow the Dylan Thomas Trail around the Maritime Quarter to Dylan Thomas Square, where you will find the Dylan Thomas Theatre and a statue of Swansea's most famous son. Check out the Dylan Thomas Web site, www.dylanthomas.com, and visit Swansea's unique **Dylan Thomas Centre,** open 1000–1630 daily.

Excursion to

Tenby

Scenic Seaside Resort

Depart from Cardiff Central Station

Distance by train: 168 km (104 miles)

Average train time: 3 hours, 9 minutes

Train information and InterCity services: (0845) 748 4950

Tourist information: Tourist Information Centre, Unit 2, Upper Park Road, Tenby SA70 7LT; *Tel:* (0183) 484 2402; *Fax:* (0183) 484 5439

www.virtualtenby.co.uk/

E-mail: tenby.tic@pembrokeshire.gov.uk

Hours: Winter, Monday–Saturday 1000–1600, closed Sunday; Summer, Monday–Friday 0930–1700, Sunday 1000–1600

Notes: To get to the tourist office, walk straight ahead from the rail station along Warren Street. Turn right onto Penally Road, then left onto Park Road. The tourist office is immediately ahead on the right.

History buffs, as well as seaside-and-sun-soakers, will enjoy this picturesque walled town and lively resort. Evidence of coins indicates that Tenby probably existed in some form during Roman times, but it was not until about 875 when it was first mentioned in a poem, referred to as Dynbych-y-Pysgod (Fortlet of the Fishes).

Take Bridge Street down to the harbor, dotted with small, colorful boats and redolent with the scents of the sea. Take a boat trip to **Caldey Island,** where excavations revealed human remains from the Stone Age. Boats run from Tenby Harbor every fifteen minutes 0930–1700 Monday through Friday and 1100–1600 Saturday. Tickets are available from the kiosk in Castle Square above the harbor. Just 3 miles south of Tenby, Caldey measures about 2 miles wide and less than a mile long. The main attraction on the island is the **Caldey Abbey,** built in 1910 by

Anglican Benedictine monks who first came to the island in 1906. The abbey was sold in 1926 to the austere Cistercian monks who occupy it today.

The tower on top of Castle Hill was first documented in 1153. Although the castle fell into ruins by 1386, Tenby continued to prosper as a port by importing wines and salt and exporting coal, culm, and cloth until the seventeenth century, when the town again suffered decline. During the Victorian era Tenby was rescued by the opening of the railway and by Sir William Paxton, among others, who developed Tenby as a resort for well-heeled tourists. Paxton's grand bathhouse promoted seawater as a cure for several ailments.

The **Tenby Museum & Art Gallery** is open daily 1000–1700; admission £4 adults, £2 children; *Tel:* (01834) 842809, www.tenbymuseum.org.uk. The Tenby Lifeboat is exhibited year-round, and the museum features rotating art exhibitions.

The town's surviving sections of its thirteenth-century walls are about 20 feet high and stretch along the base of the promontory. Armed with a map from the tourist office, you can conduct your own walking tour of this charming little town. From the famous five-arched St. George's Gate, turn right onto St. George's Street, and proceed to St. Mary's Church on the left-hand side. Most of what we see today was extensively modified in the fifteenth and nineteenth centuries.

On Quay Hill, just east of St. Mary's Church, is a rare example of a successful merchant's home during the late fifteenth century. This is the three-story **Tudor Merchant's House,** open April–October Sunday–Friday 1000–1700 (closed Saturday); *Tel:* (01834) 842279. *Admission:* £3.00 adult, £1.50 child, £7.50 family.

Cardiff–Tenby–Cardiff

DEPART Central Station	ARRIVE Tenby Station	NOTES
0904	1145	M–Sa
1104	1345	M–F
1304	1545	M–Sa
1504	1745	M–Sa
1704	1950	M–Sa
1804	2119	Su
1904	2143	M–Sa

DEPART Tenby Station	ARRIVE Central Station	NOTES
0738	1048	M–Sa
0938	1247	M–F
1141	1447	M–Sa
1223	1636	Su
1341	1647	M–Sa
1541	1847	M–Sa
1741	2051	M–Sa
1957 (1930 Su)	2249 (2249 Su)	Daily

London–Tenby

All service requires a change of trains in Cardiff; for schedules from London to Tenby, see the separate tables for London to Cardiff and Cardiff to Tenby.

APPENDIX

Calling the United Kingdom

To telephone or send a fax to the United Kingdom from the United States, you must first use the international dialing code 011. Then dial the United Kingdom country code 44. All of the area codes within Britain start with a 0, but you do not use it when you are dialing from the United States. For example, to telephone the tourist information office in Bath from the United States, dial 011 44 (870) 444 6442.

British Tourist Information Centers

Below is a listing of British tourist information centers applicable to cities appearing in this edition.

Key to Listing:

- 🚆 Train/railway
- ✶ National Express Coach
- ♿ Wheelchair/ramps
- Ⓑ Book-a-Bed-Ahead accommodations for personal callers (for same or next night) in any town with a tourist information center offering this service
- † Accommodation services available to personal callers (for same or next night)
- Ⓔ Bureau de Change currency exchange

BRITAIN
BTA British Visitor Centre

1 Regent Street
Piccadilly Circus
London SW1Y 4XT
Tel: (0207) 846 9000
Fax: (0207) 563 0302
www.visitbritain.com

ENGLAND
English Tourist Board
1 Palace Street
London
SW1E 5HX
Tel: (0207) 578 1400
www.enjoyengland.com

Bath
Bath Tourism Bureau
✱ ♿ Ⓑ † Ⓔ
Abbey Chambers
Abbey Church Yard
Bath, Somerset BA1 1LY
Tel: (0906) 711 2000
Accommodations: (0870) 420 1278
Fax: (0122) 547 7787
www.visitbath.co.uk or www.heritagecities
.com
E-mail: tourism@bathtourism.co.uk

Birmingham
Tourism Centre & Ticket Shop
✱ ♿ Ⓑ †
The Rotunda
150 New Street
Birmingham B2 4PA
Tel: (0121) 202 5115
Fax: (0121) 202 5080
www.beinbirmingham.com
E-mail: callcentre@marketingbirmingham
.com

Birmingham Convention and Visitor Bureau
✱ ♿ Ⓑ †
National Exhibition Centre
Birmingham, West Midlands B40 1NT
Tel: (0121) 202 5099

Brighton
Brighton Visitor Information Centre
Ⓑ †
Royal Pavilion Shop, Royal Pavilion
4–5 Pavilion Buildings
Brighton, East Sussex BN1 1EE
Tel: (0127) 329 0337
Fax: (0127) 329 2594
www.visitbrighton.com
E-mail: visitor.info@visitbrighton.com

Bury St. Edmunds
The Tourist Information Centre
Ⓑ †
6 Angel Hill
Bury St. Edmunds, Suffolk IP33 1UZ
Tel: (0128) 475 7083
Fax: (0128) 475 7084
www.stedmundsbury.gov.uk
E-mail: tic@stedsbc.gov.uk

Cambridge
Tourist Information Centre
✱ ♿ Ⓑ †
Peashill
Cambridge, CB2 3AD
Tel: (0871) 226 8006
Fax: (0122) 345 7588
www.visitcambridge.org
E-mail: info@visitcambridge.org

Canterbury
Canterbury Information Centre
Ⓑ †
12–13 Sun Street, The Buttermarket
Canterbury, Kent CT1 2HX
Tel: (0122) 737 8100
Fax: (0122) 737 8101
www.canterbury.co.uk
E-mail: canterburyinformation@canterbury
.co.uk

Chester
Visitor and Craft Centre
🚌 ✶ ♿ Ⓑ † Ⓔ
Vicar's Lane
Chester, Cheshire CH1 1QX
Tel: (0124) 435 1609
Fax: (0124) 440 3188
www.chester.gov.uk or www.heritagecities.com
E-mail: tourism@chester.gov.uk

Chester Centre
🚌 ✶ ♿ Ⓑ †
Town Hall
Northgate Street
Chester, Cheshire CH1 2HJ
Tel: (0124) 440 2111
Fax: (0124) 440 0420

Coventry
City of Coventry Leisure Services
🚌 ✶ ♿ Ⓑ †
Tourist Information Centre
4 Priory Row
Coventry, West Midlands CV1 5RN
Tel: (0247) 622 5616
Fax: (0247) 622 7255
www.visitcoventry.co.uk
E-mail: tic@cvone.co.uk

Dover
Dover Tourist Information Centre
🚌 ✶ ♿ Ⓑ †
Old Town Gaol
Biggin Street
Dover, Kent CT16 1DL
Tel: (0130) 420 5108
Fax: (0130) 424 5409
www.dover.gov.uk or www.whitecliffscountry.org.uk
E-mail: tic@dover.uk.com

Folkestone
Discover Folkestone
20 Bouverie Place Shopping Centre
Folkestone, Kent CT20 1AU
Tel: (0130) 325 8594
Fax: (0130) 325 9754
www.discoverfolkestone.co.uk
E-mail: cckirkham@gmail.com

Gloucester
Gloucester Tourist Office
🚌 ✶ ♿ Ⓑ †
28 Southgate Street
Gloucester GL1 2DP
Tel: (0145) 239 6572
Fax: (0145) 2504 273
www.gloucester.gov.uk/tourism
E-mail: tourism@gloucester.gov.uk

Greenwich
Tourist Information Centre
🚌 ♿ Ⓑ †
Pepys House
2 Cutty Sark Gardens
Greenwich SE10 9LW
Tel: (0870) 608 2000
Fax: (0208) 853 4607
www.greenwich.gov.uk
E-mail: tic@greenwich.gov.uk

Hastings
Hastings Tourist Office
🚌 ✶ ♿ Ⓑ †
Queens Square, Priory Meadow
Hastings, East Sussex TN34 1TL
Tel: (0142) 445 1111
Fax: (0142) 478 1186
www.visithastings.com
E-mail: hic@hastings.gov.uk

Ipswich
Tourist Information Centre
➡ ✶ ♿ Ⓑ †
St. Stephen's Church
St. Stephen's Lane
Ipswich, Suffolk IP1 1DP
Tel: (0147) 325 8070
Accommodations: (0147) 326 2018
Fax: (0147) 343 2017
www.visit-ipswich.com or www.ipswich.gov.uk
E-mail: tourist@ipswich.gov.uk

Isle of Wight
Isle of Wight Tourist Office
Ⓑ †
67 High Street
Shanklin, Isle of Wight PO37 6JJ
Tel: (0198) 381 3813
Fax: (0198) 382 3031
Accommodations: (0198) 381 3813
www.islandbreaks.co.uk
E-mail: info@islandbreaks.co.uk

King's Lynn
Tourist Information Centre
The Custom House
➡ ✶ ♿ Ⓑ †
Purfleet Quay
King's Lynn, Norfolk PE30 1HP
Tel: (0155) 376 3044
Fax: (0155) 381 9441
www.west-norfolk.gov.uk
E-mail: kings-lynn.tic@west-norfolk.gov.uk

Lincoln
The Lincoln Tourist Information Centre
✶ Ⓑ †
9 Castle Hill
Lincoln, Lincolnshire LN1 3AA
Tel: (0152) 545 5458
Fax: (0152) 254 1452
www.visitlincolnshire.com
E-mail: info@lincolnshiretourism.com

The Lincoln Tourist Information Centre
✶ Ⓑ †
21 The Cornhill
Lincoln, Lincolnshire LN1 3AA
Tel: (0152) 873 213
Fax: (0152) 254 1452

Liverpool
Merseyside Welcome Centre
➡ ♿ † Ⓔ
36–38 Whitechapel
Liverpool L2 6DZ
Tel: (0151) 233 2008 (25p/min.)
Fax: (0151) 708 0204
www.visitliverpool.com
E-mail: askme@visitliverpool.com

Tourist Information Centre
➡ ♿ † Ⓔ
Atlantic Pavilion
Albert Dock, Liverpool, Merseyside
L3 4AE
Tel: (0151) 233 2008 (25p/min.)

London
Britain Visitor Centre
Ⓑ † Ⓔ
1 Regent Street
Piccadilly Circus, London SW1Y 4XT
Tel: (0207) 846 9000
Fax: (0207) 563 0302
www.visitbritain.com

Tourist Information Centre (Heathrow)
✶ ♿ Ⓑ †
Heathrow Airport
Terminals 1, 2, 3
Underground Station Concourse
London Heathrow Airport
Middlesex TW6 2JA
Tel: (0209) 068 663344
Fax: (0207) 824 8844

Tourist Information Centre
(Camden)
Town Hall
Argyle Street, London WC1H 8NN
Tel: (0207) 974 5974
Fax: (0207) 974 3210

Tourist Information Centre (Lewisham)
🚌 ✱ ♿
Lewisham Library Building
199–201 Lewisham High Street
London SE13 6LG
Tel: (0208) 297 8317
Fax: (0208) 297 9241

Tourist Information Centre (Southwark)
🚌 ✱ † Ⓔ
London Bridge
6 Tooley Street
Tel: (0207) 403 8299
Fax: (0207) 357 6321

Tourist Information Centre (Victoria)
🚌 ✱ ♿ Ⓑ †
Victoria Station Forecourt
London SW1V 1JU
Tel: (083) 912 3456
Accommodations: (0207) 824 8844
Fax: (0207) 931 7768

Nottingham
Nottingham Tourism Centre
🚌 ♿ †
1–4 Smithy Row
Nottingham
Nottinghamshire NG1 2BY
Tel: (0844) 477 5678
www.visitnottingham.com
E-mail: tourist.information@nottingham
city.gov.uk

Oxford
Oxford Information Centre
🚌 ♿ † Ⓔ
15–16 Broad Street
Oxford, Oxfordshire OX1 3AS
Tel: (0186) 525 2200
Fax: (0186) 524 0261
www.visitoxford.org or www.oxford.gov
.uk/tourism
E-mail: tic@oxford.gov.uk

Penzance
Tourist Information Centre
🚌 ♿ †
Station Road
Penzance, Cornwall TR18 2NF
Tel: (0173) 636 2207
Fax: (0173) 636 3600
www.penzance.co.uk

Plymouth
Plymouth Tourist Information
🚌 ♿ †
Plymouth Mayflower Centre
3–5 The Barbican
Plymouth, Devon PL1 2LS
Tel: (0175) 230 6330
Fax: (0175) 225 7955
www.visitplymouth.co.uk
E-mail: barbicantic@plymouth.gov.uk

Plymouth Discovery Centre
🚌 ♿ †
Crabtree
Plymouth, Devon PL3 6RN
Tel: (0175) 226 6030
Fax: (0175) 226 6033

Portsmouth
Tourist Information Centre
Ⓑ †
The Hard
Portsmouth PO1 3QJ
Tel: (0239) 282 6722
Fax: (0239) 282 7519
www.visitportsmouth.co.uk
E-mail: tic@portsmouthcc.gov.uk

Ramsgate
Visitor Information Centre
Ⓑ †
Droit House, The Pier,
Margate
Kent, CT9 1JD
Tel: (0184) 357 7577
Fax: (0184) 358 5353
www.tourism.thanet.gov.uk
E-mail: visitorinformation@thanet.gov.uk

St. Albans
St. Albans Tourist Information Centre
♿ †
Town Hall
The Market Place
St. Albans, Hertfordshire AL3 5DJ
Tel: (0172) 786 4511
Fax: (0172) 786 3533
www.stalbans.gov.uk
E-mail: tic@stalbans.gov.uk

Salisbury
Salisbury Tourist Information Centre
♿ † Ⓔ
Fish Row
Salisbury, Wiltshire SP1 1EJ
Tel: (0172) 233 4956
Fax: (0172) 242 2059
www.visitsalisbury.com
E-mail: visitorinfo@salisbury.gov.uk

Sheffield
Sheffield Tourist Information Centre
♿ †
1 Tudor Square
Sheffield, South Yorkshire S1 2LA
Tel: (0114) 221 1900
Fax: (0114) 201 1020
www.yorkshiresouth.com
E-mail: visitor@yorkshiresouth.com

Southampton
Southampton Tourist Information Centre
♿ †
9 Civic Centre Road
Southampton SO14 7FJ
Tel: (0238) 083 3333
Fax: (0238) 083 3381
www.visit-southampton.co.uk
E-mail: tourist.information@southampton.gov.uk

Stonehenge
Stonehenge, English Heritage
First Floor Abbey Buildings
Abbey Square
Amesbury, Wiltshire SP4 7ES
Tel: (0870) 333 1181
Info Line: (0198) 062 4715
Fax: (0179) 341 4926
www.english-heritage.org.uk
See also Salisbury Tourist Information Centre

Stratford-upon-Avon
Stratford-upon-Avon Centre
♿ † Ⓔ
62 Henley Street
Stratford-upon-Avon
Warwickshire CV37 6PT
Tel: (0178) 926 4293
Fax: (0178) 929 5262
www.shakespeare-country.com or www.heritagecities.com
E-mail: stratfordtic@shakespeare-country.co.uk

Windsor
Windsor Information Centre
♿ †
24 High Street
Windsor SL4 1LH
Tel: (0175) 374 3900
Accommodations: (0175) 374 3900
Fax: (0175) 337 4929
www.windsor.gov.uk
E-mail: windsor.tic@rbwm.gov.uk

York
Tourist Information Centre
☕ † Ⓔ
1 Museum St
York, North Yorkshire YO1 7DT
Tel: (0190) 455 0099
Fax: (0190) 455 1888
www.visityork.org
E-mail: info@visityork.org

Tourist Information Centre
☕ ♿ † Ⓔ
Outer Concourse
York Railway Station
York, North Yorkshire YO1 7HB
Tel: (0190) 455 0099
Fax: (0190) 467 2753

SCOTLAND
Although the Scottish Tourist Offices do not have a code system listing specific services offered, the majority of offices are able to assist in planning where to go and what to see and in securing hotel and advance reservations for most events.

Scottish Booking & Info Centre
☕ ✶ ♿ Ⓑ † Ⓔ
P.O. Box 121
Livingston EH54 8AF
Tel: (0150) 683 2121 (outside U.K.);
(0845) 225 5121 (U.K.)
www.visitscotland.com
E-mail: info@visitscotland.com

Aberdeen
Aberdeen Visitor Information Centre
23 Union Street
Aberdeen AB11 5BP
Tel: (0122) 428 8828
Fax: (0122) 425 2219
www.aberdeen-grampian.com
E-mail: aberdeen@visitscotland.com

Ayr
Ayrshire & Arran Tourist Board
15 Skye Road
Prestwick KA9 2TA
Ayr Tourist Information Centre
22 Sandgate
Ayr KA7 1BW
Tel: (0129) 229 0300
Fax: (0129) 228 8686
www.ayrshire-arran.com
E-mail: info@ayrshire-arran.com

Dunbar
Dunbar Tourist Office Centre
143 High Street
Dunbar EH4 21ES
Tel: (0136) 886 3353
Fax: (0136) 832 222
www.dunbar.org.uk
E-mail: esic@eltb.org

Dundee
Visit Scotland Angus & Dundee
Discovery Point, Discovery Quay
Dundee, DD1 4XA
Tel: (0138) 252 7527
Fax: (0138) 252 7551
www.angusanddundee.co.uk
E-mail: dundee@visitscotland.com

Dunfermline
Tourist Information Centre
1 High Street
Dunfermline KY12 7DL
Tel: (0138) 372 0999
Fax: (0138) 362 5807
www.dunfermlineonline.net
E-mail: admin@dunfermline.info

Edinburgh
Edinburgh & Lothians Tourist Board
3 Princes Street
Edinburgh EH2 2QP
Tel: (0131) 473 3800
Fax: (0131) 473 3881
www.edinburgh.org
E-mail: esic@eltb.org

Glasgow
Greater Glasgow & Clyde Valley
Tourist Board
11 George Street
Glasgow G2 1DY
Tel: (0141) 566 0800
Fax: (0141) 566 0810
www.seeglasgow.com
E-mail: enquiries@seeglasgow.com

Inverness
The Highlands of Scotland Tourist Board
Castle Wynd
Inverness IV2 3BJ
Tel: (0146) 323 4353
Fax: (0146) 371 0609
www.inverness-scotland.com or www
.visithighlands.com
E-mail: inverness@host.co.uk

Kyle of Lochalsh
Tourist Board
Car Park
Kyle of Lochalsh IV40 8QA
Tel: (0845) 225 5121
Fax: (01506) 832 222
www.visithighlands.com
E-mail: kyle@host.co.uk

Linlithgow
Edinburgh & Lothians Tourist Board
(Linlithgow)
County Buildings, High Street
Linlithgow, West Lothian EH49 7EZ
Tel: (0150) 684 4600
Fax: (0150) 667 1373
www.linlithgow.com

Montrose (April–September)
Montrose Tourist Information Centre
Panmure Place
Montrose DD10 8HE
Tel: (0167) 673232
www.angusanddundee.co.uk
E-mail: dundee@visitscotland.com

Perth
Tourist Information Centre
Lower City Mills
West Mill Street
Perth PH3 1LQ
Tel: (0173) 845 0600
Fax: (0173) 844 4863
www.perthshire.co.uk
E-mail: perth@visitscotland.com

St. Andrews
St. Andrews Tourist Information Centre
70 Market Street
Fife KY10 9NU
Tel: (0133) 447 2021
Fax: (0133) 447 8422
www.standrews.com
E-mail: standrewstic@kftb.ossian.net

Stirling
Stirling Tourist Information Centre
41 Dumbarton Road
Stirling FK8 2QQ
Tel: (0178) 647 5019
Fax: (0178) 645 0039
www.visitscottishheartlands.com
E-mail: stirlingtic@visitscotland.com

Royal Burgh of Stirling Visitor Centre
Castle Esplanade
Stirling FK8 1EA
Tel: (0178) 647 9901
Fax: (0178) 646 1881

Stranraer
Tourist Information Centre
Burns House
Harbour Street
Stranraer DG9 7RA
Tel: (0177) 670 2595
Fax: (0177) 688 9156
www.stranraer.org
E-mail: stranraer@visitscotland.com

WALES
Welsh Tourist Board
🚌 ✶ ♿ Ⓑ † Ⓔ
Brunel House
2 Fitzalan Road
Cardiff CF2 1UY
Tel: (0292) 049 4473
www.visitwales.com
E-mail: info@tourism.wales.gov.uk

Caerphilly
Caerphilly Visitor Centre
🚌 Ⓑ †
Lower Twyn Square
Caerphilly, Mid Glamorgan CF83 1XX
Tel: (0292) 088 0011
Fax: (0292) 086 0811
www.caerphilly.gov.uk/visiting

Cardiff
Visitor Centre
🚌 Ⓑ †
The Old Library, The Hayes
Cardiff CF10 1WE
Tel: (0292) 121 1258
Fax: (0292) 023 9162
www.visitcardiff.info
E-mail: visitor@thecardiffinitiative.co.uk

Swansea
Tourist Information Centre
🚌 Ⓑ †
Plymouth Street
Swansea SA1 3QG
Tel: (0179) 246 8321
Fax: (0179) 246 4602
www.swansea.gov.uk or
www.visitswanseabay.com
E-mail: tourism@swansea.gov.uk

Tenby
Tourist Information Centre
🚌 Ⓑ †
Unit 2
Upper Park Road
Tenby SA70 7LT
Tel: (0183) 484 2402
Fax: (0183) 484 5439
www.virtualtenby.co.uk
E-mail: tenby.tic@pembrokeshire.gov.uk

Recommended Information Sources

British Tourist Authority Offices in North America
www.visitbritain.com
New York: 551 Fifth Avenue, 7th Floor, Suite 701, New York, NY 10176-0799
Tel: (212) 986-2266 or (800) GO-2-BRIT; Fax: (212) 986-1188;
E-mail: travelinfo@bta.org.uk
Chicago: 625 North Michigan Avenue, Suite 1001, Chicago, IL 60611-4977
Tel: (312) 787-0464; Fax: (312) 787-9641

National Rail Inquiries
www.nationalrail.co.uk
Rail schedules and fare information within Great Britain.
Tel: (0845) 748 4950

Scottish Tourist Board
www.visitscotland.com
Contact information same as British Tourist Authority listed above.

Wales Tourist Board
www.visitwales.com
Contact information same as British Tourist Authority listed above.

To Purchase Passes

BritRail
www.britrail.com
Tel: (866) BRITRAIL

Eurail
www.eurail.com
E-mail: orders@eurail.com

Euro Railways
www.eurorailways.com
Tel: (954) 323-8389

Rail Europe
www.raileurope.com
Tel: (800) 622-8600

Useful Phone Numbers—London

When dialing from the United States, use the codes 011 + 44 and omit the 0 from the beginning of the phone numbers listed below.

Accommodations
British Hotel Reservation Centre
13 Grosvenor Gardens
London SW1W OBD
(020) 592 3055
U.S. toll-free: (866) 279 2925
Fax: (0207) 828 6439
www.bhrconline.com
E-mail: hotels@bhrconline.com

Expotel Hotel Reservations
Kingsgate House, Kingsgate Place, London NW6 4HG
Reservations: (800) 634 3290
(0207) 328 9841
Fax: (0207) 328 8021
www.expotel.com

Victoria Station, by platform 9
(0207) 888 4646

Gatwick Station
(0129) 352 9372

King's Cross Station, adjacent to platform 8

Hotel Finders
Brookscroft House, 26 Second Avenue
London E17 9QH
(0208) 923 0918
Fax: (0208) 521 9548
www.london-guides.co.uk/hotels.php
E-mail: info@london-guides.co.uk

The London Bed & Breakfast Agency
71 Fellows Road, London NW3 3JY
(0207) 586 2768
Fax: (0207) 586 6567
www.londonbb.com
E-mail: stay@londonbb.com

The London Tourist Board
(0207) 604 2890
www.visitlondon.com

Airport Information (www.baa.co.uk)
Heathrow, general inquiries
(0870) 000 0123

London City Airport
(0207) 565 0777
www.londoncityairport.com

Gatwick (0870) 000 2468

Stansted (0870) 000 0303

American Express
30–31 Haymarket, Piccadilly Circus
(0207) 484 9610

Bike/Scooter Rentals
London Bicycle Co., 1a Gabriel's Wharf
(0207) 928 6838
www.londonbicycle.com
E-mail: mail@londonbicycle.com

On Your Bike, 52–54 Tooley Street
(0207) 378 6669
www.onyourbike.com
E-mail: london@onyourbike.com

Scootabout, 1–3 Leeke Street
(0207) 833 4607
www.hgbmotorcycles.co.uk

British Tourist Authority
British Visitor Centre
1 Regent Street, Piccadilly Circus SW1
(0208) 846 1000
www.visitbritain.com

Canadian Embassy
Canada Centre 62–65 Trafalgar Square
(0207) 258 6356

Emergency
Police or Ambulance, 999

Eurostar
(0870) 160 6600
www.eurostar.com

Express Bus Information
National Express
(0870) 580 8080
www.nationalexpress.co.uk

London Tourist Board (main office)
(0207) 932 2000
www.londontown.com

London Travel Transport Information
(0207) 222 1234

Post Office
Paddington Main Post Office
(0207) 239 2792

Rail Information
National Rail Inquiries
(0845) 748 4950 (U.K. only)
(133) 238 7601 (international callers)

River Trips and Canal Cruises
Bateaux London/Catamaran Cruises
(0207) 695 1800
www.bateauxlondon.com

George Wheeler Launches
(0207) 930 4097

King Cruises
(0800) 298 2563
www.kingcruises.com

Thames Clippers
(0870) 781 5049
www.thamesclippers.com

Thames Cruises
(0207) 740 0400
www.citycruises.com

Thames Leisure
(0207) 623 1805
www.thamesleisure.co.uk

Sleeper Reservations
Use rail inquiries No.:
in the U.K. (0845) 748 4950
outside the U.K. +44 (1332) 387601

U.S. Embassy
55 Upper Brook Street, London W1A 1AE
(0207) 499 9000
www.usembassy.org.uk

Victoria Student Travel Service
Need student I.D. to book
accommodations
(0870) 240 1010

Useful Phone Numbers—Edinburgh

Airport Information
(0870) 040 0007

American Express
139 Princes Street
(0131) 225 7881

Emergency
Fire, Police, Ambulance
999

City Sightseeing Tours
(0131) 556 2244

Student Travel Centre
(0131) 668 2221

Edinburgh Military Tattoo Ticket Office
(0131) 225 1188
www.edinburgh-tattoo.co.uk

Tourist Information
City of Edinburgh Tourist Information and Accommodations, Waverley Market, Princes Street
(0131) 473 3800

Useful Phone Numbers—Glasgow

Airport
(0870) 040 0008

American Express
115 Hope Street
(0141) 221 4366

Emergency
Ambulance, Police, Fire, and Coast Guard
999

Glasgow Travel Centre
(0141) 226 4826

First ScotRail
(0141) 332 9811

Tourist Information
Tourist Information, 35 St. Vincent Place
(0141) 204 4400

Useful Phone Numbers—Cardiff

Cardiff Bay Visitor Centre
Harbour Drive, Waterfront Park
(0292) 046 3833

Cardiff International Airport Information
Rhoose, Wales
(0144) 671 1111
Cardiff Tourist Information Centre
Cardiff Central Station, Central Square
(0291) 022 7281
Fax: (0292) 023 9162

Emergency
Ambulance, Police, Fire, and Coast Guard
999

Train-Operating Companies
www.nationalrail.co.uk

For general inquiries and timetable information, telephone the National Rail Inquiries number: within the U.K. (0845) 748 4950; outside the U.K., dial your country's international access code, plus 44-1332-387601. Web links to the individual train-operating companies are provided on www.nationalrail.co.uk.

Arriva Trains, Wales
(0845) 606 1660
www.arrivatrainswales.co.uk

c2c, Customer Services
Tel: (0845) 601 4873
www.c2c-online.co.uk

Cross country Trains
Cannon House
18 Priory Queensway
Birmingham, England B4 6BS
Tel: (0870) 010 0084
www.crosscountrytrains.co.uk

Chiltern Railways
Western House, 14 Rickfords Hill
Aylesbury HP20 2RX
Tel: (0845) 600 5165
Fax: (0129) 633 2126
www.chilternrailways.co.uk

East Midlands Trains
Nottingham, England, NG2 3DQ
Tel: (0845) 712 5678
www.eastmidlandstrains.co.uk

East Coast
Freepost RRZG-ZZZX-LKXK
Newcastle upon Tyne
NE1 5DN
Tel: (08457) 225 333
www.eastcoast.co.uk

Eurostar (UK) Customer Service
Eurostar House, Waterloo Station
London SE1 8SE
Tel: (0177) 777 7879
Bookings in the U.S.
Tel: 877-RAILPASS (724-5727)
www.eurostar.com

First Capital Connect Customer Relations
Freepost ADM3973
London SW1 AYP
Tel: (0845) 026 4700
www.firstcapitalconnect.co.uk

First Great Western, Customer Care
Milford House, 1 Milford Street
Swindon SN1 1HL
Tel: (0845) 600 5604
www.firstgreatwestern.co.uk

First Great Western Link
Venture House, 37 Blagrave Street
Reading RG1 1PZ
Tel: (0845) 330 7182
www.firstgreatwestern.co.uk

First ScotRail, Customer Service
Caledonian Chambers, 87 Union Street
Glasgow G1 3TA
Tel: (0845) 601 5929
www.firstscotrail.com/

Gatwick Express
52 Grosvenor Gardens
London SW1W 0AU
Tel: (0845) 850 1530
Fax: (0207) 973 5038
www.gatwickexpress.com

Heathrow Express
3rd Floor, 30 Eastbourne Terrace
Paddington, London W2 6LE
Tel: (0845) 600 1515
Fax: (0208) 750 6615
www.heathrowexpress.co.uk

Hull Trains
Premier House, Ferensway
Hull HU1 3UF
Tel: (0190) 452 5221
Fax: (0190) 452 5208
www.hulltrains.co.uk

London Midland
PO Box 4323
Birmingham, England B2 4JB
Tel: (0121) 634 2040
www.londonmidland.com

Merseyrail, Customer Service
Rail House, Lord Nelson Street
Liverpool L1 1JF
Tel: (0151) 702 2071
Fax: (0151) 702 3074
www.merseyrail.org

National Express East Anglia
St. Clare House, Princes Street
Ipswich IP1 1LY
Tel: (0845) 600 7245
www.nationalexpresseastanglia.com

Northern Rail, Customer Service
Main Headquarters Building, Station Rise
York Y01 6HT
Tel: (0845) 600 1159
www.northernrail.org

Silverlink Train Services
Customer Services
Main Office, Hertford House
1 Cranwood Street, London EC1V 9QA
Tel: (0845) 601 4867
Fax: (01923) 207023
www.silverlink-trains.com

Southern Trains, Customer Services
Go Ahead House, 26–28 Addiscombe Road
Croydon CR9 5GA
Tel: (0845) 127 2920
www.southernrailway.com
Southeastern Railway
P.O. Box 125, Tonbridge TN9 2ZA
Tel: (0870) 603 0405
www.southeasternrailway.co.uk

South West Trains
Friars Bridge Court
41–45 Blackfriars Road
London SE1 8NZ
Tel: (0845) 600 0650
Fax: (0207) 620 5460
www.southwesttrains.co.uk

Virgin Trains
85 Smallbrook Queensway
Birmingham B5 4HA
Tel: (0870) 789 1234
Fax: (0121) 654 7500
www.virgintrains.co.uk

A Selection of One-Way Rail Fares in Britain

Deciding whether you should purchase a BritRail Pass becomes a matter of simple arithmetic. Plan your trip to Great Britain, decide what places you want to visit, and use the fares listed below to determine if the cost of individual rail segments exceeds the cost of a BritRail Pass. Round-trip fares are slightly less than double the one-way charge. Children five to fifteen years of age, inclusive, pay half fare. Children younger than age five travel free and do not need a ticket. All fares are applicable as of press time and subject to change without prior notice. They are estimates based on the exchange rate at the time of printing, given in U.S. dollars. To convert to pounds sterling, apply current rate of exchange. For example, at press time, the rate was approximately $1.00 = £.61

ONE-WAY FARES

	First Class $	Standard Class $
From London to:		
Aberdeen	321	240
Aviemore	351	179
Ayr	356	250
Bath Spa	194	54
Birmingham	196	70
Brighton	58	44
Cambridge	63	38
Canterbury	93	49
Cardiff	245	153
Chester	250	184
Coventry	130	106
Dover	78	55
Dundee	229	134
Edinburgh	247	177
Glasgow	261	184
Gloucester	180	114
Hastings	67	44
Inverness	348	281
King's Lynn	78	49
Leamington Spa	81	47
Lincoln	168	121
Liverpool	250	147
Manchester	250	196
Nottingham	147	55

	First Class $	Standard Class $
From London to:		
Oxford	76	21
Penzance	391	101
Perth	222	194
Plymouth	286	73
Portsmouth	90	50
Salisbury	99	52
Sheffield	212	135
Southampton	103	53
Stratford-upon-Avon	191	52
Windsor	31	21
York	149	100
From Glasgow to:		
Aberdeen	119	68
Birmingham	130	53
Dundee	60	37
Edinburgh	27	19
Inverness	106	68
Manchester	227	37
Perth	39	21
Sheffield	155	70
York	212	42

Passport Information

www.travel.state.gov

You can apply for a passport (in person if you are age fourteen or older and do not meet the requirements to renew a previous passport by mail or online) at more than 8,000 facilities in the United States, including many post offices; federal, state, and probate courts; some libraries; and some municipal and county offices. Passport forms are also available for downloading from the Internet (www.travel.state.gov), and you can enter your zip code to determine which facility is closest.

Apply several months in advance if possible. It usually takes a minimum of six weeks. The National Passport Information Center (NPIC) operates an automated information number: (877) 487-2778. A recorded message describes the documents you need and the application process for obtaining a passport and gives instructions on reporting the loss or theft of your passport. For new passports (age sixteen and older), the passport application fee is $110, plus execution fee $25, for a total of $165. Younger than age sixteen, the passport application fee is $80, execution fee $25, for a total of $105. Renewal passport fees are $110.

If you are traveling in less than two weeks or if you need foreign visas, you can contact the closest regional office for an appointment, send an extra $60 for expedited service (usually this gets your passport to you in two weeks if you also pay extra for overnight delivery), or use one of the express passport services online, such as www.americanpassport.com or www.passportexpress.com. Be prepared to pay *at least triple* the normal passport fees, but you are guaranteed to get your passport as fast as 24 hours after receiving the required documents.

The regional offices and their automated appointment numbers are as follows:

Boston: Thomas P. O'Neill Federal Building, 10 Causeway Street, Suite 247, Boston, MA 02222-1094; (617) 878-0900.

Chicago: Kluczynski Office Building, 230 South Dearborn Street, Suite 380, Chicago, IL 60604-1564; (312) 341-6020.

Honolulu: Prince Kuhio Federal Building, 300 Ala Moana Boulevard, Suite 1–330, Honolulu, HI 96850.

Houston: Mickey Leland Federal Building, 1919 Smith Street, Suite 1400, Houston, TX 77002-8049; (713) 751-0294.

Los Angeles: Federal Building, 11000 Wilshire Boulevard, Suite 1000, Los Angeles, CA 90024-3615; (310) 575-5700.

Miami: Claude Pepper Federal Office Building, 51 SW First Avenue, Third Floor, Miami, FL 33130-1680; (305) 539-3600.

New Orleans: One Canal Place, 365 Canal Street, Suite 1300, New Orleans, LA 70130-6508; (877) 487-2778.

New York: Greater Manhattan Federal Building, 376 Hudson Street, New York, NY 10014; (212) 206-3500.

Norwalk: 50 Washington Street, Norwalk, CT 06854; (203) 299-5443.

Philadelphia: U.S. Customs House, 200 Chestnut Street, Room 103, Philadelphia, PA 19106-2970; (215) 418-5937.

San Francisco: 95 Hawthorne Street, Fifth Floor, San Francisco, CA 94105-3901; (415) 538-2700.

Seattle: Federal Building, 915 Second Avenue, Suite 992, Seattle, WA 98174-1091; (206) 808-5700.

Washington, D.C.: 1111 Nineteenth Street NW, Washington, DC 20524-1705; (202) 647-0518.

Tips and Trivia

Do not be surprised to see a 20 percent value-added tax (VAT) added to your bill for items purchased or services rendered. The VAT appears on just about everything, excluding bus/rail transportation.

Tipping: For luggage, generally tip £1 per bag; taxis, 10–15 percent, with a £1 minimum; for service staff in hotels, 10–20 percent if service gratuity is not included in bill. Most restaurants include a 12.5 percent gratuity on the bill. Be sure to check before tipping too generously.

Imports: You may import into Britain 200 cigarettes or 50 cigars, two liters of table wine plus one liter of liquor over 22 percent alcohol or two liters of liquor under 22 percent alcohol (e.g., fortified or sparkling wine). Two fluid ounces (60 ml) of perfume or nine ounces (250 ml) of toilet water may be imported and £145 worth of other goods including gifts and souvenirs. Regulations are strictly imposed on firearms, drugs, pornography, plants, fruit, and goods made from protected species.

Shops: Most shops are open from 0900 to 1730. Shops in smaller towns may close for one hour at lunchtime. In London, shops in the Knightsbridge area (Harrods, for example) remain open until 1900 on Wednesday, whereas those in the West End (Oxford Street, Regent Street, and Piccadilly areas) stay open until 1900 on Thursday.

Banks: Banks are usually open Monday through Friday from 0930 to 1530. Some are open on Saturday mornings. Most banks in Scotland are closed for one hour at lunchtime. The banks at London's Heathrow and Gatwick Airports are open twenty-four hours a day.

Holidays: Most banks, shops, and some museums, historic houses, and other places of interest are closed on Sunday and public holidays. Public transport services generally are reduced, especially during Christmastime. Please see the 2012/2013 Bank and Public Holidays section.

Voltage: The standard voltage is 240v AC, 50 Hz.

Climate

	Jan	Feb	Mar	Apr	May	June	July	Aug	Sept	Oct	Nov	Dec
Average Low (F)	35°	35°	37°	40°	45°	51°	55°	54°	51°	44°	39°	36°
Average High (F)	44°	45°	51°	56°	63°	69°	73°	72°	67°	58°	49°	45°
Average Rainfall (in inches)	4	3	3	2	3	3	2	3	3	3	4	4

2012/13 Bank and Public Holidays

January 2/1	New Year's Day (date observed, U.K., Rep Ireland)*
January 3	Bank Holiday (Scotland)
March 17	St. Patrick's Day (Northern Ireland, Rep Ireland)*
April 6/March 29	Good Friday
April 9/1	Easter Monday (U.K., Rep Ireland)*
May 7/6	May Day (U.K., Rep Ireland)*
June 4	Spring Bank Holiday (U.K.)*
June 8/7	June Bank Holiday (Rep Ireland)*
July 12	Battle of the Boyne: Orangeman's Day (Northern Ireland)**
August 27/26	Bank Holiday (Scotland, Rep Ireland)
August 27/26	Summer Bank Holiday (England, Wales, Isle of Man, Northern Ireland)
October 25/31	Halloween Bank Holiday (Rep Ireland)
November 30	St. Andrew's Day (Scotland)
December 27	Christmas Day (U.K., Rep Ireland)*
December 28/26	St. Stephen's Day (Rep Ireland)
December 26	Boxing Day (U.K.)*

U.K.=England, Scotland, Wales, Northern Ireland

*Bank holidays

**Subject to proclamation by the Secretary of the State for Northern Ireland

Toll-free Airline Numbers and Web Sites

(Dialing from U.S.)

Air Lingus (EI)
(800) Irish-Air/474-7424
www.aerlingus.com

Air Canada (AC)
(888) 247-2262
www.aircanada.ca

Air France (AF)
(800) 237-2747
www.airfrance.com

American Airlines, Inc. (AA)
(800) 433-7300
www.aa.com

Austrian Airlines (OS)
(800) 843-0002
www.austrianair.com

British Airways (BA)
(800) AIRWAYS
www.britishairways.com

Continental Airlines (CO)
(800) 231-0856
www.continental.com

CSA Czech Airlines (OK)
(800) 628-6107
www.czechairlines.com

Delta Air Lines, Inc. (DL)
(800) 241-4141
www.delta.com

Finnair (AY)
(800) 950-5000
www.finnair.com

Icelandair (FI)
(800) 223-5500
www.icelandair.com

KLM Royal Dutch Airlines (KL)
(800) 374-7747
www.klm.com

Lufthansa German Airlines (LH)
(800) 645-3880
www.lufthansa-usa.com

Olympic Airways (OA)
(800) 223-1226
www.olympicairlines.com

Scandinavian Airlines System (SK)
(800) 221-2350
www.scandinavian.net

Swiss International Airlines
(877) 359-7947
www.swiss.com

TAP Air Portugal (TO)
(800) 221-7370
www.tap-airportugal.pt

United Airlines, Inc. (UA)
(800) 538-2929
www.ual.com

USAirways (US)
(800) 428-4322
www.usairways.com

Virgin Atlantic Airways Ltd. (VS)
(800) 862-8621
www.virgin-atlantic.com

Entertainment Booking Agencies

Applause Theatre & Entertainment Service
(Theater, Ballet/Opera)
(800) 451-9930
Fax: (212) 397-3729
www.applause-tickets.com

Keith Prowse
(West End)
(800) 669-8687
Tel: (212) 398-1430
Fax: (212) 328-4438
www.keithprowse.com

Ticketmaster
(West End)
(800) 775-2525
Tel: (212) 307-4100
www.ticketmaster.com

Toll-free Hotel Reservation Numbers

(Dialing from U.S.)

B&B My Guest
(800) 906-4232
www.beduk.co.uk

Barclay International (apartments)
(800) 845-6636
www.barclayweb.com

Best Western Hotels
(800) 528-1234
www.bestwestern.com

Castles, Cottages & Flats
(800) 742-6030
www.castlescottages-flats.com

Elegant English Hotels
(800) 270-9206
www.eeh.co.uk

Forte Hotels
(800) 225-5843
www.roccofortehotels.com

Hilton Hotels
(800) HILTONS
www.hilton.com

In the English Manner
(apartments/cottages)
(800) 422-0799
www.english-manner.co.uk

InterContinental Hotels & Resorts
(800) 424-6835
www.ichotelsgroup.com

London B&B
(800) 872-2632
www.londonbandb.com

Hotel Book
(800) 641-0300
www.hotelbook.com

Pride of Britain
(800) 98PRIDE
www.prideofbritainhotels.com

Radisson Edwardian Hotels
(800) 333-3333
www.radisson.com

Red Carnation Hotels
(800) 424-2862
www.redcarnationhotels.com

Thistle Hotels
(800) 847-4358
www.thistle.com

Sea Travel Information

(Dialing from U.S.)

Brittany Ferries
(01144) 8703 665 333
www.brittany-ferries.co.uk

Caledonian MacBrayne
(01144) 8705 650000
www.calmac.co.uk
(Scottish Islands)

Condor Ferries
(01144) 845 345 2000
www.condorferries.co.uk
(Channel Islands)

Irish Ferries
(01144) 8705 171717
www.irishferries.com

Isle of Man Steam Packet Company
(01144) 8705 523523
www.steam-packet.com

Isles of Scilly Steamship Company
(01144) 1736 334220
www.islesofscilly-travel.co.uk

Orkney Ferries
(01144) 1856 872044
www.orkneyferries.co.uk

P&O Ferries
(01144) 8705 202020
www.poferries.com

Red Funnel Ferries
(01144) 870 444 8898
www.redfunnel.co.uk
(Isle of Wight)

Sea France
(01144) 8705 711711
www.seafrance.co.uk

Shetland Islands Council
(01144) 1806 244219
www.shetland.gov.uk/ferries/

Stena Line
(01144) 8705 707070
www.stenaline.com

Wightlink
(01144) 8705 820202
www.wightlink.co.uk

BritRail Passes

A BritRail consecutive-day or Flexipass allows unlimited travel on the entire British rail network spanning England, Scotland, and Wales. Prices are current as of press time, but are always subject to change without notice. Prices are estimates based on the exchange rate at the time of printing.

BritRail Consecutive Pass

Valid for consecutive days of rail travel throughout Britain (England, Scotland, and Wales).

	ADULT 1st Class	**ADULT** Standard Class	**SENIOR** 1st Class	**YOUTH** Standard Class	**YOUTH** 1st Class
4 days	$339	$225	$289	$179	$269
8 days	$485	$319	$409	$259	$389
15 days	$725	$485	$615	$389	$579
22 days	$919	$609	$779	$489	$735
1 month	$1,085	$725	$925	$579	$869

Senior 60+. Youth 16–25. Children 5–15, half adult fare. Children younger than age 5 travel free.

BritRail Family Passes

Receive one free child pass (age 5–15) of the same type when purchasing one adult or senior BritRail Consecutive Pass, BritRail Flexipass, BritRail Pass + Ireland, BritRail Pass 'n Drive, or BritRail Party Pass. Additional children pay half fare. Children under age 5 travel free.

BritRail Flexipass

Valid for unlimited rail travel in Britain for the days chosen within a 60-day period.

	ADULT 1st Class	ADULT Standard Class	SENIOR 1st Class	YOUTH 1st Class	YOUTH Standard Class
4 days in 2 months	$425	$285	$359	$339	$229
8 days in 2 months	$619	$415	$525	$495	$329
15 days in 2 months	$929	$625	$489	$745	$499

Senior age 60+. Youth 16–25. Children age 5–15, half adult fare. Children younger than age 5 travel free.

BritRail Pass + Ireland

Valid for travel in England, Scotland, Wales, Northern Ireland, and the Republic of Ireland.

	ADULT 1st Class	ADULT Standard Class
5 days within 1 month	$659	$445
10 days within 1 month	$1,175	$795

Children age 5–15, half adult fare; younger than age 5 travel free.

Round-trip Stena Sealink service is included between Holyhead and Dun Laoghaire, Fishguard and Rosslare, or Stranraer and Belfast via ship, HSS, or SeaLynx. Reservations are essential for Irish Sea services. Refunds not offered on dated or partially used passes; sea coupons are not refundable if unused.

BritRail England Consecutive Pass

Unlimited consecutive-day rail travel in England (Scotland and Wales are not included on the England Pass).

	ADULT 1st Class	ADULT Standard Class	SENIOR 1st Class	YOUTH Standard Class	YOUTH 1st Class
4 days	$269	$179	$229	$145	$219
8 days	$385	$259	$329	$205	$309
15 days	$579	$385	$495	$309	$465
22 days	$735	$489	$625	$389	$589
1 month	$869	$579	$739	$465	$695

Youth 16–25; senior 60+. BritRail Family Passes must be requested so each child (age 5–15) can travel free with each adult/senior pass holder. Additional children are half regular adult fare.

BritRail England Flexipass

Unlimited four, eight, or fifteen days of flexible (nonconsecutive) rail travel in a two-month period throughout England (Scotland and Wales not included).

	ADULT 1st Class	ADULT Standard Class	SENIOR 1st Class	YOUTH Standard Class	YOUTH 1st Class
4 days	$339	$229	$289	$185	$269
8 days	$495	$329	$419	$265	$395
15 days	$745	$499	$635	$399	$595

Youth 16–25; senior 60+. Family passes allow one child to travel free with each adult.

BritRail London Plus Pass

A flexipass for a large section of southern England.

	ADULT 1st Class	ADULT Standard Class
2 days within 8 days	$189	$125
4 days within 8 days	$265	$199
7 days within 15 days	$329	$239

One child age 5–15 years travels free with each full paying adult. Ask for the free BritRail Family passes. Additional children age 5–15 pay half the full adult fare. Children younger than age 5 travel free. Now extended to Bristol, Bath, and Stratford-upon-Avon. Not valid on other services via Reading operated by Great Western Trains from Paddington Station. Travel on the London Underground is not included.

BritRail Freedom of Scotland Pass

	ADULT Standard Class
4 days within 8 days	$215
8 days within 15 days	$285

Includes transportation on all Caledonian MacBrayne and Strathclyde ferries to the islands of Scotland. Discounts on some P&O ferry routes. Children younger than age 5 travel free.

Gatwick Express

	1st Class	Standard Class
One-way	$47	$33
Round-trip	$90	$56

Travel by train from Gatwick Airport to London Victoria Station. Children 5–15, half adult fare.

Great British Heritage Pass

Offers entrance to more than 600 well-known public and privately owned castles, homes, gardens, and other historic properties throughout Britain. Includes colorful guidebook and map.

	ADULT
3 days	$66
7 days	$116
15 days	$149
1 month	$199

No discounts for children. The pass is nonrefundable/nonreturnable.

Heathrow Express

	1st Class	Standard Class
One-way	$47	$33
Round-trip	$90	$58

Train travel from Heathrow Airport to London Paddington Station. Children 5–15, half adult fare.

London Pass

Entry to more than 70 major attractions, including Buckingham Palace (open August and September), St. Paul's Cathedral, and Windsor Castle, a 140-page *London Pass Guide Book*, commission-free currency exchange, free offers at restaurants, discounted telephone calls, and more. Available only with the purchase of another product.

	ADULT	CHILD
1 day	$74	$47
2 consecutive days	$99	$72
3 consecutive days	$119	$81
6 consecutive days	$158	$110

London Visitor Travelcard

Unlimited travel throughout all 6 zones of London on London Underground and buses. Three- or seven-day travel cards are available. Not valid on Heathrow Express, Gatwick, or Stansted Express.

	1 ADULT Standard Class	1 CHILD Standard Class
1 Day Central Zone	$17	$9
7 Days All Zones	$105	$53

Eurail Passes

Eurail passes entitle you to unlimited travel on Europe's extensive 100,000-mile rail network in 22 countries of Europe (England, Scotland, and Wales not included) as follows:

Austria • Belgium • Croatia • Czech Republic • Denmark • Finland • France • Germany
Greece • Hungary • Ireland (Republic of) • Italy • Luxembourg • Netherlands • Norway
Portugal • Romania • Slovenia • Spain • Sweden • Switzerland

Note: Prices are in U.S. dollars and are estimated conversions from euro prices, based on the exchange rate at press time. Please check with your retailer for updates. Prices may be slightly higher or lower. Prices listed for "additional rail days" are approximate.

Eurail Global Pass

Consecutive-day travel on any or all days together at all times.

Eurail Global Pass Saver

Rail travel for two to five people traveling for the duration of the pass. Price is per person.

	ADULT 1st Class	EURAIL Youth Pass*	
15 days	$194	$517	$675
21 days	$1,024	$667	$871
1 month	$1,261	$821	$1,072
2 months	$1,781	$1,158	$1,514
3 months	$2,196	$1,428	$1,867

Children age 4–11, half adult fare; younger than age 4 travel free.
*Available for passengers age 12–25 on their first date of travel.

Eurail Global Pass Flexi

Choose your travel days and use them within 60 days.

Eurail Global Pass Saver Flexi

Rail travel for two to five people traveling together at all times. Price is per person.

	ADULT 1st Class	Saver
10 days in 2 months	$937	$797
15 days in 2 months	$1,230	$1,046

Children age 4–11, half adult fare; younger than age 4 travel free.

Eurail Global Pass Youth Flexi*

	2nd Class
10 days in 2 months	$610
15 days in 2 months	$800

*Available for passengers age 12–25 on their first date of travel.

Eurail Select Pass

The Eurail Select Pass gives travelers the option to customize a rail pass by choosing any three, four, or five bordering Eurail countries that are connected by train or by ship. The Select Pass covers Austria, Benelux (Belgium, the Netherlands, and Luxemburg as one country), Bulgaria/Serbia/Montenegro (as one country), Denmark, Finland, France, Germany, Greece, Hungary, Italy, Norway, Portugal, Ireland (Republic of), Romania, Slovenia/Croatia (as one country), Spain, Sweden, and Switzerland.

Eurail Select Pass

Travel on any or all days for the duration of the pass in any three, four, or five adjoining Eurail pass countries.

	EURAIL SELECT PASS ADULT FIRST CLASS		
	3 Countries	4 Countries	5 Countries
5 days in 2 months	$499	$558	$615
6 days in 2 months	$551	$610	$667
8 days in 2 months	$651	$710	$769
10 days in 2 months	$755	$813	$868
15 days in 2 months	NA	NA	$1,101

Eurail Select Pass Youth*

	EURAIL SELECT PASS YOUTH*		
	3 Countries	4 Countries	5 Countries
5 days in 2 months	$325	$363	$400
6 days in 2 months	$359	$397	$434
8 days in 2 months	$424	$462	$501
10 days in 2 months	$492	$529	$565
15 days in 2 months	NA	NA	$716

*Youth price available for second-class travel passengers age 12–25. Children age 4–11, half adult fare; younger than age 4 travel free.

Eurail Select Pass Saver

For two or more persons traveling together at all times. Travel on any or all days for the duration of the pass in any three, four, or five adjoining Eurail pass countries.

	EURAIL SELECT PASS SAVER		
	3 Countries	4 Countries	5 Countries
5 days in 2 months	$424	$474	$523
6 days in 2 months	$469	$518	$567
8 days in 2 months	$554	$604	$654
10 days in 2 months	$643	$691	$738
15 days in 2 months	NA	NA	$936

Children age 4–11, half adult fare; younger than age 4 travel free.

Eurail Regional Passes

Eurail Austria–Croatia–Slovenia Pass

	ADULT 1st Class	ADULT Saverpass*	YOUTH 2nd Class
4 days in 2 months	$293	$255	$212
Additional rail days (up to 6)	$43	$38	$31

Children age 4–11, half adult fare; younger than age 4 travel free. Youth age 12–25.
* Price per person for up to five people traveling together at all times.

Eurail Austria–Czech Republic Pass

Any four days unlimited first-class rail travel within a two-month period on national rail networks of Austria and Czech Republic. Purchase up to six additional rail days.

	ADULT 1st Class	ADULT Saverpass*	YOUTH 2nd Class
4 days in 2 months	$278	$236	$181
Extra rail days	$38	$33	$25

Children age 4–11 pay half adult fare. Children younger than age 4 travel free. Youth age 12–25.
*Price per person for up to five people traveling together at all times.

Eurail Austria–Germany Pass

DAYS Within 2 Months	ADULT 1st Class	ADULT 2nd Class	ADULT Saverpass* 1st Class	ADULT Saverpass* 2nd Class	YOUTH 2nd Class
5 days	$444	$381	$381	$326	$328
6 days	$489	$418	$418	$359	$359
8 days	$582	$498	$498	$427	$428
10 days	$679	$577	$577	$498	$498

Children age 4–11 pay half adult fare. Children younger than age 4 travel free. Youth age 12–25.
*Price per person for 2–5 persons traveling together at all times.

Eurail Austria–Hungary Pass

	ADULT 1st Class	ADULT Saverpass*	YOUTH 2nd Class
4 days in 2 months	$252	$215	$164
Extra rail days	$34	$29	$23

Children age 4–11 pay half adult fare. Children younger than age 4 travel free. Youth age 12–25.
*Price per person for up to five people traveling together at all times.

Eurail Austria–Switzerland Pass

First Class rail travel in Austria and Switzerland for 4 to 10 days within 2 months. Saverpass is valid for 2 to 5 people traveling together.

	ADULT 1st Class	ADULT Saverpass*	YOUTH 2nd Class
4 days in 2 months	$278	$236	$181
Additional rail days (up to 6)	$38	$33	$25

Youth Passes are exclusively for those who are younger than age 26 on the first day of validity of their pass. Children age 4–11, half adult fare; under age 4 travel free.
*Price per person for up to five people traveling together at all times.

Balkan Flexipass

Valid for rail travel in Bulgaria, Greece, Macedonia, Montenegro, Romania, Serbia, and Turkey.

	ADULT 1st Class	SENIORS* 1st Class	YOUTH 2nd Class
5 days in 1 month	$276	$222	$165
10 days in 1 month	$482	$387	$289
15 days in 1 month	$581	$467	$349

Children age 4–11, half adult fare; younger than age 4 travel free. Youth age 12–25.
*Senior age 60 and older.

Eurail Benelux–France Pass

DAYS Within 2 months	ADULT 1st Class	ADULT 2nd Class	SAVERPASS* 1st Class	SAVERPASS* 2nd Class	YOUTH 2nd Class
4 days	$440	$381	$376	$328	$285
5 days	$484	$425	$414	$366	$321
6 days	$525	$466	$449	$402	$356
8 days	$608	$549	$518	$468	$421
10 days	$688	$633	$588	$534	$487

Children age 4–11 pay half adult fare; younger than age 4 travel free. Youth age 12–25.
*Price per person for up to five people traveling together at all times.

Eurail Benelux–Germany Pass

DAYS Within 2 months	ADULT 1st Class	ADULT 2nd Class	SAVERPASS* 1st Class	SAVERPASS* 2nd Class	YOUTH 2nd Class
5 days	$466	$350	$350	$285	$285
6 days	$515	$388	$388	$310	$310
8 days	$608	$458	$458	$366	$366
10 days	$709	$532	$532	$425	$425

Children age 4–11 pay half adult fare; younger than age 4 travel free. Youth age 12–25.
*Price per person for up to five people traveling together at all times.

Czech Republic–Germany Pass

DAYS Within 2 months	ADULT 1st Class	ADULT 2nd Class	SAVERPASS* 1st Class	SAVERPASS* 2nd Class	YOUTH 2nd Class
5 days	$433	$357	$356	$305	$305
6 days	$482	$397	$395	$338	$338
8 days	$562	$468	$466	$406	$406
10 days	$646	$541	$539	$470	$470

Children age 4–11 pay half adult fare; younger than age 4 travel free. Youth age 12–25.
*Price per person for up to five people traveling together at all times.

Eurail Denmark–Germany Pass

Unlimited 1st- or 2nd-class rail travel in Germany and Denmark.

DAYS Within 2 months	ADULT 1st Class	ADULT 2nd Class	SAVERPASS* 1st Class	SAVERPASS* 2nd Class	YOUTH 2nd Class
4 days	$380	$310	$310	$239	$238
5 days	$427	$350	$350	$269	$269
6 days	$473	$388	$388	$295	$295
8 days	$570	$466	$466	$338	$338
10 days	$685	$520	$520	$383	$383

*Price per person for 2 to 5 people traveling together.
Children age 4–11 pay half adult fare; younger than age 4 travel free. Youth age 12–25.

European East Pass

Valid for rail travel in Austria, Czech Republic, Hungary, Poland, and Slovakia.

	1st Class	2nd Class
5 days in 1 month	$340	$234
Additional days	$39	$32

Up to 5 additional days can be added. Children age 4–11, half adult fare; younger than age 4 travel free.

France–Germany Pass

DAYS Within 2 months	ADULT 1st Class	ADULT 2nd Class	SAVERPASS* 1st Class	SAVERPASS* 2nd Class	YOUTH 2nd Class
4 days	$449	$406	$406	$368	$314
5 days	$498	$447	$447	$404	$347
6 days	$544	$491	$491	$435	$383
8 days	$638	$575	$575	$501	$449
10 days	$733	$660	$660	$575	$518

Children age 4–11 pay half adult fare; younger than age 4 travel free. Youth age 12–25.
*Price per person for up to five people traveling together at all times.

Eurail France–Italy Pass

Unlimited rail travel on national networks of France and Italy.

DAYS Within 2 months	ADULT 1st Class	ADULT 2nd Class	SAVERPASS* 1st Class	SAVERPASS* 2nd Class	YOUTH 2nd Class
4 days	$409	$349	$349	$297	$265
5 days	$458	$288	$388	$330	$298
6 days	$504	$428	$428	$364	$328
7 days	$551	$470	$470	$401	$359
8 days	$600	$510	$510	$433	$388
9 days	$648	$549	$549	$468	$421
10 days	$695	$591	$591	$501	$452

*Price per person for up to five people traveling together at all times. Youth is under 26.

Eurail France–Spain Pass

Unlimited rail travel on national networks of France and Spain.

DAYS OF TRAVEL Within 2 months	ADULT 1st Class	ADULT 2nd Class	SAVERPASS* 1st Class	SAVERPASS* 2nd Class	YOUTH 2nd Class
4 days	$409	$349	$349	$297	$265
5 days	$458	$388	$388	$330	$298
6 days	$504	$428	$428	$364	$328
7 days	$551	$470	$470	$401	$359
8 days	$600	$510	$510	$433	$388
9 days	$648	$549	$549	$468	$421
10 days	$695	$591	$591	$501	$452

*Price per person for up to five people traveling together at all times. Youth is under 26.

Eurail France–Switzerland Pass

	ADULT 1st Class	SAVERPASS* 1st Class	YOUTH 2nd Class
4 days	$444	$376	$312
5 days	$492	$420	$347
6 days	$543	$466	$383
7 days	$591	$506	$418
8 days	$641	$546	$452
9 days	$693	$589	$487
10 days	$742	$631	$518

Children age 4–11, half adult fare or saver price; younger than age 4 travel free. Youth younger than age 26.

*Price per person for 2 to 5 people traveling together at all times.

Eurail Germany–Poland Pass

DAYS Within 2 months	ADULT 1st Class	ADULT 2nd Class	SAVERPASS* 1st Class	SAVERPASS* 2nd Class	YOUTH** 2nd Class
5 days	$459	$394	$394	$333	$335
6 days	$504	$433	$435	$369	$369
8 days	$598	$515	$515	$437	$439
10 days	$688	$596	$596	$503	$503

*Price per person based on 2 to 5 people traveling together at all times.

**Younger than age 26.

Eurail Germany–Switzerland Pass

DAYS Within 2 months	ADULT 1st Class	SAVERPASS* 1st Class	YOUTH 2nd Class
5 days	$473	$404	$333
6 days	$522	$444	$368
8 days	$615	$527	$433
10 days	$712	$608	$501

*Price per person for 2 to 5 people traveling together at all times. One child (age 4–11) and one adult traveling together qualify for Saverpass.

Children age 3 and younger than travel for free; children age 4–11 travel for half the adult fare.

Eurail Greece–Italy Pass

Unlimited 1st- or 2nd-Class rail travel in Greece and Italy.

	ADULT 1st Class	SAVERPASS* 1st Class	YOUTH 2nd Class
4 days in 2 months	$390	$331	$253
Additional rail days (up to 6)	$38	$34	$26

*Price per person for 2 to 5 people traveling together.

Children age 4–11 pay half adult fare; younger than age 4 travel free. Youth age 12–25.

Unlimited travel on the train networks of CH (Hellenic State railways) and Trenitalia, plus a return crossing between Ancona/Bari and Igoumenitsa/Patras on board the Superfast Ferries ships, or between Brindisi and Igoumenitsa/Corfu/Patras on board the Hellenic Mediterranean lines (HML) and Blue Star Ferries ships, for the period of validity of the pass.

Eurail Hungary–Croatia–Slovenia Pass

DAYS Within 2 months	ADULT 1st Class	SAVERPASS* 1st Class	YOUTH 2nd Class
5 days	$269	$229	$189
6 days	$297	$252	$208
8 days	$349	$297	$245
10 days	$401	$341	$281

Youth younger than age 26.

Children age 4–11, half adult fare; younger than age 4 travel free.

*Price per person based on 2 to 5 people traveling together at all times.

Eurail Hungary–Romania Pass

Unlimited rail travel in Romania and Hungary for 5, 6, 8, or 10 days in two months.

DAYS Within 2 months	ADULT 1st Class	SAVERPASS* 1st Class	YOUTH 2nd Class
5 days	$283	$241	$199
6 days	$310	$265	$218
8 days	$366	$311	$257
10 days	$420	$357	$294

Youth younger than age 26.

Children age 4–11, half adult fare; younger than age 4 travel free.

*Price per person for 2 to 5 people traveling together at all times.

Eurail Italy–Spain Pass

DAYS Within 2 months	ADULT 1st Class	SAVERPASS* 1st Class	YOUTH 2nd Class
4 days	$390	$331	$253
6 days	$468	$399	$304
8 days	$546	$466	$356
10 days	$624	$534	$407

Youth younger than age 26.

*Price per person for 2 to 5 people traveling together at all times.

Eurail Portugal–Spain Pass

	ADULT 1st Class	SAVERPASS* 1st Class
3 days in 2 months	$347	$295
Additional rail days (up to 7)	$45	$38

Purchase up to seven additional rail days. Children age 4–11, half adult fare; younger than age 4 travel free. *Price per person based on 2 to 5 people traveling together.

Eurail Scandinavia Pass

Valid for unlimited rail travel in Denmark, Finland, Norway, and Sweden.

	ADULT 2nd Class	ADULT SAVER 2nd Class	YOUTH 2nd Class
4 days in 1 month	$350	$298	$263
5 days in 1 month	$389	$331	$292
6 days in 1 month	$443	$377	$333
8 days in 1 month	$490	$417	$368
10 days in 1 month	$545	$463	$409

Youth age 12–25. Children age 4–11, half adult fare; younger than age 4 travel free.

Eurail Country Passes

Austria Pass

The Austria country pass allows 15 days in which to use 3 to 8 travel days in either 1st or 2nd class.

	ADULT 1st Class	ADULT 2nd Class
3 days	$241	$170
4 days	$278	$196
5 days	$306	$215
6 days	$335	$236
7 days	$365	$256
8 days	$393	$276

Children pay half adult fare.

Benelux Pass

	ADULT 1st Class	ADULT 2nd Class	SAVERPASS* 1st Class	SAVERPASS* 2nd Class	YOUTH 2nd Class
5 days in one month	$399	$264	$340	$225	$180

Children age 4–11 pay half adult fare; younger than age 4 travel free. Youth age 12–25.
*Price per person for up to five people traveling together at all times.

Eurail Bulgaria Pass

	ADULT 1st Class	ADULT 2nd Class
3 days in one month	$139	$104
Additional rail days (up to 5)	$52	$38

Children age 4–11 pay half adult fare; younger than 4 travel free. Youth age 12–25.

Eurail Croatia Pass

Valid on Croatian Railways for 3, 4, 6, or 8 days of rail travel within 1 month in 1st or 2nd class.

DAYS Within 1 month	ADULT 1st Class	ADULT 2nd Class	SAVERPASS* 1st Class	SAVERPASS* 2nd Class	YOUTH 2nd Class
3 days	$167	$133	$142	$113	$96
4 days	$224	$169	$191	$144	$113
6 days	$297	$224	$253	$191	$150
8 days	$353	$262	$300	$223	$167

Children age 4–11 pay half adult fare; younger than 4 travel free. Youth younger than 26.
*Price per person for 2 to 5 people traveling together at all times.

Czech Republic Pass

Valid for 3, 4, 6, or 8 days of rail travel in a 1-month period.

	ADULT 1st Class	ADULT 2nd Class	YOUTH 2nd Class
3 days	$167	$125	$83
4 days	$231	$172	$115
6 days	$328	$244	$162
8 days	$389	$289	$192

Children age 4–11 half adult fare; younger than age 4 travel free. Youth age 12–25.

Eurail Denmark Pass

Valid for 3 or 7 days of rail travel within a 1-month period.

	ADULT 1st Class	ADULT 2nd Class	YOUTH 2nd Class
3 days	$203	$133	$100
7 days	$316	$206	$155

Children age 4–11 half adult fare; younger than age 4 travel free. Youth age 12–25.
*Price per person for 2 or more persons traveling together at all times.

Eurail Finland Pass

Valid for 3, 5, or 10 days of 1st- or 2nd-class travel within a 1-month period.

	ADULT 1st Class	ADULT 2nd Class
3 days	$289	$194
5 days	$384	$258
10 days	$521	$350

Children age 6–16 half adult fare; younger than age 6 travel free.

France Railpass

Valid for 3–9 days of 1st- or 2nd-class travel within a 1-month period.

	ADULT 1st Class	ADULT 2nd Class	SAVERPASS* ADULT 1st Class	SAVERPASS* ADULT 2nd Class	YOUTH 1st Class	YOUTH 2nd Class
3 days	$322	$260	$275	$224	$227	$192
4 days	$371	$302	$316	$259	$260	$222
5 days	$417	$340	$356	$292	$294	$253
6 days	$463	$376	$394	$324	$327	$280
7 days	$508	$410	$432	$352	$360	$310
8 days	$552	$444	$470	$383	$392	$338
9 days	$597	$478	$508	$411	$424	$365

Children age 4–11 half adult fare; younger than age 4 travel free. Youth younger than age 26.
*Price per person for 3 or more persons traveling together at all times.

German Railpass

Valid for 4–10 flexible days of travel within a 1-month period.

	ADULT 1st Class Single	ADULT 1st Class Twin*	ADULT 2nd Class Single	ADULT 2nd Class Twin*	YOUTH 2nd Class
4 days	$356	$538	$273	$406	$218
5 days	$389	$598	$293	$436	$232
6 days	$435	$660	$322	$482	$250
7 days	$482	$722	$354	$528	$264
8 days	$525	$784	$383	$578	$279
9 days	$577	$844	$418	$622	$296
10 days	$624	$908	$447	$668	$311

Children age 4–11 half adult fare; younger than age 4 travel free. Youth younger than age 26.
*Twinpass prices are per person for 2 people traveling together at all times.

Greece Railpass

Valid for any 3–10 days of 1st-class rail travel in Greece within a 1-month period.

	ADULT 1st Class	YOUTH 1st Class
3 days	$157	$140
4 days	$207	$185
5 days	$240	$214
6 days	$289	$257
7 days	$337	$301
8 days	$388	$345
9 days	$436	$388
10 days	$486	$434

Children age 4–11 half adult fare; younger than age 4 travel free. Youth younger than age 26.

Eurail Hungary Pass

Available for 5 days of travel within a 15-day period or 10 days of travel within a 1-month period.

	ADULT 1st Class	SAVERPASS* 1st Class	YOUTH 2nd Class
5 days within 15 days	$117	$101	$88
10 days within 1 month	$162	$146	$111

Children age 6–14, half adult fare. Youth age 15–25.

* Price per person for 2 or more persons traveling together at all times.

Eurail Ireland Pass

Valid for any 5 days of rail travel in Ireland within a 1-month period.

	ADULT 2nd Class	SENIOR 2nd Class	YOUTH 2nd Class
5 days within 1 month	$335	$252	$286

Children age 4–11, half adult fare; younger than age 4 travel free. Youth younger than age 26. Senior age 60 or older.

Eurail Italy Pass

Valid for 3, 4, 5, 6, 7, 8, 9, or 10 days of rail travel within a 2-month period.

DAYS Within 2 months	ADULT 1st Class	ADULT 2nd Class	SAVERPASS* 1st Class	SAVERPASS* 2nd Class	YOUTH 2nd Class
3 days	$278	$227	$237	$192	$169
4 days	$309	$251	$263	$215	$188
5 days	$346	$280	$294	$239	$210
6 days	$377	$306	$320	$259	$229
7 days	$411	$334	$351	$284	$250
8 days	$444	$361	$379	$308	$270
9 days	$479	$389	$408	$330	$291
10 days	$513	$415	$435	$353	$311

Children age 4–11 half adult fare; younger than age 4 travel free. Youth younger than age 26.
*Price per person for 2 or more persons traveling together at all times.

Eurail Norway Pass

Valid for 3, 4, 5, 6, or 8 days of 2nd-class rail travel within Norway.

DAYS Within 1 month	ADULT 2nd Class	YOUTH 2nd Class
3 days	$287	$216
4 days	$311	$234
5 days	$344	$259
6 days	$391	$294
8 days	$436	$328

Up to 2 children travel free with each adult pass; more than 2 children age 4–15 pay half adult fare; younger than age 4 travel free. Youth passes for students under 26 years old.

Eurail Poland Pass

Valid for 5, 8, 10, or 15 days of rail travel in Poland within a 1-month period.

DAYS Within 1 month	ADULT 1st Class	ADULT 2nd Class	YOUTH 1st Class	YOUTH 2nd Class
5 days	$178	$138	$125	$97
8 days	$250	$195	$176	$137
10 days	$283	$219	$199	$154
15 days	$393	$302	$276	$213

Younger than age 4 travel free. Youth younger than age 26.

Eurail Portugal Pass

Valid for 3, 4, or 6 days of 1st-class rail travel within a 1-month period.

DAYS Within 1 month	ADULT 1st Class
3 days	$158
4 days	$204
6 days	$269

Children age 4–11, half adult fare; younger than age 4 travel free (unless a separate seat is requested).

Eurail Romania Pass

Valid for 5 or 10 days of rail travel within a 2-month period in 1st class (2nd class for Youth).

DAYS Within 2 months	ADULT 1st Class	SAVERPASS* 1st Class	YOUTH 2nd Class
5 days	$207	$177	$166
10 days	$361	$308	$290

Children age 4–11 half adult fare; younger than age 4 travel free. Youth younger than age 26.

Eurail Slovenia Pass

DAYS Within 1 month	ADULT 1st Class	ADULT 2nd Class	YOUTH 2nd Class
3 days	$101	$76	$66
4 days	$143	$108	$92
6 days	$204	$153	$131
8 days	$245	$184	$157

Children age 4–11 half adult fare; younger than age 4 travel free.

Eurail Spain Pass

Valid for 3–10 days of 1st- or 2nd-class rail travel within a 2-month period.

DAYS Within 2 months	ADULT 1st Class	ADULT 2nd Class
3 days	$304	$244
4 days	$346	$277
5 days	$391	$313
6 days	$436	$349
7 days	$481	$386
8 days	$526	$422
9 days	$473	$459
10 days	$618	$495

Children age 4–11 half adult fare; younger than age 4 travel free.

Sweden Pass

Valid for 3, 4, 5, 6, or 8 days of 1st- or 2nd-class rail travel within a 1-month period.

DAYS Within 1 month	ADULT 1st Class	ADULT 2nd Class	YOUTH 2nd Class
3 days	$374	$289	$217
4 days	$401	$310	$233
5 days	$447	$345	$259
6 days	$506	$390	$293
8 days	$565	$435	$327

Up to 2 free child passes with purchase of each adult pass; children age 4–15 half adult fare. Youth younger than age 26.
Pass does not include supplement on x2000 train.

Swiss Card (ideal for skiers)

Valid for one round-trip rail journey plus 50% discount on Swiss railways, lake steamers, postal buses, and most mountain railroads within a 1-month validity period.

	1st Class	2nd Class
1 month—1 round-trip	$289	$207

Children younger than age 16, free with parent. Children age 6–15 not accompanied by parent, half adult fare. Children younger than age 6 travel free.

Swiss Pass

Valid for consecutive-day unlimited travel. Choice of first class or second class. Free Swiss Family Card: Children younger than age 16 travel free when accompanied by at least one parent; half adult fare when not accompanied by parent. Includes travel on lake steamers, transportation on 35 city systems, postal and private bus lines.

CONSECUTIVE DAYS OF TRAVEL	1st Class	2nd Class	SAVERPASS* 1st Class	SAVERPASS* 2nd Class	YOUTH** 1st Class	YOUTH** 2nd Class
4 days	$441	$294	$375	$249	$332	$221
8 days	$638	$425	$543	$362	$479	$319
15 days	$771	$514	$655	$436	$579	$386
22 days	$888	$592	$755	$503	$666	$444
1 month	$979	$652	$831	$554	$734	$489

*Price per person based on two or more adults traveling together at all times; children younger than age 16 travel free when accompanied by a parent.

**For persons ages 16–25.

Swiss Transfer Ticket

Great for skiers or for those who will stay in one place. Provides for one round-trip ticket from any Swiss airport to any Swiss destination within a 1-month period.

	1st Class	2nd Class
1 day in 1 month	$218	$145

Children younger than age 16 travel free when accompanied by at least one parent; otherwise, children age 6–15, half adult fare. Children younger than age 6 travel free.

Rail/Drive Passes

BritRail Pass 'n Drive

Valid for any 6 days (4 rail, 2 car) within 2 months. No additional rail days can be added. Additional car days up to 5 maximum.

CAR CATEGORY	2 ADULTS*		ADDITIONAL CAR DAY
	1st Class	Standard Class	
Compact	$1,049	$749	$63
Intermediate	$1,067	$767	$72
Compact automatic	$1,111	$813	$94
Intermediate automatic	$1,138	$838	$107

CAR CATEGORY	1 ADULT*	
	1st Class	Standard Class
Compact	$587	$437
Intermediate	$605	$455
Compact automatic	$649	$499
Intermediate automatic	$676	$526

Discounted fare for children 5–15. Children younger than age 5 travel free. Extra car days for one adult are the same as for two adults.

*Prices include both persons.

Eurail Drive Pass

Any 6 days travel (4 days 1st-class rail and 2 days Hertz car rental) within a 2-month period to explore Austria, Belgium, Denmark, Finland, France, Germany, Greece, Hungary, Italy, Luxembourg, the Netherlands, Norway, Portugal, Republic of Ireland, Spain, Sweden, and Switzerland. Customize your trip by adding an unlimited number of car rental days.

	1 ADULT 1st class	2 ADULTS 1st class
Compact	$639	$1,110
Economy	$594	$1,064
Intermediate	$664	$1,136
Small Automatic*	$711	$1,182

*Automatic available only in major locations. Automatic cars not available in France. Includes local tax on car rental. Third and fourth person sharing the car receive a special rate per person. Discounted fare for children 4–11.

Eurail Select Pass 'n Drive

Any 5 days (3 rail, 2 Hertz car rental) within 2 months in any of the 3 or 4 bordering countries selected. Add up to 7 additional rail days and an unlimited number of car days.

3 COUNTRIES

CAR TYPE	ADULT Single	ADULT Twin**	ADDITIONAL CAR DAY
Economy	$536	$950	$62
Compact	$581	$994	$84
Intermediate	$606	$1,020	$98
Small Automatic*	$654	$1,168	$122

Child age 4–11 rate is half the adult sharing rate.
*Small automatic with Hertz only in major locations.
**Price is for 2 travelers. Third and fourth adult will receive a discounted rate.
Automatics are not available in France, Bulgaria, Croatia, Finland, Greece, and Romania. Car rental portion includes unlimited mileage and VAT (value-added tax). CDW (collision damage waiver) insurance not included.

4 COUNTRIES

CAR TYPE	ADULT Single	ADULT Twin**	ADDITIONAL CAR DAY
Economy	$583	$1,044	$62
Compact	$628	$1,088	$84
Intermediate	$654	$1,114	$98
Small automatic*	$701	$1,162	$122

Child age 4–11 rate is half the adult sharing rate.
*Small automatic with Hertz only in major locations.
**Price per person for 2 travelers. Third and fourth adult will receive a discounted rate.
Automatics are not available in France, Bulgaria, Croatia, Finland, Greece, and Romania. Car rental portion includes unlimited mileage and VAT (value-added tax). CDW (collision damage waiver) insurance not included.

France Rail 'n Drive

Two days of 1st-class rail travel and 2 days of car rental in France within a 1-month period. Up to 3 additional rail days and unlimited Avis car rental days may be purchased.

CAR TYPE	1 ADULT 1st Class	2 ADULTS 1st Class	ADDITIONAL CAR DAYS
Compact	$326	$542	$55
Economy	$309	$525	$47
Full Size	$411	$627	$98
Intermediate	$349	$565	$67
Luxury Automatic	$571	—	$178
Additional Rail Days	$42	$83	—

Note: Third and fourth person sharing car, reduced rates apply. Pass is valid only with Avis. Pass must be validated within 6 months of the date of purchase. Special fares on Eurostar journeys. Children ages 4–11, reduced rates.

German Rail 'n Drive

Any 2 days unlimited rail travel in Germany and 2 days Hertz car rental with unlimited mileage and local tax included. Choose between 4 car categories (3 with manual transmission and 1 automatic). Unlimited additional car days. Up to 2 additional rail days. Third and fourth person and/or children age 5–11 sharing car need only purchase German Railpasses.

CAR TYPE	1 ADULT 1st Class	1 ADULT 2nd Class	2 ADULTS 1st Class	2 ADULTS 2nd Class	ADDITIONAL CAR DAYS
Compact					
2 days in 1 month	$308	$265	$483	$397	$65
3 days in 1 month	$368	$312	$603	$491	$65
4 days in 1 month	$434	$361	$735	$589	$65
Intermediate					
2 days in 1 month	$298	$255	$473	$387	$62
3 days in 1 month	$358	$302	$593	$481	$62
4 days in 1 month	$424	$351	$725	$579	$62
Intermediate					
2 days in 1 month	$326	$283	$501	$415	$76
3 days in 1 month	$386	$330	$621	$509	$76
4 days in 1 month	$452	$379	$753	$607	$76

Italy Rail 'n Drive

Valid for 4 days of unlimited rail travel and 2 days of car rental within 2 months for travel in Italy. An unlimited number of car days may be added. Additional rail days are available.

CAR CATEGORY	ADULT		2 ADULTS*		ADDITIONAL CAR DAY
	1st Class	2nd Class	1st Class	2nd Class	
Compact	$503	$444	$816	$698	$96
Economy	$463	$403	$776	$658	$76
Intermediate	$558	$498	$872	$752	$122
Economy Automatic**	$521	$462	$834	$716	$104

Third and fourth persons sharing car or children need only purchase a Eurail Italy Pass.
*Total price for both adults.
**Automatic transmission available at select locations.

Spain Rail 'n Drive

Choice of 3, 4, 5, 6, 7, 8, 9, or 10 days of unlimited rail travel and 2 days of car rental within 2 months of travel in Spain. Up to 2 additional rail days and unlimited car days available. Note: Only 5 days are listed below. Additional rail days are available.

CAR CATEGORY	ADULT		2 ADULTS*		ADDITIONAL CAR DAY
	1st Class	2nd Class	1st Class	2nd Class	
Compact	$415	$354	$722	$600	$56
Intermediate	$471	$410	$778	$656	$84
Intermediate Automatic**	$545	$484	$852	$730	$120

Third and fourth person sharing car need only purchase Spain Pass. Need only purchase rail passes for children.
*Price for both persons.
**Automatic transmission available at select locations.

Security

Rail Pass Security

Entitles traveler to a 100% reimbursement on the unused portion of the rail pass if lost or stolen while traveling in Britain or Europe.

$20 per pass

Rail Pass/Rail & Drive Security

This program entitles travelers to a 100% reimbursement on the unused portion of a rail pass or a combination Rail pass/Rail 'n Drive program if lost or stolen while traveling in Britain or Europe.

$20 per rail pass or for the driver
$20 for each additional person